THE
GOTHIC

BLACKWELL GUIDES TO LITERATURE

Series editor: Jonathan Wordsworth

The English Renaissance	*Andrew Hadfield*
Children's Literature	*Peter Hunt*
The Gothic	*David Punter and Glennis Byron*
Twentieth-Century American Poetry	*Christopher MacGowan*

THE GOTHIC

David Punter and Glennis Byron

Blackwell
Publishing

BLACKWELL PUBLISHING
350 Main Street, Malden, MA 02148-5020, USA
9600 Garsington Road, Oxford OX4 2DQ, UK
550 Swanston Street, Carlton, Victoria 3053, Australia

First published 2004 by Blackwell Publishing Ltd

5   2007

Library of Congress Cataloging-in-Publication Data

Punter, David.
The Gothic / David Punter and Glennis Byron.
p. cm. – (Blackwell guides to literature)
Includes bibliographical references and index.
ISBN 0-631-22062-3 (hardcover : alk. paper) – ISBN 0-631-22063-1
(pbk. : alk. paper)
1. Horror tales, English – History and criticism.   2. Horror tales,
American – History and criticism.   3. Gothic revival (Literature) –
United States.   4. Gothic revival (Literature) – Great Britain.   I. Byron,
Glennis, 1955–   II. Title.   III. Series.

PR830.T3P856 2004
823'.0872909 – dc21
2003012537

ISBN-13: 978-0-631-22062-6 (hardcover : alk. paper) – ISBN-13: 978-0-631-22063-3 (pbk. : alk.
paper)

A catalogue record for this title is available from the British Library.

Set in 10/12.5 Galliard
by SNP Best-set Typesetter Ltd, Hong Kong
Printed and bound in Singapore
by Markono Print Media Pte Ltd

For further information on
Blackwell Publishing, visit our website:
www.blackwellpublishing.com

Contents

How to Use This Book ix

Chronology xi

Introduction xviii

Backgrounds and Contexts 1

Civilization and the Goths 3
Gothic in the Eighteenth Century 7
Gothic and Romantic 13
Science, Industry and the Gothic 20
Victorian Gothic 26
Art and Architecture 32
Gothic and Decadence 39
Imperial Gothic 44
Gothic Postmodernism 50
Postcolonial Gothic 54
Goths and Gothic Subcultures 59
Gothic Film 65
Gothic and the Graphic Novel 71

Writers of Gothic 77

William Harrison Ainsworth (1805–1882) 79
Jane Austen (1775–1817) 80
J. G. Ballard (1930–) 82
Iain Banks (1954–) 83
John Banville (1945–) 84
Clive Barker (1952–) 85

Contents

William Beckford (1760–1844)   87
E. F. Benson (1867–1940)   88
Ambrose Bierce (1842–1914)   89
Algernon Blackwood (1869–1951)   90
Robert Bloch (1917–1994)   91
Elizabeth Bowen (1899–1973)   92
Mary Elizabeth Braddon (1835–1915)   94
Charlotte Brontë (1816–1855) and Emily Brontë
   (1818–1848)   95
Charles Brockden Brown (1771–1810)   97
Edward George Bulwer-Lytton (1803–1873)   98
James Branch Cabell (1879–1958)   99
Ramsey Campbell (1946–)   100
Angela Carter (1940–1992)   101
Robert W. Chambers (1865–1933)   103
Wilkie Collins (1824–1889)   104
Marie Corelli (1855–1924)   105
Charlotte Dacre (1771/1772?–1825)   106
Walter de la Mare (1873–1956)   108
August Derleth (1909–1971)   109
Charles Dickens (1812–1870)   110
'Isak Dinesen' (1885–1962)   111
Arthur Conan Doyle (1859–1930)   113
Lord Dunsany (1878–1957)   114
Bret Easton Ellis (1964–)   115
William Faulkner (1897–1962)   116
Elizabeth Gaskell (1810–1865)   118
William Gibson (1948–)   119
William Godwin (1756–1836)   120
H. Rider Haggard (1856–1925)   121
Nathaniel Hawthorne (1804–1864)   123
James Herbert (1943–)   124
William Hope Hodgson (1877–1918)   125
E. T. A. Hoffmann (1776–1822)   127
James Hogg (1770–1835)   128
Washington Irving (1783–1859)   129
G. P. R. James (1799–1860)   130
Henry James (1843–1916)   131
M. R. James (1862–1936)   132
Stephen King (1947–)   134

Rudyard Kipling (1865–1936)   135
Francis Lathom (1777–1832)   136
J. Sheridan Le Fanu (1814–1873)   137
Sophia Lee (1750–1824)   138
Vernon Lee (1856–1935)   140
M. G. Lewis (1775–1818)   141
David Lindsay (1878–1945)   142
H. P. Lovecraft (1890–1937)   143
George MacDonald (1824–1905)   144
Arthur Machen (1863–1947)   146
James Macpherson (1736–1796)   147
Richard Matheson (1926–)   148
Charles Robert Maturin (1780–1824)   149
Herman Melville (1819–1891)   150
Joyce Carol Oates (1938–)   152
Margaret Oliphant (1828–1897)   153
Mervyn Peake (1911–1968)   154
Edgar Allan Poe (1809–1849)   155
John Polidori (1795–1821)   157
Ann Radcliffe (1764–1823)   158
Clara Reeve (1729–1807)   159
G. W. M. Reynolds (1814–1879)   160
Anne Rice (1941–)   162
Walter Scott (1771–1832)   163
Mary Wollstonecraft Shelley (1797–1851)   164
Charlotte Smith (1740–1806)   165
Robert Louis Stevenson (1850–1894)   166
Bram Stoker (1847–1912)   167
Horace Walpole (1717–1797)   169
H. G. Wells (1866–1946)   170
Edith Wharton (1862–1937)   171
Oscar Wilde (1854–1900)   172

Key Works   175

Horace Walpole, *The Castle of Otranto* (1764)   177
William Beckford, *Vathek* (1786)   181
Ann Radcliffe, *The Mysteries of Udolpho* (1794)   185
William Godwin, *Caleb Williams* (1794)   190
M. G. Lewis, *The Monk* (1796)   194
Mary Wollstonecraft Shelley, *Frankenstein* (1818, revised 1831)   198

Contents

Charles Robert Maturin, *Melmoth the Wanderer* (1820)   203

James Hogg, *The Private Memoirs and Confessions of a
Justified Sinner* (1824)   208

Emily Brontë, *Wuthering Heights* (1847)   212

Wilkie Collins, *The Woman in White* (1860)   217

J. Sheridan Le Fanu, *Uncle Silas* (1864)   222

Robert Louis Stevenson, *The Strange Case of Dr Jekyll and
Mr Hyde* (1886)   226

Bram Stoker, *Dracula* (1897)   230

Henry James, *The Turn of the Screw* (1898)   235

Robert Bloch, *Psycho* (1959)   240

Anne Rice, *Interview with the Vampire* (1976)   244

Stephen King, *The Shining* (1977)   248

Bret Easton Ellis, *American Psycho* (1991)   253

Themes and Topics   257

The Haunted Castle   259

The Monster   263

The Vampire   268

Persecution and Paranoia   273

Female Gothic   278

The Uncanny   283

The History of Abuse   288

Hallucination and the Narcotic   293

Guide to Further Reading   298

Index   305

How to Use This Book

This book is intended primarily for advanced undergraduate and post-graduate students and aims to introduce the reader to the most significant works, issues and debates within the field of Gothic studies while at the same time pointing to potential areas for future research.

The entries in the first section, 'Backgrounds and Contexts', are designed to serve two main functions. First, they consider some of the revolutions in taste that fostered the emergence of the Gothic in the eighteenth century and the social and political changes – such as industrialism or imperialism – that influenced its subsequent development up to the present day. Second, while the emphasis of the book as a whole is on the literary Gothic, in this section the student will also find an introduction to the various manifestations of Gothic in fields other than literature, including art, architecture, film and Gothic subcultures.

Precisely what constitutes the Gothic, of course, is – and will no doubt remain – a highly contested issue. The works of the seventy-eight authors in the next section, 'Writers of Gothic', however, selected mainly for their individual significance in shaping the evolution of the form, can nevertheless be said to offer representative examples of its dominant modes and its various subgenres. Here are included writers of ghost stories and horror fiction, writers not only of the 'classic' Gothic novel but also of such forms as urban, techno-, Southern and postmodern Gothic. The main concerns in this section are to identify what is distinctive about each writer's work in terms of the Gothic, pointing to specific texts that can be considered in some way typical of the writer's particular brand of Gothic, and to suggest how that writer is influenced by – and an influence upon – the developing Gothic tradition.

'Writers of Gothic' is followed by 'Key Works', and the texts selected for extended commentary here are those which are generally agreed to have exerted the most influence upon the ways in which the tradition has evolved and which are now most usually taught in university courses on the Gothic. While this section should further demonstrate the wide variety of modes and subgenres that have been considered 'Gothic', it should also allow for the tracing of the development of key motifs over the centuries and suggest the connections between these frequently quite disparate texts. To facilitate the identification of connections and developments further, the final section on 'Themes and Topics' focuses on a selection of recurrent figures and concerns, such as the vampire or the uncanny, while, like 'Key Works', providing examples of differing critical approaches to the Gothic.

The four main sections are designed to build upon each other and facilitate a gradual expansion of knowledge. One might begin, for example, by considering the extended analysis of a particular text in 'Key Works' – say, Ann Radcliffe's *The Mysteries of Udolpho*. From there one could move to consider how the text fits into Radcliffe's literary career by consulting 'Writers of Gothic', identify its connections with the developing Gothic of the eighteenth century in 'Backgrounds and Contexts', and finally explore the evolution of some of the text's major motifs and concerns by consulting such entries as 'Female Gothic' and 'The Haunted Castle' in 'Themes and Topics'. The notes '(q.v.)' or '(qq.v.)' cross-refer readers to author(s), work(s) or issue(s) discussed elsewhere in the guide in order to aid further the identification of links and connections. A chronology is provided which lists the most significant works of Gothic literature and film from 1757 to 2000, and here some trends can be observed suggest some interesting similarities and differences in the treatment of Gothic within these two fields. Finally, a word about bibliographies and further study: each entry in each section offers a bibliography that is specific to the issue, text or author in question; in the case of individual authors these have been limited, for reasons of space, to three key entries. These bibliographies are supplemented by a comprehensive 'Guide to Further Reading' with sections on collections of Gothic writing, collections of Gothic criticism, general studies of the Gothic, and Gothic bibliographies. Students wanting to explore Gothic resources further using the internet could not do better than to start with Jack G. Voller's 'The Literary Gothic' (www.litgothic.com/index_html.html), a guide to all things concerned with literary Gothicism, which offers information about authors, texts, web sites, book reviews and much more, including valuable links to numerous e-texts of important and often overlooked works of Gothic interest.

CHRONOLOGY

1757	Edmund Burke, *A Philosophical Enquiry into the Origin of Our Ideas of the Sublime and the Beautiful*
1762	Richard Hurd, *Letters on Chivalry and Romance*
1764	Horace Walpole, *The Castle of Otranto* (reissued in 1765 with a new preface and subtitle *A Gothic Story*)
1768	Horace Walpole, *The Mysterious Mother*
1773	John Aikin and Anna Laetitia Aikin Barbauld, 'On the Pleasure Derived from Objects of Terror; with Sir Bertrand, a Fragment'
1777	Clara Reeve, *The Champion of Virtue: A Gothic Story* (reissued in 1778 as *The Old English Baron*)
1783	Sophia Lee, *The Recess*, vol. 1 (finished in 1785)
1786	William Beckford, *Vathek*
1788	Charlotte Smith, *Emmeline, the Orphan of the Castle*
1789	Ann Radcliffe, *The Castles of Athlin and Dunbayne*; Charlotte Smith, *Ethelinde; or, The Recluse of the Lake*
1790	Ann Radcliffe, *A Sicilian Romance*
1791	Ann Radcliffe, *The Romance of the Forest*; Horace Walpole, *The Mysterious Mother*
1793	Eliza Parsons, *Castle of Wolfenbach: A German Story*; Charlotte Smith, *The Old Manor House*
1794	Lawrence Flammenberg, *The Necromancer*; William Godwin, *Things as They Are; or, The Adventures of Caleb Williams*; Ann Radcliffe, *The Mysteries of Udolpho*; Regina Maria Roche, *The Children of the Abbey: A Tale*
1796	Carl Grosse, *Horrid Mysteries*; M. G. Lewis, *The Monk*; Eliza Parsons, *The Mysterious Warning: A German Tale*

1797	William Beckford, *Azemia*; Ann Radcliffe, *The Italian*
1798	Charles Brockden Brown, *Wieland; or, The Transformation*; Samuel Taylor Coleridge, 'The Rime of the Ancient Mariner'; Francis Lathom, *The Midnight Bell*; Matthew Lewis, *The Castle Spectre*; Regina Maria Roche, *Clermont: A Tale*; Eleanor Sleath, *The Orphan of the Rhine*
1799	Charles Brockden Brown, *Edgar Huntley; or, The Memoirs of a Sleepwalker* and *Ormond; or, The Secret Witness*; William Godwin, *St Leon: A Tale of the Sixteenth Century*
1805	Charlotte Dacre, *Confessions of the Nun of St Omer*
1806	Charlotte Dacre, *Zofloya, or The Moor*
1807	Charles Robert Maturin, *The Fatal Revenge; or, The Family of Montorio*
1810	Percy Bysshe Shelley, *Zastrozzi*
1811	Percy Bysshe Shelley, *St Irvyne*
1813	Lord Byron, *The Giaour*
1816	E. T. A. Hoffmann, 'The Sandman'; Charles Robert Maturin, *Bertram; or, The Castle of St Aldobrand*
1817	Lord Byron, *Manfred*; E. T. A. Hoffman, *Nachstücke* (*Night Pieces*)
1818	Jane Austen, *Northanger Abbey*; James Hogg, *The Brownie of Bodsbeck*; Thomas Love Peacock, *Nightmare Abbey*; Mary Wollstonecraft Shelley, *Frankenstein*
1819	John Polidori, *The Vampyre*; Percy Bysshe Shelley, *The Cenci*
1819–20	Washington Irving, *The Sketch Book of Geoffrey Crayon, Gent.*
1820	Charles Robert Maturin, *Melmoth the Wanderer*; J. R. Planché, *The Vampyre, or, The Bride of the Isles: A Romantic Melodrama in Two Acts*
1824	James Hogg, *The Private Memoirs and Confessions of a Justified Sinner*; Washington Irving, *Tales of a Traveller*
1826	Ann Radcliffe, 'On the Supernatural in Poetry' and *Gaston de Blondeville*
1827	Edward George Bulwer-Lytton, *Falkland*
1830	Walter Scott, *Letters on Demonology and Witchcraft*
1832	Washington Irving, *The Alhambra*; Edward George Bulwer-Lytton, *Eugene Aram*
1833	Edward George Bulwer-Lytton, *Godolphin*
1837	Nathaniel Hawthorne, *Twice-Told Tales*
1838	Charles Dickens, *Oliver Twist*; Edgar Allan Poe, *The Narrative of Arthur Gordon Pym of Nantucket* and 'Ligeia'

1839	Edgar Allan Poe, 'The Fall of the House of Usher'
1840	William Harrison Ainsworth, *The Tower of London: An Historical Romance*; Edgar Allan Poe, *Tales of the Grotesque and Arabesque*
1841	Charles Dickens, *The Old Curiosity Shop*
1843	Edgar Allan Poe, 'The Black Cat' and 'The Pit and the Pendulum'
1844–8	G. W. M. Reynolds, *The Mysteries of London*
1845	G. W. M. Reynolds, *Faust* (serialized until 1846)
1846	Nathaniel Hawthorne, *Mosses from an Old Manse*; Edward George Bulwer-Lytton, *Lucretia*; Edgar Allan Poe, 'The Cask of Amontillado'
1847	Charlotte Brontë, *Jane Eyre*; Emily Brontë, *Wuthering Heights*; James Malcolm Rymer, *Varney the Vampire, or The Feast of Blood*
1848–56	G. W. M. Reynolds, *The Mysteries of the Courts of London*
1849	William Harrison Ainsworth, *The Lancashire Witches*
1850	Nathaniel Hawthorne, *The Scarlet Letter*
1851	Nathaniel Hawthorne, *The House of the Seven Gables*; J. Sheridan Le Fanu, *Ghost Stories and Tales of Mystery*
1852	Herman Melville, *Pierre; or, the Ambiguities*
1853	Charlotte Brontë, *Villette*
1856	Wilkie Collins, *After Dark*; Herman Melville, *The Piazza Tales*
1858	George MacDonald, *Phantastes*
1859	Edward George Bulwer-Lytton, 'The Haunted and the Haunters'; George Eliot, 'The Lifted Veil'
1860	Wilkie Collins, *The Woman in White*
1862	Mary Elizabeth Braddon, *Lady Audley's Secret*
1864	J. Sheridan Le Fanu, *Uncle Silas*
1865	Charles Dickens, *Our Mutual Friend*
1866	Wilkie Collins, *Armadale*
1868	Wilkie Collins, *The Moonstone*
1870	Charles Dickens, *The Mystery of Edwin Drood*
1871	J. Sheridan Le Fanu, 'Carmilla'
1872	J. Sheridan Le Fanu, *In a Glass Darkly*
1878	Wilkie Collins, *The Haunted Hotel: A Mystery of Modern Venice*
1880	Margaret Oliphant, 'The Beleaguered City'
1882–8	Margaret Oliphant, *Little Pilgrim* series
1884	Robert Louis Stevenson, *The Body-Snatcher*
1885	H. Rider Haggard, *King Solomon's Mines*; Margaret Oliphant, 'Old Lady Mary'

1886   Robert Louis Stevenson, *The Strange Case of Dr Jekyll and Mr Hyde*

1888   Rudyard Kipling, *Plain Tales From the Hills* and *The Phantom Rickshaw and Other Tales*

1890   Vernon Lee, *Hauntings*; Oscar Wilde, *The Picture of Dorian Gray* (in *Lippincott's Magazine*, with expanded version in book form in 1891)

1891   Ambrose Bierce, *Tales of Soldiers and Civilians*

1892   Ambrose Bierce, *In the Midst of Life*; Charlotte Perkins Gilman, 'The Yellow Wallpaper'

1893   Ambrose Bierce, *Can Such Things Be?*

1894   Arthur Machen, *The Great God Pan* and *The Inmost Light*

1895   Robert W. Chambers, *The King in Yellow*; Marie Corelli, *The Sorrows of Satan*; Arthur Machen, *The Three Imposters*; George MacDonald, *Lilith*

1896   H. G. Wells, *The Island of Dr Moreau*; Margaret Oliphant, 'The Library Window'

1897   Richard Marsh, *The Beetle*; Bram Stoker, *Dracula*

1898   Henry James, *The Turn of the Screw*

1903   A. C. Benson, *The Hill of Trouble*; Bram Stoker, *The Jewel of Seven Stars*

1904   M. R. James, *Ghost Stories of an Antiquary*

1905   Lord Dunsany, *The Gods of Pegana*

1906   Algernon Blackwood, *The Empty House and Other Ghost Stories*

1907   William Hope Hodgson, *The Boats of the 'Glen Carrig'*; Arthur Machen, *The Hill of Dreams*

1910   Edith Wharton, *Tales of Men and Ghosts*

1911   F. Marion Crawford, *Wandering Ghosts*; M. R. James, *More Ghost Stories of an Antiquary*; Oliver Onions, *Widdershins*; Bram Stoker, *The Lair of the White Worm*

1912   E. F. Benson, *The Room in the Tower and Other Stories*

1919   James Branch Cabell, *Jurgen*; Sigmund Freud, 'The Uncanny'; Robert Wiene, dir. *The Cabinet of Dr Caligari*

1922   Arthur Conan Doyle, *Tales of Twilight and the Unseen* and *Tales of Terror and Mystery*; David Lindsay, *The Haunted Woman*; F. W. Murnau, dir. *Nosferatu: Ein Symphonie Des Grauens*

1923   E. F. Benson, *Visible and Invisible*; Walter de la Mare, *The Riddle and Other Stories*

1926	Cynthia Asquith, *The Ghost Book*; Walter de la Mare, *The Connoisseur and Other Stories*; Mary Wollstonecraft Shelley, *The Last Man*
1927	H. P. Lovecraft, *The Case of Charles Dexter Ward: A Novel of Terror*; Fritz Lang, dir. *Metropolis*
1929	Ernest Jones, *On the Nightmare*
1931	William Faulkner, *Sanctuary*; M. R. James, *Collected Ghost Stories*; Todd Browning, dir. *Dracula*; Reuben Mamoulian, dir. *Dr Jekyll and Mr Hyde*; James Whale, dir. *Frankenstein*
1932	William Faulkner, *Light in August*; Carl Dreyer, dir. *Vampyr*; Victor Halperin, dir. *White Zombie*
1935	James Whale, dir. *Bride of Frankenstein*
1936	William Faulkner, *Absalom! Absalom!*
1937	Edith Wharton, *Ghosts*
1938	Daphne du Maurier, *Rebecca*
1940	Alfred Hitchcock, dir. *Rebecca*
1941	August Derleth, *Someone in the Dark*
1942	Jacques Tourneur, dir. *Cat People*
1943	Jacques Tourneur, dir. *I Walked with a Zombie*
1944	Lewis Allen, dir. *The Uninvited*
1945	Elizabeth Bowen, *The Demon Lover, and Other Stories*; H. P. Lovecraft and August Derleth, *The Lurker at the Threshold*
1946	Mervyn Peake, *Titus Groan*
1950	Mervyn Peake, *Gormenghast*
1954	Isak Dinesen, *Seven Gothic Tales*; Richard Matheson, *I Am Legend*
1956	Don Siegel, dir. *Invasion of the Body Snatchers*
1957	Terence Fisher, dir. *Dracula*
1959	Robert Bloch, *Psycho*; Shirley Jackson, *The Haunting of Hill House*; Mervyn Peake, *Titus Alone*
1960	Roger Corman, dir. *The House of Usher*; Alfred Hitchcock, dir. *Psycho*; Michael Powell, dir. *Peeping Tom*; Wolf Rilla, dir. *Village of the Damned*
1961	Roger Corman, dir. *The Pit and the Pendulum*
1963	August Derleth, *Mr George and Other Odd Persons*; Robert Wise, dir. *The Haunting*
1965	Roman Polanski, dir. *Repulsion*
1967	Ira Levin, *Rosemary's Baby*
1968	Joyce Carol Oates, *Expensive People*; George A. Romero, dir. *Night of the Living Dead*; Roman Polanski, dir. *Rosemary's Baby*

1970   J. G. Ballard, *The Atrocity Exhibition*; Roy Ward Baker, dir. *The Vampire Lovers*

1971   William Peter Blatty, *The Exorcist*; Thomas Tryon, *The Other*; Boris Sagal, dir. *The Omega Man*

1973   John Banville, *Birchwood*; William Friedkin, dir. *The Exorcist*; Robin Hardy, dir. *The Wicker Man*

1974   Stephen King, *Carrie*; James Herbert, *The Rats*; Tobe Hooper, dir. *The Texas Chain Saw Massacre*

1975   James Herbert, *The Fog*; Stephen King, *'Salem's Lot*; Fred Saberhagen, *The Dracula Tape*; David Cronenberg, dir. *Shivers*; Brian Forbes, dir. *The Stepford Wives*

1976   August Derleth, *Dwellers in Darkness*; Anne Rice, *Interview with the Vampire*; David Seltzer, *The Omen*; Richard Donner, dir. *The Omen*; Brian de Palma, dir. *Carrie*; George A. Romero, dir. *Martin*

1977   Stephen King, *The Shining*; Jim Sharman, dir. *The Rocky Horror Picture Show*

1978   Whitley Strieber, *The Wolfen*; John Carpenter, dir. *Halloween*; Wes Craven, dir. *The Hills Have Eyes*; George A. Romero, dir. *Dawn of the Dead*

1979   Angela Carter, *The Bloody Chamber*; Peter Straub, *Ghost Story*; Werner Herzog, dir. *Nosferatu: Phantom der Nacht*; George A. Romero, dir. *Dawn of the Dead, Day of the Dead*; Ridley Scott, dir. *Alien*

1980   Ramsay Campbell, *To Wake the Dead*; Suzy McKee Charnas, *The Vampire Tapestry*; David Cronenberg, dir. *Scanners;* Sean S. Cunningham, dir. *Friday the 13th*; Stanley Kubrick, dir. *The Shining*

1981   Thomas Harris, *Red Dragon*; Whitley Strieber, *The Hunger*; John Irvin, dir. *Ghost Story*; John Landis, dir. *An American Werewolf in London*

1982   William S. Burroughs, *Cities of the Red Night*; Tobe Hooper, dir. *Poltergeist*

1983   Susan Hill, *The Woman in Black*; Stephen King, *Pet Sematary*; Tony Scott, dir. *The Hunger*

1984   Iain Banks, *The Wasp Factory*; William Gibson, *Neuromancer*; Jody Scott, *I, Vampire*; S. P. Somtow, *Vampire Junction*; Wes Craven, dir. *A Nightmare on Elm Street*

1985   Paul Auster, *City of Glass*; Anne Rice, *The Vampire Lestat*; Tom Holland, dir. *Fright Night*

1986   Iain Banks, *The Bridge*; John Banville, *Mefisto*; David Lynch, dir. *Blue Velvet*; John McNaughton, dir. *Henry: Portrait of a Serial Killer*

1987   Clive Barker, *Weaveworld*; Stephen King, *The Tommyknockers* and *Misery*; Alan Moore and Dave Gibbons, *Watchmen*; Toni Morrison, *Beloved*; Alan Parker, dir. *Angel Heart*; Joel Schumacher, dir. *The Lost Boys*; Kathryn Bigelow, dir. *Near Dark*

1988   Clive Barker, *The Books of Blood*; Neil Gaiman, *The Sandman: No. 1*; Amitav Ghosh, *The Shadow Lines*; Barbara Hambly, *Those Who Hunt the Night*; Thomas Harris, *Silence of the Lambs*; David Cronenberg, dir. *Dead Ringers*

1989   John Banville, *The Book of Evidence*

1990   Iain Banks, *The Wasp Factory*; Tim Burton, dir. *Edward Scissorhands*

1991   Bret Easton Ellis, *American Psycho*; Jewelle Gomez, *The Gilda Stories*; Jonathan Demme, dir. *The Silence of the Lambs*

1992   Iain Banks, *The Bridge*; Poppy Z. Brite, *Lost Souls*; Ramsey Campbell, *The Claw*; Dan Simmons, *Children of the Night*; Francis Ford Coppola, dir. *Bram Stoker's Dracula*; Bernard Rose, dir. *Candyman*

1993   Iain Banks, *Complicity*; Ramsay Campbell, *The Long Lost*

1994   Neil Gaiman, *Brief Lives*

1995   Joyce Carol Oates, *Zombie*; David Fincher, dir. *Se7en*

1996   James Robinson, *Witchcraft*; David Cronenberg, dir. *Crash*; Robert Rodriguez, dir. *From Dusk Till Dawn*

1997   Iain Banks, *A Song of Stone*

2000   Mary Harron, dir. *American Psycho*

Introduction

Since the late 1970s, the Gothic has become a highly popular field of academic study. Scores of books have been published, both on the Gothic in general, and on particular subgenres and authors. A journal, *Gothic Studies*, has been established, and is connected to the International Gothic Association, a body which exists to promote the study of the Gothic.

Perhaps despite, or perhaps because of, this concentration of critical activity, the Gothic remains a notoriously difficult field to define. In this volume, we have chosen to treat it broadly. Nobody would dispute that the early writers in the genre, such as Ann Radcliffe, M. G. Lewis or Charles Robert Maturin, fall squarely within the Gothic tradition; after that, though, various critical claims and counter-claims have been made, and it is for the student and reader to evaluate these claims and to find out for themselves which of the many definitions and descriptions seem most apposite.

Clearly it is possible to speak of the Gothic as a historical phenomenon, originating (in its literary sense, but not necessarily in other senses) in the late eighteenth century. Equally, it has seemed to many critics more useful to think of it in terms of a psychological argument, to do with the ways in which otherwise repressed fears are represented in textual form. A more radical claim would be that there are very few actual literary texts which are 'Gothic'; that the Gothic is more to do with particular moments, tropes, repeated motifs that can be found scattered, or disseminated, through the modern western literary tradition. Then again, one might want to think of Gothic, especially in its more modern manifestations, in terms of a collection of subgenres: the ghost story, the horror story, the 'techno-Gothic' – all of these would be ways of writing that have obvious connections with the 'original' Gothic, but their differences might be seen as at least as important as their similarities.

Yet despite these differences – and it is obviously a very long way from Ann Radcliffe to William Gibson – one can also point to the extraordinary persistence of certain motifs – the vampire, for example, or the monstrous potential of science and technology – and as well to the way in which these motifs seem to continue to be recycled in the 'Gothic textual body'. Sometimes this can be to genuinely shocking effect; at other times the habit Gothic seems to have of preying upon, consuming and recycling itself can lead to more or less consciously comic effects – as in, for example, Hammer horror films.

Perhaps the Gothic is an entirely serious attempt to get to grips with difficulties in social organization, or in the organization of the psyche; perhaps it is a rather down-market or debased form of tragedy, akin to melodrama; perhaps it is an escapist form, in which the reader is encouraged to avoid rather than to confront fear and anxiety. Certainly different critics have espoused all of these possibilities and more. Equally certainly, however, there is currently an intense and invigorating debate about these issues, and we hope that this book will help readers to understand something of this debate and of the causes of it.

It is also clear that the issue of the Gothic is alive (if not entirely well) in western cultures in the early twenty-first century, in the form of popular 'Goth' culture as well as, for example, in the apparently endless remaking and reshaping of vampire myth in literature and film. The study of the Gothic, therefore, is – like, of course, the study of any literary genre – not something that can be pursued in academic isolation; the study of the Gothic opens windows onto all manner of aspects of social and psychological life. Whether it does so in an entirely distinctive way, or whether the binding together of many different phenomena under the heading 'Gothic' is a matter of critical convenience – or even perhaps, of critics writing themselves into these phenomena – is again a matter for the individual reader or student to decide.

It is sometimes said that Gothic has flourished at times of actual or potential social upheaval – in the late eighteenth and early nineteenth centuries, for example, or at the end of the nineteenth century – but it would also be possible to ask what periods of recent western history could not be described in this way. Certainly Gothic offers horrors to the reader; but it can be argued that the horrors it offers are as nothing to the horrors of war or even of conventional domestic life. Gothic is above all, perhaps, a way of representation: nothing that Ann Radcliffe's heroines suffer could possibly match the continuing actual sufferings of whole continents in recent times.

Gothic is, perhaps, a staggering, limping, lurching form, akin to the monsters it so frequently describes. Some of its writers deserve to be granted real literary stature; many more do not. Some are repetitive almost beyond belief. Some Gothic works are vivid and genuinely haunting; others seem to inhabit a world of cardboard characters and clichéd settings. This, though, would again be true of any literary form; we may choose to judge it by its acknowledged masters and mistresses, or we may wish to look broadly at the whole repertoire.

In this book we have chosen the broad approach, but it is important to emphasize that this necessarily raises as many questions as it answers. We do not attempt here to define the Gothic, but rather to present some of its parameters, and to describe some of the terrain that lies within those parameters. In the end, the question remains, as it must, one of critical judgement; and we hope that the materials assembled here will help readers with that judgement, and enable them to refine and develop their own notion of what – for them – the Gothic is.

BACKGROUNDS AND CONTEXTS

Civilization and the Goths

Historically, the Goths were one of several Germanic tribes instrumental in the fall of the Roman Empire. In the absence of early written records, little can be said with much certainty about them, although archaeologists have confirmed their early settlement in the Baltic and their gradual migration down to the Black Sea. The Goths made their first incursion into Roman territory during the third century, and eventually, under Alaric, took Rome in AD 410, subsequently establishing kingdoms in France and Italy. The first extant history of the Goths is Jordanes's *Getica* (551), and here an etymological confusion begins. As Samuel Kliger (1945) has shown, Jordanes aimed to glorify the Thracian tribe, the Getes, from whom he sprang, and therefore identified them with the more impressive tribe of the Goths. In addition, he gave credence to the idea of a general northern identity, and all those tribes later called 'Germanic' or 'Teutonic' came to be known collectively as the 'Goths'.

Far more important than any sketchy history of the actual Goths that can be reconstructed, however, are the myths that developed around them, and the varying aesthetic and political agendas that these myths were subsequently appropriated to serve. 'Gothic' became a highly mobile term, remaining constant only in the way it functioned to establish a set of polarities revolving primarily around the concepts of the primitive and the civilized. Initially, because the Goths left no literature or art of their own, they came to be remembered only as the invaders and destroyers of the great Roman civilization. Since very little was known about the medieval world generally during the Renaissance, the idea of the 'Dark Ages' that followed the fall of Rome soon expanded to include the medieval period generally, up to about the middle of the seventeenth century, and 'Gothic' became a term applied to all things medieval. When Italian art historians of the early

Renaissance first used the term 'Gothic' in an aesthetic sense, they erroneously attributed a style of architecture (q.v.) to those Germanic tribes that sacked Rome, and identified this style as barbaric, disordered and irrational in opposition to the classical style. By the eighteenth century a Goth had come to be defined, in the terms of Dr Johnson's *Dictionary* of 1775, as 'one not civilised, one deficient in general knowledge, a barbarian', and the medieval or Gothic age as a cultural wasteland, primitive and superstitious. This equation of the Gothic with a barbaric medieval past served not only to establish through difference the superiority of the more classical traditions of Greece and Rome, but also to confirm the virtues of the equally civilized, ordered and rational present.

During the eighteenth century, however, the Gothic also began to be invested with a set of different and contradictory values in both aesthetic (see 'Gothic in the Eighteenth Century' below) and political terms. This resulted from the reclamation of a native English past that played a crucial role in the eighteenth-century development of both a literary and a political nationalism. The history of the term 'Gothic' actually begins in political discussion, where the project of producing the past as barbaric and superstitious had begun to be contested as early as the sixteenth century (Smith 1987). Since the term had expanded to include all the Germanic tribes, including those who invaded Britain in the fifth century, it was possible to offer an alternative, if mythical, construction of the Gothic past as the site of a true national, democratic and civilized heritage. Here the past becomes idealized to provide not a site of difference, but a site of continuity.

In establishing this alternative myth of Gothic origins, commentators drew upon such sources as the Roman historian Tacitus' *Germania* (AD 98). What Tacitus said about the Germanic tribes generally came to be particularly associated with the Goths, and he depicted them as brave, virtuous and, as demonstrated by their representative system of government and their invention of the jury system, possessing a strong belief in justice and liberty. The belief that the English constitution originated with the Anglo-Saxons was common, if contested; it was, however, given renewed authority in the eighteenth century by the influential historian Charles-Louis de Secondat Montesquieu in his *Spirit of the Laws* (1748, trans. 1750) when, citing Tacitus as his source, he famously commented that the English idea of political government derives from the Germans and their 'beautiful system . . . invented first in the woods' (in Clery and Miles 2000: 61). According to the Whig view of history, such moments as the signing of the Magna Carta and the Revolution of 1688 were ones when a tradition of freedom that had been displaced with the French invasion of 1066 was reaffirmed. The Glorious Revolution had consequently not introduced an entirely new social order, but rather recovered an original social order that had been replaced by foreign authoritarian rule. In this rethinking of history, rather than being seen as the despoilers of civilized values, the Goths were celebrated as the *source* of these values. As James Thomson wrote in his poem 'Liberty' (1735–6), the Goths were those who reinstated the liberty once held but lost by a decadent Rome. In settling Britain they 'brought a happy government along; / Formed by that freedom which, with secret voice, / Impartial nature teaches all her sons' (4.682–4). Similarly, Edmund Burke's *Reflections on the Revolution in France* (1790) continually recalls the Gothic heritage – which he discusses in terms of 'chivalry' – to assert the superiority of a civilized England over a barbaric France. The Goths were now seen to have laid the very foundations of a democratic, rational British society, and the Gothic to be the site of a uniquely British culture and politics.

The myth of the Goths, then, can be seen in various ways to have been, as Mark Madoff observes, 'a product of fantasy invented to serve specific political and emotional purposes' (1979: 337). Like the Goths themselves, 'Gothic' as a term is endlessly mobile; simultaneously, its essential function remains unchanged. As the brief history of the terms 'Goth' and 'Gothic' outlined above suggests, the Gothic is identified with the primitive for specific ideological purposes, and these are achieved in two main ways. In one, the Gothic is associated with the barbaric and uncivilized in order to define that which is other to the values of the civilized present. Alternatively, the Gothic is still associated with the primitive but this primitive has now become identified with the true, but lost, foundations of a culture. The Gothic past is consequently seen as retaining not only more power and vigour than the present, but also, in a strange way, more truly civilized values. What remains constant throughout the developing political use of the term is that the Gothic always remains the symbolic site of a culture's discursive struggle to define and claim possession of the civilized, and to abject, or throw off, what is seen as other to that civilized self.

Bibliography

Clery, E. J. and Miles, Robert 2000: *Gothic Documents: A Sourcebook, 1700–1820.* Manchester: Manchester University Press.

Holbrook, William C. 1941: 'The Adjective *Gothique* in the Eighteenth Century.' *Modern Language Notes*, 56, 498–503.

Kliger, Samuel 1945: 'The "Goths" in England: An Introduction to the Gothic Vogue in Eighteenth-Century Aesthetic Discussion.' *Modern Philology*, 47, 107–17.

Kliger, Samuel 1952: *The Goths in England: A Study in Seventeenth and Eighteenth Century Thought.* Cambridge, MA: Harvard University Press.

Madoff, Mark 1979: 'The Useful Myth of Gothic Ancestry.' *Studies in Eighteenth-Century Culture*, 9, 337–50.

Smith, R. J. 1987: *The Gothic Bequest: Medieval Institutions in British Thought, 1688–1863.* Cambridge: Cambridge University Press.

Sowerby, Robin 2000: 'The Goths in History and Pre-Gothic Gothic.' In David Punter (ed.), *A Companion to the Gothic.* Oxford: Blackwell, 15–26.

Gothic in the
Eighteenth Century

The birth of Gothic as a genre of fiction, the 'Gothic novel', and all its numerous successors came about as a direct result of changes in cultural emphasis in the eighteenth century. The reputation of the eighteenth century has mainly been as an age of reliance on reason, as a time when enlightenment was seen as possible and the rational explanation of natural and human activities formed an agenda in the service of which most of the European intellectuals of the age worked. However, as is always the case with such simple histories of ideas, this inevitably tells only part of the story.

During the eighteenth century, there was, for example, a shift in the meanings and connotations of the word 'Gothic'. Whereas previously it had referred specifically to the 'Goths' (q.v.) themselves, or at least to later imaginings of them, to the barbarian northern tribes who played so reviled a part in the collapse of the Roman Empire, less weight came to be placed on the presumed geographical significance of the word and correspondingly more on the historical. Here, however, there was a serious difficulty, for very little was actually known in the later eighteenth century about the history of the Dark Ages, or indeed about medieval history. From being a term suggestive of more or less unknown features of the Dark Ages, 'Gothic' broadened out to become descriptive of anything medieval – in fact, of all things preceding about the middle of the seventeenth century.

Another connotation was attached to this: if 'Gothic' meant to do with what was perceived as barbaric and to do with the medieval world, it could be seen to follow that it was a term which could be used in structural opposition to 'classical'. Where the classical was well ordered, the Gothic was chaotic; where the classical was simple and pure, Gothic was ornate and convoluted; where the classics offered a world of clear rules and limits, Gothic represented excess and exaggeration, the product of the wild and the uncivilized, a world that constantly tended to overflow cultural boundaries.

These extensions in, or reversals of, meaning have a perceptible logic; but what started to happen in the middle of the eighteenth century had less to do with logic and more to do with a shift in cultural values. For while the word 'Gothic' retained this central stock of meanings, the value placed upon them began to alter radically. It is not possible to put a precise date on this change, but it was one of huge dimensions which affected whole areas of architectural, artistic and literary culture in Britain and also in some parts of mainland Europe; for what happened was that the 'medieval', the primitive, the wild, became invested with positive value in and for itself and came to be seen as representing virtues and qualities that the 'modern' world needed.

Gothic stood for the old-fashioned as opposed to the modern; the barbaric as opposed to the civilized; crudity as opposed to elegance; old English barons as opposed to the cosmopolitan gentry; often for the English and provincial as opposed to the European or Frenchified, for the vernacular as opposed to an 'imposed' culture. Gothic was the archaic, the pagan, that which was prior to, or was opposed to, or resisted the establishment of civilized values and a well-regulated society. And various writers, starting from this point, began to make out a case for the importance of these Gothic qualities and to claim, specifically, that the fruits of primitivism and barbarism possessed a vigour, a sense of grandeur that was sorely needed in English culture. Furthermore, these writers began to argue that there were whole areas of English cultural history which had been ignored in conventional reconstructions of the past, and that the way to breathe life into the culture was by re-establishing relations with this forgotten, 'Gothic' history.

Many of the crucial texts which made this point were written in the 1760s. The most important of all was *Letters on Chivalry and Romance* (1762), by Bishop Hurd. Hurd was a littérateur, an amateur and an antiquarian rather than a serious critic, but he summarized a very widespread flow of thought in his enquiry into the nature and value of the Gothic. Perhaps the best-known passage goes as follows:

> The greatest geniuses of our own and foreign countries, such as Ariosto and Tasso in Italy, and Spenser and Milton in England, were seduced by these barbarities of their forefathers, were even charmed by the Gothic Romances. Was this caprice and absurdity in them? Or, may there not be something in the Gothic Romance peculiarly suited to the views of a genius, and to the ends of poetry. (Hurd 1963: 4)

The arts of our forefathers and the folk traditions on which they drew, Hurd is saying, may have been ill formed and may indeed not have conformed to rules which we have since come to regard as constitutive of aesthetic success and propriety; but perhaps this very rudeness and wildness can be construed as itself a source of power – a power that Spenser, Shakespeare and Milton saw and which we may not be able to reclaim unless we come to value it and see it more clearly.

It is not simple to pin down precisely who the 'forefathers' were to whom Hurd refers, but critics agree that there were four principal areas of past literature that were brought back into cultural acceptability and prominence under the aegis of this early 'revival of the Gothic'. First, there was the genuinely ancient British heritage, in so far as any of it was available in the eighteenth century. Thomas Gray regarded himself as well read in old Welsh poetry; James Macpherson (q.v.) in his 'translations' of the imaginary Gaelic poet Ossian saw himself as referring back to ancient British 'tradition'; Thomas Percy's important translation in 1770 of P. H. Mallet's *Northern Antiquities* was designed to reacquaint its readers with large areas of the ancient history of northern Europe.

Second, there was a revival of interest in ballads. Percy's crucial collection, *Reliques of Ancient English Poetry*, was published in 1765, and it was the re-establishment of the credentials of this form of 'folk-poetry' which was to lead on to the interest of the major romantics in ballad-like poems, through works like William Blake's 'Gwin, King of Norway', written in the 1770s, to Samuel Taylor Coleridge's 'Ancient Mariner' (1798), and thence to John Keats's 'La Belle Dame sans Merci' and Percy Bysshe Shelley's *Mask of Anarchy*, both written in 1819.

Third, Gothic was taken to include English medieval poetry. Best known by far were the works of Chaucer, which were given a scholarly edition by Thomas Tyrwhitt in 1775–8. And fourth, Gothic included, at least for some writers and critics, the major work of Spenser and of the Elizabethans, whose strength, it now came to be thought, had been buried under the achievements of the mid-seventeenth century. This shift of value was at its apogee in the 1790s. It was not, of course, the case that Gothic ever became a universal standard of taste, but by that time the arguments that supported it were being given their fullest articulation and the stage was set for Gothic to develop as the basis for a literary form.

As we have said, however, the literary effects of this change in values were by no means the whole of the picture. The other principal application of the term 'Gothic' was, as it still is, in the field of architecture (q.v.), and here it was used to refer to medieval architecture, principally churches and cathedrals, from about the twelfth to the sixteenth centuries. Alongside its taste for 'ancient' literature, the late eighteenth century acquired a pronounced taste for medieval buildings, whether real or fake. Wealthy land-owners even went to the extent of building Gothic ruins, ready-made, in the grounds of their mansions, and occasionally to the expense of hiring hermits to live in custom-made adjacent cells. The most famous example of Gothic building in the period was Horace Walpole's (q.v.) Strawberry Hill, a Gothic castle in appearance even if surprisingly small in scale. By far the most impressive, however, must have been William Beckford's (q.v.) Fonthill Abbey, which collapsed under the weight of its own vast tower. What later flowed from this taste was to be the 'Gothicizing' mania of the Victorians.

When examining the emergence of the Gothic in the eighteenth century, it is helpful to contrast it with the concept of Augustanism, which took its name from the Augustan period of the Roman Empire. The latter-day, eighteenth-century Augustans saw their period of national history as analogous to this past age in that their own too seemed to them a silver age: that is, they saw it as being poised between splendid, 'golden' achievements in the past and a possible future collapse into a barbarian age, of bronze. According to Augustan theory, the barbarians are forever at the gates; the writer's role must therefore be to maintain cultural defences against this cultural encroachment.

Crucial to the Augustan ideal, as embodied in, to take a major example, Alexander Pope, is that the early classical poets had already found out and indeed described the secrets of the natural world; it would therefore be presumptuous of a poet or any other writer to claim to be discovering novelty; the task was instead to express old truths in increasingly beautiful and arresting forms. But it is also important to notice that as early as the 1740s we can trace the development of a form of poetry which was radically different from anything Pope advocated, and which came to be called 'graveyard poetry'. Graveyard poetry is significant here because it prefigures the Gothic novel in several ways, and its emergence was sudden and dramatic: Edward Young's massive *Night Thoughts* came out between 1742 and 1745; Robert Blair's *The Grave* in 1743; James Hervey's major work, *Meditations among the Tombs*, between 1745 and 1747; Thomas Warton's *On the Pleasures of Melancholy* in 1747; and Gray's famous *Elegy in a Country Church-Yard* in 1751.

What these works focus on, in sharp contradistinction to Pope's, is the severe limitations of human pretensions to rational understanding of the purposes and workings of the cosmos. Graveyard poetry constitutes an implicit attack on those who, like Pope, claim that nature's purpose is merely to serve human needs. For the graveyard poet, the nature of destiny and the evolution of the future are far less comprehensible than this. Although written largely about death, these works also serve a subtly different purpose of challenging the certainties of human progress to which Pope and many of his contemporaries subscribed, and suggest a far more dubious awareness

10

of the limitations of human knowledge and the necessity of owning to the inevitability of human frailty.

A well-known and typical passage which illustrates the way in which these poets anticipated the evolution of Gothic can be found in Thomas Parnell's 'Night-Piece on Death' (1833, first published 1722):

> By the blue taper's trembling light,
> No more I waste the wakeful night,
> Intent with endless view to pore
> The schoolmen and the sages o'er:
> Their books from wisdom widely stray,
> Or point at best the longest way.
> I'll seek a readier path, and go
> Where wisdom's surely taught below. (1–7)

Quiet though his language may appear to be, Parnell is saying something quite radical for the times. Unlike Pope, he is not impressed with the attempts made by reason to define the limits and aspirations of the human species. To learn wisdom, it is necessary to take a quicker and more frightening path, which is the path not of reason but of intense feeling; one can best – or perhaps only – learn the secrets of life (if one really wishes to, and has the strength to) from prolonged and absorbed meditation on its extreme limit: death. Here we see, among other things, a harbinger of the thrill of entering forbidden, thanatic realms which would later become the province of the Gothic novel.

Thus in Parnell's poetry, in Young's, and indeed in all the better examples of graveyard poetry, the value of reason is replaced by a valuation of feeling, and what this leads to is a sense of the sublime, in which the mind is overwhelmed by, or swoons before, something greater than itself. What is crucial, however, is that this 'something greater' is also inevitably accompanied by terror. The essential text here is the major eighteenth-century treatise on the sublime, Edmund Burke's *Origin of Our Ideas of the Sublime and Beautiful* (1757). It is Burke who first significantly effects the crucial connection between sublimity and terror:

> Whatever is fitted in any sort to excite the ideas of pain, and danger, that is to say, whatever is in any sort terrible, or is conversant about terrible subjects, or operates in a manner analogous to terror, is a source of the *sublime*; that is, it is productive of the strongest emotion which the mind is capable of feeling. (1958: 39)

In these words, Burke seems even to connect the very nature of mind with the capacity for experiencing terror, so that this capacity becomes an essential mark of our humanness. The Enlightenment conviction that man can understand his own circumstances has never, indeed, disappeared from the history of ideas; but what the Gothic does is to entertain the fear or rather, to follow Burke, the terror that such an enterprise may not in fact be possible, that there is something inherent in our very mortality that dooms us to a life of incomprehension, a life in which we are forever sunk in mysteries and unable to escape from the deathly consequences of our physical form.

Bibliography

Burke, Edmund 1958: *A Philosophical Enquiry into the Origin of Our Ideas of the Sublime and Beautiful*, ed. J. T. Boulton. London: Routledge and Kegan Paul.

Hurd, Richard 1963: *Letters on Chivalry and Romance*, ed. Hoyt Trowbridge. Los Angeles: Augustan Reprint Society.

Punter, David 1996: *The Literature of Terror: A History of Gothic Fictions from 1765 to the Present Day*. 2nd edn. 2 vols. London: Longman.

Smith, R. J. 1987: *The Gothic Bequest: Medieval Institutions in British Thought 1688–1863*. Cambridge: Cambridge University Press.

Gothic and Romantic

The canon of writing during the 'romantic' period has changed radically over recent years (McGann 1994), but most of those writers traditionally considered to be the major romantic poets were influenced by, and played a part in shaping, the evolution of Gothic, and here we give some of the best-known examples. In the case of William Blake (although, of course, his status as a 'romantic' poet is hotly disputed), his early work includes imitations of Spenser and of other writers rehabilitated by the Gothic revival. Blake had a strong interest in the ballad form, as we can see from such conventional works as 'Fair Elenor' (1783) and, rather differently, from the thematically highly complex but formally simple works in the Pickering Manuscript, such as 'The Mental Traveller'. Some of the prose pieces in the *Poetical Sketches* (1783) appear to have been influenced by 'Ossian', and there is also an influence from the graveyard poets, evidenced outstandingly in Blake's illustrations to Edward Young and Robert Blair but also in the constant preoccupation with 'graveyard vocabulary', as strong in *Vala, or, The Four Zoas* (1795–1804) and *The Keys to the Gates* (*c*.1818) as in his earlier work.

A notable example of this last occurs in a passage in *Thel* (1789), where the eponymous protagonist is exploring the psychic depths:

> The eternal gates' terrific porter lifted the northern bar.
> Thel entered in and saw the secrets of the land unknown.
> She saw the couches of the dead, and where the fibrous roots
> Of every heart on earth infixes deep its restless twists –
> A land of sorrows and of tears where never smile was seen.
>
> She wandered in the land of clouds, through valleys dark, listening
> Dolours and lamentations; waiting oft beside a dewy grave
> She stood in silence, listening to the voices of the ground,
> Till to her own grave plot she came. (4.1–9)

This graveyard language, the emphases on secrets, the 'land unknown', the 'voices of the ground' as well as the focus, throughout the poem, on the innocent, vulnerable heroine who is travelling through dangerous realms clearly point us towards the Gothic in terms of plot as well as scenario. The insistence that wisdom can be learned only from an encounter with death takes us directly back to a poet like Parnell; but the insistence that this is a 'narrative of the psyche', a journey through the mind, moves the reader forward to the psychological nuances of nineteenth-century Gothic.

As frequently in Blake, this Gothic discourse also carries directly political inflections. There are obvious examples in his most direct poetic account of historical events, *The French Revolution* (1791). There is a moment, for example, when the poem depicts the inmates of the Bastille:

> In the tower named *Order*, an old man, whose white beard covered the
>   stone floor like weeds
> On the margin of the sea, shrivelled up by heat of day and cold of night;
>   his den was short
> And narrow as a grave dug for a child, with spiders' webs wove,
>   and with slime
> Of ancient horrors covered, for snakes and scorpions are his companions.
>   (1.38–40)

And around this passage there are references to skeletons, the 'eternal worm' (1.34), a man 'Chained hand and foot, round his neck an iron band, bound to the impregnable wall' (1.27). Here the emphasis, as so frequently in the Gothic novel in the hands of, for example, Ann Radcliffe or M. G. Lewis (qq.v.), is on tyranny and its effects, on the horrific and seemingly limitless powers of the despot.

When we turn to Samuel Taylor Coleridge, we find less emphasis on this political dimension and more on psychological mood, in the characteristically Coleridgean range of dejection, disappointment and melancholy. In more formal terms, we also find Ossianic poetic prose, and a series of ballads, from 'Anna and Harland' (1790) to 'Alice du Clos' (1828). In 'The Destiny of Nations' (1796), another well-known location, the poetry of Gray and Young forms a background to a set of meditations on history inextricably linked to the key Gothic theme of the ruin, in lines like:

> As through the dark vaults of some mouldered Tower
> (Which, fearful to approach, the evening kind
> Circles at distance in his homeward way)
> The winds breathe hollow, deemed the plaining groan
> Of prisoned spirits. (305–9)

This view of the past as peopled by ghosts which haunt the present demonstrates that, although Blake was aware of the antecedents of Gothic, Coleridge was already conscious of it in its more contemporary forms: of Radcliffe's novels, many of whose features appear in 'The Old Man of the Alps' (1798); of Lewis, in 'The Mad Monk' (1800); and, very importantly, of the German father of English Gothic, Friedrich Schiller, to whom he addressed these well-known lines:

> Ah Bard tremendous in sublimity!
> Could I behold thee in thy loftier mood
> Wand'ring at eve with finely-frenzied eye
> Beneath some vast old tempest-swinging wood!
> Awhile with mute awe gazing I would brood:
> Then weep aloud in a wild ecstacy! (9–14)

Whereas Blake is concerned with a way of articulating the effects of social and political repression, Coleridge is in the end more concerned with finding correlatives for his personal psychological predicament, his melancholia. The tone of alienation that pervades his work is struck in the 'lines' written at Shurton Bars (1795):

> And there in black soul-jaundic'd fit
> A sad gloom-pamper'd Man to sit,
>   And listen to the roar:
> When mountain Surges bellowing deep
> With an uncouth monster leap
>   Plung'd foaming on the shore. (49–54)

The numerous ghosts and spectres in Coleridge's poetry were, critics usually opine, related to his own pervasive feeling of guilt; 'The Pains of Sleep' (1803) is very close to Young's *Night Thoughts* (1742–5), not only in the structure of feeling which it manifests, but also in the exaggerated, lurid terms in which Coleridge tries to objectify his nightmares:

> But yester-night I prayed aloud
> In anguish and in agony,
> Up-starting from the fiendish crowd
> Of shapes and thoughts that tortured me:
> A lurid light, a trampling throng,
> Sense of intolerable wrong,
> And whom I scorned, those only strong! (14–20)

It is perhaps also worth adding that this sense of guilt and persecution, which continues into work as late as 'Limbo' (1817) and beyond, has been seen as distinctively modern in its awareness of its own psychological origins; Coleridge was well aware that the ghosts that tortured him were of his own imagining, but he was equally aware that this in no way lessened their potency. The connection between psychological and political plight typical of the Gothic is none the less evident, in, for example, the poem known as 'The Dungeon' (1797), with its 'savage faces, at the clanking hour / Seen through the steams and vapour of his dungeon, / By the lamp's dismal twilight!' (14–16).

Percy Bysshe Shelley was of all the major romantics the most immersed in Gothic writing, even though from time to time he tries to reject it. Quite apart from his complicated role in relation to Mary Wollstonecraft Shelley's *Frankenstein* (qq.v.), he also clearly shows the influences of Lewis, William Godwin and Charlotte Dacre (qq.v.) in the two short Gothic romances, *Zastrozzi* (1810) and *St Irvyne* (1811), which he wrote in his youth. Like Coleridge, he was also heavily influenced – for instance in *The Revolt of Islam* (1817) and *The Cenci* (1819) – by Schiller and the German Gothics, whose works were praised and reviled in England at the time. He was, according to Mary Shelley, 'a lover of the wild and wonderful in literature; but had not fostered these tastes at their genuine sources – the romances of chivalry of the middle ages; but in the perusal of such German works as were current in those days' (*Queen Mab*, n. 9). This was certainly true, but what Shelley found in the Germans was principally a sanction for the portrayal of extreme, 'wild', violent situations, particularly again in *The Cenci*, and a pretext for employing these means for the display of political situations. A crucial text for Shelley, again, was Schiller's *Die Räuber* (1777–80), in which what we might now think of as Gothic or even melodramatic descriptions are used in the service of the directly political lesson that social violence is the product of social injustice. *Queen Mab* (1813), *The Cenci* and *The Revolt of Islam* all hinge on this argument, which becomes part of a broader Gothic and romantic argument that the outlaw, the bandit, is behaving in a justifiable fashion when he is responding to the impositions of an unjust and unjustifiable society. But the conjunction of Gothic vocabulary and political thinking has been seen at its strongest in the poem Shelley was writing at the time of his death, *The Triumph of Life* (1822), and particularly in this passage:

> The earth was gray with phantoms, and the air
> Was peopled with dim forms, as when there hovers

16

A flock of vampire-bats before the glare
Of the tropic sun, bringing, ere evening,
Strange night upon some Indian isle; – thus were

Phantoms diffused around; and some did fling
Shadows of shadows, yet unlike themselves,
Behind them; some like eaglets on the wing

Were lost in the white day; others like elves
Danced in a thousand unimagined shapes
Upon the sunny streams and grassy shelves;

And others sate chattering like restless apes
In vulgar bands,
Some made a cradle of the ermined capes

Of kingly mantles; some across the tiar
Of pontiffs sate like vultures; others played
Under the crown which girt with empire

A baby's or an idiot's brow, and made
Their nests in it. The old anatomies
Sate hatching their bare broods under the shade

Of demon wings, and laughed from their dead eyes
To re-assume the delegated power,
Arrayed in which those worms did monarchise,

Who made this earth their charnel.

Here phantoms, skeletons, 'the old anatomies' serve to mock the things of this earth, as the graveyard poets had insisted; but Shelley's work moves in a different direction by demonstrating that these typically Gothic phantoms have a specific relation to earthly tyranny and injustice.

Lord Byron's poetry is full of Gothic allusions. The ballad form is represented in 'Oscar of Alva' (1807); the by now almost traditional imitation of 'Ossian' in 'The Death of Calmar and Orla' (1807); 'Chaucerian' medieval archaism in *Childe Harold's Pilgrimage* (1813). In fact there is in Byron, in keeping with his consistently ambivalent engagement with the role of the aristocracy, a prevalent concern with the nature of feudalism, and also with monasticism, as in *Lara* (1814) and 'The Song of the Black Friar' from *Don Juan* (1819–24), which reminds the reader again of Radcliffe and Lewis. Many critics have seen Byron himself – or, better, one aspect of Byron or of the Byron myth as developed by himself but equally by others – as the apotheosis of the fearless, terrifying, outlaw hero who occurs all the time in the Gothic novel from *The Mysteries of Udolpho* to *Dracula* (qq.v.). It needs to be said, however, that Byron's attitude towards the Gothic was frequently satirical. 'The horrid crags, by toppling convent crowned' in *Childe Harold*, and the description of Newstead Abbey –

> Yes! In thy gloomy cells and shades profound,
>   The monk abjur'd a world, he ne'er could view;
> Or blood-stain'd Guilt repenting, solace found,
>   Or Innocence, from stern Oppression, flew (21–4)

– have been cited as straightforward references to the Gothic conventions, but the famous description of the apparition towards the end of *Don Juan* is clearly intended to provoke a more ironic reaction:

> It was no mouse – but lo! a monk, arrayed
>   In cowl and beads, and dusky garb, appeared,
> Now in the moonlight, and now lapsed in shade,
>   With steps that trod as heavy, yet unheard;
> His garments only a slight murmur made;
>   He moved as shadowy as the Sisters weird,
> But slowly; and as he passed Juan by,
> Glanced, without pausing, on him a bright eye. (16.160–7)

Byron's attitude towards Gothic, then, is complex. On some occasions he uses it for purposes similar to Shelley's, to indict political and religious repression; but Byron's attitude to the past is less certain – some would say less didactic – than Shelley's. There is a sense of aristocratic nostalgia which sits uneasily alongside the political radicalism throughout Byron's work, and which is reflected, among other ways, in his use of the Gothic.

John Keats's relation to the Gothic is in some ways the most marginal, but in others the most simple: where there are Gothic references in his poetry, they tend to be directly to an older world of chivalry, without the dark inflection that more usually characterizes Gothic. He was certainly interested in the 'old Britain' that might be reconstructed from sources as diverse as Spenser and Bishop Hurd. Yet even with Keats we find passages in, for example, *Isabella, or, The Pot of Basil* (1818) which show clearly how deeply rooted some of the darker Gothic assumptions had become:

> Who hath not loiter'd in a green church-yard,
>   And let his spirit, like a demon-mole,
> Work through the clayey soil and gravel hard,

> To see scull, coffin'd bones, and funeral stole;
> Pitying each form that hungry Death hath marr'd,
> And filling it once more with human soul? (353–8)

The question for Keats was about how far the apparently pure visible forms of medieval chivalry covered over – or brought with them – a very different vision of the world. He expresses this doubt at greatest length in *Endymion* (1817):

> Groanings swell'd
> Poisonous about my ears, and louder grew,
> The nearer I approach'd a flame's gaunt blue,
> That glar'd before me through a thorny brake.
> The fire, like the eye of gordian snake,
> Bewitch'd me towards; and I soon was near
> A sight too fearful for the feel of fear:
> In thicket hid I curs'd the haggard scene –
> The banquet of my arms, my arbour queen,
> Seated upon an uptorn forest root;
> And all around her shapes, wizard and brute,
> Laughing, and wailing, groveling, serpenting,
> Showing tooth, tusk, venom-bag, and sting!
> O such deformities! (3.489–502)

Such passages as this carry the authentic tone of Gothic nightmare. So indeed do others in Keats, perhaps most enduringly the fearsome revelation of 'La Belle Dame sans Merci' (1820), and they bring us to what was clearly seen in the period as a crucial question about the Gothic and its relation to the past, namely to what extent such terrifying visions are to be taken as necessary correctives to the conventional descriptions of the past.

Bibliography

Hume, Robert D. 1969: 'Gothic Versus Romantic: A Revaluation of the Gothic Novel.' *Publications of the Modern Language Association*, 84, 282–90.

Janowitz, Anne 1990: *England's Ruins: Poetic Purpose and the National Landscape.* Oxford: Blackwell.

McGann, Jerome J. (ed.) 1994: *The New Oxford Book of Romantic Period Verse.* Oxford: Oxford University Press.

Punter, David 1996: *The Literature of Terror: A History of Gothic Fictions from 1765 to the Present Day.* 2nd edn. 2 vols. London: Longman.

Science, Industry
and the Gothic

The Gothic novel began to emerge at a time when the forces of industrialization were transforming the very structures of society. As Britain gradually changed from an agricultural into an industrial society, there was a steady movement of the population out of rural areas into the urban-centred industrial world. The traditional social system collapsed as new types of work and new social roles were established. Emergent capitalism led to a growing sense of isolation and alienation, as increasing mechanization divorced workers from the products of their labour, and the urban centres disconnected them from the natural world. The very ideas of what it meant to be human were disturbed in the face of increasing regimentation and mechanistic roles. Notably, as Jerrold E. Hogle remarks, it is precisely at this moment that Mary Wollstonecraft Shelley's *Frankenstein* (qq.v.) emphasizes the horror of her creature's artificiality: the human is replaced by an automaton manufactured from fragments (Hogle 1998).

Discoveries in the sciences only served to aggravate a sense of alienation and further disturb notions of human identity. During the later eighteenth century, traditional metaphysical and theological investigations into the meaning of life began to be displaced by secular and materialist explorations of its origins and nature. In 1771, Joseph Priestley observed that placing mice in a bell jar depleted the air and led to their suffocation, while sprigs of mint refreshed the air and made the mice lively; eight years later, Antoine Lavoisier interpreted Priestley's data to provide the first understanding of the processes of respiration. Many scientists, however, remained reluctant to accept a theory that made human life dependent upon the vegetative world; the idea that life might be either maintained or initiated simply through material causes challenged all traditional beliefs about humanity's unique position within the world.

By 1814, a debate over what came to be known as the 'life-principle' had caused a rift in the sciences, encapsulated primarily in the differing positions of John Abernethy, president of the Royal College of Surgeons, and his pupil William Lawrence, appointed as second professor at the college in 1815. Lawrence advocated a strictly materialist position. Abernethy, wanting to retain some metaphysical elements in common with religious beliefs, conversely argued that such concepts as 'organization', function' and 'matter' could not entirely explain life: something else was required, some 'subtle, active vital principle' that might be linked to the concept of the immortal soul.

As soon as science begins to disturb notions of the human, it becomes a site of particular interest to the Gothic writer. The question that preoccupies Mary Shelley's prototypical Gothic scientist Victor Frankenstein, namely 'Whence . . . did the principle of life proceed', was a matter of intense debate during the years in which *Frankenstein* was first conceived and written, and it was a debate with which Shelley was demonstrably familiar. Marilyn Butler (1994) suggests that Victor's reference to infusing 'a spark of being into the lifeless thing that lay at my feet' may indicate the kind of 'galvanic battery' used in early electrical experiments in which attempts were made to revive dead animals or hanged criminals. Furthermore, she observes, clear signs in the original 1818 text of *Frankenstein* indicate that Shelley sided primarily with Lawrence and the materialist position.

The publication of Lawrence's *Lectures on Physiology, Zoology and the Natural History of Man* in 1819, however, led to a public outcry, and Lawrence was suspended by the Royal College of Surgeons and forced to withdraw the book. During the following years it was repeatedly pirated and reproduced, but Lawrence was unable to claim copyright under a ruling of 1818 that prohibited such claims in cases like Lawrence's *Lectures*, considered to be 'hostile to natural and revealed religion'. The eventual notoriety of Lawrence's work, Butler argues, probably had much to do with Shelley's revisions. What she added to *Frankenstein* was 'usually reverent', and what she cut, including 'doubt thrown on a non-material mind or spirit, and a divine Creator', was precisely what was found most offensive in Lawrence's theories (Butler 1994: li). In its connection to the 'life-principle' debate, therefore, *Frankenstein* can be seen to set out for the first time the concern that dominates Gothic's engagement with both science and industry over the following centuries: the disruption of accepted notions of the human.

As the nineteenth century progressed, the damaging effects of industrialism became increasingly clear and had much to do with the emergence of a new site of Gothic horror: the city. In Victorian Gothic (q.v.), the castles and abbeys of the eighteenth century give way to labyrinthine streets, sinister rookeries, opium dens, and the filth and stench of the squalid slums. Gothic motifs are appropriated to convey the horror of this world not only in the fiction of such authors as Charles Dickens and G. W. M. Reynolds (qq.v.), but also in the work of sociologists and journalists, including Friedrich Engels's *The Condition of the Working Class in England in 1844* (1845) and William Booth's *In Darkest England and the Way Out* (1890). The savage and primitive are shown to exist in the very heart of the modern, civilized metropolis.

While capitalism theoretically promotes individual self-improvement – most notably suggested at the time by Samuel Smiles's highly popular how-to book, *Self-Help* (1859), as well as numerous fictional narratives of the self-made man – in practise, such opportunities were by no means available to all. This discrepancy between the ideal and the practise is often considered to account for the high incidence of crime in our capitalist world, and it is certainly notable that with the establishment of a capitalist society a new Gothic villain, the criminal, begins to emerge.

The development of new sciences began to offer possible ways of theorizing deviance, and Gothicized criminality by linking it to the past. In the process, there was a further questioning, even a dismantling, of conventional ideas concerning the human. Most obviously, perhaps, evolutionary theories began to challenge any belief in the integrity and superiority of the human species. With the emergence of criminal anthropology, even more disturbing theories of atavism began to be proposed. The very nature of the civilized was thrown into question as these sciences began to identify vestiges of the past within the bodies of the present. As the Italian criminal anthropologist Cesare Lombroso maintained in 1876, the 'criminal is an atavistic being who reproduces in his person the ferocious instincts of primitive humanity and the inferior animals' (Lombroso-Derrero 1911: xiv). Just as a cultivated garden rose will revert to the original dog rose when neglected, so, he argued, a human may, under certain conditions, revert to a more primitive state, and the savage of the past consequently survive in the midst of civilization.

One of the first works of Gothic fiction to engage with these ideas is Robert Louis Stevenson's *The Strange Case of Doctor Jekyll and Mr Hyde* (qq.v.). As evolutionary theories established that the emergence of the civilized was dependent upon the prior existence of the savage, so Jekyll discovers that the retention of his civilized and respectable exterior is dependent upon the existence of Hyde. The split provides a literal embodiment of the difference between, and mutual dependency of, the civilized and the primitive. Significantly, evil is written upon the face of Hyde and signs of 'deformity and decay' upon his body, pointing to ways in which the developments of criminal anthropology could be reassuring: they suggested that the criminal or the insane could be identified through physical characteristics or behaviour, and consequently implied the possibility of containing what was deviant.

As he explains in the introduction to his daughter's 1911 English summary of his work, *Criminal Man*, Lombroso's moment of 'revelation' came when, conducting a post mortem on a criminal, he opened up the skull to find a distinct depression comparable to that in lower animal forms: a sign of reversion, a vestige of the primitive. At this moment he realized 'the problem of the nature of the criminal', and saw the explanation for both the distinctive physical traits and the behavioural tendencies that he observed:

> Thus were explained anatomically the enormous jaws, high cheek-bones, prominent superciliary arches, solitary lines in the palms, extreme size of the orbits, handle-shaped or sessile ears found in criminals, savages, and apes, insensibility to pain, extremely acute sight, tattooing, excessive idleness, love of orgies, and the irresistible craving for evil for its own sake, the desire not only to extinguish life in the victim, but to mutilate the corpse, tear its flesh, and drink its blood. (Lombroso-Derrero 1911: xxv)

While this may seem more reminiscent of the werewolf than the vampire (q.v.), in other sections Lombroso pays particular attention to the excessive development of the lateral incisors in criminals, and it is such descriptions that allow Mina in Bram Stoker's *Dracula* (qq.v.) to identify the Count as 'a criminal and of criminal type', and consequently to predict his behaviour.

While on the one hand such new sciences offered ways of fixing lines of difference, and consequently of locating and possibly containing the threat of the deviant, at the same time they suggested other less reassuring possibilities. As Kelly Hurley has most notably demonstrated, these scientific discourses emphasized the potential changeability of the human. Numerous Gothic fictions of the Decadence (q.v.) consequently focus on monstrous metamorphic bodies, on what Hurley identifies as the 'abhuman', bodies that have 'lost their claim to a discrete and integral identity, a fully human existence' (2002: 190).

Even in Stoker's *Dracula*, where there is hope that the classifications of criminal anthropology may identify and thereby contain the deviant, categories are repeatedly shown to break down, suggesting the need to move away from materialist explanations and to engage with the more shadowy arena of the mind. 'Mental physiology' or early psychiatry began to emerge during the later nineteenth century, and the growing interest in this field

23

played a pivotal role in identifying the threat to social and psychic order as internal. Gothic fiction increasingly began to suggest that the chaos and disruption previously located mainly in such external forces as vampire or monster (qq.v.) was actually produced within the mind of the human subject. In Wilde's *The Picture of Dorian Gray* (1890, rev. 1891) and Stevenson's *Dr Jekyll and Mr Hyde*, it may be the self that is manifest in the double but that double is nevertheless still given a physical and verifiable form. In such works as Henry James's *The Turn of the Screw* (qq.v.) and Charlotte Perkins Gilman's 'The Yellow Wallpaper' (1892), however, and in the stories of Vernon Lee and Walter de la Mare (qq.v.), there is frequently increasing ambiguity and a more sophisticated exploration of psychological processes. Not surprisingly, the scientist who began to appear in twentieth-century Gothic fiction is frequently a psychologist.

There was a return of interest to the more materialist sciences, however, during the second half of the twentieth century as the technological explosion created a new set of anxieties that are reproduced and intensified in the Gothic. With advances in weaponry, for example, the proposition that the end of the world was near no longer seemed quite so fantastical. During the 1950s, transfiguring radiation became a common trope in popular horror, often combined with the idea of the last man on earth, initially used in Mary Shelley's 1826 novel, *The Last Man*. In Richard Matheson's (q.v.) *I am Legend* (1954), for example, the protagonist is the sole survivor in a world of vampires created by an irradiated virus, the product of nuclear testing.

What might appear most notable about Gothic fiction's engagement with technology today is the way in which notions of the human continue to be disrupted. The horror of the artificial human, first proposed in Shelley's *Frankenstein*, re-emerges in an up-to-date form with the possibility of new kinds of simulated life, with cyborgs, animated machines, and reproduction by computer or genetic engineering. 'What is expelled in the fantastic flight to hyperreality', Fred Botting suggests, 'is the "meat", the term employed by cyberpunk writers to denote the formless bodily excess of no use to machines' (1999: 150). In Rudy Rucker's *Wetware* (1994), the drug 'Merge' can not only decompose the body at a molecular level, but also reconstitute genes in order to produce hybrid monstrosities. With the disturbing monstrous transformations of the previous fin de siècle, the abhuman can ultimately be rejected, abjected, and the human recovered, the 'normal' body reinstated as the limit and basis of identity. Now, the 'dominant form and meaning of humanity' is simply 'meat', no more than 'a lumpen mass of consumptive and rotting desires' (Botting 1999: 152). We can be 'meat or machine . . . enjoy the horrors of excessive corporeality or the image-

24

saturated void of virtuality' (152), Botting concludes. If there is nothing else left to recover or reinstate, science may well have taken the Gothic to its limits.

Bibliography

Botting, Fred 1999: 'Future Horror (the Redundancy of Gothic).' *Gothic Studies*, 1 (2), 139–55.

Butler, Marilyn 1994: 'Introduction.' In Mary Shelley, *Frankenstein: or the Modern Prometheus. The 1818 Text.* Oxford: Oxford University Press, ix–li.

Hogle, Jerrold E. 1998: '*Frankenstein* as Neo-Gothic: From the Ghost of the Counterfeit to the Monster of Abjection.' In Tilottama Rajan and Julia Wright (eds), *Romanticism, History, and the Possibilities of Genre: Re-forming Literature, 1789–1837.* Cambridge: Cambridge University Press, 176–210.

Hurley, Kelly 2002: 'British Gothic Fiction, 1885–1930.' In Jerrold E. Hogle (ed.), *The Cambridge Companion to Gothic Fiction.* Cambridge: Cambridge University Press, 189–207.

Lombroso-Derrero, Gina 1911: *Criminal Man According to the Classification of Cesare Lombroso.* London: Putnam.

Victorian Gothic

It is generally agreed that the period of the 'classic' Gothic novel, narrowly defined as a historical genre, came to an end early in the nineteenth century. The exact moment is variously identified as the publication of Mary Wollstonecraft Shelley's *Frankenstein* (qq.v.) in 1818 or Charles Robert Maturin's *Melmoth the Wanderer* (qq.v.) in 1820. As a mode, however, the Gothic continued to return throughout the nineteenth century, dispersed into a variety of fictional forms, before re-emerging with full force once more during the period identified as the Decadence (q.v.).

Victorian Gothic is marked primarily by the domestication of Gothic figures, spaces and themes: horrors become explicitly located within the world of the contemporary reader. The romantic Gothic villain is transformed as monks, bandits and threatening aristocratic foreigners give way to criminals, madmen and scientists. The exotic and historical settings that serve to distance the horrors from the world of the reader in earlier Gothic are replaced with something more disturbingly familiar: the bourgeois domestic world or the new urban landscape.

This domestication of the Gothic is partly the result of its appropriation by the sensation novel. Beginning in the early 1860s with the publication of Wilkie Collins's *The Woman in White* (qq.v.), Ellen Wood's *East Lynne* (1861) and Mary Elizabeth Braddon's (q.v.) *Lady Audley's Secret* (1862), sensation fiction focuses on the bourgeois world and is characteristically preoccupied with domestic crime and disorder. Generally speaking, Gothic sensation novels fall into two main categories. Some novelists, often male, work within the female Gothic (q.v.) tradition of the heroine imprisoned within the home or some substitute institution. These texts demonstrate a particular interest in questions of identity and the transgression of borderlines. In *The Woman in White*, for example, gendered boundaries are explored

through representations of Marian, Fosco and Frederick Fairlie, and definitions of sanity and insanity through the pairing of Laura and Anne.

Transgression becomes even more central to the second main type of
Gothic sensation fiction, where it is associated with the sensational spectacle
of the mad or criminal female protagonist. The women tend to assume the
roles of both heroine and monster (q.v.), and provoke anxieties about the
instability of identity and the breakdown of gender roles. Behind the façade
of the modest and respectable Victorian woman lurk both the bigamous and
murderous Lucy Graham in Braddon's *Lady Audley's Secret*, considered by
many critics to be one of the most noxious books of its time, and the even
more disturbing murderess, adulteress and forger Lydia Gwilt, of Collins's
Armadale, clearly a worthy descendant of Victoria in Charlotte Dacre's (q.v.)
Zofloya (1805).

The primary way in which sensation novelists transformed the Gothic
during this period is indicated by Henry James's (q.v.) comments on Collins
in an essay entitled 'Miss Braddon'. Collins, James writes, is concerned with

> those most mysterious of mysteries, the mysteries which are at our own doors.
> The innovation gave a new impetus to the literature of horrors . . . Instead of
> the terrors of 'Udolpho', we were treated to the terrors of the cheerful country-
> house and the busy London lodgings. And there is no doubt that these were
> infinitely the more terrible. (1865: 593)

James's description might equally be applied to another genre with Gothic
connections that became popular at mid-century: the ghost story. Victorian
ghost stories typically centre on the irruption of the supernatural into the
familiar, comfortable and – as suggested by the very titles of such stories as
J. Sheridan Le Fanu's (q.v.)'Green Tea' (1869), Collins's 'A Terribly Strange
Bed' (1852) and Elizabeth Gaskell's (q.v.) 'The Old Nurse's Story' (1852)
– the mundane everyday world. The prevalence of ghost stories at this time
was partly the result of the emergence of many new periodicals and literary
magazines in the wake of the mid-century expansion of the publishing industry – Charles Dickens (q.v.), for example, published many ghost stories in
the magazines he edited, *Household Words* and *All the Year Round*. Their
popularity is often attributed to the rise of positivistic science and the decline
of religion in the increasingly materialist and secular nineteenth century:
ghosts challenge or at least question the authority of science and reason, and
as Julia Briggs suggests in *Night Visitors* (1977), could be seen as an oddly
reassuring, if nevertheless disturbing, proof of something beyond. A growing
interest in spiritualism and the occult, along with a proliferation of societies
for psychical research, prompted the publication of numerous stories of

supposedly 'true' hauntings, including Catherine Crowe's *The Night Side of Nature* (1848). Crowe suggested that as evolutionary theory had revealed a new world of marvels, so the fantastic was beginning to appear more and more real, and there is a clear movement towards naturalizing the fantastic in many ghost stories of the time. In Edward George Bulwer-Lytton's (q.v.) 'The Haunted and the Haunters: or, the House and the Brain' (1859), for example, the ordinary London house is not haunted by a conventional spirit. Rather, the haunting is the result of a former disgruntled servant who put a compass into the house with the written instruction 'so moves the needle, so work my will'.

Interestingly, many of the best ghost stories were written by authors, like Gaskell and Margaret Oliphant (q.v.), more usually associated with realism; the intrusion of the supernatural seems to be so much more shocking in a story that exploits realist strategies. And while both sensation and supernatural fiction can be seen to participate in the domestication of the Gothic, this was actually a movement initiated much earlier in the novels of writers who began to appropriate Gothic elements in the service of the realist agenda. William Harrison Ainsworth (q.v.) began the movement towards domestication with a consciously Gothic treatment of England in such historical novels as *The Tower of London* (1840), while Dickens and G. W. M. Reynolds (q.v.) took this one step further by constructing a Gothic England relocated within a contemporary city setting. Reynolds, the author of such melodramatic supernatural tales as *Wagner, the Wehr-Wolf* (1846–7), produced a nightmarish version of what is often termed urban Gothic in *The Mysteries of London* (1845–8). Reynolds's main target is the depraved aristocracy, but he also points to the dismal effects of a corrupt system upon the poor and presents a London marked primarily by disease and dirt and odious stenches, a claustrophobic polluted world of 'everlasting cloud'.

In such novels as *Oliver Twist* (1838), *Bleak House* (1852–3) and *Little Dorrit* (1855–7), Dickens similarly appropriates the Gothic in the service of both realism and polemic. In his 1841 preface to *Oliver Twist*, he rejects the romantic representations of Newgate novels, with their glamorization of the life of the outlaw, in favour of simple depictions of 'the everyday existence of a Thief'. His concern, he claims, is with the lessons taught by the 'cold wet shelterless midnight streets of London; the foul and frowsy dens, where vice is closely packed and lacks the room to turn; the haunts of hunger and disease'. Nevertheless, it is the Gothic that facilitates this realist agenda. The city, with its dark, narrow, winding streets and hidden byways replacing the labyrinthine passages of the earlier castles and convents, is established as a site of menace through the importation of various traditional Gothic motifs and scenarios. This is not to say that the terrors described duplicate those experienced by earlier Gothic protagonists: they are, rather, quite specific to the modern urban experience. When Oliver is dragged into a 'labyrinth of dark narrow courts', he is trapped within a criminal world that is the product of a Victorian social system.

This focus on the contemporary world does not mean that Gothic relinquishes its interest in the past. At the same time as it is appropriated to represent new social problems, it also offers a space in which the past can persist in a modified form. Indeed, Robert Mighall convincingly argues that Victorian Gothic fiction is 'obsessed with identifying and depicting the threatening reminders or scandalous vestiges of an age from which the present is relieved to have distanced itself'. These reminders or vestiges can be variously found in the prisons, lunatic asylums and slums, and also in the bodies or minds of 'criminals, deviants, or relatively "normal" subjects' (Mighall 1999: 26). He shows how numerous narratives of mid-century, for example, began to concern themselves with the idea of a family curse, a characteristic Gothic motif since Horace Walpole's *The Castle of Otranto* (qq.v.). Emerging at precisely the moment when contemporary science was looking to hereditary disease to explain moral dysfunction, however, these narratives transform the original motif: in such works as Collins's 'Mad Monkton' (1855) supernatural explanations are replaced by a materialist emphasis on pathological function (Mighall 1999: 78–9).

The past also remains a significant motif in both sensation and supernatural fiction, but again in a slightly modified form, with an emphasis on recent, rather than distant, events. Gothic sensation fiction focuses on family secrets and the immediate past of its transgressive protagonists. In a revision of Collins's plot in *The Woman in White*, for example, the male protagonist of Braddon's *Lady Audley's Secret* eventually arranges to have Lucy incarcerated in a lunatic asylum. This is not because anyone is really convinced she has inherited a taint of insanity from her mother, but because her criminal past would bring scandal to a respectable family. Hidden away, Lucy herself becomes the secret past of the Audleys.

Ghost stories also frequently focus on the family secrets of a recent past. In Gaskell's 'The Old Nurse's Story', for example, the home of Miss Furnivall is haunted by the phantoms of her sister, her sister's child, and the father who drove them out to meet their death in the snow. But as the re-enactment of past events shows, there can be an even closer relationship between the haunter and the haunted than this. While old Miss Furnivall pleads 'O father! Father! Spare the little innocent child', another phantom materializes, her younger self, looking upon the scene as she once did in approval, 'stony and deadly serene'. Similarly, in *The Haunted House*, included in the Christmas production of *All the Year Round* for 1859, a story is offered for each room in the house, but all the occupiers turn out to be haunted by nothing more than some troubling aspect of their past selves.

A number of Victorian ghost stories do, however, eliminate the role of the past altogether. In Le Fanu's 'Green Tea' (1869), there is the possibility that what haunts the protagonist is no more than an aspect of his repressed self. Such a change in the ghost story would seem in line with Terry Castle's theory about 'spectral technology'. According to Castle, the development of this technology resulted in a relocation of the supernatural during the late eighteenth and early nineteenth centuries. The mind itself became 'a kind of supernatural space, filled with intrusive spectral presences' (1995: 164).

This idea is certainly suggested by many of the Victorian writers who appropriated the Gothic in the service of a more powerful psychological realism. Following Robert Heilman's influential article on 'Charlotte Brontë's "New" Gothic', many critics have noted that the Brontës (q.v.) in particular use elements of the Gothic in order to suggest the powerful, irrational and potentially dangerous forces of the mind. Emily Brontë's *Wuthering Heights* (q.v.), for example, presents Catherine as a restless ghost, while Heathcliff, a brooding Gothic villain, is variously described as vampire, fiend and ghoul. These Gothic motifs work not so much to suggest the supernatural as to convey a powerful sense of desire and connection in the two characters. In Charlotte Brontë's *Jane Eyre* (1847) the Gothic emerges primarily in the figure of Bertha Mason, the hero-villain Rochester's first, mad wife, imprisoned on the third storey. Bertha comes to function both as an externalization of Rochester's guilt over a dubious past, and as a double for Jane, an embodiment of her rebellion, and Bertha must consequently be destroyed before Jane and Rochester can be finally united. While such early critics as Heilman saw the Gothic elements in such novels as functioning primarily in the service of the intensification of feeling, later critics have recognized that they also serve other purposes. The Gothic nature of Jane's experiences when she is locked in the Red Room, for example, conveys a powerful sense of her fears, but also dramatically confirms her vision of herself as a victim. Gothic is activated here, as it is repeatedly during the Victorian age, not only to convey a powerful sense of psychological disturbance, but also in the service of a penetrating social critique.

Bibliography

Botting, Fred 1996: *Gothic*. London: Routledge.
Briggs, Julia 1977: *Night Visitors: The Rise and Fall of the English Ghost Story*. London: Faber and Faber.

Castle, Terry 1995: *The Female Thermometer: Eighteenth-Century Culture and the Invention of the Uncanny.* Oxford: Oxford University Press.

Heilman, Robert B. 1958: 'Charlotte Brontë's "New" Gothic.' In Robert Rathburn and Martin Steinman (eds), *From Jane Austen to Joseph Conrad.* Minneapolis: University of Minnesota Press, 118–32.

James, Henry 1865: 'Miss Braddon.' *Nation,* 9 Nov., 593–5.

Mighall, Robert 1999: *A Geography of Victorian Gothic Fiction: Mapping History's Nightmare.* Oxford: Oxford University Press.

Milbank, A. 1992: *Daughters of the House: Modes of the Gothic in Victorian Fiction.* Houndmills: Macmillan.

Milbank, A. 2002: 'The Victorian Gothic in English Novels and Stories, 1830–1880.' In Jerrold E. Hogle (ed.), *The Cambridge Companion to Gothic Fiction.* Cambridge: Cambridge University Press, 145–65.

Pykett, Lyn 1994: *The Sensation Novel: From The Woman in White to The Moonstone.* Plymouth: Northcote House.

Robbins, Ruth and Wolfreys, Julian (eds) 2000: *Victorian Gothic: Literary and Cultural Manifestations in the Nineteenth Century.* Houndmills: Palgrave.

Schmitt, Cannon 2002: 'The Gothic Romance in the Victorian Period.' In Patrick Brantlinger and William B. Thesing (eds), *A Companion to the Victorian Novel.* Oxford: Blackwell, 302–17.

Wolfreys, Julian 2002: *Victorian Hauntings: Spectrality, Gothic, the Uncanny and Literature.* Basingstoke: Palgrave.

Art and Architecture

Medieval Gothic Architecture

As an aesthetic term, 'Gothic' was first used by Italian art historians during the early Renaissance to describe European art and architecture from the middle of the twelfth to the sixteenth centuries. The comments of one of these critics, Giorgio Vasari in his *Lives of the Artists* (1550), indicate the main attitude of the time to this 'monstrous and barbarous' style of architecture, which ignores 'every familiar idea of order'. After inveighing against the piling up of tabernacles and pinnacles, ornate decoration and pointed arches, he concludes that this medieval manner of building

> was invented by the Goths, who, after the destruction of the ancient buildings and the dying out of architects because of the wars, afterwards built – those who survived – edifices in this manner; these men fashioned the vaults with pointed arches of quarter circles and filled all Italy with these damnable buildings . . . God preserve every land from the invasion of such ideas. (in Frankl 1960: 290–1)

While Vasari no doubt knew that the Goths (q.v.) were not actually responsible for the buildings he was describing, the terms 'Goth' and 'Gothic' were already beginning to be used to designate anything medieval and to establish through difference the superiority of the classical ideals that the Renaissance world was attempting to re-establish.

In architecture, as in fiction, it is difficult to be precise about what constitutes the Gothic. A style that flourished over four centuries, it is generally divided into three main periods. It began at the monastery of St Denis near Paris with the patronage of the Abbot Suger in the early twelfth century, and

32

the style soon spread across Europe, being adapted and reinvented in various ways in different countries. The second phase of Gothic architecture was redefined primarily in Italy, and the final phase, which coincided with the beginnings of the Renaissance, was centred mainly on Burgundy, Flanders and Germany.

The origins of the Gothic style are often considered to lie in the problems presented by the vaulting of churches in stone: the weight of the solid vault pushed the walls outwards and resulted in collapse, and so the ribbed vault was introduced. A skeleton structure of rib and shaft was developed to lighten the weight of the vault, and the pointed arch to reduce outside pressure. This use of pointed arches in ribbed vaults then created thrusts at certain fixed points that were neutralized by the counter-thrusts of flying buttresses (arched bars supported by stone columns set outside the walls of the building). A purely mechanical explanation, however, does not account for many other features of Gothic buildings. It does not explain, for example, the attempts to heighten the naves and replace walls with stained glass in order to allow intense light to flood the building. Nor does it explain why buttresses, flying buttresses, shafts, finials and pinnacles are combined to create an impression of infinite subdivisions, or why walls are transformed into complex networks through the use of geometrical tracery (decorative stonework) and stained glass.

Various attempts have consequently been made to suggest the underlying 'meaning' or 'purpose' of these Gothic structures, although many art historians reject such speculation, since there is little contemporary medieval commentary to back up any conclusions (Martindale 1996: 7–13). On the whole, however, these attempts seem – perhaps inevitably – to reveal more about the commentators and their own agendas than about the architecture itself. There is, for example, the early forest theory (Frankl 1960: 275), which connects Gothic with the natural world and argues that the pointed arch and the dematerialization of the stone through tracery give a sense of living growth. For some German romantic writers, Gothic buildings were consequently icons of the primitive and the natural Edenic world. The nineteenth-century Catholic architect Augustus Pugin, on the other hand, considered height or the vertical principle as emblematic of the resurrection. Others more generally identify this vertical principle and the upward thrust of the Gothic as a visual expression of the spiritual quest for heaven. For John Ruskin, Gothic style suggested creativity and freedom of expression and was set in contrast to the soulless mechanical reproductions of the Victorian age. For socialist commentators like Wilhelm Hausenstein in 1916, the Gothic expresses the subordination of the individual to Christian society as a whole and is consequently 'collectivist'.

Attempts have also been made to link a Gothic style of architecture with the Gothic mode in fiction. G. R. Thompson, for example, connects the ideas of terror and horror as described in Ann Radcliffe's (q.v.) 'On the Supernatural in Poetry' (1826) to the effects produced by the Gothic cathedral. According to Radcliffe, 'Terror and horror are so far opposite, that the first expands the soul, and awakens the faculties to a high degree of life; the other contracts, freezes, and nearly annihilates them.' For Thompson, the 'central image for these paradoxes in the Gothic is the cathedral itself, for it has both an outward, upward movement towards the heavens, and an inward, downward motion, convoluting in upon itself in labyrinthine passages and dark recesses, descending to catacombs deep in the earth' (1974: 4).

Gothic Revival

The idea that the classical style of architecture was superior to the medieval or Gothic remained dominant until the eighteenth century, when a revival of interest in Gothic architecture accompanied a more general reassessment of the arts and culture of the medieval world (see 'Gothic in the Eighteenth Century' above). By mid-century, Batty Langley had domesticated the Gothic for eighteenth-century use in such works as *Gothick Architecture Improved by Rules and Proportions* (1747). Despite the reference to rules, Langley tended to focus on reproducible detail rather than structural principles in a manner typical of the approach to Gothic in the early Revival, and as Horace Walpole's (q.v.) Strawberry Hill, usually considered the first domestic Gothic Revival building, well demonstrates, this tends to lead to a sense of theatrical pastiche. While inspired by authentic and primarily ecclesiastical sources, Walpole copies from an eclectic variety of different Gothic styles. There is a reliance on dramatic effect rather than real Gothic structures: pointed vaults and windows, piers and columns and stained glass all combine to create the impression of a stage set. Artefacts are divorced from their foundations and turned into signs disconnected from their original substance, Jerrold E. Hogle (2002) points out, and such insistent counterfeiting is also present in Gothic fiction from the start. Walpole's *The Castle of Otranto* (q.v.) not only pretends in its first edition to be a translation of an old manuscript, but is also full of ghosts of what is already artificial, such as the walking figure of a portrait. The use of hollowed-out references to the past allows the Gothic to be filled with 'antiquated repositories into which modern quandaries can be projected and abjected simultaneously' (Hogle 2002: 15–16).

Interest in Gothic architecture increased during the early nineteenth century, when attention turned from domestic buildings to churches. The

Church Building Act of 1818 led to the building of many new churches, most of which were in a Gothic style. Study of the origins and principles of Gothic style also intensified, with Thomas Rickman eventually establishing the basic terminology which continues to be used today in his *Attempt to Discriminate the Styles of English Architecture* (1819). Rickman distinguished Early English (twelfth-century: the choir at Canterbury; the nave at Wells); Decorated (*c.*1230–1350: the nave at York); and Perpendicular (1350 to the end of the Middle Ages: chapels at Windsor, Westminster, King's College).

The key player in the Victorian Gothic revival was the architect and designer Pugin, and his attitude towards the medieval world is clearly suggested by the rather lengthy title of his best-known work: *Contrasts: Or a Parallel Between the Noble Edifices of the Middle Ages, and Corresponding Buildings of the Present Day: Shewing the Present Decay of Taste* (1836). Pugin is concerned not just with architecture but with social conditions: insisting on an organic relationship between architecture and social organization, he presents the Middle Ages as an ideal age of faith and social responsibility. In *Contrasts*, for example, a modern utilitarian workhouse is set against a noble monastic building used in the Middle Ages for the relief of the poor, to suggest the clear superiority of the latter, both aesthetically and morally. Pugin also turned the emphasis away from the decorative and towards functionality. There are two main principles in architecture, he claims in *The True Principles of Pointed or Christian Architecture* (1844): 'First, that there should be no features about a building which are not necessary for convenience, construction or propriety; second, that all ornament should consist of enrichment of the essential construction of the building.' For Pugin, however, a Catholic convert, the idea of the functional included the doctrinal, and he introduced elements that were somewhat problematic for the primarily Protestant Victorians. Reclaiming the Gothic style was for them reclaiming a national and democratic heritage, but there were nevertheless already anxieties about Gothic's associations with Catholicism that Pugin's designs only intensified. The more elitist elements involved in, for example, high altars and screen divisions between clergy and congregation were particularly worrying for many Victorians. 'They saw mischief lurking in every pointed niche', as Charles Eastlake observed in his 1872 *A History of the Gothic Revival*, 'and heresy peeping from behind every Gothic pillar' (1980: 268).

Ruskin, however, another key figure in the Victorian Gothic Revival, was able to transmit and popularize many of Pugin's ideas by detaching them from Catholic ideology, turning attention more towards secular buildings, and returning to an insistence on the democratic nature of the Gothic. In his essay 'On the Nature of the Gothic' in *The Stones of Venice* (1851–3),

Ruskin insists on imperfection as the sign of life in art, and exploits the Gothic in his attack on modern industrialization. The medieval workman, he argues, is able to express his individuality in a way the modern factory worker cannot. For Ruskin, the Gothic, as the architecture of imperfection, demonstrates signs of life and liberty in those who worked the stone. By the end of the century, however, Ruskin's ideas had been turned completely around by many, and he himself had revised many of his opinions. In the work of Thomas Hardy, most notably *Jude the Obscure* (1895), Gothic buildings are seen as nothing more than signs of an outdated and feudal world, and of the modern world's obsession with this hierarchical past and consequent denial both of progress and of social justice. With the emergence of Modernism, the Gothic Revival in architecture ends.

Gothic Art

If a discussion of Gothic architecture is problematic because of the wide diversity of styles and interpretations, a discussion of Gothic art is even more so and tends to necessitate a shift in emphasis. In the early Gothic period of the twelfth century, there was limited scope for painting. Instead of wall paintings, stained glass windows predominated. Illuminated manuscripts and illustrated romances might be seen to provide evidence of a Gothic art, but many critics suggest the primary influence is Byzantine. Similarly, it is debatable whether the general development of painting, beginning with Giotto in the early fourteenth century, can actually be described as Gothic. While some would link the stylization and linear quality of such early paintings to Gothic, others see in them a new understanding of nature and a striving for the classical ideal that would mark them as early Renaissance.

As a result, when speaking today of Gothic art as opposed to Gothic architecture, we are more likely to be referring to a kind of art that visually engages with many of the ideas and forms associated with Gothic fiction. This is an art that can be seen to originate in much the same period as the Gothic novel, to respond similarly to the emphasis on reason and order during the Enlightenment, and to move into the exploration of psychological states. The best known of these artists is the Swiss-born John Henry Fuseli, who came to London and became a professor at the Royal Academy. While other revolutionary artists of the time reacted against the neoclassical principles of the Royal Academy by returning to the natural world, Fuseli looked to dreams and visions. He distorts and exaggerates form to suggest projections of troubled minds. As one critic famously observed in the *New Monthly Magazine* for 1831, 'It was he who made real and visible to us the vague and insubstantial phantoms which haunt like dim dreams the oppressed imagination' (quoted in Jasper 1992: 105). The first of several versions of Fuseli's most popular work, *The Nightmare*, was exhibited at the Royal Academy in 1782. It depicts a woman stretched out across a bed sleeping, the covers thrown off, and her arms flung up over her head. On her torso crouches an incubus, and peering through the curtain is a horse, the 'nightmare' of the title, with its eyes gleaming and its teeth bared. The painting, increasingly erotic as different versions progressed, suggests both terror and a vague sense of oppression.

Another eighteenth-century painting frequently identified with the Gothic is the Spanish artist Goya's 'The Sleep of Reason Produces Monsters' (1799), which depicts a sleeping man slumped over a desk in a posture suggestive of desperation, with his head hidden in his arms. Paper and a pen on the table suggest he is a writer, and bats hover around and above him, appearing simultaneously to emerge from and to threaten him. Goya's own manuscript notes on a trial proof of the work, suggesting a movement towards psychological theories of repression, emphasize the message of his picture: 'Fantasy abandoned by reason produces impossible monsters; united with it, she is the mother of the arts and origin of its marvels.'

During the nineteenth century, the darker side of the psyche continues to be explored by fairy painters like Richard Dadd, in such works as *The Fairy-Feller's Master Stroke* (1864), and by Gustav Doré in the illustrations he did for Dante's *Inferno* in 1861 and for Samuel Taylor Coleridge's 'The Rime of the Ancient Mariner' in 1875. On the whole, however, the dominance of genre scenes and romantic historical pieces tended to work against the expression of a Gothic sensibility in Victorian art. In the early twentieth century, Gothic elements could be found in various movements, particularly those that can be seen as a darker underside to and a rejection of Modernism. Surrealism, for example, offered a celebration of irrationality, insanity and hysteria in order to convey or release unconscious desires, nightmares and phobias, and critics of the movement even occasionally even used Gothic as a synonym for Surrealism – usually, it must be said, in a pejorative sense.

In art, however, perhaps the most significant emergence of a Gothic sensibility may be located in the late twentieth century and associated with a more widespread cultural revival of interest in the Gothic. The 1997 exhibition *Gothic*, organized by the Institute of Contemporary Art in Boston and curated by Christoph Grunenberg, demonstrated the fascination of contemporary artists with the dark and uncanny side of the human psyche. In his introduction to the book that accompanied this exhibition, a book full of fabulous reproductions of the works discussed, Grunenberg explicitly locates this art in the context of both past Gothic fiction and the current renewed interest in the Gothic. The production of horror and terror in con-temporary Gothic art, he shows, is achieved through a 'plurality of stylistic modes and presentational strategies' (Grunenberg 1997: 168). While some artists exploit crude, fragmented, often repulsive and contorted forms, others prefer detached and controlled form in the service of excessive and violent images. Gothic therefore emerges in both the formless and horrific images of the mutilated and diseased body, as in Cindy Sherman's photographs, and in the reconfigurations of everyday domestic objects or body parts to produce disturbingly uncanny effects, as in the work of Robert Gober. 'The old Gothic themes of the uncanny, the fantastic and pathological and the tension between the artificial and organic are infused with new potency', Grunenberg summarizes, 'as contemporary artists address concerns about the body, disease, voyeurism and power' (Grunenberg 1997: 168).

What seems to link many of the works reproduced in Grunenberg's book is the way in which they produce horror mainly through the disturbance of the mundane and the familiar. Suggesting that something is going dreadfully wrong in the everyday world, they promote fears not about the past but about the future, about the looming prospect of total social and bodily dis-integration. In this respect, Gothic art of today participates in much the same anxieties as emerge in many other contemporary Gothic forms: the future has become the primary site of threat and dissolution, as devastating, in its own way, as any sinister Gothic past.

Bibliography

Clark, Kenneth 1962: *The Gothic Revival: An Essay in the History of Taste*. London: John Murray.

Eastlake, Charles 1980: *History of the Gothic Revival*. Leicester: Leicester University Press.

Frankl, Paul 1960: *The Gothic: Literary Sources and Interpretations through Eight Centuries*. Princeton, NJ: Princeton University Press.

Grunenberg, Christoph (ed.) 1997: *Gothic: Transmutations of Horror in Late Twentieth Century Art*. Cambridge, MA: MIT Press.

Hogle, Jerrold E. 2002: 'Introduction.' In Hogle (ed.), *The Cambridge Companion to Gothic Fiction*. Cambridge: Cambridge University Press, 1–20.

Jasper, David 1992: 'The Fantastic.' In Jean Raimond and J. R. Watson (eds), *A Handbook to English Romanticism*. Houndmills: Macmillan, 103–5.

Martindale, Andrew 1996: *Gothic Art*. London: Thames and Hudson.

Thompson, G. R. (ed.) 1974: *The Gothic Imagination: Essays in Dark Romanticism*. Washington: Washington State University Press.

GOTHIC AND DECADENCE

The Gothic is frequently considered to be a genre that re-emerges with particular force during times of cultural crisis and which serves to negotiate the anxieties of the age by working through them in a displaced form. Such a theory would certainly be supported by the sudden resurgence of Gothic in the late nineteenth century. The age which produced some of our most enduring cultural myths, including Robert Louis Stevenson's *Dr Jekyll and Mr Hyde* (qq.v.), Oscar Wilde's (q.v.) *The Picture of Dorian Gray* (1890, rev. 1891) and Bram Stoker's *Dracula* (qq.v.), was also a time marked by growing fears about national, social and psychic decay.

England was an imperial power in decline, threatened by the rise of such new players as Germany and the United States, experiencing doubts about the morality of the imperial mission, and faced with growing unrest in the colonies. At home, the social and psychological effects of the Industrial Revolution were becoming all too clear as crime and disease were rife in the overcrowded city slums. The traditional values and family structures upon which the middle class had based its moral superiority were disintegrating, challenged by the emergence of such figures as the 'New Woman' and the homosexual. Gothic texts of the late 1880s and 1890s consequently come to be linked primarily by a focus on the idea of degeneration.

Anxieties about the nation are both managed and aggravated by the emergence of what Patrick Brantlinger terms 'imperial Gothic' (q.v.), a 'blend of adventure story with Gothic elements' (1988: 227). There is, as in the original Gothic, an interest in the foreign, but rather than looking to Europe, there is a movement out into the Empire. One of the primary anxieties of this imperial Gothic is that encounters between the English and their colonized subjects may well result in the civilized human reverting to the barbaric. A related and equally worrying fear is that England itself will be invaded and contaminated by the alien world. Such imperial Gothic narratives articulate anxieties about the integrity of the nation, about the possibility of the 'primitive' infecting the civilized world.

But it is not just a matter of some external force infecting England. As in much previous Victorian Gothic (q.v.), the city itself, particularly London, heart of the supposedly civilized world, continues to be represented as a site of cultural decay and a source of menace. William Booth's influential survey of the degraded living conditions of the poor, *In Darkest England and the Way Out* (1890), tellingly echoes the title of Henry Stanley's then recently published *In Darkest Africa*. It was not necessary to travel as far as Stanley, Booth implies, to find a realm of darkness: it could also be found in the heart of the city slums. The presence of the primitive is clearly suggested in Stevenson's *Dr Jekyll and Mr Hyde* as the city resounds with a 'low growl', and when Wilde's Dorian Gray wanders through 'dimly-lit streets, past gaunt black-shadowed archways and evil-looking houses', he is challenged by 'grotesque children' and drunkards chattering like 'monstrous apes'.

In the new fictional Gothic landscape of the city, however, it is not primarily the criminal underworld or the poor that are implicated as a source of horror. The focus is usually far more on the middle classes, and on exposing what underlies the surfaces of the supposedly civilized and respectable world. The crimes of Helen Vaughan, who engineers the suicides of five respectable gentlemen in Arthur Machen's (q.v.) *The Great God Pan* (1894), for example, are significantly labelled the 'West End Horrors'. They are said to be far more horrific than the East End Horrors, the brutal murders of five prostitutes by Jack the Ripper in the Whitechapel area during 1888.

One of many monstrous (q.v.) females with a desire for power in Gothic fiction of the time, Helen embodies not only anxieties about the potential decline of the middle classes generally, but also, more specifically, anxieties about the breakdown of middle-class gender ideology. The emergence and demands of the New Woman aggravated such fears, and Gothic texts of the time repeatedly produce powerful and sexually aggressive females as alien or monstrous, setting them in opposition to the 'pure' woman in an attempt to stabilize gendered identity. Nevertheless, the stability of such an opposition is also repeatedly undermined as the pure woman metamorphoses into the evil. In *Dracula* (q.v.), for example, the naively coquettish Lucy mutates into a 'nightmare' of 'voluptuous wantonness', and the text suggests that Dracula himself is only a catalyst which allows for the release of an uncontrollable and passionate self within.

If, as Robert Miles and other recent critics have suggested, the Gothic generally represents 'the self finding itself dispossessed in its own house, in a condition of rupture, disjunction, fragmentation' (Miles 2002: 3), then this is a concern which is increasingly intensified in the works of this period. The idea that the supposedly civilized subject harbours something alien within is particularly emphasized by the return of the double or *Doppelgänger* in such works as *Dr Jekyll and Mr Hyde* and *The Picture of Dorian Gray*. In both these cases, however, it is suggested that the real problem is not the existence of some more primitive and passionate internal self, but the force with which that self must be repressed in accordance with social conventions. Dorian, who sells his soul for eternal youth while his portrait ages and decays in his place, is warned of the dangers of repression by Sir Henry: 'The only way to get rid of a temptation is to yield to it. Resist it, and your soul grows sick with longing for the things it has forbidden to itself, with desire for what its monstrous laws have made monstrous and unlawful.' As in the case of Jekyll, repression has the potential to produce a split in the psyche. However, although we are encouraged to think in terms of duality by the oppositions of Jekyll and Hyde and of Dorian and his portrait, the texts also imply it is not simply a *split* that is at issue but a more complex fragmentation of the subject. As Dorian suggests, man may well be not a stable unified subject, but a 'complex, multiform creature'.

Multiplicity, an even more disturbing concept than duality, is repeatedly suggested in decadent Gothic texts through the representation of metamorphic bodies or what Kelly Hurley (1996) identifies as the 'abhuman'. The abhuman may be a body that retains traces of human identity but has become, or is in the process of becoming, something quite different. Alternatively, it may be some indefinable 'thing' that is mimicking the human, appropriating the human form. Either way, it is the integrity of human identity that is threatened; these are liminal bodies, occupying the space between the terms of such oppositions as human and beast, male and female, civilized and primitive. Examples of such disturbing bodies abound in Gothic of the time, most obviously perhaps in the beast people of H. G. Wells's (q.v.) *The Island of Dr Moreau* (1896). The protagonist, Prendick, is initially puzzled by their uncanny effect, by a sense of familiarity and yet of strangeness. When he discovers that they are the products of 'Moreau's horrible skill', he becomes increasingly repulsed by these disturbing hybrids, and by what they suggest about the instability of the human subject. Prendick's attempts to reinstate 'sane' and stable boundaries between the human and the beast, however, fail; when he returns to civilization the people he meets appear like beast-people, and he fears that they, like Moreau's creatures, will begin to revert.

The majority of these abhuman bodies are the product not of supernatural forces but of scientifically explainable processes, and it is the scientist who becomes the pre-eminent figure in the Gothic fiction of the period.

Many forms of materialist science, including criminal anthropology, had attempted to provide tools for identifying and categorizing what was alien and abnormal, the agents of dissolution and decline. What we now call criminal profiling was first attempted at this time in the hunt for Jack the Ripper. But science did not just offer reassuring ways of locating and defining difference, it could also function in various ways as a transgressive and disruptive force, challenging the stability and integrity of the human subject (see also 'Science, Industry and the Gothic' above).

Fears about the integrity of the self are forcefully articulated at this time through the emergence of what some critics call 'Darwinian Gothic'. Evolutionary theories had dissolved the previously accepted boundaries between human and animal. Darwin's claim in *The Descent of Man* (1871) that man was descended from a hairy-tailed quadruped which had in turn evolved out of a series of diverse forms, ultimately leading back to a fish-like being, disturbingly challenged any belief in the integrity and superiority of the human species. Furthermore, it led to the conclusion that if something could evolve it could also devolve or degenerate, whether it were individual, society or nation. The destabilizing effects of such thought are at least partly responsible for the body becoming a particular site of anxiety in the Gothic of this time, and the possibility of sliding down the evolutionary ladder is perhaps most horrifyingly suggested by the physical metamorphosis of the dying Helen in *The Great God Pan*. A doctor who witnesses the sight reports how the human body, 'thought to be unchangeable and permanent', begins to melt and dissolve. And what is primarily horrific is not that Helen changes from 'woman to man, from man to beast', but that she then changes from beast to worse than beast, into some 'horrible and unspeakable shape' that lies outside any stable and reassuring binary thought.

Significantly, Helen is the result of experimental neuro-surgery carried out by Dr Raymond on her quite ordinary human mother. Moreau is not only a vivisectionist; he also practises behaviour modification, and is clearly familiar with much contemporary thought in the field of mental physiology. As science moved away from its materialist base during this period to explore the less tangible arena of the mind, it contributed even further to the idea that the threat to order had its origins in human nature. The threat represented by Helen may well have less to do with the supernatural than with the simple liberation from repression. As the operation on her mother Mary allows her to see beyond the veil of this world to the 'real' world it hides, exposes her, perhaps, to the full forces of the unconscious, so Helen seems to have been born without any social or psychic restraints.

In *Degeneration*, one of the most notorious non-fictional texts of the Decadence, Max Nordau proclaimed the end of an era: 'Over the earth the shadows creep with deepening gloom, wrapping all objects in a mysterious dimness, in which all certainty is destroyed and any guess seems plausible. Forms lose their outlines, and are dissolved in floating mist' (1895: 5–6). Not only does Nordau clearly appropriate Gothic elements to convey a sense of cultural decline, he also precisely puts his finger on what may well be the primary fear that haunts the age, a fear that is simultaneously managed and intensified by the Gothic fiction of the time. Repeatedly, we are offered the spectacle of devolution and decay, of chaos and multiplicity. Forms and boundaries dissolve as comforting certainties mutate into questions. The Gothic horror of the Decadence is the horror of dissolution, of the nation, of society and, ultimately, as we move into the Modernist world, of the human subject itself.

Bibliography

Brantlinger, Patrick 1988: *Rule of Darkness: British Literature and Imperialism, 1830–1914.* Ithaca, NY: Cornell University Press.

Byron, Glennis 2000: 'Gothic in the 1890s.' In David Punter (ed.), *A Companion to the Gothic.* Oxford: Blackwell, 132–41.

Halberstam, Judith 1995: *Skin Shows: Gothic Horror and the Technology of Monsters.* Durham, NC: Duke University Press.

Hurley, Kelly 1996: *The Gothic Body: Sexuality, Materialism, and Degeneration at the Fin de Siècle.* Cambridge: Cambridge University Press.

Miles, Robert 2000: *Gothic Writing, 1750–1820: A Genealogy.* Manchester: Manchester University Press.

Navarette, Susan J. 1998: *The Shape of Fear: Horror and the Fin de Siècle Culture of Decadence.* Lexington, KY: University Press of Kentucky.

Nordau, Max 1895: *Degeneration.* London: Heinemann.

Schmitt, Cannon 2002: 'The Gothic Romance in the Victorian Period.' In Patrick Brantlinger and William B. Thesing (eds), *A Companion to the Victorian Novel.* Oxford: Blackwell, 302–17.

İmperial Gothic

The concept of 'imperial Gothic' can be – and has been – interpreted in a number of different ways. It can be seen, for example, as a phenomenon occurring within 'imperial fiction' in general. 'Imperial fiction' suggests itself principally as a description of a particular kind of fiction in which imperial exploration and power figure centrally or largely in the text, as they do in the works of, for example, H. Rider Haggard and Rudyard Kipling (qq.v.); alongside these semi-canonical imperial writers one would also need to set an entire subgenre of nineteenth- and twentieth-century fiction, mostly aimed at school-age boys, where themes of adventure and discovery occur in empire settings.

Some critics, however, would want to extend this idea of 'imperial fiction' considerably by drawing attention to the numerous works, from the nineteenth century in particular, where the empire plays a more disguised role; the emblematic text here might be Charlotte Brontë's (q.v.) *Jane Eyre* (1847), where the Caribbean forms the implicit backdrop to the career of Brontë's hero-villain, Rochester, and to the emergence of the figure of his first wife, the original 'madwoman in the attic'. Others would want to broaden the field to include texts, like H.G. Wells's (q.v.) *The Island of Doctor Moreau* (1896), where the connection to concepts of empire – and, inextricably, racial difference – are more complexly symbolically coded. Others, again, would want to focus on the way in which some works with an empire background interrogate imperial values rather than overtly supporting them, although such distinctions have proved very difficult to make; there is, for example, continuing critical discussion about the ideological force of Kipling's stories, and even more about the multiple meanings to be found in rereadings of Joseph Conrad's *Heart of Darkness* (1902) (Achebe 1977).

The intersections between Gothic and this 'imperial field' are many and various. Most of the Irish author Bram Stoker's (q.v.) books, for example,

44

have imperial connections in what one might take to be the 'conventional' sense of empire – that is, as relating to what Victorians would have seen as 'far-flung corners of the earth' – even leaving aside the further connections that emerge when one considers the interactions of British and Irish history as themselves imbued with imperial content. This, then, would be a case of an obviously Gothic writer – like M. G. Lewis (q.v.) before him, whose wealth was founded on classic imperial exploitation (Peck 1961) – involved with imperial issues. Another approach would be based on the ways in which many nineteenth-century involvements with empire become themselves 'Gothicized', in the sense that the racial or national 'other' comes to be seen from a Gothic perspective, endowed with diabolical, monstrous or merely melodramatically powerful qualities, as would be the case with Haggard and others.

The Island of Doctor Moreau, to take a first example, is a story that is set on an island where we are introduced to the figure of Dr Moreau, who, exiled from Europe, is apparently undertaking biological experiments. At first the protagonist Prendick assumes that these experiments are designed, by a process of vivisection, to reduce human beings to the condition of the beast; the case turns out to be that what Moreau is actually trying to do is to turn the beast into the human, with limited and eventually terrifying results. What us crucial in the scenario, however, is that there is an emphatic distinction between the white men who are conducting the experiments and the 'beast-men' who are symbolically assimilated to the condition of the 'native'. A well-noted and crucial scene occurs when Moreau, his assistant Montgomery and Prendick, threatened with revolt and accompanied by one of the more 'domesticated' of the creatures, go forth to reassert their control and encounter the beast-men coming out of the jungle towards them:

> As soon as they had approached within a distance of perhaps thirty yards they halted, and bowing on knees and elbows, began flinging the white dust upon their heads. Imagine the scene if you can. We three blue-clad men, with our misshapen black-faced attendant, standing in a wide expanse of sunlit yellow dust under the blazing blue sky, and surrounded by this circle of crouching and gesticulating monstrosities, some almost human, save in their subtle expressions and gestures, some like cripples, some so strangely distorted as to resemble nothing but the denizens of our wildest dreams.

What this passage clearly signifies is a scenario of imperial domination and submission, a fantasy of the 'otherness', familiar to us now from postcolonial criticism, of a primal encounter with the native. It is significant also that

Moreau, throughout the text, is described as 'white', both white-haired and white-faced; Prendick is described as 'chalky'; the 'white dust' with which the beast-men cover themselves can be seen as a sign of racial submission. The anxieties that Prendick entertains throughout about what Moreau is doing have also to be seen in the general context of Victorian anxieties about evolution, or rather about the contamination that might result if less 'developed' races and species are allowed their own self-determination; it is in this way that the 'imperial' themes of *Doctor Moreau* interact with a prevalent set of 'Darwinian' themes.

That *Doctor Moreau* is a Gothic text would seem beyond doubt: Moreau himself can be seen as a Frankensteinian seeker, a man who has, like Victor Frankenstein, put family ties and relationships behind him in the search for forbidden knowledge. Unlike Frankenstein, however, he openly acknowledges that part of the process in which he is engaged necessitates the use of pain, and the status of pain as an instrument of imperial domination becomes surprisingly open within the text. In Moreau's hands the 'other' is reduced to the status of an object, to be formed or reshaped at will. We can see here a metaphor for the ways in which the violence of empire has so frequently been translocated, reterritorialized onto an 'empty' island; this again accords with a certain imperial discourse, in which the land that falls under the rule of empire is perceived as 'empty' because its previous inhabitants – native American, Australian aboriginal – are denied the status of the human. This is a logic that one can compare with a mass of *Boys' Own* stories, where the dangers to be encountered in the name of the spread of 'civilization' may include wild animals or human natives, but no real distinction is made between them.

One of the great models for these narratives is Rider Haggard's *King Solomon's Mines* (1885). The opening paragraph, fictitiously penned by the narrator Allan Quatermain, summarizes a host of imperial themes:

> It is a curious thing that at my age – fifty-five last birthday – I should find myself taking up a pen to try and write a history. I wonder what sort of history it will be when I have done it, if I ever come to the end of the trip! I have done a good many things in my life, which seems a long one to me, owing to my having begun so young, perhaps. At an age when other boys are at school, I was earning my living as a trader in the old Colony. I have been trading, hunting, fighting, or mining ever since. And yet it is only eight months ago that I made my pile.

The myth of the imperial adventurer is of an 'unlettered' man none the less finding in the empire ways of advancement that might not be available at home – it is further suggested (and this is part of the appeal of the genre) that even a boy might be able to succeed in this world. This relates, of course, to a many-sided myth. In the first place, there is the idea that the empire provides a kind of playground and at the same time a source of potential wealth to those not in a position to obtain it at home – the younger sons of noble families, for example. There is also the idea that operating in the empire can become a kind of test, a *rite de passage*, from which the adventurer can return wiser and stronger, having tested out his manhood on a necessary enemy. Over against this, however, but also supporting the 'romance of empire', there is the idea that wealth gained in the empire is somehow disreputable, that even to go to the 'ends of the earth' implies a certain stain on the character, a declaration that one has gone somewhere where not too many questions will be asked.

But what the empire also becomes, in *King Solomon's Mines* and elsewhere, is a site of the at least apparently supernatural. A famous scene takes place in a cave:

> Let the reader picture to himself the hall of the vastest cathedral he ever stood in, windowless indeed, but dimly lighted from above . . . and he will get some idea of the size of the enormous cave in which we stood, with the difference that this cathedral designed of nature was loftier and wider than any built by man.

This site of natural sublimity affects the narrator much as cathedrals and castles have affected characters throughout Gothic fiction, but the reaction is intensified by what is found in one of the side 'chapels':

> There at the end of the long stone table, holding in his skeleton fingers a great white spear, sat *Death* himself, shaped in the form of a colossal human skeleton, fifteen feet or more in height. High above his head he held the spear, as though in the act to strike; one bony hand rested on the stone table before him, in the position a man assumes on rising from his seat, whilst his frame was bent forward so that the vertebrae of the neck and the grinning, gleaming skull projected towards us, and fixed its hollow eye-places upon us, the jaws a little open, as though it was about to speak.

The description becomes even more lurid, but the point is that it portrays precisely the culmination of Quatermain's own fears and anxieties; as in so many Gothic tales, what he is seeing is the projection of his own fantasies, the death, in this case, that is proposed as the doom of the white man who makes a mistake in the 'heart of darkness' – while all the time that 'mistake' is precisely an effect of the white man's misprision of the other, the impossibility, for the imperialist, of seeing the racial and exploited other as a fellow human being.

A further form taken by the 'imperial Gothic' might be referred to under that catch-all heading, 'The Empire Writes Back' (Ashcroft, Griffiths and Tiffin 1989), and covers that genre of stories in which something from the empire – some artefact, or some half-suppressed memory, or some deed whose consequences have not yet been felt – returns from the 'far corners of the earth' to pursue the adventurer. There are plenty of such stories in the oeuvre of Arthur Conan Doyle (q.v.); an emblematic one would be one of the Sherlock Holmes short stories, 'The Speckled Band' (1892). Here Holmes is called in to investigate a death which could not have taken place through any obvious external intrusion; the dead girl's last word, 'the speckled band', initially mistaken by Holmes as a reference to a group of gypsies, eventually reveals itself as referring to a snake which has been used to kill her and which bids fair to be used again. Holmes, naturally, not only works this out but drives the snake back to destroy its owner.

This owner, the girl's stepfather, the evilly named Dr Grimesby Roylott, is a huge and violent man who has been a doctor in Calcutta but who has been repatriated after a prison sentence for killing his 'native butler'. We know from the outset that he is fond of 'Indian animals', and that a baboon (later mistaken by Holmes and Watson for a 'hideous and distorted child') and a cheetah roam the grounds of Stoke Moran, Roylott's half-ruined Gothic pile. What is crucial in the story, considered as an example of imperial Gothic, is that not only does Roylott therefore use as a means of murder a creature 'reimported' from the empire – a swamp adder, 'the deadliest snake in India', as Holmes claims – but Roylott's violence and indeed partial success as a murderer are attributed precisely to a residual imperial influence: he is, Holmes says, 'a clever and ruthless man who had had an Eastern training'.

Quite what this 'Eastern training' has amounted to is not a question the text is equipped overtly to answer: there is a slippage, ideologically essential in the imperial context, between the idea that Roylott has the necessary 'equipment' to deal with the perhaps desperate exigencies of 'service' in the east, and the rather different, but in the end more convincing, idea that he has been in some way contaminated, infected, penetrated by eastern ideas, that he has himself 'gone native' – the myth of the 'assassin' is not far away. This 'orientalist' vision therefore bears the ultimate responsibility for his own condition and for the death of his stepdaughter; it is as though, mysteriously, the east is to blame for the events. It also ultimately performs an act of narrative dehumanization on Roylott himself: 'I am no doubt indirectly responsible for Dr Grimesby Roylott's death', Holmes finally says to Watson, 'and I cannot say that it is likely to weigh heavily upon my conscience.'

The empire is thus portrayed here and elsewhere as a place where distorted visions may occur, where the 'normal' boundaries of the civilized world slip away or are constantly under siege. Just as the castles of the 'original Gothic' existed as fastnesses to repel encroaching invaders, so do the colonial enclaves of imperial Gothic exist as outposts in the surrounding dark; but what interests the Gothic is not so much the survival of these outposts as the menaces which may come to destroy them, the 'return' of the imperial repressed.

Bibliography

Achebe, Chinua 1977: 'An Image of Africa: Racism in Conrad's *Heart of Darkness.*' *Massachusetts Review*, 18, 782–94.

Ashcroft, William, Griffiths, Gareth and Tiffin, Helen (eds) 1989: *The Empire Writes Back: Theory and Practice in Post-Colonial Literatures.* London: Routledge.

Peck, Louis F. 1961: *A Life of Matthew G. Lewis.* Cambridge, MA: Harvard University Press.

Smith, Andrew, and Hughes, William (eds) 2003: *Empire and the Gothic: The Politics of Genre.* London: Palgrave.

Gothic Postmodernism

A story by Russell Hoban called 'The Ghost Horse of Genghis Khan' (1992) begins, like so many ghost stories, in a Gothic study:

> There were shadowy places and lamplit places in the study. There were maps on the wall. There was a human skeleton that made gentle clacking sounds as you moved it. There were three pendulum clocks that struck the hours at different times when they were running. Now they were stopped at different times. There was a model of a Portuguese fishing boat, there was a stuffed barn owl. There were rocks and seashells from many places and a stone from a Crusader fort in Galilee with chisel marks on it.

This realm, however, a realm of the antiquarian or of the reterritorialization of the displaced object, is unable to sustain itself in isolation. It overflows, it crumbles and buckles before a superflux of meaning which we might reasonably regard as postmodern. As John, the young protagonist of the story, reads a further story – one that his father has been writing and has left unfinished in the typewriter – the father lies unconscious in a hospital. Somehow John finds himself both dreaming and carrying on with the writing of this story, which is of how Genghis Khan was saved from death by a ghost horse. There is a sense in which, in a move characteristic of the complex relations between the Gothic and the postmodern, the ghost horse invades the realm of modernity – represented in the hospital, the fibrillators and endotracheal tubes – asserting a connection, through dream and fantasy, that threatens to make a mockery of the precise territorializing of the 'maps on the wall'.

Gothic has always had to do with disruptions of scale and perspective, with a terrain that we might, again following Hoban, refer to as 'the moment under the moment'. No point on the map is exactly where or what it seems;

50

on the contrary, it opens into other spaces, and it does not even do that in a stable fashion. What might have been an opening last night into another world may now be closed, absent, terrifying in the quality of its unyieldingness. What we find in the numerous conjunctions of Gothic and the postmodern is a certain sliding of location, a series of transfers and translocations from one place to another, so that our sense of the stability of the map is – as indeed it has been since the first fantasy of a Gothic castle (q.v.) – forever under siege, guaranteed to us only by manuscripts whose own provenance and completeness are deeply uncertain.

What we also find is a certain attention to the divisions and doublings of the self. A curious dialogue takes place in Hoban's story, between John and John's mind. John's mind 'was much older than the boy', we are told; 'it was as ancient as the stars, it remembered all sorts of things that John had never known'. Just so, the traditional Gothic castle could be seen as embodying a past that goes back behind – or beneath – the 'moment' of the subject, that asserts a different kind of continuity, even if it is one that can be known only under the sign of the secret, only in the 'shadows' of the darkened study, or, as Hoban puts it, in 'the shadows and the long night and the herds of the dead'.

There is here, then, a double sense of dislocated space and threatened subjectivity. We can find a similar conjunction in an emblematic postmodern text, Paul Auster's *City of Glass* (1985), which will be discussed in greater detail in the section on 'Persecution and Paranoia' below; but to move to a second, and perhaps more obviously Gothic, 'location': Iain Banks's *Complicity* (1993), a postmodern novel of the double and of the draining of identity, is told in a rare mixture of first- and second-person narrative voices. Furthermore, it offers a highly Gothic hotel as one of its central locations. We are introduced to it by a sign, a sign that has 'been there for years, ever since they opened the new road, and it says "Strome Ferry – no ferry", and that just says it all'. What we then have here is a sign that is no sign, a sign – rather like the lost manuscript beloved of Gothic tradition – that cancels itself in the very act of utterance, a sign that depicts, or indicates, a location that is no more, that belongs to a different regime, a different order of the past.

Just so the hotel itself seems to belong to the past, to a ruinous Gothic realm of rot and decay:

> The ballroom smells damp. It is illuminated only by the light shining from the stairwell and the desk lamp on the old trestle table which holds the computer. Torn, bleached-looking curtains hang at the sides of the six tall window bays. My breath smokes in front of me and mists on the cold glass. All the panes are dirty and some are cracked. A couple have been replaced with hardboard. In

51

two of the window bays there are buckets to catch drips but one of them has
overflowed and caused a puddle to form around it . . . [It] is scattered with
cheap wooden chairs, tables, rolls of ancient, mouldy-smelling carpets, a couple
of old motorbikes and lots of bits of motorbikes standing or lying on oil-stained
sheets.

Somewhere here, as frequently in Banks, the relics of a feudal order remain
to haunt the decay of the present in a neo-Gothic reprise. But here the faded
curtains are matched by a new, barbaric invasion represented by the motorbikes and, indeed, 'what looks and smells like an industrial-standard deep-
fat frier'; the interplay of past and present is further complicated as the past
seeks to claim the ruins of the contemporary for its own.

In the novel, it is as if the condition of the ballroom – and of the hotel
in general – represents a frozen moment, a moment of incompatibility and
conflict. In this context, the subject can gain no firm purchase; all that can
be done is to 'take up a position', to insert oneself in one way or another
into the contradictory Gothic matrix the room and the hotel represent. But
the structure of the text goes further than this, and prevents the reader from
knowing exactly who or what it is that is inhabiting – or perhaps being produced by, being given substance by – this haunted place. The passage above
suggests a 'first person'; but there is also a 'second person' at large in the
hotel (as, in a different sense, there is in the Overlook Hotel in Stephen
King's *The Shining* [qq.v.]) perhaps occupying some other set of dimensions,
moving on trajectories that never intersect. From this ghostly second-person
perspective, for example, the ballroom looks the same yet also different. 'The
old motorbikes, tables, chairs and carpets . . . look like forlorn toys in some
long-neglected doll's house':

At one end of the dark corridor . . . a door lies ajar . . . In the corner of the
room the dumb waiter contains a selection of logs of various sizes. You take
the biggest of the logs, which is about the size of a man's arm, and walk softly
across the room to the bedroom door. You go through and stand listening to
the rain and the wind, and – just audible – the noise of a man breathing slowly
and rhythmically in the bed. You hold the log in front of you as you walk
towards the bed.

Complicity, then, is indeed the theme here: what would it be like, the text
asks, to be a 'you' formed in the image of the hotel itself, to be an effect of
one's own place, to feel no compunction as the log comes bloodily down
since all has been already predetermined, staged as the consequence of a specific conjunction in this time and space, a time and space in which the shards
and fragments that make up the destroyed hotel prove impossible to hold

together, where the psychoses that these Gothic locations themselves hold close to their hearts detonate?

In these two examples, from Hoban and Banks, as later in the example from Auster, I have tried to show how the complications of postmodern writing, particularly in the areas of subjectivity and location (the inner and outer worlds), reflect back onto and into the Gothic, how the uncertainties of a world in which narrative is never sure or reliable not only suggest an origin in the Gothic but also resort to Gothic means in the development of the texts themselves. The postmodern, one might suggest, is the site of a certain 'haunting', and in this sense can never free itself from the ghosts of the past, even if it takes as its task the constant (and constantly dubious) reconstruction of that past. One might also suggest that the involvement of the postmodern with notions like the Derridean 'trace' and Lacanian '*méconnaissance*' provides further evidence that the distortion of perspective which is a constant hallmark of Gothic fiction finds a further 'home' in the postmodern, and that this twist of history has precisely to do with the advent and fate of modernity; with the Gothic's 'origin' as a counter-discourse to the modernizing impulse of the Enlightenment, and with postmodernism's complex rebuttal and development of Modernism's own post-Enlightenment progressive dictates.

Bibliography

Eagleton, Terry 1996: *The Illusions of Postmodernism*. Oxford: Blackwell.
Jencks, Charles 1996: *What is Postmodernism?* 4th edn. London: Academy Editions.
Nicol, Bran (ed.) 2002: *Postmodernism and the Contemporary Novel: A Reader*. Edinburgh: Edinburgh University Press.

Postcolonial Gothic

At first glance a connection between the Gothic and the postcolonial might seem difficult to establish, particularly in view of the emergence of the Gothic as a phenomenon specifically within European history, or rather perhaps within certain distorted perspectives on that history. But in fact we could say that 'distortion' is precisely the sign under which we might principally describe a form of 'postcolonial Gothic' that has become increasingly prevalent since the early 1980s.

For it could reasonably be said that the term 'postcolonial' itself has an inevitably distorting effect. In one sense this can be seen as unavoidable in that the postcolonial world itself is distorted; not, that is, in the sense of having been twisted away from some recognizable master-trajectory or severed from an imaginary origin, but in deeper senses to do with obfuscations of desire, impossible hybridities, the haunting ineradicability of paths not taken. The cultures and histories of colonized nations are shadowed by the fantasized possibility of alternative histories, the sense of what might have been if the violence of colonization had not come to eradicate or pervert the traces of 'independent development' – even if, at the same time, we need to recognize that the notion of 'independence' is itself, politically as well as psychologically, a myth.

'Gothic', as we know, is also a 'haunted' term. It is true that there may be dangers in attempting to use the term 'Gothic' in a postcolonial context, but it needs also to be remembered with what alarming frequency the Gothic has called into being its own other. Its very 'European-ness', its embroilment in shifting boundaries, migratory flights, feudal points of order, strongholds of reason falling in a relentless series to the approach of the barbarians, all of this is precisely what produced the American Gothic tradition from Charles Brockden Brown (q.v.) on, just as more recently it has answered, or

54

been answered by, a call from within the postcolonial – whether one thinks of the crazed and labyrinthine intricacies of Salman Rushdie's architectures, or of the bizarre and claustrophobic worlds of Margaret Atwood.

One way of approaching these issues would be by beginning from the supposition that Gothic represents a specific view of history. One might refer to this view as an 'expressionistic' one, a view that abandons minutiae and details in favour of the grand gesture, history as sublimity, the melodrama of rise and fall, a view in which terror and pity are the moving forces; but it would also be a more troubling view, for it would have to deal with the impossibility of escape from history, with the recurrent sense in Gothic fiction that the past can never be left behind, that it will reappear and exact a necessary price.

We might refer to this, then, as history written according to a certain logic: a logic of the phantom, the revenant, a logic of haunting, and it is here that we might see the connection with the postcolonial coming most clearly into view. The very structure of the term 'postcolonial' itself, its apparent insistence on a time 'after', on an 'aftermath', exposes itself precisely to the threat of return, falls under the sign of an unavoidable repetition; the attempt to make, for example, the nation in a new form is inevitably accompanied by the traces of the past, by half-buried histories of exile, transportation, emigration, all the panoply of the removal and transplantation of peoples which has been throughout history the essence of the colonial endeavour.

One of the most obvious texts here, although it might not at first glance seem to be set in a 'postcolonial' context, would be Toni Morrison's *Beloved* (1987). *Beloved* is centred on a revenant, the returned figure of a baby that has been killed by its own mother. The reason for this killing constitutes the central conundrum, the enigma, the unanswerable question of the text, for the mother, Sethe, has killed her baby because she thought that death was preferable to the slavery that would be its lot were it to survive. This much is clear; what is also clear is the extended series of descriptions of the state of the slave that take up a large part of the book. Beyond this, however, there is a certain penumbra of unclarity. For example, although there are obvious signs that the strange figure known as Beloved, arriving unexpectedly on Sethe's doorstep, is in *some* sense the phantom of the dead baby, the question remains: in *what* sense? For a ghost, she is extremely physical; there are also suggestions that perhaps the characters' identification of her with the dead baby is a red herring, that perhaps Beloved is simply a sponger, or deranged. To go a little further than this, though, perhaps one might suggest that this does not matter: the logic of the revenant is that it cannot be laid to rest and will return, and whether this is a physical, supernatural or merely symbolic return is in the end not important.

What is important is that the multiple and complex violences and hatreds engendered by slavery – considered here as the most extreme form of the colony – cannot be laid to rest; and that this is where the postcolonial might reasonably remind the reader of the Gothic, which is an arena in which these shadow battles, struggles between versions of history, have been fought out in a European context. *Beloved*, among many other things, insists on the implacability of trauma, on the concept that the damage done to individuals by refusal to treat them as selves in their own right will itself result in a specific version of the general impossibility of escape from the past. Only that which is treated as human, the text seems to say, can be properly buried; if you try to bury that which has been denied its human rights to begin with, then there is no possibility that the stone will remain in place. This then comes as an alternative logic that circumvents the conventional logic of guilt or blame: it does not in the end matter whether or not Sethe is morally responsible for the death of her daughter, for the inexorability of history and the ghost works at a deeper level than this, boring its way up from the sacred ground, insisting on making its presence felt – again – no matter what practises are used, what apologies are issued, in the attempt to repel the Gothic, to lay the spectres of the past.

The past, on this view of history, is of course right in our midst; we see it in the form of contemporary debates around cultural and racial blame and apology, and hence the nature of recriminations and restitutions, the insistence on the memorial, the monument to suffering, even though the only form such a monument perhaps can or should appropriately take is the form of a ruin. To pursue these issues further, we can take a particular example, Amitav Ghosh's *The Shadow Lines*, published in 1988. This is a highly complex book. It involves a nameless narrator who lives his life partly through his fantasies about his older cousin Tridib; these fantasies are so strong for him that he is able to imagine in enormous detail time that Tridib has spent in London, even before he goes there himself. One of the questions behind the book concerns this question of fantasy: the narrator's other cousin Ila has travelled widely but apparently remembers nothing, but behind this there lies the question of what it is that one wishes to remember. For as we learn more about the history of the family, so we see more clearly the multiple deracinations and displacements to which they have been subject, principally of course as the result of the partition of the subcontinent as a final farewell act of the British imperial drama.

If, however, we are to look at *The Shadow Lines* from a Gothic perspective, then these problematic histories come to us in certain recognizable ways. They come, for example, as ruins. Tridib, it seems, has had his own sexual awakening while seeing a couple making love in the ruins of a London cinema during the Second World War. Later he writes to May, daughter of the English family with whom he was staying at the time; bizarrely, he tells her of this incident. At first deciding that the letter is pornographic, May later accepts his invitation to visit him in Calcutta, and they find themselves going to the Victoria Memorial. May hates it at first glance, presumably seeing it as a symbol of imperial domination. 'It shouldn't be here', she says, 'It's an act of violence. It's obscene.' But Tridib disagrees. 'No it's not', he says. 'This is *our* ruin, that's what we've been looking for.'

An entire postcolonial history is condensed into these phrases. The question put is: if all relationships between cultures, between races, between histories have been ruined – by warfare, by empire, or both – then what is it that might be able to survive such general devastation, what might there be that 'remains' amid these ruins? Ghosh's characterization of the events clearly states that the presence of the Victoria Memorial is 'ruinous', in more than one sense; but the question remains as to what might be born, or reborn, out of these ruins, the 'ruins of empire', what might truly be the possibilities of any 'postcolonial' under these circumstances. But the question also remains of what might be permanently destroyed – for the narrator, at least:

> I never went there again in that old mood of cheerful expectancy. I knew there was something else in that building now, some other meaning, a meaning I couldn't fathom, but which I knew existed, despite me. It became a haunted site: I could not go there without hearing Tridib's soft voice whispering: This is our ruin, this is where we meet.

Of course, the question of *what* haunts this site – the phantom of unexplained sexuality, or the trace of inexplicable foreign domination – is left delicately suspended, as is the origin of most hauntings in Gothic fiction; but in any case the haunting is complete, the shadow lines are drawn. Under these circumstances, the only way the narrator can go in order to understand his own individual and cultural past is, in a Gothic trope, down to the cellar, where he takes Ila in an attempt to understand more by reliving the innocent yet curiously menacing games of their childhood. Once there, however,

> [t]hose empty corners filled up with remembered forms, with the ghosts who had been handed down to me by time . . . They were all around me, we were together at last, not ghosts at all: the ghostliness was merely the absence of time and distance – for that is all that a ghost is, a presence displaced in time.

This 'ghosting' provides a kind of solution: under these conditions the very different material circumstances, the difference of cultural experience, between the secluded narrator and the materialistic and westernized Ila can be in some sense overcome; but this is a mere phantom victory – a pseudo-'victorious' statue – and the violations of empire cannot be laid to rest so simply. The narrator may assert that the 'difference' of the ghost is simply one of time, and it is certainly true that the notion of the ghost presupposes a displacement in time, but below this there are also other displacements, ones more to do with location and territory than with time, states of the imagination in which the statue of Queen Victoria is absent, or ghosted, a mere spectre that can be blown away at the slightest threat of new-found 'independence'.

This, however, would be an over-optimistic account of the narrative trajectory of *The Shadow Lines*, as it would be of any number of other postcolonial writings, from the fiction of Amos Tutuola and Joan Riley to the poetry of Derek Walcott and Edward Kamau Brathwaite; for as *The Shadow Lines* develops, it becomes obvious that the Gothic process of ghosting has infected even the very process of narrative. 'And what of the story?', the narrator asks, echoing as he does so the words of Tridib as he seeks, against the background of bombs and war-time destruction, the narrative promised him by his English host Snipe:

> And what of the story?
> I see it in the mouths of the ghosts that surround me in the cellar: of Snipe, telling it to Tridib, of Tridib telling it to Ila and me, in that underground room in Raibajar; I see myself, three years later, taking May, the young May, to visit the house in Raibajar the day before she left for Dhaka with my grandmother and Tridib.

The story of the postcolonial, then – here as elsewhere – is in the mouths of ghosts; the effect of empire has been the dematerialization of whole cultures, and the Gothic tropes of the ghost, the phantom, the revenant, gain curious new life from the need to assert continuity where the lessons of conventional history and geography would claim that all continuity has been broken by the imperial trauma.

Bibliography

Inden, Ronald 1990: *Imagining India*. Oxford: Blackwell.

Loomba, Ania and Suvir Kaul 1994: *On India: Writing History, Culture, Post-Coloniality*. Stirling: Oxford Literary Review.

Punter, David 2000: *Postcolonial Imaginings: Fictions of a New World Order*. Edinburgh: Edinburgh University Press.

GOTHS AND GOTHIC SUBCULTURES

Gothic subcultures have their roots in the Britain of the late 1970s and early 1980s, when a style of 'dark', atmospheric and introspective music began to emerge out of and in opposition to punk, glam rock and new romantic. The 1979 release of 'Bela Lugosi's Dead' by Bauhaus provides the definitive moment, with respect to both sound and image, for the start of the first generation of Goths. At first, the single appeared to escape categorization. It featured high reverb on top of a dub-reggae beat, and the whispered repetition of such phrases as 'Bela Lugosi's dead' and 'Undead, undead, undead', sometimes giving way to a vibrato reminiscent of David Bowie that complemented the glam-rock theatricality of the performance. Punk musical elements such as distorted guitar effects and reggae bass-lines were used, but with a slower tempo and eerie atmospherics (Gunn 1999: 37). Initially it was described as post-punk or minimalist punk, but these labels were soon replaced by 'Gothic'.

Other influential bands of the time included the Cure, the Damned and Specimen, and a London nightclub run by the members of Specimen, the Batcave, began to provide a venue for the new music. Perhaps most influential, however, were Siouxsie and the Banshees, in terms of both what James Hannaham calls Siouxsie's 'powerful vibrato howl' (in Grunenberg 1997: 96) and her appearance – at least after it had shifted from the appropriation of Nazi imagery to a less politically provocative dark femininity. Gothic soon became as easily distinguished as a style as it did as a music, if not more so, a style characterized primarily by black velvets, lace, fishnets, and silver jewellery based on religious and occult themes, and complemented by dyed black hair, white makeup and dark slashes of lipstick.

There are varying opinions about who originally called the music Gothic; Siouxsie Sioux is sometimes said to have first used the term to describe the new direction taken by the band in the 1981 album *Ju Ju*, but there are many rival claims. It was nevertheless the British music press who popularized the label both to describe and to help construct an emerging music genre. When a new set of bands appeared during the mid- and late 1980s, many decisively aligned themselves with Gothic. The Gothic rock of such bands as the Sisters of Mercy, more accessible and less extreme than such earlier bands as Specimen, soon attracted wider interest. Many of them were given mainstream media coverage and the music became more widely available.

Interest in Gothic declined during the early 1990s as the music press turned their attention to such new movements as the indie scene. Gothic music became increasingly influenced by other styles, and the earlier guitar-based sound, with its emphasis on minor chords, minimalist rhythms and slower tempos, often merged with electronic chords and dance beats. At this point, terminology begins to bewilder. Some commentators today argue that Gothic describes a set of subgenres and subcultures, including Goth, metal and industrial, with common elements, which may sometimes merge musically to produce such hybrid forms as industrial Gothic. Primarily for the sake of clarity, this is the position taken here. Others, however, equate Gothic with Goth, and see this as quite distinct from metal and industrial. At the same time, they introduce such other terms as 'darkwave' or 'ethereal Goth', stretching the boundaries of Gothic, as Joshua Gunn notes, 'to include a wide array of sounds and styles on the basis of some crucial similarity to a more centrist gothic band of the past' (1999: 43). Clearly, any study of Gothic subcultures and their music is at present drastically complicated by an ongoing struggle both to establish and to expand generic boundaries.

The project is further problematized by the way in which, since the 1990s, Gothic music has filtered into the mainstream and became increasingly commercialized. Goth clothes have been similarly appropriated by mainstream fashion and appeared on the catwalk and in national chain shops. One negative effect of Gothic subcultures becoming more high profile is that they are frequently implicated in the moral panic attacks so often directed at youth cultures; when two teenagers opened fire on fellow pupils at the Columbine High School in Denver in April 1999, to give the most notorious example, they were mistakenly identified with a Goth youth culture because of the music found in their homes. As many critics have since pointed out, however, violence and aggression are quite at odds with the values of the Goth scene. This is even indicated by the way in which Gothic music is frequently described in terms that echo academic distinctions between the female Gothic (q.v.) of Ann Radcliffe (q.v.) and the male Gothic of M. G. Lewis (q.v.). James Hannaham, for example, distinguishes heavy metal, 'aggressive, sexist, and therefore "masculine"', from Goth, with its 'softer, more accepting, "feminine" cast' (in Grunenberg 1997: 81), while Alicia Porter makes a similar distinction between the feminine of Goth and the masculine of industrial.

Whether there may be further and more significant connections between Gothic subcultures and the academic world of Gothic studies is a question critics are beginning to suggest needs to be explored. Sara Martin, for example, argues that

> if Gothic youth subcultures can be regarded as the practical result of a particular interpretation of the philosophy of Gothic texts, and Gothic texts are the field of research of Gothic Studies, Gothic youth subcultures – themselves producers of new Gothic texts – could (perhaps should) be also part of Gothic Studies. (2002: 28)

Within the popular market, attempts to bring the Gothic tradition together with Gothic subcultures have already been made. Gavin Baddeley, for example, combines a whirlwind tour through Gothic literature and film with a general discussion of the origins and development of Goth music and a section on style. However, although he asserts that Goth is 'much more than an image – it is an aesthetic, a viewpoint, even a lifestyle, its tradition a legacy of subversion and shadow', it is not clear what the 'viewpoint' might be. Claiming that the very name of the Goth subculture 'pays due but ironic homage to the architectural and literary ambitions of Beckford and Walpole' (2002:10, 17), Baddeley ultimately leaves the impression that, for the present generation at least, the relationship of Goth to the Gothic tradition is mainly parodic.

Martin is more specific in her suppositions, and suggests a more serious underlying purpose. Gothic in terms of subcultures, she argues, 'seems to have taken the place of the cultural paradigm usually associated to [*sic*] rebelliousness and youth, namely, Romanticism'. It provides a means of expressing discomfort with 'the realities of the late capitalist, post-modern Western world'. Gothic scholars, she further proposes, may make 'important contributions to the understanding of these social phenomena, for we have been exploring for several decades the metaphorical use of Gothic as an expression of social and political anxieties' (2002: 38).

If Goth is taken as just one of various Gothic subcultures, then the Goth scene itself may not offer the most promising focus for such research. While some commentators suggest there is some kind of underlying Goth ideology, 'mindset' or common 'values', there seems to be little agreement about precisely what this might involve. Most internet sites tend to define Goth primarily in terms of clothing and musical preference. The insistent artificiality of Goth style might seem to suggest a continuation of the counterfeiting tendency which has characterized Gothic since the eighteenth-century Gothic Revival (see 'Art and Architecture' above), an emptying out of the past in order to produce, in Jerrold E. Hogle's words, 'antiquated repositories into which modern quandaries can be projected and abjected simultaneously' (2002: 15–16). Recent sociological studies of the present Goth subculture, however, have not on the whole supported this idea. Paul Hodkinson, for example, confirms that in 'the case of the goth scene, shared tastes and norms manifested themselves primarily in the arena of style', and his research found 'no underlying shared structural, psychological or political meaning to be discerned from the style' (2002: 35, 62). On the contrary, he adds, responses in interviews and questionnaires demonstrated a 'particular tendency for hostility toward the suggestion that their appearance suggested anything about their character, outlook or behaviour'. It was usually insisted that 'style was held to be significant in and of itself as a set of enthusiastic preferences located within, and not beyond, the sphere of the aesthetic' (2002: 62). In Dick Hebdige's terms, Goth seems to be a 'spectacular subculture', a subculture 'concerned first and foremost with consumption . . . It communicates through commodities' (1979: 94–5). Goth style may externalize a rejection of mainstream society, but primarily in facilitating a sense of consistent and collective distinctiveness, rather than in the service of any coherent social or political statement. Furthermore, the Goth emphasis on commodities would seem to suggest a far closer connection with mainstream society than might initially be apparent.

While the study of Gothic subcultures requires attention to 'both the lifestyle and the textual production – literary and non-literary' (Martin 2002: 29), the study of the former is, at present, fraught with difficulties for academics. As attendance at any International Gothic Association conference would confirm, for most, fieldwork would be, to say the least, difficult. The problem will only be resolved for Gothic studies when more young scholars who are already positioned to some degree within the Gothic scene begin to do academic work. In the meantime, texts rather than lifestyles would seem to offer the most viable focus of research. A number of the writers already beginning to be studied in the universities, including Poppy Z. Brite, Caitlin Kernan and Christa Faust, have, or have had, connections with Gothic subcultures. The graphic novel (q.v.), another new focus of academic study, also has close links with these subcultures, and there is a small but growing industry of graphic novels written by and for a primarily Gothic audience, including those issued by Slave Labour, such as *Gloom Cookie* and *Lenore*, and most notably Jhonen Vasquez's *Johnny the Homicidal Maniac* and its spin-offs.

It is, however, the music of the various Gothic subcultures, the lyrics and related videos, that may offer the most promising areas of research. Many Gothic lyrics appropriate and reinterpret traditional Gothic texts, often in the service of social critique. Diamanda Galas, for example, reworks Edgar Allan Poe (q.v.) in the trilogy *The Divine Punishment* (1986), *Saint of the Pit* (1986) and *You Must Be Certain of the Devil* (1988), known collectively as *The Masque of the Red Death* (Mute Records), in order to explore attitudes towards Aids, particularly the attitudes of the church. Cultural critics and historians, most notably James Hannaham and Csaba Toth, have already begun the study of Gothic music, and often draw upon the work done in Gothic studies to facilitate their research. Once again, however, Goth does not seem the most promising focus for any exploration of the ways in which Gothic music may express social and political anxieties. As James Hannaham (1997) confirms in 'Bela Lugosi's Dead and I Don't Feel So Good Either: Goth and the Glorification of Suffering in Rock Music', for many of these early bands, Gothic was primarily a matter of style. The privileging of style over substance is certainly both strategy and theme in the seminal Goth song 'Bela Lugosi's Dead', with Lugosi reduced to representation as the distinction between actor and character collapses.

Other early bands, however, often those who retained links to their punk roots and incorporated Gothic less as a matter of style and more as the dominant sensibility in their sounds and lyrics, reveal a clearer political agenda in their rejection of the values of the postmodern late capitalist world. Joy Division's explorations of madness, alienation and isolation in *Unknown Pleasures* (1979), for example, have a strong political engagement. Pioneering the use of echoing reverb as a metaphor for emptiness, Joy Division set their lyrics against the bleak background of a depressed postindustrial Britain. Ian Curtis's lyrics not only describe the alienation of the self from society, however, James Hannaham observes, but also suggest the way in which 'numbness and surrender divide the self' (94), providing a new take on the Gothic motif of the double. Csaba Toth's 'Like Cancer in the System: Industrial Gothic, Nine Inch Nails, and Videotape' (in Grunenberg 1997), drawing partly upon Judith Halberstam's work on the technology of monsters (q.v.), makes some particularly interesting links between contemporary Gothic studies and industrial Gothic. Industrial Gothic videos released by such artists as Nine Inch Nails, Psychic TV and Test Department, Toth argues, show a postindustrial world in which 'boundaries between the "normal" and the pathologized "other" collapse, and the "normal" is often more dreadful than its "unnatural" opposite'. As Toth's reading of the video 'Burn' interestingly demonstrates, the strategy found in so much contemporary Gothic fiction is also 'a narrative strategy endemic in contemporary industrial art culture' (in Grunenberg 1997: 88). It may well be, then, that the relationship between Gothic studies and Gothic subcultures will become a productive area of research for new Gothic scholars.

Bibliography

Baddeley, Gavin 2002: *Goth Chic: A Connoisseur's Guide to Dark Culture*. London: Plexus.

Grunenberg, Christoph (ed.) 1997: *Gothic: Transmutations of Horror in Late Twentieth Century Art*. Cambridge, MA.: MIT Press.

Gunn, Joshua 1999: 'Gothic Music and the Inevitability of Genre.' *Popular Music and Society*, 23 (1), 31–50.

Hannaham, James 1997: 'Bela Lugosi's Dead and I Don't Feel So Good Either: Goth and the Glorification of Suffering in Rock Music'. In Christoph Grunenberg (ed.), *Gothic: Transmutations of Horror in Late Twentieth Century Art*. Cambridge, MA.: MIT Press, 118–13, 96–2 (pages numbered backwards).

Hebdige, Dick 1979: *Subculture: The Meaning of Style*. New York: Methuen.

Hodkinson, Paul 2002: *Goth: Identity, Style and Subculture*. Oxford: Berg.

Hogle, Jerrold E. 2002: 'Introduction.' In Hogle (ed.), *The Cambridge Companion to Gothic Fiction*. Cambridge: Cambridge University Press, 1–20.

Martin, Sara 2002: 'Gothic Scholars Don't Wear Black: Gothic Studies and Gothic Subcultures.' *Gothic Studies*, 4 (1), 28–43.

Porter, Alicia (accessed 2002): *A Study of Gothic Subculture*. www.gothics.org/subculture/index.html.

Goᴛʜɪᴄ Fɪʟᴍ

The enduring – indeed, some would say the growing – appeal of the horror film owes a great deal to its roots in the Gothic: in Gothic fiction itself, with its endless recycling of narratives from Mary Wollstonecraft Shelley, Edgar Allan Poe, Bram Stoker, Robert Louis Stevenson (qq.v.) and many others, and also in terms of a kind of melodramatic expressionism of style that is unmistakably Gothic in its cultural and structural force. There are many ways of trying to provide a history of the horror film, but this version is based on David Punter's in *The Literature of Terror*, and seeks to break the history down into seven phases (Punter 1996: II, 96–118, 149–56).

The first wave of popular horror films was made in the US in the 1930s, mostly by Universal Studios, and relied heavily on such directors as Tod Browning and James Whale, as well as the acting of such iconic figures as Boris Karloff and Bela Lugosi. The years 1931–3 saw the appearance not only of Browning's version of *Dracula* and Whale's of *Frankenstein*, but also of Reuben Mamoulian's splendid version of *Dr Jekyll and Mr Hyde* (which remains to date the most frequently filmed of all Gothic fictions); Schoedsack and Pichel's *The Most Dangerous Game*; Erle C. Kenton's *Island of Lost Souls*; Victor Halperin's *White Zombie*; Karl Freund's *The Mummy*; and of course *King Kong*, a key twentieth-century myth, also directed by Schoedsack and Pichel.

One crucial feature which connects many of these films is their dependence on Gothic literary sources; but there are other, more important aspects which justify defining them as a subgenre in their own right. First, there is the genuine complexity of their attitudes towards the monstrous (q.v.). In *Frankenstein* and *King Kong*, of course, we are now all too familiar with the ambiguous emotional effects which these early directors were able to produce; but the Mamoulian *Jekyll and Hyde* is also complex in terms of audience response, largely because of the sensitive playing of Fredric March as Jekyll and Hyde. *The Most Dangerous Game* is crammed with Gothic echoes as it brings to the screen a fresh and significant image of the displaced, anachronistic and bloodthirsty aristocrat. *White Zombie* is a film with a perhaps appropriately somnambulistic style, yet also, in accordance with its Gothic roots, an insistence on social and political dimensions. These films were also photographically inventive: realistic or unrealistic as the settings may supposedly be, they are linked by their creation of a remarkable set of persistent images of doom, whether in the first graveyard scene of *Franken-stein* or in the endless revolution of the zombie-powered mill-wheel in *White Zombie*.

As a second phase, there is an upsurge of horror films in the 1950s, typically with a science-fiction bias and an all too obvious political content; here the succession of extended images which emerges is designed to encode arguments about the Cold War, about fears of invasion from the east, about the dangers of technologization, and above all about the perceived threat to US individualism from communism. In these films it would be regrettably fair to say that the earlier complexities of style and response seem to come for a time to be systematically eliminated from the genre. The typical product of the 1950s lies on the edge of horror and science fiction: it confronts order with disruption in a simplistic fashion, usually by allowing some kind of generalized human society – or rather, perhaps, a collection of individuals – to stand unquestioned and by putting up against it an alien being or species which never stands a chance. The examples are legion, and include *Flying Disc Men from Mars* (1950), *Radar Men from the Moon* (1952), *War of the Worlds* (1952), *The Beast from 20,000 Fathoms* (1953), *It Came from Outer Space* (1953), *Invaders from Mars* (1953), *Killers from Space* (1953), *Creature from the Black Lagoon* (1954) and *The Monster from the Ocean Floor* (1954). All of these films enact the defeat of an alien power; very often what this alien power comes to offer is interpreted as some form of mind control, which means that the films all serve as exemplars of a specific form of 'freedom', which is shown as inherently strong enough to resist all threat. It is easy to read in this phenomenon a certain defensiveness quite specific to the US, a Cold War paranoia which seems to necessitate a continual acting out of physical, mental or moral invasion and of strategies for resistance; the pleasure of the defeat of the monster is rarely psychologized but left as a way of protecting home, hearth and family.

One of the strands which the horror film pursues in the next decade, the 1960s, is typified in the achievement of Roger Corman, a horror auteur of

enormous significance, who figures among other things as a major rein-
terpreter of Edgar Allan Poe (q.v.). Corman was one of the most prolific di-
rector/producers in the history of cinema, but he turned his hand most
consistently to horror between 1960 and 1964. During these years he
made a cycle of seven films (*The House of Usher* [1960], *The Pit and the
Pendulum* [1961], *The Premature Burial* [1961], *Tales of Terror* [1962], *The
Haunted Palace* [1963], *The Masque of the Red Death* [1964] and *The Tomb
of Ligeia* [1964]) which are usually referred to as the Poe cycle. But although
in each of the films it is true that Corman adapts elements of Poe's stories
(except in *The Haunted Palace*, which is based on H. P. Lovecraft's [q.v.]
The Case of Charles Dexter Ward [1927–8]), Corman is forced, by the brevity
of the stories themselves and the assumptions audiences make regarding
narrative film, to add a great deal to them, and he also makes little attempt,
except in *The Tomb of Ligeia*, to invoke the drowsy, opiated tone of Poe, so
that the films remain in a very real sense Corman's own. To criticize him as
an exploiter of Poe would, however, be beside the point: the cycle is very
much a self-consistent set of horror films, with their own detailed and impressive *mise-en-scène*, within which elements of Poe are embedded but remade
in ways that specifically resonate with key motifs in 1960s' culture.

It has, however, been said that the initiative with regard to horror film
had largely passed in the 1960s to Britain, where the notorious Hammer
Studios (named not for a blunt instrument, as is commonly thought, but for
the millionaire who was their initial source of financing) began a whole series
of further interpretations of the classic Gothic narratives. Hammer Studios
also made a less well-known but equally important series of examinations of
psychopathology: examples include *Taste of Fear* (1960), *Maniac* (1962),
Paranoia (1963), *Fanatic* (1965) and *The Anniversary* (1967).

Although Corman's work and the horror films made by Hammer, which
were most frequently directed by Terence Fisher, have often been contrasted,
there are nevertheless similarities. The mingled response of fear and laughter which marks, for example, Dracula's fifteenth 'resurrection' is the sure
mark of a 'Goth' cult; these films reflect a situation where the rules are clearly
known, and because of this the film-maker is free to move knowingly among
the many variations possible on a theme.

Yet in the long run what has come to seem most remarkable about the
Hammer films is their place in a specifically English cultural life. The roots
of Hammer's treatment of the Frankenstein and Dracula myths lie directly
in the earlier Gothic, considered again from the vantage point of the 1960s.
Hammer horror is, like Corman's, self-ironizing; but what is important is
that this is only a similarity of means, and the ends of Corman and Fisher
remain radically different. Hammer's films do not on the whole embark on

the tricky balancing of good and evil that Corman attempts; what has been more shocking in Hammer films, especially the later ones, has rather been the explicitness with which successive directors presented the connections between violence and sexuality, an explicitness which, within the earlier tradition, might take one back to M. G. Lewis (q.v.) rather than to Poe.

Corman's films and Hammer's, however, remain to a large extent a recycling of old themes, and there is something of a strain evident in their attempts to render their fears and anxieties up to date. A very different kind of horror film was being made at the same time, best represented in the work of Alfred Hitchcock, Roman Polanski and Michael Powell, which might be best described in terms of an emphasis on the revelation of the terror of everyday life. Here we have films – not specifically related to each other, or to the earlier Gothic tradition – that appear initially to turn their backs on explicit Gothic settings and strive to prise apart the bland surfaces of common interaction to disclose the anxieties and aggressions that lie beneath.

Three emblematic films here might be Hitchcock's *Psycho* (1960), Powell's *Peeping Tom* (1960) and Polanski's *Repulsion* (1965). Each of these three films is, at root, a study in paranoia. Each of them also posits a correlation between paranoia and a thwarting in the relation between the ordered and the chaotic. Each of them, in the search for a visual equivalent for a psychological state, finds a setting which in the end, however, relates closely to traditional Gothic imagery. In *Psycho* it is the house, with its cellars and mysterious doors, which has come down to us as pure American Gothic. In *Peeping Tom* it is the film-processing laboratory which, in a remarkably self-referential trope, becomes a substitute for the hero's homelessness, shot as it is in half-tones and impossible as it is to discern its physical limits; what we have here is the laboratory of generations of Frankensteins, in which the endless attempt is continued to discern the secrets of creation, but here translated into cinema's own concerns and scenario. Catherine Deneuve's apartment in *Repulsion*, albeit outwardly contemporary, is capable at times of sprouting supernatural apparitions worthy of the direst secrets of *Udolpho* (q.v.).

The sixth category, beginning in the 1970s, would be well typified by *The Exorcist* (1973), and would include films which have been widely seen as exploitative yet which, were we to follow through any argument about the social significance of the forms of terror, should be considered in a more detailed way. What is common to these films is an apparent return to age-old themes of satanism and possession. *The Exorcist* itself is visibly a Gothic work in its trappings, and not a Gothic relieved with the ironic spice of comedy. In other words, and in sharp contrast to almost all the other works mentioned, it is a work which professes not knowledge but ignorance, ignorance of the psychological ambivalence of the vocabulary of Gothic images. Yet this is itself perhaps a further level of 'forgery', and reminds us of how much Gothic has had to do with forgery and the fake through the centuries (Hogle 1994): W. P. Blatty, the writer and producer who appears to have had most say in the shape of the film, seems in fact to be all too well aware of the manipulative potential of film, but chooses to delude us into believing in what appears on the surface to be a certain literal-mindedness. It is doctors and psychiatrists themselves who in the film recommend that the case of 12-year-old Regan MacNeil be referred to the exorcists; thus the audience is put in the position not of interpreting horror symbolism as commentary on psychological disorder, but of accepting it as the outward and visible sign-system of the Devil.

But perhaps this is to make too much of the text of *The Exorcist*, which might be best viewed as largely a sequence of special effects, the narrative submerged during the actual viewing experience, and deliberately so. The audience envisaged, unlike that of many of the earlier horror films referred to above, is thus a passive one; from being a potential mode of enquiry into the limits and conditions of the human, horror has here become a pure spectacle which demands – and indeed permits – almost nothing by way of judgement on the part of the spectator.

The seventh and final phase of horror film to mention, the most recent, is perhaps beginning to reverse this trend, and shows an ironic self-consciousness at work that none the less does not eschew bur rather glories in film's exploitative potential. In this category would be included several long-running series, including the *Friday the 13th* and *Nightmare on Elm Street* sequences. In *Friday the 13th* (1980), for example, a modernized version of the Gothic panoply is present in full force: the isolated campsite, the mysterious snake under the bed, the dead telephones, the jeep stuck in the swamp, most especially the lashing storm which rages for the whole of the second half of the film. All the key moments involve, as would also be the case in the more recent *Blair Witch Project* (1999), a wandering hand-held camera, familiar from previous generations of Gothic film as representing the vantage point of the killer himself or herself. To say that *behind* this lurks a prurient sexual concern would be to overestimate the film's subtlety; the gloating shots of perfect young flesh, the scene in which one young lover lies murdered in a top bunk while her partner is innocently below, are in no way withheld from view but form, along with scantily dressed bodies, a running refrain to murder by axe, knife and arrow. The wounded mother who is a key protagonist of the film carries around with her an entire arsenal of weaponry, and it could be said that, given the woodenness of the acting and the indistinguishability of the teenagers, the only attempt at differentiation, in this as in so many other contemporary teen-scream films, lies in the choice of the mode of death.

The questions raised by Gothic in film thus seem to be twofold: first, there is the question of the explicit, of what is *shown*, and the extent to which this can be compatible with the issues of secrecy with which the traditional Gothic has always been concerned. Second, there is a question of history, of how far it has proved possible to produce new sources of horror without having recourse to older models.

Bibliography

Clover, Carol J. 1992: *Men, Women and Chain-Saws: Gender in the Modern Horror Film*. London: BFI.

Hogle, Jerrold E. 1994: 'The Ghost of the Counterfeit in the Genesis of the Gothic.' In Allan Lloyd Smith and Victor Sage (eds), *Gothick: Origins and Innovations*. Amsterdam: Rodopi, 23–33.

Hutchings, Peter 1993: *Hammer and Beyond: The British Horror Film*. Manchester: Manchester University Press.

Jones, Darryl 2002: *Horror: A Thematic History in Fiction and Film*. London: Arnold.

Punter, David 1996: *The Literature of Terror: A History of Gothic Fictions from 1765 to the Present Day*. 2nd edn. 2 vols. London: Longman.

GOTHIC AND THE
GRAPHIC NOVEL

The graphic novel, it is sometimes said, is no more than an overgrown comic, a regressive and mindless form of entertainment; but this is certainly not true of the best of them. *Watchmen* (1987), by Alan Moore and Dave Gibbons, is one of the most remarkable achievements to date in this new form, and a highly sophisticated text in its own right, involving a type of 'syncopation' of word and image which slows and complicates the narrative thrust and makes for a genuine depth of reading. This is further enhanced by the way in which the text is a tissue of referentiality, taking us back to William Blake, Friedrich Nietzsche and of course the Gothic and romantic traditions as frequently as to Bob Dylan. The test of such a text might be to ask: could what it does be done in any other way? Is it merely hybridizing existent forms? Here I think it is clear that *Watchmen* has evolved its own form; in the corners of the pictures there are always other narratives, other fragments of story, which are then continually picked up and rethreaded later in the text.

However, it could still be said that this display of technical virtuosity is expended on a topic of scant interest, since the story itself concerns precisely the question of comic-book heroes, especially when they are past their sell-by date. It could alternatively be argued that this is inevitable in the genre; that the question then becomes one of how the text recycles and adapts these pre-existing materials, just as 'literary' texts prove themselves through their reuse and adaptation of the trace, through the way in which they can give added resonance to past texts, the 'manuscripts' of Gothic, which are, at the end of the day, the focus of their interest.

The figure of the news vendor who provides the common man's commentary on events in *Watchmen* is continually falling through the black holes of his own words as he tries to grasp the apocalyptic nature of the political background, which is the Soviet invasion of Afghanistan and the consequent fear of global war. 'Don't people see the *signs?*' he asks, 'Don't they know where this is *headed?*', but the visual content makes it clear that we also have to see these 'signs' not merely as social portents but also as material signs and 'headlines', precisely the stuff of the newspapers which he is forever half-comprehendingly reading; and when he adds, '*See? Apathy!* Everybody escapin' into comic books an' TV! Makes me sick . . . I mean, all this, it could all be *gone*: people, cars, TV shows, magazines . . . Even the word "gone" would be gone', then we glimpse an intensity of involvement with the spread of media influence in general which would be very difficult to achieve in any other form.

Self-referentiality, a concern with personal and social terror, the shameless exploitation of the exotic and the disastrous: all these give *Watchmen* a distinctly Gothic feel, which is even stronger in a 1994 graphic novel by the master of the genre, Neil Gaiman, called *Brief Lives*. Here we are in a world not of costumed heroes but of the gods, or rather, in a new mythology of the seven 'Endless' who lie even further back behind the gods, and perhaps their names can best give us an idea of the parameters of the world in which they move: Destiny, Death, Dream, Destruction, Desire, Despair and Delirium – although we also note that, at some previous time, before dislocation or before the Fall, Delirium's true name was 'Delight'. The action hinges on Destruction's abandonment of his quasi-divine tasks in the face of the far greater destructiveness unleashed on the world through human scientific and technological discovery, a remake of the Frankenstein myth. Again we have here the highly complex textuality typical of the Gothic (these 'brief lives' are also, for example, those of John Aubrey [1626–95], who made a collection of notes, anecdotes and gossip about his contemporaries, gathered together under the title *Brief Lives*), looking back precisely to the Gothic masters, Blake, Samuel Taylor Coleridge and the marquis de Sade among others.

Much as in Blake's *Vala, or, The Four Zoas* (1795–1804), the disappearance or rather dereliction of duty of Destruction unseats the balance of the world. Delirium in particular, the youngest of the Endless, embarks on a search for him, and is assisted by Dream. Dream has his own reasons for embarking on his journey for, as Morpheus, he has unfinished business with his son Orpheus, who exists now only as a severed head in a tiny Greek shrine; Dream knows that he has to complete the task of releasing Orpheus from his bondage into life, into death, and the release of Destruction from the world enables him also to do this.

Brief Lives is a more violent text than *Watchmen*, and yet the stylization of the artwork keeps this within strict boundaries. Certainly neither can be regarded as a 'comic book', if the comparison is supposed to be either with children's comics or with the 1960s' 'head comix', largely because both graphic novels owe a sombre allegiance to a far wider mythic tradition, and are largely free from the manic glee in destruction large and small which characterizes so much of the 'comic' world. Neither are they in any sense light-hearted texts; on the contrary, one of the faults which both share is an unremitting solemnity which at first sits oddly with the form. At the end of the day, however, perhaps what they remind us of is that a culture which relies on the visual image at least as much as on the written or spoken word, and in which the majority of newspapers are themselves now given over to the image as the amount of newsprint in the tabloids shrinks year by year, is as much in need of applicable interpretation as the more traditional forms; and it is this serious work at the interface of word and image which the graphic novels, at their best, are performing, while at the same time they carry forward an expressionist tradition in which the extreme emotions are personified and thrown into violent interaction.

Another of Gaiman's graphic novels – the ninth volume, in fact, of a much longer work called *The Sandman* – is *The Kindly Ones* (1996), which contains an introduction by Frank McConnell, in which he talks a little about Gaiman's narrative techniques – and in which, it is also fair to say, he takes care to establish a discourse which refuses academic purchase on the text. The 'kindly ones' of the title are the fates, and McConnell draws our attention to the way in which their conversation is *ab initio* constructed to 'refer to the act of telling'. To quote McConnell, partly quoting Gaiman:

> 'What are you making him then', asks Clotho of Lachesis in the third frame of the first chapter. 'I can't say that I'm terribly certain, my popsy', she replies, 'but it's a fine yarn, and I don't doubt that it'll suit, go with *anything*, this will'. The story begins as a story about storytelling . . . In fact, eight of the thirteen chapters begin, in the first frame, with a thread of some sort running across the panel, and with a comment that applies equally to the telling of the tale and to the tale itself.

McConnell's interpretation of this process brings us again face to face with Gothic complexities of tale-telling, and we can see this in more detail in a different work, *Witchcraft* (1996), by a team headed by writer James Robinson. *Witchcraft* is essentially a Gothic feminist revenge story running across different time-frames. In Roman Britain, a group of benevolent witches is set upon by a gang of (male) barbarians. One of those who is raped and killed cries out in the moment before her death to the goddesses. Here the figure of the three-in-one recurs, not exactly the Fates this time but the triplicity that is held to have preceded the Christian usurpation of the trinity

– and they are forced to provide opportunities for revenge, even though this is not immediately possible at the time. The story then unfolds in a variety of different scenarios as the character Ursula and her killer are reborn in various different guises; on each occasion until the last one the achievement of vengeance is thwarted, but finally that vengeance is achieved and the previous aggressor is sent back into the past, to relive endlessly the very pain he has inflicted on others, to endure as the perpetually repeated victim of sexual violence.

One strength of the text lies in the repertoire of delay. By this I do not mean merely the delaying devices conventionally employed to prevent an early denouement, but rather the way in which a parallel is achieved between narrative delay and the delay necessary in the reading process in order to keep our attention moving between word and picture. But it is also true that, like Gothic, this graphic novel weaves its own explanations around historical events. For example, there is a long passage which deals with the life of the adventurer Richard Burton, who is figured as the current reincarnation of Ursula. The violent barbarian figures as a man called Ithal, who is having an affair with Burton's mother. When Burton confronts him he is hideously humiliated by Ithal, and this is seen as the motivation behind Burton's later career; coming across Ithal again in later life, and thereby encountering a further chance of revenge, he again flunks it in favour of fame and fortune, and the vengeance goes unachieved. Yet because, of course, the text does not take linear historical time seriously, these events become merely items or instances in a longer history, in this case of gender oppression.

Witchcraft, we may say, sets out to provide an interpretative master-narrative by means of which particular events can be explained, a typically Gothic alternative to history. Thus the shards and fragments of its dialogue, which operate in a postmodern dispersive fashion at a local level, all tend towards a unification of narrative. The same cannot be said of the many graphic novels that exist in what we have already identified as the aftermath of the superheroes. Another instance of this subgenre would be the series of texts written by Grant Morrison under the title of *The Invisibles*. The Invisibles are, as it were, superheroes for our age, postmodern superheroes who are prone to moments of extreme doubt about what they are doing and why they are doing it. To put it another way, these superheroes are, like so many Gothic protagonists, robbed of narrative agency: as they go about their everyday work of killing and salvation, they are never sure whether in fact they are enacting someone else's narrative: whether, indeed, their story has already been written – and drawn – for them.

The obvious irony of this position – because, of course, their perception is correct – is underlined in a volume of *The Invisibles* called *Counting to*

None (1999) by a character called King Mob, who is looking, for reasons too complicated to explain here, for a time machine. 'Sometimes I wonder if the time machine *causes* the end of everything', he says, and we can hardly fail to pick up the resonance of the time machine as the process of narrative itself, as the process whereby freedom is destroyed in the very act of recounting:

> Maybe it was something that never should have been made, like the *bomb* . . .
> I'm shooting people and it never seems to *end*. It was all those *Moorcock* books;
> I wanted to be *Jerry Cornelius*, the English assassin. I wanted the guns and the
> cars and the girls and the chaos. Shit. I've ended up a *murderer*, my karma's
> a bloody *minefield*.

But lack of knowledge is not an option, just as unreading Michael Moorcock is an impossibility. Whatever fate is traced in texts like *The Invisibles*, it is ineluctable; like any Gothic hero, the protagonists are doomed by forces beyond their control, and even their self-awareness and scepticism cannot help them to escape from the horror of their position.

Bibliography

Eisner, Will 1996: *Graphic Storytelling and Visual Narrative*. Florida: Poorhouse Press.
McCloud, Scott 2000: *Reinventing Comics*. New York: Paradox Press.

Writers of Gothic

William Harrison Ainsworth
(1805–1882)

William Harrison Ainsworth was one of the most popular and prolific of Victorian writers, reckoned in his time alongside Charles Dickens (q.v.) in his hold on the public imagination. Born in Lancashire, Ainsworth published a long series of historical novels, including *Rookwood* (1834), *Jack Sheppard* (1839), *The Tower of London: An Historical Romance* (1840), *Old St Paul's* (1841) and *Windsor Castle* (1843); a well-known and sociable figure in his earlier years, he became increasingly retiring in the 1850s and later.

Many of his novels make use of Gothic and supernatural machinery, from ghosts and spectres to crypts and underground passages; this can be particularly vividly seen in *The Tower of London*, where the question might fairly be asked as to whether it is really a historical novel at all, so fantastical become the dimensions and intricacies of the tower as it is explored in more and more detail throughout the text. Certainly Ainsworth is interested, here and elsewhere, in taking up supernatural legends, especially those which have clung tenaciously to great old buildings, and constructing his narratives around them.

The Lancashire Witches (1849), which many critics have regarded as Ainsworth's most compelling work, takes as its theme the actual Lancashire witch trials of 1613, referred to in some detail in Walter Scott's (q.v.) *Letters on Demonology and Witchcraft* (1830), and weaves them into a gripping narrative. The book's faults are those habitual to Ainsworth: poor dialogue, an over-reliance on costume details and some lack of clarity in the lines of the story; nevertheless, there are various descriptive passages which could be compared with those in Ann Radcliffe (q.v.), and given extra conviction by Ainsworth's familiarity with and love of the country he is describing.

The influences of Radcliffe, M. G. Lewis (q.v.) and Scott can be found throughout his work, not only in the novels but also in the short stories he published early in his career, such as 'The Pirate', 'Adventure in the South Seas', 'The Fortress of Saguntum' (1829) and 'The Spectre Bride' (1822), stories which, taken as a group, provide an interesting bridge between the more exotic aspects of Lewis's work and the later exoticism of Robert Louis Stevenson's (q.v.).

Bibliography

Buckley, Matthew 2002: 'Sensations of Celebrity: *Jack Sheppard* and the Mass Audience.' *Victorian Studies*, 44 (3), 423–63.

Maxwell, Richard 1978: 'City Life and the Novel: Hugo, Ainsworth, Dickens.' *Comparative Literature*, 30, 157–71.

Worth, George J. 1972: *William Harrison Ainsworth*. New York: Twayne.

Jane Austen

(1775–1817)

While such works as *Sense and Sensibility* (1811), *Pride and Prejudice* (1813) and *Emma* (1816) would seem to place Jane Austen worlds away from anything we might conceivably identify as Gothic, she nevertheless made one significant contribution to the tradition with *Northanger Abbey*. Although not published until 1818, *Northanger Abbey* was completed in 1798, a time when the Gothic novel had reached the peak of its popularity but was also beginning to be increasingly attacked and satirized by its critics. Austen, however, does not want to dismiss the Gothic novel completely – she gives full credit to its imaginative powers – but only to moderate the excesses of the Gothic sensibility and show the need to discipline 'an imagination resolved on alarm'.

Catherine Morland, the 'heroine', or perhaps anti-heroine, has an obsession with Gothic novels that leads her to construct thrilling fantasies about what she will find at Northanger Abbey when she is invited to stay there, but all her expectations are successively deflated as she finds domestic comfort and a distressing absence of 'dirt and cobwebs'; a promising 'hidden manuscript' turns out to be nothing more than a mundane shopping list, and the wife of General Tilney, owner of the abbey, is discovered to have died of nothing more than interesting than natural causes. As Austen's narrator gently concludes, 'Charming as were all Mrs Radcliffe's works, and charming even as were the works of all her imitators, it was not in them perhaps that human nature, at least in the midland counties of England, was to be looked for.'

While many critics have read Austen's parody as a relatively straightforward demonstration of Catherine's need to distinguish fantasy from reality, an education in which she is guided by the general's son, Henry Tilney, others have pointed out that Austen is, nevertheless, suggesting that fantasy and reality are not completely inimical. Many of the underlying fears of Radcliffean Gothic, particularly the fear of patriarchal authority, are proven to be quite valid. The autocratic General Tilney may not have murdered his wife, but as he most clearly reveals when he unceremoniously tosses Catherine out of Northanger, he is nevertheless an unpleasant and mercenary man.

Austen may be primarily concerned with the works of Ann Radcliffe (q.v.), but the seven 'horrid' novels that Catherine's acquaintance Isabella Thorpe recommends demonstrate that Austen had a wide knowledge of the Gothic genre. These novels – Lawrence Flammenberg's *The Necromancer, or, The Tale of the Black Forest* (1794), Karl Grosse's *Horrid Mysteries* (1796), Francis Lathom's (q.v.) *The Midnight Bell* (1798), Eliza Parsons's *Castle of Wolfenbach: A German Story* (1793) and *The Mysterious Warning: A German Tale* (1796), Eleanor Sleath's *The Orphan of the Rhine* (1798), and Regina Maria Roche's *Clermont* (1798) – were considered to be Austen's parodic inventions until they were discovered by the bibliographer Michael Sadleir in the 1920s.

Bibliography

Roberts, Bette B. 1989: 'The Horrid Novels: *The Mysteries of Udolpho* and *Northanger Abbey.*' In Kenneth W. Graham (ed.), *Gothic Fictions: Prohibition/Transgression.* New York: AMS Press, 89–111.

Sadleir, Michael 1927: *The Northanger Novels: A Footnote to Jane Austen.* London: English Association Pamphlet No. 68.

Wallace, Tara Ghoshal 1988: '*Northanger Abbey* and the Limits of Parody.' *Studies in the Novel,* 20, 262–73.

J. G. BALLARD

(1930–)

The idea that J. G. Ballard might suitably be considered a Gothic writer might initially seem perverse; he is best known now as the author of *Empire of the Sun* (1984), in which, in a thinly disguised form, he recounts his boyhood experiences in a Japanese prisoner-of-war camp in Shanghai. His earliest work consisted of science fiction stories, mostly published in pulp magazines, but even then standing out from the mass of similar work by virtue of the intensity with which he depicted the dissolution of the individual.

At the centre of Ballard's concerns lies an awareness of the frightening malleability of the human, of the ways in which fears, technological and otherwise, can destroy all semblance of individual difference. *The Atrocity Exhibition* (1970), perhaps his most challenging work, is laid out like a series of newspaper paragraphs, grouped around a series of obsessive images – the death of John F. Kennedy, the fate of Marilyn Monroe, the wars and tortures of the twentieth century – and any notion of a stable protagonist is continually undermined by a series of name changes that makes the reader unsure from what perspective he or she is observing this accumulation of western nightmares.

That Ballard is a postmodern writer would thus be incontestable; the Gothic element arises as we pursue his figures through the terrifying labyrinths of a world where there is little except persecution (q.v.) – persecution not directly by the forces of political tyranny but more subtly by a relentless erosion of human difference in favour of a stock of public imagery that cannot be evaded but continues to assail the individual at every turn. If we were now to refer to a subgenre of 'techno-Gothic', then Ballard would be the originator: his notion of technology is not to do with external machines but with the inner mechanization of response, and with the doubts that follow as to whether what we are seeing is in fact a question of human feeling or rather one of an implanted repertoire of behaviours that, in the end, make us doubt the meaning of our own humanity.

Bibliography

Aldiss, Brian 1971: 'The Wounded Land: J. G. Ballard.' In Thomas D. Clareson (ed.), *The Other Side of Realism: Essays on Modern Fantasy and Science*

Fiction. Bowling Green, OH: Bowling Green State University Popular Press, 116–30.

Goddard, James and David Pringle 1976: *J. G. Ballard: The First Twenty Years.* Hayes: Bran's Head Press.

Perry, Nick 1970: 'Homo Hydrogenesis: Notes on the Work of J. G. Ballard.' *Riverside Quarterly*, 4, 98–105.

Iaiп Baпks

(1954–)

Iain Banks is an extraordinarily prolific Scottish writer who writes under two names. As Iain M. Banks, he is the author of a series of science fiction novels, including *Consider Phlebas* (1988), *The Player of Games* (1989), *State of the Art* (1989), *Use of Weapons* (1990), *Against a Dark Background* (1993), *Feersum Endjinn* (1994), *Excession* (1996) and *Inversions* (1998). As Iain Banks, his novels have been more diverse, and several of them have acquired a reputation as the products of a peculiarly dark imagination. *The Wasp Factory* (1990), for example, is the first-person narrative of one Frank Cauldhame. Frank lives on a small Scottish island with his father; he has already killed three people, and spends much of his time torturing and killing animals. Off in the distance, Frank's brother is gradually approaching the island, having escaped from an asylum. The revelatory denouement is remarkable; perhaps even more so is the half-playful, half-menacing tone in which Frank addresses the reader, sucking us into his own pathology even while we are appalled and repulsed both by the mayhem he causes and also by the parodically distorted reasoning which leads him towards death and destruction.

The Bridge (1992), perhaps Banks's best-known novel, takes place on a number of levels, which are eventually revealed as united in the sense that they all occur within the comatose consciousness of John Orr, who is recovering from a serious car accident. Thus the whole text can be seen as a medley of dreams, in which the narrator's psyche – or perhaps parts of that psyche – play different roles. One of these roles is as the Barbarian, a terrifyingly violent 'superhero' who moves through worlds of myth uncomprehendingly, slaying everything that crosses his path and speaking entertainingly in a broad Glaswegian accent.

Complicity (1993) again tells a daringly complex narrative, this time alternating between the conventional first-person narrative of a cocaine-sniffing, burned-out journalist called Cameron Colley and, remarkably, a second-person narrative not assigned to anybody by name but evidently recounting the exploits of a serial murderer. The 'complicity' of the title is of two kinds: is Colley complicit in these murders, even to the extent of *being* the murderer, whether he 'knows' it or not; and what is our situation as readers confronted with these scenarios of violence, many of which are committed against people who are themselves covert and unpunished criminals of the nastiest kind?

Bibliography

MacGillivray, Alan 1996: 'The Worlds of Iain Banks.' *Laverock*, 2, 22–7.

Martin Alegre, Sara 2000: 'Consider Banks: Iain (M.) Banks's *The Wasp Factory* and *Consider Phlebas*.' *Revista Canaria de Estudios Ingleses*, 41, 197–205.

Middleton, Tim 1999: 'The Works of Iain M. Banks: A Critical Introduction.' *Foundation: The International Review of Science Fiction*, 28 (76), 5–16.

John Banville

(1945–)

John Banville, an Irish writer, was literary editor of the *Irish Times* from 1988 to 1998. Since his first novel, *Long Lankin*, was published in 1970 he has written a series of other fictions, plays and short stories. His best-known novels include *Doctor Copernicus* (1976), *Kepler* (1981), *Mefisto* (1986), *The Book of Evidence* (1989) and *Ghosts* (1993).

Banville's literary style is instantly recognizable: allusive, sceptical, yet veering into moments of poetic richness, it enables the reader to enter into worlds where nothing is quite certain or quite what it seems to be. *The Book of Evidence*, for example, is a first-person narrative told by an imprisoned murderer, in which he looks back over the events which have brought him to this pass. And yet perhaps what he recalls has no real validity; for Banville, as for many other Gothic and postmodern writers, the irony is that there is no secure body of 'evidence' to be found in some objective, external past, rather the restless movement of memory continually rearranging, reordering, supplying new stories, new narratives. Furthermore in *The Book of Evidence* even these stories, often contradictory in themselves, slide in and out of a prevailingly dreamlike atmosphere which often has the effect of making it seem as though the events, if indeed they have happened at all, have only done so under the condition of dream, as part of a sliding away, a continual evasion of truths that cannot be caught or held securely within the text.

These motifs of the instability of the past and the unreliability of the text are present also in such others of Banville's fictions as *Mefisto*, where we might see a central fable in the figure of a man who stops suddenly and lifts his head, 'as if waking in fear out of a muddled dream, my heart thudding dully, while around me in the deepening stillness a sort of presence struggles to materialise'. It is the surrounding presence of these phantom forms – even though they frequently fail to materialize at all – which produces the Gothic texture of Banville's fictions, a texture in which the weave between the living and the dead, the historical and the imagined, is so close that it is impossible to separate one from the other.

Bibliography

Berensmeyer, Ingo 2000: *John Banville: Fictions of Order: Authority, Authorship, Authenticity*. Heidelberg: Carl Winter Universitätsverlag.

D'Hoker, Elke 2000: 'Books of Revelation: Epiphany in John Banville's Science Tetralogy and *Birchwood*.' *Irish University Review*, 30 (1), 32–50.

McMinn, Joseph 2000: 'Versions of Banville: Versions of Modernism.' In Liam Harte and Michael Parker (eds), *Contemporary Irish Fiction: Themes, Tropes, Theories*. Houndmills: Macmillan, 79–99.

CLIVE BARKER

(1952–)

Clive Barker is one of Britain's best-known contemporary writers of popular horror fiction. He began his career as a playwright, and his subsequent interests can be gauged from the titles and topics of some of these plays: *The History of the Devil*, *Frankenstein in Love*, a play about Goya called *Colossus* (published together as *Incarnations* in 1995). His next venture was into short stories, culminating in the six volumes of tales known as *The Books of Blood* (1988). Several of these stories were adapted for the screen, something Barker also tried himself when in 1987 he directed a version of his novella *The Hellbound Heart*, producing the well-known film *Hellraiser* and, inevitably, its several sequels.

Clive Barker (1952–)

It would be fair to say that Barker's work now covers the full gamut of textual and related production, from the original novels which he continues to write himself, of which the best known are probably *Weaveworld* (1987) and *Imajica* (1991), through the continuing succession of films (q.v.), and onto comic books and graphic novels (q.v.) based, often tenuously, on his work or, at least, on the 'mythology' which is perceived as underpinning that work. He has also recently written more plays and had a one-man art exhibition.

It would be fair to say that Barker's fictions have epic ambitions: they are enormously long, packed with incident, and often range freely across vast swathes of time. More significant, however, would be the range of supernatural terrors that he conjures up. It would not be entirely accurate to call him a sadistic writer, but clearly he has been concerned throughout his work with pain and the limits of pain, with what the human body can endure and with what humans can inflict upon each other. In this respect, it might be said that he produces a kind of contemporary, popular version of Charles Robert Maturin (q.v.), an unending series of examples of torture; on the other hand, he is far less like Maturin – and more, if we were to pursue some somewhat unlikely analogies, like Edward George Bulwer-Lytton (q.v.) – in his continuing interest in the figure of the secret society, the suppressed story, the overarching plot that lies in some supernatural realm beyond the world's apparent events.

Bibliography

Goh, Robbie B. H. 2000: 'Consuming Spaces: Clive Barker, William Gibson and the Cultural Poetics of Postmodern Fantasy.' *Social Semiotics*, 10 (1), 21–39.

Joshi, S. T. 1991: 'Clive Barker: Sex, Death and Fantasy.' *Studies in Weird Fiction*, 9, 2–12.

McRoy, Jay 2002: 'There are No Limits: Splatterpunk, Clive Barker, and the Body *in extremis*.' *Paradoxa: Studies in World Literary Genres*, 17, 130–50.

WILLIAM BECKFORD
(1760–1844)

William Beckford's relation to the Gothic tradition is somewhat oblique, and rests largely on his 1786 novel *Vathek* (q.v.), which is not really a Gothic novel but rather an orientalist tale, although its anti-realism and its insistence on grandiloquent effects suggest that, if not Gothic in itself, it can certainly be seen to participate in the revolution of taste in the 1780s and 1790s that fostered the emergence of the Gothic.

Beckford was an extremely wealthy man, and his ambitions were by no means entirely literary. He was above all a collector of the strange and the exotic, and to house his collections he built a Gothic 'abbey' at Fonthill, outside Bath. We have many reports of its grandeur in its heyday; but perhaps what is paradoxically best known about it is that, after Beckford had been forced to sell it in order to service debts, its magnificent central tower collapsed, providing a kind of allegory of the themes of aspiration and fall which could be seen as encapsulating the dizzying, sublime yet disastrous perspectives of the Gothic.

Vathek itself is a short novel which recounts the story of the Caliph Vathek, who, partly led on by his mother, is tempted by a figure known as the Giaour (but clearly a satanic emissary) who shows him a series of strange talismans which will convey power on him. Thus tempted he performs human sacrifices, and the Giaour then leads him on a journey. The end of the journey is at Istakhar and the Halls of Eblis; here, as the reader probably expects, Vathek does indeed discover the talismans and all manner of other treasures, but he also discovers the terrible price that he – and all others who have sought wealth and power through tyranny and murder – now has to pay. It is a curious book, which sometimes seems uncertain of its own direction but which on the other hand succeeds well in conveying a distinctly exotic atmosphere of a kind that was genuinely new in the 1780s. As it moves between terror and high humour, the reader is never quite certain how seriously events are meant to be taken, and yet it is, paradoxically, this sophisticated alternation of tone, reminiscent in itself of the dandyish aspect of Beckford, that gives the book its strength and its unique appeal.

Bibliography

Brockman, H. A. N. 1956: *The Caliph of Fonthill*. London: Laurie.

Gemmett, Robert J. 1977: *William Beckford*. Boston: G. K. Hall.
Saglia, Diego 2002: 'William Beckford's "Sparks of Orientalism and the Material/ Discursive Orient of British Romanticism.' *Textual Practice*, 16 (1), 75–92.

E. F. Benson
(1867–1940)

Now perhaps best known for his series of books featuring Emmeline Lucas (Lucia) and her social rival, Elizabeth Mapp, Edward Frederic Benson was a prolific author, producing biographies, histories and memoirs as well as numerous works of fiction. Several of his novels have supernatural elements: *The Judgment Books* (1895), for example, plays a variation on Wilde's (q.v.) *The Picture of Dorian Gray* (1890, rev. 1891) in its concern with the evil influence exerted upon an artist through his own self-portrait; family curses form the focus of such novels as *The Luck of the Vails* (1901) and *The Inheritor* (1930); in *Across the Stream* (1919) the protagonist is haunted by a demon in the shape of his dead brother; and *Raven's Brood* (1934) is a story of witchcraft set in the English countryside.

It is now generally considered, however, that none of these novels is as successful as Benson's supernatural short stories, many of which have become anthology standards. His first collection was *The Room in the Tower and Other Stories* (1912), and the much-reprinted title story aptly demonstrates Benson's ability to produce a chilling and claustrophobic nightmare out of the most mundane and ordinary world. The protagonist here is troubled for over fifteen years by variations on a recurrent dream in which he is inexplicably at the house of Jack Stone, a schoolfellow whom he scarcely knew. There is always the same sense of 'dreadful oppression and foreboding' and the silence is broken each time as the mother says to him, 'Jack will show you your room: I have given you the room in the tower.' As in most of Benson's stories, psychological horror ultimately gives way to physical horror, and Mrs Stone, with her 'narrow, leering eyes' and 'demon-like mouth', is revealed as a suicide turned into a vampire (q.v.). Benson's other classic vampire tale is 'Mrs Amworth', first published in his finest collection of stories, *Visible and Invisible* (1923). Now relocated to a quiet English village, the vampire appears in the guise of the 'vigorous and genial' widow of an Indian civil servant. The highly jolly and sociable Mrs Amworth is surely one of the strangest and most disturbing of all vampires ever to have floated, 'nodding and smiling', outside a window. It is perhaps notable that both the evil forces in these stories are women, and some critics have detected elements of misogyny and sadism in these and several other of Benson's supernatural tales.

Bibliography

Masters, Brian 1991: *The Life of E. F. Benson*. London: Chatto and Windus.

AMBROSE BIERCE

(1842–1914)

Ambrose Bierce was an American journalist and man of letters who published two collections of short stories, *Tales of Soldiers and Civilians* (1891) and *Can Such Things Be?* (1893). The stories are brief, violent and grisly, and in many cases contain supernatural, or at least inexplicable, elements. Typical is 'The Famous Gilson Bequest' (1893), which begins with the small-town trial and hanging of one Milton Gilson for horse-stealing and other crimes. Gilson's will bequeaths his all to his main enemy, Brentshaw, on one condition: that if anyone can come forward and *prove* Gilson's criminality, the estate will pass to that person. Brentshaw, of course, therefore wastes his life in earnest defence of Gilson's reputation. In the end he goes, prematurely aged and broken, to visit Gilson's grave, to find it open, and has a vision of the dead man's ghost, engaged in stealing the ashes of the other occupants of the graveyard. Until now the narrator has remained equivocal about Gilson's guilt, but now we know that his dishonesty was real and has infected not only Brentshaw but the whole town.

Perhaps Bierce's best-known story is 'An Occurrence at Owl Creek Bridge' (1891), in which the protagonist appears to survive an attempt at hanging him for treachery, only for it to be revealed at the end that his apparent escape and subsequent travel to safety have been mere fantasy and that he in fact died as planned. Some of the other stories, however, operate rather differently and indeed may better be seen as prose poems. 'An Inhabitant of Carcosa' (1893), for example, presents a man who finds himself isolated amid unrecognized ruins, thus repeating a frequent 'romantic' motif; but the fragments around him seem also to fragment the tale itself and no explanation is proffered of his mysterious translation.

Perhaps the peculiar horror of Bierce's vision derives from its bleakness: any moment of apparent revelation is likely to be immediately undercut; any hope that the world of spirits or the afterlife might provide justice or recompense for injustice here on earth is cast aside, as the afterworld is revealed to be at least as gruesome as its predecessor.

Bibliography

Davidson, Cathy N. 1982: *Critical Essays on Ambrose Bierce*. Boston: G. K. Hall.
Gale, Robert L. 2001: *An Ambrose Bierce Companion*. Westport, CT: Greenwood Press.
Grenander, Mary E. 1971: *Ambrose Bierce*. New York: Twayne.

ALGERNON BLACKWOOD
(1869–1951)

Algernon Blackwood published a large number of short stories in the first two and a half decades of the twentieth century, as well as some rather less successful novels and a substantial body of works for children. What is distinctive about his writing should probably be seen to follow from the fact that he is one of the few writers of Gothic fiction actually to have believed in the supernatural: an early adherence to Buddhism is modified into an interest in the Order of the Golden Dawn, and subsequently into a personal brand of mysticism which is intensified rather than challenged by extensive reading in psychology.

His stories are allusive, often opaque, but informed by thrilling depictions of natural forces which are only partially transmutable into words. In a typical story, 'The Man Whom the Trees Loved' (1912), the protagonist, a man who has spent his life caring for trees, is eventually claimed by them as one of their own: the transcendence of human concerns that this implies is carefully balanced against his wife's powerful sense of loss as he vanishes into a greater, farther world where individuality will be subsumed into a wider, dreaming life. In one of Blackwood's novels, *The Human Chord* (1928), an attempt is made to utter a harmonic which will not only call down the gods but will transmute the utterers themselves into gods. The attempt fails, but the reader is left in little doubt where Blackwood's sympathies lie.

Blackwood was secretive about his life, at least until his last years, when he became, oddly, a well-known radio personality in Britain; much of his life was spent abroad, especially in the wildernesses of Canada and Europe, and this sense of the wild lies at the heart of virtually all his best work. Where so many writers of the Gothic rely upon the terrors of claustrophobia, Blackwood's tales are more concerned with the fear of wide open spaces, with what visitations might come when one is alone with the elements; in the best of those tales, the achievement is concomitant with death, but whether this ending of the physical body is coterminous with spiritual death is a question handled with tact and a sense of the ineradicable nature of longing.

Bibliography

Briggs, Julia 1977: *Night Visitors: The Rise and Fall of the English Ghost Story.* London: Faber and Faber.

Hudson, Derek 1961: 'A Study of Algernon Blackwood.' *Essays and Studies,* 14, 109–14.

Punter, David 1996: *The Literature of Terror: A History of Gothic Fictions from 1765 to the Present Day.* Vol. 2: *The Modern Gothic.* 2nd edn. London: Longman.

ROBERT BLOCH
(1917–1994)

Robert Bloch's interest in horror was first prompted by *Weird Tales,* a pulp magazine specializing in tales of the macabre and supernatural, and particularly by the stories of H. P. Lovecraft (q.v.). Bloch wrote more than two hundred short stories, primarily fantasy, horror and science fiction, as well as twenty-two novels and various non-fiction articles. After experimenting with such subjects as voodoo in 'Mother of Serpents' (1936), demonic possession in 'Fiddler's Fee' (1940) and black magic in 'Return to the Sabbat' (1941), Bloch turned his attention to psychological horror in the mid-1940s.

Much of his subsequent work reveals a fascination with the mind of the psychopathic killer and with the ability of the psychotic to merge into the everyday world. This interest is first shown in the short story, 'Yours Truly, Jack the Ripper', published in 1943. The story was twice adapted for the radio, and led to Bloch's own radio series, *Stay Tuned for Terror,* in 1945.

His first novel, *The Scarf* (1947), takes the reader directly into the mind of the killer with its first-person narrative: Daniel Morley, a young writer, begins by taking out his frustrations and anger with the women he knows through his typewriter, but soon begins to use the red scarf of the title. As the women become characters in his books, so they become characters in his mind, and he has no hesitation in killing what he considers a fiction.

In 1955, already established as a screenwriter in Hollywood, Bloch began writing for *Alfred Hitchcock Presents*, and in 1959, he produced the novel for which he is best known today, *Psycho* (q.v.), inspired in part by Wisconsin serial killer Ed Gein. Made into a film (q.v.) by Alfred Hitchcock in 1960, *Psycho* became one of the most powerful and influential horror myths of the twentieth century. Bloch's subsequent novels include two rather undistinguished sequels to *Psycho*; a historical horror novel, *American Gothic* (1974); a Lovecraftian fantasy, *Strange Eons* (1978); and *The Jekyll Legacy* (1990), written with André Norton, a sequel to Robert Louis Stevenson's (q.v.) classic Gothic story.

Bibliography

Bloch, Robert 1993: *Once Around the Bloch: An Unauthorized Biography*. New York: St Martin's Press.

Matheson, Richard and Mainhardt, Ricia 1995: *Robert Bloch: Appreciations of the Master*. New York: Tor.

Punter, David 1990: 'Robert Bloch's *Psycho*: Some Pathological Contexts.' In Brian Docherty (ed.), *American Horror Fiction: From Brockden Brown to Stephen King*. New York: St Martin's Press, 92–106.

ELIZABETH BOWEN

(1899–1973)

Elizabeth Bowen is best known for her novels, including *The House in Paris* (1935) and *The Heat of the Day* (1948), rather than specifically as a Gothic writer; none the less, all of her work suggests a certain haunting quality, whether it be haunting by unresolved issues from the past or by ghosts of the present.

From the point of view of the Gothic, her most important work is contained in *The Demon Lover, and Other Stories*. This volume was published in

1945, and the date is significant; the war forms a largely implicit backdrop to these tales of unrequited and half-buried love, although whether this is the First or Second World War, or rather a meditation on the hallucinatory strangeness engendered by war in general, remains unclear. Perhaps the best-known story is 'The Demon Lover', which succinctly takes the reader into the world of a woman who gets an unwelcome reminder of a rash promise she made to a man who was in fact killed many years ago, in the First World War; as we may perhaps predict, this wraith reappears in her life, but the unexpected manner in which he does so is shocking in its suddenness.

But if the Gothic is significant in Bowen, it is probably less so in terms of individual stories than in the general sense of the phantomatic that haunts her work. The 'great houses' that characterize her fiction are given, naturally, a present existence, but this 'presence' is always accompanied by a certain – or rather, perhaps, uncertain – history, often only half-known to the characters but remaining, as it were, just out of vision, never fully comprehensible. Bowen, we might say, is a writer of 'Gothic love'; in other words, of kinds of love that are difficult to distinguish from obsession, that are unable to respect the boundaries of life and death and that challenge – as ghostly fiction always does – linear views of history. In Bowen's scenarios, the present continually shades off into memories of the past, or even of fantasized pasts in which the 'course of the heart' might well have been different.

Bibliography

Bennett, Andrew and Nicholas Royle 1995: *Elizabeth Bowen and the Dissolution of the Novel: Still Lives*. London: Macmillan.

Ellmann, Maud 2001: 'Elizabeth Bowen: The Shadowy Fifth.' In Rod Mengham and N. H. Reeve (eds), *The Fiction of the 1940s: Stories of Survival*. Houndmills: Macmillan, 1–25.

Punter, David 2001: 'Hungry Ghosts and Foreign Bodies.' In Andrew Smith and Jeff Wallace (eds), *Gothic Modernisms*. London: Palgrave, 11–28.

MARY ELIZABETH BRADDON

(1835–1915)

Born in Soho, Braddon began her career by defying all Victorian notions about acceptable behaviour for middle-class women, supporting herself and her mother by going on the stage. By 1860, however, she had given up acting to write anonymous thrillers for the penny-dreadfuls. She lived with the publisher John Maxwell, and wrote constantly to help earn money to support herself, Maxwell, their five illegitimate children, and Maxwell's children from his legal marriage – his wife was confined in a Dublin insane asylum. This goes some way towards explaining her extraordinary output: Braddon wrote over eighty novels, including the best-selling *Lady Audley's Secret* (1862), *Aurora Floyd* (1863), *John Marchmont's Legacy* (1863) and *Gerard, Or the World, The Flesh, and the Devil* (1891), a reworking of Goethe's *Faust*. She also produced nine plays and numerous short stories and articles as well as editing several magazines, including *Temple Bar* and *Belgravia*. Braddon is now best known, however, as one of the most successful of Victorian sensation novelists.

Sensation fiction, sometimes called 'domesticated Gothic' because of the way in which it transfers Gothic events to the heart of a supposedly respectable Victorian society, focuses upon secrets, social taboos, the irrational elements of the psyche, and questions of identity. Murder, adultery, bigamy, blackmail, fraud and disguise are common components of the plot. In *Lady Audley's Secret*, the title character, after being abandoned to poverty by her husband, leaves her child and creates a new identity for herself; she remarries into a wealthy family, and then, when her first husband returns, she tries – somewhat understandably, perhaps – to murder him in order to preserve her new status. When ultimately discovered, she is confined to an asylum and becomes the dark secret of the Audley family's past.

Braddon also produced a number of ghost stories which have become anthology standards, most notably 'The Cold Embrace' (1860), which like her sensation fiction pushes at the fragile veneer of social convention and focuses on the psychological, suggesting that the haunting may well be only in the mind, the ghostly embrace no more than a manifestation of guilt and remorse. She also made an unusual contribution to vampire (q.v.) literature with 'Good Lady Ducayne' (1896), a tale that reveals her fascination with theories of blood transfusion, and is typical of much of her work in the way a detached and ironic narrative voice is set against the sensational subject matter of the story.

Bibliography

Briganti, Chiara 1991: 'Gothic Maidens and Sensation Women: Lady Audley's Journey from the Ruined Mansion to the Madhouse.' *Victorian Literature and Culture*, 19, 189–211.

Tromp, Marlene, Gilbert, Pamela K. and Haynie, Aeron (eds) 2000: *Beyond Sensation: Mary Elizabeth Braddon in Context*. Albany, NY: State University of New York Press.

Wolff, Robert Lee 1979: *Sensational Victorian: The Life and Fiction of Mary Elizabeth Braddon*. New York: Garland.

CHARLOTTE BRONTË (1816–1855) AND EMILY BRONTË (1818–1848)

Daughters of Patrick Brontë, the curate of Haworth in Yorkshire, Charlotte and Emily Brontë were first exposed to the Gothic through their avid reading of the supernatural tales and poems published in the literary annuals and in *Blackwood's* magazine. Gothic elements are notable in their juvenilia, in Emily's early poems about Gondal, a gloomy realm that she invented with her sister Anne, and in Charlotte's stories about the imaginary kingdom of Angria, which she invented with her brother Branwell. Charlotte also produced one early and rather humorous ghost story, 'Napoleon and the Spectre' (1833), with a playfully vengeful ghost described in a delightfully lurid manner as having a swollen, protruding tongue, black and bloody, and bulging, bloodshot eyes.

As many critics have noted, while the Brontës appropriate many Gothic conventions and motifs in their later novels, they also transform these in significant ways. Not only are their heroines far more complex and independent than the traditional Gothic heroine, but they tend to reject the bland and virtuous hero usually offered as a reward for such a heroine's seemingly endless troubles. They much prefer the more problematic Byronic hero-villains who are their soul mates, but who nevertheless offer a much-feared threat to their fiercely defended independence.

95

In Emily's main contribution to the Gothic, *Wuthering Heights* (q.v.), the first Catherine is presented primarily as a restless ghost, while Heathcliff is alternately described as vampire (q.v.), fiend and ghost. These motifs, however, suggest not so much the supernatural as the psychological; *Wuthering Heights* appropriates Gothic motifs in order to explore questions of desire, obsession and fear. Charlotte's work moves further in the direction of realism, but nevertheless draws heavily upon the Gothic in developing the psychology of her characters. This is evident, for example, in *Villette* (1853), where a ghostly nun, although eventually exposed as a hoax, still plays a significant role in developing the central themes of emotional and sexual frustration. The use of the Gothic is particularly notable, however, in Charlotte's most acclaimed work, *Jane Eyre* (1847). Jane, the protagonist and narrator, relates the story of her rebellion against her orphaned and outcast state, her search for affection and companionship, and her eventual marriage to Rochester. Her move towards this union is impeded by Bertha Mason, Rochester's mad wife, a ghostly – and ghastly – figure imprisoned in the third storey of his home. Although the Gothic emerges in such notable early scenes as Jane's imprisonment within the Red Room, it is the moment when she first hears the 'preternatural laughter' of the madwoman that marks the most decisive intrusion of the Gothic mode. Bertha functions both as an embodiment of Rochester's dubious past, continually rising up in the present, and as a double for Jane. Brontë's use of the Gothic in *Jane Eyre* has been of particular interest to feminist critics, who have seen the third storey of Thornfield as representative of Jane's consciousness, and the madwoman Bertha as the embodiment of female rage.

Bibliography

Alexander, Christine 1993: '"The Kingdom of Gloom": Charlotte Brontë, the Annuals, and the Gothic.' *Nineteenth-Century Literature*, 47, 409–36.

Gilbert, Sandra M. and Gubar, Susan 1979: *The Madwoman in the Attic*. New Haven, CT: Yale University Press.

Heilman, Robert B. 1958: 'Charlotte Brontë's "New Gothic".' In Robert Rathburn and Martin Steinman (eds), *From Jane Austen to Joseph Conrad*. Minneapolis: University of Minnesota Press, 118–32.

CHARLES BROCKDEN BROWN
(1771–1810)

Charles Brockden Brown is often referred to as America's first professional man of letters. Influenced by William Godwin (q.v.) and the Enlightenment thinkers, Brown was himself a considerable influence on the Shelleys (see 'Mary Wollstonecraft Shelley') among others. What is perhaps most interesting about his work is that, while it professes on the surface to attempt a justification of rationalism, it frequently ends by undermining reason's claims, and producing a world of persecution (q.v.) and terror that bears comparison with the world of Godwin's *Things as They Are; or the Adventures of Caleb Williams* (q.v.) or, perhaps even closer, that of James Hogg's *The Private Memoirs and Confessions of a Justified Sinner* (q.v.).

By far Brown's most interesting novel is *Wieland; or, The Transformation* (1798), which tells the story of a melancholy young man, Theodore, who is moved to terrible actions, including the murder of his family and his own eventual suicide, by 'voices'. These voices, and the events they spark, are explained in a variety of complicated ways, not all of them perhaps entirely harmonious one with another. At one level the 'voices' are the product of a rationalist friend of Theodore's called Carwin, who has the gift of ventriloquism and who claims to be using it to test – and presumably eventually expose – Theodore's religious credulity. But Brown also suggests that Theodore would not have been deceived by these practices in the first place were it not for his already credulous disposition and his religiose self-deception.

One can therefore see that *Wieland* functions as a warning against religious excess; but at the same time it seems also to point out to the reader the dangers of the kind of cold logic Carwin claims to be using to disabuse Theodore of his delusions; in a way that parallels Hogg's *Confessions*, the reader is left unsure as to whether Carwin is the mundane, reasonable figure he claims to be or some kind of demonic incarnation. What also needs to be said about *Wieland*, as about others of Brown's novels, is that although in the portrayal of terror and persecution it draws firmly on the nascent Gothic tradition, it is also the case that this tradition is crucially relocated into a recognizable contemporary world.

Bibliography

Bennett, Charles E. 1980: 'Charles Brockden Brown and the International Novel.' *Studies in the Novel*, 12 (1), 62–4.

Schneck, Peter 2002: 'Wieland's Testimony: Charles Brockden Brown and the Rhetoric of Evidence.' *REAL: The Yearbook of Research in English and American Literature*, 18, 167–213.

Watts, Steven 1994: *The Romance of Real Life: Charles Brockden Brown and the Origins of American Culture*. Baltimore, MD: Johns Hopkins University Press.

EDWARD GEORGE BULWER-LYTTON

(1803–1873)

Edward Bulwer-Lytton's novels are now much neglected, but certainly during the 1830s he was regarded as one of the most significant and serious of British novelists, and he was for a time one of the most successful. He wrote in many different genres – or rather, perhaps, most of his novels effectively 'crossed' styles and subgenres one with another.

Some of his earliest work, for example, appears to be 'silver-fork' fiction, novels of fashionable society, but the most obvious example, *Pelham* (1828), in fact transgresses the boundaries of that rather indulgent school and plunges into considerably darker waters. *Eugene Aram* (1832), *Godolphin* (1833) and *Lucretia* (1846), similarly, all deal to an extent in Gothic themes, but what is crucial about Bulwer-Lytton's work is that in it these themes are no longer displaced, as they were in the work of Ann Radcliffe and M. G. Lewis (qq.v.), into the badlands of Catholic Mediterranean Europe and/or into the distances of past centuries but are acted out in contemporary Britain, and usually specifically in London.

The class position of these novels is thus odd: on the one hand, Bulwer-Lytton himself was an aristocrat and it is obviously the case that the novels demonstrate a familiarity with the upper classes, while on the other hand some of the scenes of low life are worthy of comparison with Charles Dickens (q.v.). Perhaps one should say that it is precisely in the contrast between these two worlds that the real vigour of these earlier novels can be found. The story of Bulwer-Lytton's writing, however, is one of gradual retreat from these more immediate and pressing concerns, in which the Gothic is used to represent something of the real horror of everyday life, into a more misty world, informed by his Rosicrucian and other mystical interests, which often returns the reader to a more old-fashioned, eighteenth-century emphasis on, for example, the Faustian pact with the devil and its dire consequences, but at the same time sacrifices much of the narrative drive which still makes the earlier work eminently readable.

Bibliography

Christensen, Allan Conrad 1976: *Edward Bulwer-Lytton: The Fiction of New Regions.* Athens, GA: University of Georgia Press.

Mulvey-Roberts, Marie 2001: 'Fame, Notoriety and Madness: Edward Bulwer-Lytton Paying the Price of Greatness.' *Critical Survey*, 13 (2), 115–34.

Wolff, Robert Lee 1971: *Strange Stories, and Other Explorations in Victorian Fiction.* Boston: Gambit.

JAMES BRANCH CABELL

(1879–1958)

James Branch Cabell was a writer from the South of the US whose work combines elements of fantasy with satire and mockery, especially of realist conventions and assumptions. It might be best to describe him as a 'high romantic' writer, except that there runs through his work a self-awareness, even a self-absorption, which prevents him from ever fully falling for the admiration of fantasy and imagination that he so loudly proclaims in his prefaces and in his comments on his own and (more rarely) others' writings.

His major novels were *The Cream of the Jest* (1917), *Jurgen* (1919), *Figures of Earth* (1921), *The High Place* (1923) and *Something about Eve* (1927). All of them centre, in one way or another, on a quest, usually to find something beyond the confines of the 'real' world, something that exists off the map that we conventionally use to guide us. But the question of whether this quest is ever truly successful is usually enveloped in irony; although his characters may escape to other lands, which are variably pleasurable or terrifying, they are nevertheless under a constraint to return. The unresolved question would then be: do these flights of fancy in some way menace or weaken the realm of reality, or is it that they are merely dreams that are cast into the outer darkness upon our awakening?

Cabell's views on modern life were harsh, and it has been tempting for many critics to see his scorn as an after-effect of conditions in the 'New South', and therefore to see him as a harbinger of Southern Gothic. His principal critical success came with the publication of *Jurgen*, but in a fittingly ironic move it was this same novel that was promptly banned for two and a half years – perhaps on the grounds of an account of sexual adventuring that may have seemed transgressive at the time, but perhaps also because the novel sets itself starkly against realist critical canons. Cabell's writing may occasionally seem over-rich to the point of lushness, but it is also laced with an acerbic dismissal of hypocrisy, from which the writer does not always exempt even himself.

Bibliography

Davis, Joe Lee 1962: *James Branch Cabell*. New York: Twayne.

Inge, M. Thomas and Edgar E. MacDonald (eds) 1983: *James Branch Cabell: Centennial Essays*. Baton Rouge: Louisiana State University Press.

Tarrant, Desmond 1967: *James Branch Cabell: The Dream and the Reality*. Norman: University of Oklahoma Press.

RAMSEY CAMPBELL

(1946–)

Ramsey Campbell was born in Liverpool and began writing horror fiction at a very early age, largely under the influence of the works of H. P. Lovecraft (q.v.) and his many successors and imitators. Campbell has evolved into an extremely prolific and popular writer of novels and short stories; many critics would say that the short works represent the better part of his output, on the grounds that while he is excellent at creating innovative scenarios for terror, his skills seem less when he is trying to work through long narratives or to develop our sympathetic interest in characters and their fate.

Perhaps, though, what is most singular about Campbell's work is the settings. It could be argued that the whole process of Gothic fiction over the last two hundred years has been gradually towards more and more immediate locations, so that those fears that one would in previous times only have encountered if one had taken the dangerous step of leaving the safe shores of Britain have increasingly come to infest the most mundane of environments. And Campbell's settings are indeed mundane – a council estate, a block of flats, an urban underpass – while his characters, who have most usually done nothing whatever (or nothing they know of) to deserve the ghastly fates that universally befall them, are the most ordinary of people, who rarely have any insight into the origin or purposes of the forces of evil that have awakened around them – until the last minute; but during the last minute there is rarely time for reflection.

His best-known novels include *To Wake the Dead* (1980; later known as *The Parasite*) and *The Long Lost* (1993); his collections of short stories include *The Height of the Scream* (1976), *Dark Feasts* (1987) and *Waking Nightmares* (1991). At the heart of his principal themes there lies a concern with the relations between inner and outer worlds: a constant questioning as to whether the appalling images that constantly arise before his characters with lethal consequences have origins in an outer world of anguish and suffering, or whether they are projections of aspects of the self that have never (fortunately) previously seen the light of day. In the end, it seems this question cannot be answered; all there is to conclude the encounter between the natural and the supernatural is a rapidly stifled scream.

Bibliography

Joshi, S. T. 2001: *Ramsey Campbell and Modern Horror Fiction*. Liverpool: Liverpool University Press.

King, Stephen 1981: *Danse Macabre*. New York: Everest House.

Ménégaldo, Gilles 1996: 'Gothic Convention and Modernity in Ramsey Campbell's Short Fiction.' In Victor Sage and Allan Lloyd Smith (eds), *Modern Gothic: A Reader*. Manchester; Manchester University Press, 188–97.

Angela Carter

(1940–1992)

During her relatively short life, Angela Carter became one of the best-known British novelists of the late twentieth century. Her reputation is based largely on her novels, from *Shadow Dance* (1965) and *The Magic Toyshop* (1967), through *The Infernal Desire Machines of Doctor Hoffman* (1972) and *The Passion of New Eve* (1977), to *Nights at the Circus* (1984) and *Wise Children* (1992). But she also published several acclaimed books of short stories, most notably *The Bloody Chamber* (1979), and other works of cultural criticism, of which *The Sadeian Woman* (1982) is the best known and, because of what has been seen as its equivocal position regarding feminism and women's victimhood, also the most reviled.

The content of the stories in *The Bloody Chamber* can be effectively judged from some of their titles: 'The Courtship of Mr Lyon', 'Puss-in-Boots', 'The Erl-King', 'The Werewolf'. In a prose which is often hypnotically somnambulistic Carter retells old legends and fairy stories, but always from an unusual point of view and usually with a twist on the accepted interpretations. This background of myth and legend also figures largely in the novels, which are populated by vampire counts, morbid clowns, glass women. A prevailing image is the circus – the circus of night, the circus of desire, a place where conventional boundaries between man and beast, between face and mask, between appearance and reality, bend and warp – which is taken as the archetypal image for a version of 'magic realism' that refuses to recognize limitations or restrictions.

What Carter also does, right through her works, is encourage the reader into a series of games with the text. *The Passion of New Eve*, for example, confronts us with a protagonist who apparently changes gender – or rather, has his/her gender forcibly changed – and this creates an intricately puzzling textual world. In *Nights at the Circus* the central character, a performer known as Fevvers, may or may not have wings: the ending of the novel leads us to expect that this question will be resolved, but in fact a layer of ambiguity remains, as it does throughout these highly self-conscious and beautifully artificed fictions.

Bibliography

Parker, Emma 2000: 'The Consumption of Angela Carter: Women, Food and Power.' *Ariel: A Review of International English Literature*, 31 (3), 141–69.

Roemer, Danielle M. and Bacchilega, Cristina (eds) 1998: *Angela Carter and the Fairy Tale*. Detroit: Wayne State University Press.

Sage, Lorna 1994: *Angela Carter*. Plymouth: Northcote House with the British Council.

ROBERT W. CHAMBERS
(1865–1933)

One of the best-known popular writers of late nineteenth- and early twentieth-century America, Robert W. Chambers wrote very few stories which can be considered Gothic, almost all of them published in 1895 in a volume called *The King in Yellow*. Most of his work was in the form of 'society' novels and historical novels, and almost all of them have vanished from public and critical view.

The stories in *The King in Yellow*, however, have a certain strange power. In one respect, like Edgar Allan Poe (q.v.), Chambers occupies a curious relation to 'Modernism'; the stories rarely feel like completed wholes but more like partially assembled fragments, in the course of which many of the seemingly important questions are left open. Vague pieces of mythology – some ancient, some lifted from other 'invented' mythologies such as those of Ambrose Bierce (q.v.) – are introduced only to fade again from sight. At the end of 'The Yellow Sign', for example, a figure appears 'and the bolts rotted at his touch', but the doctor who is called to explain 'a horrible decomposed heap on the floor' has 'no theory, no explanation'. The stories are themselves 'tatters', one of Chambers's favourite words, fragmentary manifestations of evil which are not *produced* by dislocation of sensibility, although that dislocation tears gaps in the world through which evil may come – and through which may also come, from time to time, a decadent beauty which it is death or madness to behold.

'The Repairer of Reputations' is an internal study of megalomaniac insanity and mental disintegration; 'The Demoiselle d'Ys' concerns an encounter with a long-dead woman; in 'The Mask' the boundaries between the real and the artificial are explored in a setting and manner reminiscent of Oscar Wilde's (q.v.) *The Picture of Dorian Gray* (1890, rev. 1891). Throughout, there is a certain lushness of prose, an indulgent caressing of the reader's fears, which in the end overwhelms the rather vestigial attempts at narrative, and which leaves the reader with a sense of terror, a lingering feeling, or indeed scent, of the macabre rather than with a clear picture of the story the writer appears to be attempting to convey.

Bibliography

Emmert, Scott D. 1999: 'A Jaundiced View of America: Robert W. Chambers and *The King in Yellow.*' *Journal of American Culture*, 22 (2), 39–44.

Punter, David 1996: *The Literature of Terror: A History of Gothic Fictions from 1765 to the Present Day.* Vol. 2: *The Modern Gothic.* 2nd edn. London: Longman.

WILKIE COLLINS
(1824–1889)

Collins is perhaps the best known of all writers of the Victorian sensation novel, a hybrid genre that emerged during the 1860s and combined elements of the Gothic with domestic realism. His twenty-three novels and novellas, including most notably *The Woman in White* (q.v.) and *The Moonstone* (1868), and his numerous short tales of terror, frequently appropriate Gothic conventions and motifs in order to transform what is familiar and comfortable into something strange and menacing.

In 'A Terribly Strange Bed', for example, included in the collection *After Dark* (1856), the most mundane of household objects transforms into an animated and malevolent machine that attempts to crush the narrator. These stories frequently avoid any clear conclusions about the nature of the apparently supernatural manifestations through the use of unreliable narrators. 'The Dream Woman', one in a series of ten linked stories in *The Queen of Hearts* (1859), is typical in this respect. The woman of the title is a knife-wielding figure who repeatedly appears at the narrator's bedside; whether she is just a product of nightmare or an actual spectral presence is never determined. In the sensational conclusion, a climax with echoes of Edgar Allan Poe's (q.v.) 'Ligeia', she returns in a new form as the narrator's eyes open to see 'The Dream-Woman again? No! His wife; the living reality, with the dream-spectre's face, in the dream spectre's attitude; the fair arm up, the knife clasped in the delicate white hand.' The reader is left here to ponder precisely what the implications of this highly suggestive moment might be.

The dream also plays a crucial role in *Armadale* (1866), long neglected but gradually being recognized as one of Collins's most Gothic works. Playing an interesting variation on James's Hogg's *The Private Memoirs and Confessions of a Justified Sinner* (q.v.), *Armadale* offers Ozias Midwinter as the evil double who nearly drives the hero, Allan Armadale, insane. Questions of identity are central here, and, as in most of Collins's fiction, closely linked to questions of property, of possession and dispossession. But there is also something more to it than this, as Alan Armadale's dream, which strangely reproduces not his own but Midwinter's anxieties, most clearly implies. While rational explanations are repeatedly offered for such puzzling moments, Collins nevertheless constantly subverts these explanations to suggest something far more troubling, something that takes us away from the ordinary world of property and possession and further into the realm of the psyche. As the confusion of identity reaches bewildering proportions, only the coolly villainous Lydia Gwilt retains any grip on a stable identity; a superficially respectable middle-class Victorian woman whose malevolence easily matches that of M. G. Lewis's (q.v.) Mathilda or Charlotte Dacre's (q.v.) Victoria, Gwilt is probably Collins's finest creation, and certainly the centre of the book's interest.

Bibliography

Heller, Wendy Tamar 1992: *Dead Secrets: Wilkie Collins and the Female Gothic.* New Haven, CT: Yale University Press.
Pykett, Lyn (ed.) 1998: *Wilkie Collins: New Casebook.* Houndmills: Macmillan.
Thoms, Peter 1992: *The Windings of the Labyrinth: Quest and Structure in the Major Novels of Wilkie Collins.* Athens, OH: Ohio University Press.

Marie Corelli
(1855–1924)

Born Mary (or Minnie) Mills in Perth, Scotland, Marie Corelli adopted her pseudonym as a stage name during a brief career as a concert pianist. She claimed to have begun writing as a result of an unspecified 'peculiar psychic occurrence', and in Gothic terms Corelli is primarily of interest for her reworking of Gothic motifs in the service of her explorations in the occult. Her first novel, *A Romance of Two Worlds* (1886), is, like most of her works, cross-generic: a combination of science fiction and the occult, it concerns a visionary dream in which the heroine, a pianist, encounters the magician Heliobas. While this and the following *Vendetta, Or The Story of One Forgotten* (1886) were scornfully dismissed by the critics, her sequel to the story of Heliobas, *Ardath, The Story of a Dead Self* (1889), made her a celebrity.

The Soul of Lilith (1892), which concludes the Heliobas trilogy, is a rewriting of the Faust theme with echoes of the Pygmalion myth: a sorcerer binds the soul of a dying girl to her body in order to create a female familiar.

Other works relevant to the Gothic include *Barabbas* (1893), a revisionary fantasy of the Crucifixion, and its first sequel, *The Sorrows of Satan* (1895), which presents Satan as a misunderstood adventurer in modern London; the latter's sales broke all records in publishing history. Corelli also wrote short supernatural stories, the best of which can be found in *Cameos* (1895). The restraints imposed by the short story form had a salutory effect on Corelli's writing, and such ghost stories as 'The Lady with the Carnations' lack her usual excesses.

Although critics remained derisive, and ridiculed – in most cases justifiably it must be said – her work for its sentimentality and verbosity, the public, including William Gladstone, Queen Victoria, and thousands of other readers across both Britain and America, found Corelli's outrageous fantasies irresistible. She was one of the most prolific and certainly the most commercially successful novelists of her time, and many of her works were being adapted by silent film-makers (see 'Gothic Film') well into the 1920s. In India, where her popularity has remained constant up to the present, a version of *Vendetta* called *Intequam* was made in 1969. A recent more general resurgence of interest in Corelli since the late 1960s means that many of her works are once again in print.

Bibliography

Federico, Annette R. 2000: *Idol of Suburbia: Marie Corelli and Late-Victorian Literary Culture*. Charlottesville: University Press of Virginia.

Ransom, Teresa 1999: *Miss Marie Corelli, Queen of Victorian Bestsellers*. Stroud: Sutton.

CHARLOTTE DACRE
(1771/1772?–1825)

Little is known about Charlotte Dacre's life; even her date of birth is uncertain. She was the daughter of a Jewish banker and political radical, Jonathan King, and his first wife Deborah, and eventually married the editor of the *Morning Post*, Nicholas Byrne. In 1805, Dacre published a two-volume book of poems, *Hours of Solitude*, primarily concerned with love, but also including several depictions of insanity and a number of horror ballads, many of which exploit the motif of the demon lover. Her Gothic verse reveals the influence both of the German poet Gottfried August Bürger, whose influential supernatural ballad 'Lenore' had been translated into English in 1795, and of M. G. Lewis (q.v.), author of *The Monk* (q.v.). Dacre's first novel, *The Confessions of the Nun of St Omer* (1805), was dedicated to Lewis.

With *Zofloya, or The Moor* (1806), long neglected but gradually assuming an important place in the Gothic canon, Dacre discarded her pseudonym, 'Rosa Matilda', and began publishing under her own name. Ambitious and oversexed, the protagonist Victoria has frequently been seen as a female version of Lewis's notorious Ambrosio, and in a manner reminiscent of Ambrosio is encouraged to commit increasingly fiendish and illicit acts; not, however, by a demon, but by Lucifer himself, disguised as a seductive Moor. Frustrated passions are given form, under his guidance, in increasingly horrific acts of violence. Victoria murders her husband, drugs and rapes his brother when he rejects her, and tortures, kills and cuts up his fiancée, the 'fairy-like' Lilla, with particularly worrying gusto. Eventually Victoria is, again like Ambrosio, thrown into an abyss by her satanic lover. *Zofloya* is of particular interest for its challenge to the conventional gendered types of Gothic fiction, its construction of the racial other, and its complex engagement with questions of evil. Although Dacre begins by promising to reveal the causes behind events, the explanation for Victoria's evil is left unclear, variously identified as nature, nurture and supernatural intervention. Her dreams repeatedly anticipate the action, perhaps indicating a movement towards more psychological sophistication, a suggestion that Zofloya is, above all, an embodiment of the darker forces within Victoria herself.

Bibliography

Carciun, Adriana 1995: '"I Hasten to Be Disembodied": Charlotte Dacre, the Demon Lover, and Representations of the Body.' *European Romantic Review*, 6, 75–97.

Dunn, James A. 1998: 'Charlotte Dacre and the Feminisation of Violence.' *Nineteenth-Century Literature*, 53, 307–27.

Hoeveler, Diane Long 1997: 'Charlotte Dacre's *Zofloya*: A Case Study in Miscegenation as Sexual and Racial Nausea.' *European Romantic Review*, 8, 185–99.

WALTER DE LA MARE
(1873–1956)

In the life and work of Walter de la Mare, it is possible to discern a curious disjunction. Outwardly a family man, sociable, and publicly highly regarded during at least the early and middle phases of his career, he none the less wrote a long series of works which are almost universally recounted from the position of the outsider. In his poems, novels and even more particularly short stories, it is often as though the author himself becomes a kind of ghost, looking in at a world that is barely comprehensible while behind his back, as it were, there hovers another world that is known only by equally cryptic signs.

De la Mare is a supreme – perhaps *the* supreme – writer of the liminal. In *The Riddle and Other Stories* (1923), *The Connoisseur and Other Stories* (1926), *On the Edge* (1930) and *The Wind Blows Over* (1936), the reader finds worlds that constantly hover on the edge of intelligibility; yet, in the end, the possibility of making full or acceptable sense of these intimations and tremblings is withheld. To regard these stories as Gothic is to point to their indecipherability, their resistance to rational explanation; but de la Mare's ghosts – if ghosts they are – are among the most subtle, the least fully presented, of all the many ghosts to be encountered within the tradition.

Perhaps this sense of the liminal in de la Mare is also significantly conjured by bearing in mind the peculiarity of his construction of his own audience, for he was also a well-known 'writer for children', even though many of his works seem precisely to express the extreme difficulty, first, of being a child, and second, of recalling what childhood might have been like. Certainly in the stories childhood does not emerge as a Wordsworthian place of innocence and freedom; rather, it is a place which casts long, dark shadows through adulthood, shadows that are impossible to banish, yet which serve to give an extraordinary plangency of tone to these most challenging and problematic of all Gothic writings.

Bibliography

McCrosson, Doris 1966: *Walter de la Mare*. New York: Twayne.
Punter, David 1996: *The Literature of Terror: A History of Gothic Fictions from 1765 to the Present Day*. Vol. 2: *The Modern Gothic*. 2nd edn. London: Longman.

Wills, John H. 1964: 'Architecture of Reality: The Short Stories of Walter de la Mare.' *North Dakota Quarterly*, 32, 85–92.

AUGUST DERLETH

(1909–1971)

Born in Sauk City, Wisconsin, the writer, editor and publisher August William Derleth was a remarkably prolific author. His first short story, 'Bat's Belfry', was published in *Weird Tales* in 1926 and is a traditional vampire (q.v.) story written as a collection of letters and diary entries. As well as contributing macabre fiction regularly to *Weird Tales*, Derleth wrote detective fiction and numerous historical novels, short stories, journals and poems, known collectively as the Sac Prairie Cycle. While lacking any supernatural or horrific content, these works nevertheless demonstrate some links with the Gothic through their portraits of people disturbed or obsessed, faced with madness either in themselves or in others.

After the death of his mentor H. P. Lovecraft (q.v.), Derleth became the co-founder, with Dennis Wandrei, of Arkham House, initially formed in 1939 to publish Lovecraft's work. Derleth also published many Lovecraft pastiches, stories using Lovecraft's settings and concepts, heavily influenced by the Cthulhu Mythos cycle. In addition, and somewhat controversially, he published a number of stories such as *The Lurker at the Threshold* (1945) which he claimed to be 'posthumous collaborations', that is, works completed by Derleth from notes and story fragments left by Lovecraft.

Derleth's own horror fiction, produced mainly for *Weird Tales*, was collected in several volumes, beginning with *Someone in the Dark* (1941) and ending with the posthumous *Harrigan's File* (1975) and *Dwellers in Darkness* (1976). Although heavily influenced by Lovecraft, his stories are undeniably of inferior quality. Like Lovecraft, Derleth is primarily concerned with the production of horrific effects, things that will send the reader, like Dorgan and the narrator in 'The Dweller in Darkness', 'screaming voicelessly' from what is revealed to us. He has an unfortunate tendency, however, to reduce all potentially ambiguous situations and moral struggles to a simple conflict of good and evil, with good invariably rewarded and evil punished. This view of the universe, at odds with Lovecraft's more amoral vision, has been pejoratively described as the Derleth Mythos. Derleth's best collection is often considered to be *Mr George and Other Odd Persons* (1963) – in itself rather odd in that it was published under the pseudonym Stephen Grendon but had a photograph of Derleth on the dust-jacket – which contains a number of quite effective stories of supernatural revenge characterized by moments of the laconic black humour that is so often one of Derleth's saving graces. Today, however, his importance primarily lies in the crucial role he played in reviving interest in Lovecraft and for his work as an editor: such early anthologies as *Sleep No More* (1944) and *Who Knocks* (1946) made available many neglected classics of horror fiction, and are still considered as models of their kind.

Bibliography

Stephens, Jim 1992: *An August Derleth Reader*. Madison: Prairie Oak Press.
Wilson, Alison M. 1983: *August Derleth: A Bibliography*. Metuchen, N.J.: Scarecrow Press.

CHARLES DICKENS
(1812–1870)

Dickens, of course, is a writer of far too great a stature to be bound by genres; the various modes of writing which he took up he fused and moulded into a style utterly distinctive, in which a certain kind of social realism and the grotesquerie of melodrama enter into a seemingly impossible alliance. But this style is none the less inevitably dependent on antecedents, and these certainly included the neo-Gothic realm of the Newgate novel, as practised by Edward George Bulwer-Lytton and William Harrison Ainsworth (qq.v.). Dickens was also well aware of the work of Ann Radcliffe (q.v.), a connection one can probably see most clearly in novels like *Barnaby Rudge* (1841).

Dickens was from the outset perceived as a novelist of sensation, with a taste for terror and intimately linked to the Victorian passion for melodrama. He commissioned ghost stories for his magazine *All the Year Round*, and wrote two notable ones himself, 'The Trial for Murder' (1865) and 'The Signalman' (1866). But it is in novels like *Oliver Twist* (1838) and *The Old Curiosity Shop* (1841) that we see most clearly the replaying of the key Gothic theme of youthful innocence surrounded and persecuted by the forces of darkness, as in his emblematic description of his purposes in the creation of the figure of Little Nell: 'I had it always in my fancy to surround the lonely figure of the child with grotesque and wild . . . companions, and to gather about her innocent face and pure intentions, associates as strange and uncongenial as the grim objects that are about her bed when her history is first foreshadowed.'

Here we have, as it were, Radcliffe's Emily or M. G. Lewis's (q.v.) Antonia rewritten for Victorian England, with the outlandishness of Italian castles and Spanish monasteries replaced by the parallel outlandishness of the 'curiosity shop' itself, and the lowering violence of Catholic noblemen updated and curiously distorted into the deranged and deformed figure of Quilp. Dickens's use of the Gothic, we might say, was in many ways more knowing than that of his forebears, and certainly it was more clearly and directly aligned with a sense of social purpose; but what his debt to the Gothic also underlines is the strength of the tradition, the continuity from not only the early Gothic novels but even earlier, from the chapbooks of murders and violent crimes which also affect the tradition and form part of the backdrop to the melodrama of the Dickensian nineteenth century.

Bibliography

Frank, Lawrence 1999: 'News from the Dead: Archaeology, Detection and *The Mystery of Edwin Drood.*' *Dickens Studies Annual: Essays on Victorian Fiction*, 28, 65–102.

Hobsbaum, Philip 1972: *A Reader's Guide to Charles Dickens.* London: Thames and Hudson.

Stone, Harry 1980: *Dickens and the Invisible World.* London: Macmillan.

'İsak Dinesen'

(1885–1962)

'Isak Dinesen' was the pen name of the author Karen Blixen, and her interest in terms of the Gothic derives from her volume *Seven Gothic Tales* (1954). Her use of the term 'Gothic', however, is unusual, and has little or nothing to do with horror or terror. It is rather the case that it harks back to older conceptions of the Gothic, in the sense of a fascination with social and cultural forms which have passed away, even if they continue to leave their long shadows across the present.

There is a kind of mourning in Dinesen, a mourning for notions of honour and privilege that might – perhaps – have been more alive in more feudal, less democratic days. The world, so her stories imply, has become fatally corrupted, and this in turn challenges the location of the artist, forced to survive amid the depredations of commerce. That she is a kind of idealist there can be no doubt; yet at the same time the ruefulness, the faintly ironic wistfulness of the tales suggests that she recognizes that this idealism has no real place in the present world.

It is important to bear in mind, however, that there is a significant connection in Dinesen between the passing away of an age and the social position of women. Most of the stories are told from a female perspective, and so the world of the past is viewed through a specific lens, one that is always slightly out of line with the apparent certainties of the past order. This makes it difficult precisely to situate her emphasis on elegance and delicacy, or rather on the disappearance of those qualities from contemporary life; her opinions on politics, and perhaps especially on sexual politics, are notoriously difficult to pin down amid the strange panoply of her stories. Perhaps what is most significant about the Gothic in relation to Dinesen is its insistence that the 'official' story of the past which is told in the history books is not the only version available; our memories, individual and collective, are less reliable than we know, and are always inflected by mourning and nostalgia.

Bibliography

Brantly, Susan C. 2002: *Understanding Isak Dinesen*. Columbia, SC: University of South Carolina Press.

Pelensky, Olga Anastasia (ed.) 1993: *Isak Dinesen: Critical Views*. Athens, OH: Ohio University Press.

Stoddart, Helen 1996: 'Isak Dinesen and the Fiction of Gothic Gravity.' In Victor Sage and Allan Lloyd Smith (eds), *Modern Gothic: A Reader*. Manchester: Manchester University Press, 81–8.

ARTHUR CONAN DOYLE

(1859–1930)

Better known for the long series of Sherlock Holmes stories, and the inde-fatigable writer of works in a wide range of genres, Arthur Conan Doyle was also one of the most significant figures in the development of the English ghost or horror story. Some of the Sherlock Holmes tales themselves, of course, and especially the later ones, could fairly be regarded as horror stories, but Conan Doyle's more significant contribution to Gothic-related genres came in the stories which were republished in 1922 as *Tales of Twilight and the Unseen* and *Tales of Terror and Mystery*.

There are four major influences on Conan Doyle's tales of terror. The first is the work of the sensation novelists Wilkie Collins and J. Sheridan LeFanu (qq.v.). In many ways one can see the stories as microcosmic attempts to follow in the footsteps of such writers, but the second influence, Edgar Allan Poe (q.v.), was clearly in the end more congenial to Conan Doyle's powers and habits – indeed, there are several stories, such as 'The Brown Hand' (1899), that almost appear to begin at least as pastiches of Poe. The other two shaping influences are more cultural and ideological than literary. There is the concern with empire and the exotic that runs through so many of the tales – for example, 'The Brazilian Cat' (1898) and 'Lot No. 249' (1892) – and which provides a typically late Victorian twist to traditional Gothic themes. And there is also Conan Doyle's own deep involvement with spiritualism, apparent in stories such as 'The Horror of the Heights' (1913), which informs some of his writing on telepathy and the existence of other worlds.

Are these stories ghost stories or horror stories? Mostly, we should probably say, the latter, in that the strange and macabre events that occur have often the most physical of manifestations. It is particular *objects*, often displaced objects, that are more frequently the source of terror than imperceptible night visitors: we might, curiously in view of Conan Doyle's spiritualism, see in this a manifestation of the Victorian age's obsession with the material, such that fear arises not from some realm *beyond* but rather from the threat of instability in precisely what might otherwise appear perfectly solid and reliable.

Bibliography

Hendershot, Cyndy 1996: 'The Animal Without: Masculinity and Imperialism in *The Island of Doctor Moreau* and "The Adventure of the Speckled Band".' *Nineteenth-Century Studies*, 10, 1–32.

Otis, Laura 1999: *Membranes: Metaphors of Invasion in Nineteenth-Century Literature, Science and Politics*. Baltimore, MD: Johns Hopkins University Press.

Wynne, Catherine 2002: 'Philanthropies and Villainies: The Conflict of the Imperial and the Anti-Imperial in Conan Doyle.' In Stacy Gillis and Philippa Gates (eds), *The Devil Himself: Villainy in Detective Fiction and Film*. Westport, CT: Greenwood Press, 69–80.

LORD DUNSANY

(1878–1957)

Lord Dunsany was an Irish aristocrat, though born in London and educated at Eton and Sandhurst. He was during his lifetime one of the best known of fantasy writers, and the bulk of his work belongs more properly within the domain of fantasy than of Gothic, in the specific senses that, first, it deals in the creation of lighter rather than darker worlds and, second, he is attached to happy endings almost to the point of self-parody.

A large part of his output was in the form of short stories, sometimes loosely bound together by, for example, a common narrator or, more often, a common fantasy location. His first two books, *The Gods of Pegana* (1905) and *Time and the Gods* (1906), are set in a specific mythical realm; the five books he wrote concerning a character known as Jorkens are all told by a notorious liar in his London club.

In Dunsany's work, then, it is less a matter of imaginary worlds intruding on conventional reality, more a question of being translated wholesale – as in such later fantasy as that of J. R. R. Tolkien – into a different realm. Nevertheless, there are inevitably moments when the dark imagination cannot be dismissed, as in, for example, *The Charwoman's Shadow* (1926). Here the central trope concerns a new version of the pact with the devil: the evil magician does not seek his victims' souls but their shadows, which he keeps in a 'box of shadows'; although the novel ends in characteristically upbeat fashion, the image of the writhing, captive shadows is not one easily forgotten.

The Blessing of Pan (1927) aptly summarizes some of the complexities at the heart of Dunsany's apparently simple work. It is an account of the reappearance of pagan religion in a village, and of the consequent collapse not only of Christianity but also of the whole apparatus of machinery and money that is assumed to go with it. But whether this uprising of something more primitive represents any kind of solution to what Dunsany saw as the desiccation and alienation of 'modern' life remains, in the end, for the reader to judge.

Bibliography

Amory, Mark 1972: *Biography of Lord Dunsany*. London: Collins.
Duperray, Max 1993: 'Lord Dunsany Revisited.' *Studies in Weird Fiction*, 13, 10–15.
Littlefield, Hazel 1959: *Lord Dunsany: King of Dreams*. New York: Exposition Press.

BRET EASTON ELLIS
(1964–)

Bret Easton Ellis is probably best known for the book and subsequent film (q.v.) of *American Psycho* (q.v.). *American Psycho* is the first-person narrative of a Wall Street banker who is also a torturer, serial killer and cannibal. The extraordinary power of the book comes from three sources. First, there is the remarkably graphic depiction of violence; second, there is the absolutely blank style in which this is conveyed; and third, there is the utter impossibility of the protagonist, Patrick Bateman, ever being exposed. He has, as it were, protective clothing: it is impossible for most people in the text to believe him capable of his crimes, while for others to admit such a possibility would risk, for example, downgrading local property prices, and must therefore be avoided at all costs.

Equally interesting, and only slightly less violent, is Ellis's *Glamorama* (1998), a novel about Victor, a man with, as it were, no memory, a man whose descent into a virtual world both paralyses him with terror and yet at the same time seems a natural, even inescapable, continuation of the 'virtual life' which is all he has ever led – and which, by extension, is all that is on offer in contemporary New York. What Victor comes to realize is that the hollowness characteristic of his everyday life in the upper echelons of hip

New York society is an all-pervasive hollowness; that the technology of virtuality has destroyed any hope of secure linear history, whether of the individual or of the community. Indeed, perhaps individuals no longer exist at all in any meaningful sense; perhaps the world in which we are adrift is one in which we no longer have any guarantee of individual uniqueness. Maybe, then, what Ellis is recapitulating is at least partly the Gothic anxiety about the draining of subjectivity, about the ways in which people can become monstrous (q.v.) – but in these cases without anybody (except, of course, the reader) noticing. Despite their graphic quality, in one sense the reverse of melodrama, Ellis's novels posit deranged or psychopathic heroes whose activities go entirely unnoticed because they are so indistinguishable from the general texture of contemporary urban life.

Bibliography

Abel, Marco 2001: 'Judgement is Not an Exit: Toward an Affective Criticism of Violence with *American Psycho.*' *Angelaki*, 6 (3), 137–54.

Blazer, Alex 2002: 'Chasms of Reality, Aberrations of Identity: Defining the Postmodern through Bret Easton's *American Psycho.*' *Americana: The Journal of American Popular Culture*, 1 (2), n.p.

Freccero, Carla 1997: 'Historical Violence, Censorship and the Serial Killer: The Case of *American Psycho.*' *Diacritics*, 27 (2), 44–58.

WilliAm FAULKNER

(1897–1962)

American short story writer and novelist, Faulkner is best known for his Yoknapatawpha cycle, set in a fictionalized region of Mississippi and spanning the decades from the American Civil War through to the Depression; this series began with *Sartoris* in 1929 (reissued in 1973 as *Flags in the Dust*) and ended with *The Mansion* in 1959. Faulkner is often considered the progenitor of a subgenre called Southern Gothic, which appropriates elements of the traditional Gothic, combines them with the particular concerns of the American South, and is characterized by an emphasis on the grotesque, the macabre and, very often, the violent. Faulkner presents a Gothicized version of the American South, investigating madness, decay and despair, and the continuing pressures of the past upon the present, particularly with respect to the lost ideals of a dispossessed Southern aristocracy and to the continuance of racial hostilities. Of particular interest for the Gothic are *Sanctuary* (1931), the rather lurid story of Temple Drake, an Alabama debutante; *Light in August* (1932), concerning the life of Joe Christmas, an orphan of ambiguous ancestry who believes himself to be part black; and *Absalom! Absalom!* (1936), the story of Thomas Sutpen and the effect of his actions on future generations, perhaps Faulkner's most compelling examination of race, gender and the burdens of the past.

Many of Faulkner's short stories also clearly belong within a Gothic tradition, most notably the much anthologized 'A Rose for Emily' (1930), the remarkable story of Emily Grierson, an ageing spinster in Jefferson. An unnamed narrator relates in a seemingly haphazard fashion key moments in Emily's life, including the death of her father and a brief relationship with a Yankee road paver, Homer Barron. A 'fallen monument' of Southern gentility, Emily and her house, 'lifting its stubborn and coquettish decay above the cotton wagons and the gasoline pumps – an eyesore among eyesores', provide a haunting account of the insidious corruption at the heart of a dismantled Southern aristocracy. It is a story of Gothic revenge – or perhaps a story of Gothic love: this is something that the disturbing conclusion ultimately leaves for the reader to decide.

Bibliography

Jarraway, David R. 1998: 'The Gothic Import of Faulkner's "Black Son" in *Light in August.*' In Robert K. Martin and Eric Savoy (eds), *American Gothic: New Interventions in a National Narrative.* Iowa City: University of Iowa Press, 57–74.

Kerr, Elizabeth M. 1979: *William Faulkner's Gothic Domain.* New York: Kennikat.

Martin, Robert K. 1998: 'Haunted by Jim Crow: Gothic Fictions by Hawthorne and Faulkner.' In Robert K. Martin and Eric Savoy (eds), *American Gothic: New Interventions in a National Narrative.* Iowa City: University of Iowa Press, 129–42.

ELIZABETH GASKELL
(1810–1865)

Elizabeth Gaskell is associated primarily with literary realism and known mainly for her social problem novels and her chronicles of industrial life, including *Mary Barton* (1848) and *North and South* (1855). She was, however, also a highly gifted writer of supernatural tales, and is considered to have had a significant influence on the development of the Victorian ghost story, particularly in setting out some of the ways in which the supernatural could be used to explore women's particular concerns.

'The Old Nurse's Story' (1852), an anthology standard, demonstrates many of the essential features of the typical Victorian ghost story, with its homely, domesticated detail and its restrained treatment of the supernatural. Like most of Gaskell's supernatural tales, it has a rural setting – as opposed to the urban environment of her social problem works – and its primary interest is in the disruptions caused by sexuality and jealousy and in repressive patriarchal power. Less frequently reprinted but equally accomplished are 'The Poor Clare' (1856) and 'Lois the Witch' (1859), stories in which Gaskell explores women's problematic relationships with power through the figure of the witch, and, in 'The Poor Clare', reworks the motif of the double to critique repressive sexual ideology. The curse of the protagonist, Bridget, ambiguously described in 'The Poor Clare' as 'no common woman' but 'one powerful for good as for evil', falls on Lucy, a girl who is, unknown to her, her own granddaughter, the child of her seduced daughter Mary. Lucy, demure and compliant, is subsequently haunted by a monstrous double, 'a ghastly resemblance, complete in likeness...but with a loathsome demon soul looking out of the grey eyes'. The haunting is ostensibly explained, in the manner of Horace Walpole (q.v.), by reference to the biblical text that 'the sins of the father shall be visited upon the children' – that is, Lucy is suffering for her father's crimes in seducing her mother – but it can also, more interestingly, be seen as making visible the split in women effected by Victorian middle-class gender ideology. As these stories demonstrate, the supernatural allowed for a much easier treatment of certain themes – such as sexuality and illegitimacy – that Gaskell felt the need to deal with far more cautiously in the realist mode with her fallen woman novel, *Ruth* (1853).

Bibliography

Dickerson, Vanessa 1996: *Victorian Ghosts in the Noontide: Women Writers and the Supernatural.* Columbia: University of Missouri Press.
Stoneman, Patsy 1987: *Elizabeth Gaskell.* Bloomington: Indiana University Press.
Uglow, Jenny 1993: *Elizabeth Gaskell: A Habit of Stories.* London: Faber and Faber.

WILLIAM GIBSON
(1948–)

The publication in the symbolic year 1984 of William Gibson's *Neuromancer* revolutionized the possibilities of cyber-fiction. His imagining of a highly, if patchily, technologized world of the near future sparked off an immediate debate about the directions of science. After this has come a lengthy stream of further fictions, including *Burning Chrome* (1986), *Count Zero* (1986), *Mona Lisa Overdrive* (1988), *Virtual Light* (1993), *Idoru* (1996) and others.

What they all have in common is a racy, hard-boiled style obviously influenced by Raymond Chandler and by film noir; the protagonist of *Neuromancer*, Case, is a 'console cowboy', a techno-maverick caught up in wars involving corporate forces and artificial intelligences which are wildly beyond his understanding. The potency of technology is half-glimpsed, but it is obvious that it dwarfs human powers, and this would be where the Gothic quality of Gibson's work resides. Quite apart from the prevalence of monsters (q.v.) of all kinds, there is also the pervasiveness of a paranoia (q.v.) engendered by the knowledge that power is passing away, or has already passed away, from the human subject and is now in the hands of much vaster forces.

These forces, of course, are in this instance multinational, corporate, incalculably wealthy; in these senses their supernatural quality is not the same as it would have been for earlier Gothic writers, but none the less they serve to relativize the human individual and to suggest that there are ghosts in the machine which are not susceptible of being fully viewed by human intelligence. Gibson's fiction is, in this sense, Gothic for our times: full of horrific potential, yet always offset by the ironic, wisecracking figure of the human subject who can walk these 'mean streets' without being destroyed by the superhuman powers being unleashed around him. Alongside the 'human' aspect of the story, there is always another story going on: when Case deploys his full expertise and dives, as it were, into the heart of the machine, pits his wits against the might of the computer, he is representing a small strike against an overarching power, a small resistance to the power of those who occupy unassailable positions in the ruling order of the world; as the persecuted heroes and heroines of earlier Gothic fiction deployed their small skills against the apparently supernatural power of their enemies, and as in *Frankenstein* (q.v.) the power of technological creation is pitted in the end against the alternative – if no more palatable – residual powers of the human.

Bibliography

Annesley, James 2001: 'Netscapes: Gibson, Globalisation and the Representation of New Media.' *Forum for Modern Language Studies*, 37 (2), 218–29.

Myers, Tony 2001: 'The Postmodern Imaginary in William Gibson's *Neuromancer*.' *Modern Fiction Studies*, 47 (4), 887–909.

Tomas, David 2000: 'The Technophilic Body: On Technicity in William Gibson's Cyborg Culture.' In David Bell and Barbara M. Kennedy (eds), *The Cybercultures Reader*. London: Routledge, 175–89.

WILLIAM GODWIN
(1756–1836)

One of the most influential political radicals of his time, Godwin was the son of a Dissenting minister, educated as a Calvinist and ordained as a Unitarian minister. He then became an atheist and a passionate rationalist, professing a belief in human perfectability and natural justice through the cultivation of reason. In 1797 he married Mary Wollstonecraft, author of *A Vindication of the Rights of Woman* (1792); a year later she died giving birth to their daughter Mary, the future wife of Percy Bysshe Shelley and the author of *Frankenstein* (qq.v.). Godwin was the author of the *Enquiry Concerning Political Justice* (1793), and Mary Wollstonecraft Shelley's *Frankenstein* owes much to this political treatise, particularly in its demonstration that character is produced by circumstance.

Godwin's main contributions to the Gothic are *Things as They Are; or, The Adventures of Caleb Williams* (q.v.), with its brooding atmosphere of religious terror and its exploration of guilt and persecution (q.v.), and *St Leon: A Tale of the Sixteenth Century* (1799). Although the former is generally considered to offer a more profoundly Gothic psychology, the latter is the more obviously Gothic of the two works in its appropriation of Gothic conventions and its use of the supernatural. Reginald St Leon is a Promethean overreacher who receives the gift of the philosopher's stone and eternal life from a Wandering Jew figure. St Leon's own subsequent wanderings bring only torment to both himself and others: he is imprisoned by the Inquisition, murders his faithful servant, and is confined in a subterranean vault. Too late, he finds that he longs only for the domestic world he once rejected. In contrast to the sharp political and religious criticism found in *Caleb Williams*, *St Leon* ultimately offers a far more conservative moral that demonstrates the modification of Godwin's radical beliefs and seems unequivocally offered in good faith: 'Live in the midst of your family; cultivate domestic affection . . . be assured that you will then be found no contemptible or unbeneficial member of the community at large.' It would remain for Mary Shelley to problematize these domestic affections celebrated by her father with her own Promethean overreacher, Victor Frankenstein.

Bibliography

Clemit, Pamela 1993: *The Godwinian Novel: The Rational Fictions of Godwin, Brockden Brown, Mary Shelley*. Oxford: Clarendon Press.
Lévy, Ellen 1996: 'The Philosophical Gothic of *St Leon*.' *Caliban*, 33, 51–62.
Marshall, Peter H. 1984: *William Godwin*. New Haven, CT: Yale University Press.

H. RIDER HAGGARD
(1856–1925)

As well as being a foremost exponent of the supernatural, both in his fiction and apparently in his own beliefs, Rider Haggard was also one of the prime figures of late Victorian fantasy. Generations of writers of *Boys' Own* fiction, not to mention scores of writers and film-makers (see 'Gothic Film') obsessed with depicting 'lost worlds', owe a debt to Haggard, creator of *King Solomon's Mines* (1885), *She* (1886) and *Ayesha* (1905).

As an alternative account, we might also say that Haggard is the major exponent of 'imperial Gothic' (q.v.). In other words, his works make a major connection between imperial and colonial concerns, particularly in Africa, and the exercise of the supernatural. It has of course been part of the paraphernalia of empire to invest the 'colonized other' with supernatural powers, partly no doubt in order to explain the west's occasional defeat by 'native' forces; but Haggard draws this connection tighter by locating the supernatural, the magical, directly in the 'lost worlds' of his imagination.

These 'lost worlds', interestingly, are places that are in some ways 'beyond' the conventional antinomies of dark and light, good and evil, which otherwise inform Haggard's work; they are places where space and, more particularly, time become distorted and unaccountable, Gothic spaces where there is no certainty left as to where or when we are. Haggard, of course, is playing upon the conventional (for his time) association between colonized people and the primitive or primordial; but what is more interesting is the way in which he submits this to a curiously cyclical view of history, within which the dead are capable of rising up and the perceptions of his white characters, far from being in secure command of all they convey, become confused, indeed hallucinated (q.v.), by the complexities of the scenes upon which they unwittingly enter.

It would, of course, be impossible to ignore the fact that Haggard, just as he was an apologist of sorts for empire, was even more an apologist for patriarchy; in his fiction all the age-old Gothic doubts about the frightening power of women are laid bare in almost embarrassingly simple fashion. But what perhaps remains important about Haggard is the connection he makes between this fear of feminine power and the supernatural; his rational heroes quail before this supernatural conjunction even while they are claiming to have conquered all that they see.

Bibliography

Cohen, Morton 1960: *Rider Haggard: His Life and Works*. London: Hutchinson.

Cunningham, Gail 2000: 'Masculinities in the Age of the New Woman: From *She* to "Vee".' In Alcindo Pinheiro de Sousa, Luisa-Maria Flora and Teresa de Ataide Malafai (eds), *The Crossroads of Gender and Century Endings*. Lisbon: Colibri, 109–24.

Ellis, Peter Berresford 1978: *H. Rider Haggard: A Voice from the Infinite*. London: Routledge.

Παthαηίεl Ηαωτhοrηε

(1804–1864)

Born in Salem, Massachusetts, Hawthorne came from an old New England family with close links to the notorious history of the area: two of his ancestors were magistrates involved in the seventeenth-century witch hunts and active in the persecution of the Quakers, and local history consistently played a significant role in Hawthorne's writing. Hawthorne considered himself primarily a producer of romances, or fantastic tales, in opposition to the dominant trend of realist stories of contemporary life. Edgar Allan Poe (q.v.) and Hawthorne are usually considered to be the major American Gothic writers of the mid-nineteenth century, and while both emphasize the psychological, their Gothic works are strikingly distinct. In contrast to Poe's usually vague and unspecified Gothic environments, Hawthorne's explorations of isolation, obsession and guilt – both familial and national – are imbued with a very concrete sense of a specific time and place.

Of all Hawthorne's novels, *The House of the Seven Gables* (1851) might be considered the most Gothic – it is certainly a key text in demonstrating the reworking of European Gothic motifs for American requirements. Like Horace Walpole's *The Castle of Otranto* (qq.v.), it has an ancestral crime and a curse, but the traditional Gothic castle is replaced by a family home, a house haunted by residues of the past days of American colonization and inhabited by a family in decline. Walpole's portraits give way to daguerrotype photography, demonic possession is replaced by mesmerism, and ultimately all mysteries are explained: even the deaths attributed to the curse turn out to be the result of apoplexy. Hawthorne's updated version of the haunted castle (q.v.) is also set firmly in the commercial world of Salem, and the concerns of the story, centring on the theft of a piece of land on which the house was built, are very much those of this modern American world.

The reworking of Gothic motifs is also evident throughout Hawthorne's short stories, many of which deal with religious intolerance and hypocrisy. In 'The Minister's Black Veil', for example, Hawthorne appropriates his central motif from Ann Radcliffe's *Mysteries of Udolpho* (qq.v.). In *Udolpho*, the veil serves primarily to create suspense; when Hawthorne transfers it to the face of the Reverend Mr Hooper, however, it assumes new significance, becoming simultaneously suggestive of both guilt and mourning. The best of Hawthorne's short stories, including the much anthologized 'Young

Goodman Brown', are found in *Mosses from an Old Manse* (1846), a collection which Melville, in an 1850 review, famously identified as marked by a 'great power of blackness' derived from the 'Calvinistic sense of Innate Depravity and Original Sin'. A later collection, *The Snow-Image, and Other Tales* (1852), continues to explore this blackness in such tales as 'The Man of Adamant', a sinister story of psychosis hidden under a mask of religious piety: a radical Puritan preacher, with 'a plan of salvation . . . so narrow, that, like a plank in a tempestuous sea, it could avail no sinner but himself', eventually becomes a calcified corpse, undergoing a physical transformation that shockingly literalizes his spiritual condition.

Bibliography

Frank, Albert von (ed.) 1991: *Critical Essays on Hawthorne's Short Stories*. Boston: G. K. Hall.

Martin, Robert K. 1998: 'Haunted by Jim Crow: Gothic Fictions by Hawthorne and Faulkner.' In Robert K. Martin and Eric Savoy (eds), *American Gothic: New Interventions in a National Narrative*. Iowa City: University of Iowa Press, 129–42.

Ringe, Donald A. 1982: *American Gothic: Imagination and Reason in Nineteenth-Century Fiction*. Lexington, KY: University Press of Kentucky.

JAMES HERBERT
(1943–)

Herbert, best-selling writer of horror fiction and often seen as Britain's answer to Stephen King (q.v.) – and sometimes less charitably as the poor man's Stephen King – has produced over twenty novels and is also the author of *Dark Places* (1993), a primarily photographic book about Britain's most haunted houses. Herbert's style is variously praised by his supporters for its clarity and lucidity, and dismissed by his critics as riddled with clichés and marked by monotonous repetition. Millions of readers have nevertheless, as his promotional material never fails to remind us, found his novels compulsive reading.

The novels are usually set in either London or the south of England, and the most Gothic of these in a sense could be said to look back to *Frankenstein* (q.v.) in their concerns with the powers of darkness as unleashed by science. In his first book, for example, *The Rats* (1974), rash scientific experiments lead to

London being overrun by a mutant strain of rats about the size of a small dog which begin to hunt in packs and kill humans, while in *The Fog* (1975) another irresponsible professor causes havoc with 'mutated mycoplasma' and turns most of the population of London into killing machines. The boundary between 'civilisation and naked animal behaviour' is one of Herbert's primary concerns, with such things as fog or darkness serving to release the animal within. There is typically a strong emphasis on – and celebration of – the heroic individualist, and the plots tend to centre on a youthful suburban protagonist who is set against the system, repeatedly demonstrating that, as we are told in *The Fog*, 'Despite all the technological advances of science, it seemed survival still depended on the action of a man. One man.'

Particularly in his more recent works, Herbert deals as much with the ghostly or the fantastic as with the horrific. *Once* (2001) offers an encounter with the good and evil of the faeries, while *Nobody True* (2003) concerns a man who returns from an out-of-body experience to discover he has been murdered, and, freed from his body, embarks on a quest to find his murderer. A number of Herbert's novels have been made into films (q.v.), including *The Fog* and the first book in his David Ash series, *Haunted* (1988), an effective traditional ghost story in which a sceptical psychic investigator is called in to investigate a haunted house and encounters a rather odd family.

Bibliography

Cabell, Craig 2001: *Biography of James Herbert*. London: Sidgwick and Jackson.
Grixti, Joseph 1989: *Terrors of Uncertainty: The Cultural Contexts of Horror Fiction*. London: Routledge.
Jones, Stephen (ed.) 1992: *James Herbert: By Horror Haunted*. London: Hodder and Stoughton.

William Hope Hodgson
(1877–1918)

William Hope Hodgson spent many years of his life at sea, and an almost psychopathic terror of, and anger against, the sea pervades many of his works. Never particularly well known as a writer, he led a life of considerable struggle and was killed at Ypres near the end of the First World War. His works are among the strangest horror writings in the canon, and consist mainly of four novels, *The Boats of the 'Glen Carrig'* (1907), *The House on the Border-land* (1908), *The Ghost Pirates* (1909) and *The Night Land* (1912), and a volume of short stories, *Carnacki, the Ghost-Finder* (1913).

Some critics have suggested that Hodgson could barely write, and there is some unavoidable truth in this. *The Boats of the 'Glen Carrig'* is so oddly structured as to be hardly a novel at all. *The Night Land* is two or three times the length it should be and almost impenetrably written, in a new language Hodgson invented (but should not have done). The whole corpus suffers from huge problems of characterization, stemming largely from a complete absence of any ability to portray any human emotion except stark terror. But seen from another angle, these are the outward and visible signs of the appalling set of visions Hodgson is trying to convey: visions, essentially, of a human world of decreasing strength and coherence trapped between various encroaching forces of supernatural evil. It is almost impossible to read Hodgson – even his short stories – without becoming aware that these visions have a pathological origin, or perhaps many such: where there is power in the texts, it is the power of the single transfixed or transfixing image – the power, in other words, of trauma. One actual image that occurs more than once in his works is that of malign stone deities that advance on the outposts of civilization an inch at a time over the millennia: in the face of this vision of slow, inexorable attrition, perhaps mere human narrative seemed too petty to Hodgson to be worthy of notice. At any rate, these are remarkable works, and although it may sound as though they are too freak-ish to count within any tradition, however loosely defined, it does appear that Hodgson was quite well read in earlier horror fiction. Certainly his own work gained the always dubious and sometimes counter-productive accolade of being admired by H. P. Lovecraft (q.v.).

Bibliography

Bell, Ian 1986: 'A Dream of Darkness: William Hope Hodgson's *The Night Land.*' *Studies in Weird Fiction*, 1 (1), 13–18.

Everts, R. Alain 1973: 'William Hope Hodgson, Master of Fantasy.' *Shadow*, 19, 20.

Hurley, Kelly 2001: 'The Modernist Abominations of William Hope Hodgson.' In Andrew Smith and Jeff Wallace (eds), *Gothic Modernisms*. London: Palgrave, 129–49.

E. T. A. Hoffmann
(1776–1822)

Writer and composer Ernst Theodor Amadeus Hoffmann – he changed his third name, Wilhem, to Amadeus in homage to the composer Mozart – was a key figure in the German romantic movement. He was an enthusiastic reader of Gothic fiction, and his own Gothic novel – *Die Elixiere des Teufels* (*The Devil's Elixir*) (1815–16) – was directly inspired by M. G. Lewis's *The Monk* (qq.v.). Drawing upon the fiction of the discovered manuscript, the story concerns a Capuchin monk, Brother Medardus, who is tempted by a mysterious elixir said to have been wrested from the devil by St Anthony and subsequently pursues a career of crime and lust rivalling that of Lewis's Ambrosio. In this 'analysis of a man who did not know where he began or ended', however, Hoffmann complicates the story with a continual series of doublings, not only with Medardus, who pursues and is pursued by his own double, but also with nearly all the characters Medardus encounters.

Hoffmann's reputation primarily rests on his fantastical short stories, and here too, the duality of perception and experience is a recurrent concern. The worlds of fantasy and reality become closely interwoven, even confused, in such stories as the early 'Ritter Gluck' (1809), which offers competing interpretations of madness and possession in the story of a musician who believes he is the composer Gluck, and in the far darker and better-known stories of 'The Sandman' and 'The Entail' (1816–17).

Hoffmann's psychological refashionings of Gothic motifs had a wide influence, particularly upon such American Gothic writers as Washington Irving, Nathaniel Hawthorne and Edgar Allan Poe (qq.v.). Hoffmann's explorations of dreams, doubles and insanity have also attracted many psychoanalytical readings; *Die Elixire des Teufels* influenced Carl Jung's theory of archetypes, while even more notably, an interpretation of Hoffmann's 'The Sandman' is central to Sigmund Freud's essay on 'The Uncanny' (1919) (see 'The Uncanny' below). Finally, although Hoffmann himself is usually considered something of a second-rate composer – his most acclaimed musical work is the opera *Undine* – his stories have nevertheless formed the basis for many operas and ballets, including Delibes's *Coppélia* and Tchaikovsky's *Nutcracker Suite* and, of course, Offenbach's *Tales of Hoffmann*.

Bibliography

McGlathery, James 1997: *E. T. A. Hoffmann*. New York: Twayne.
Wright, Elizabeth 1978: *E. T. A. Hoffmann and the Rhetoric of Terror*. London: University of London Press.

JAMES HOGG
(1770–1835)

Although James Hogg's main contribution to Gothic is usually considered to be *The Private Memoirs and Confessions of a Justified Sinner* (q.v.), in fact almost all of his work involves supernatural events and Gothic themes. Known in his lifetime as the 'Ettrick Shepherd' and regarded as virtually uneducated (although it would be more accurate to regard him as a self-taught late starter), he retained throughout his works a healthy and lively respect for the world of spirits, who consequently play a considerable part in his novels, short stories and poems.

The Brownie of Bodsbeck (1818), for example, is at one level a straight-forward historical novel, set in the year 1685 and dealing in the monstrous (q.v.) behaviour of Graham of Claverhouse. However, the Brownie, initially treated merely as the stuff of local folk-lore, comes to occupy a central space in the tale. Stories like 'Adam Bell' (1820) and 'The Barber of Duncow' (1831) use ghosts to great effect; sometimes these are ghosts in the conventional sense, but Hogg is also interested in other kinds of apparition which represent people still living.

He is also interested in the psychological implications of belief in the supernatural: 'The Brownie of the Black Haggs' (1828), for example, concerns a supernatural being who, like Gil-Martin in the *Justified Sinner*, may be as much a projection of the principal character's state of mind as an objective entity. Indeed, in Hogg's work the line between psychological obsession and supernatural visitation is a very fine one, and frequently crossed.

In his work, it is possible to trace the intimate historical connection between the emergence of the Gothic and the older traditions of the folk-tale; just as the Gothic novel is to an extent foreshadowed by the antiquarianism of Bishop Percy and others (see 'Gothic in the Eighteenth Century'), so in Hogg Gothic effects are a kind of superstructure on top of an older set of beliefs. What is crucial in his work is the vertiginous sense he

128

gives us not only of not knowing what to believe ourselves, but even of not knowing what structure of belief is being proffered by the narrator, as he sways between old acceptance and a more modern, and even sometimes satirical, scepticism.

Bibliography

Gifford, Douglas 1976: *James Hogg*. Edinburgh: Ramsay Head Press.
Lee, L. L. 1966: 'The Devil's Figure: James Hogg's *Justified Sinner*.' *Studies in Scottish Literature*, 13, 15–23.
Smith, Nelson C. 1980: *James Hogg*. Boston: Twayne.

WASHINGTON IRVING

(1783–1859)

Irving, frequently described as the father of the American short story and the first American writer to achieve international fame, was born in New York City, but spent twenty years of his adult life in Europe. He frequently reworks European folk-tales to create new legends for America, as in such well-known stories as 'Rip Van Winkle' and 'The Legend of Sleepy Hollow' (both 1819–20), and his Gothic tales are usually characterized by both wit and scepticism. While the more exotically set stories collected in *The Alhambra* (1832) are quite unambiguously concerned with the spectral world, more typically Irving's tales either hover between supernatural or natural explanations or ultimately offer a rational, and frequently humorous, resolution.

One of his most frequently anthologized works, 'The Adventure of the German Student' from the collection *Tales of a Traveller* (1824), exemplifies this tendency towards a sceptical rationalization of the supernatural. Set during the French Revolution, the tale concerns a young student who, returning late to his lodgings, finds a beautiful woman – of whom he has been previously dreaming – weeping by a guillotine. He takes her home, where they declare their love and, in accordance with 'the liberal doctrines of the day', agree to dispense with the formalities of marriage. The next day, he finds her lying dead across the bed; the police are summoned and to the student's query they reply that they do indeed know her: she had been guillotined the day before. The student – understandably – goes mad and is confined to an asylum. In the final lines, one of the story's auditors asks if the tale was factual. 'A fact not to be doubted', the teller of the tale responds, throwing sudden doubt upon his authority, 'The student told it me himself. I saw him in a mad-house in Paris.'

With his typically urbane tone, Irving repeatedly takes the reader from the apparently supernatural event to the psychological explanation, and encourages attention to the frequently suspect and irrational motives of his characters. In this respect he can be said to anticipate the even more complex investigations of the psyche that are subsequently offered by such later Gothic short story writers as Edgar Allan Poe and Henry James (qq.v.).

Bibliography

Bell, Michael Davitt 1980: *The Development of American Romance: The Sacrifice of Relation*. Chicago: University of Chicago Press.

Bowden, Mary Weatherspoon 1981: *Washington Irving*. Boston: Twayne.

Thompson, G. R. 1983: 'Washington Irving and the American Ghost Story.' In Howard Kerr, John W. Crowley and Charles Crow (eds), *The Haunted Dusk: American Supernatural Fiction, 1820–1920*. Athens, GA: University of Georgia Press, 13–36.

G. P. R. JAMES
(1799–1860)

G. P. R. James was a prolific mid-nineteenth-century historical novelist of extraordinary popularity: the Parlour and Railway Libraries published no fewer than forty-seven of his novels. He was first brought to public attention by Walter Scott (q.v.), who saw and approved of James's early novel *Richelieu* (1829). Among his works are some that are rather clearly influenced by the supernatural Gothic, such as *The Ruined City* (1828) and *The Castle of Ehrenstein* (1847); but most of the others – *Henry of Guise* (1839), for example, or *Leonora d'Orco* (1857), or *Mary of Burgundy* (1833) – are Gothic in the rather different sense that they are exercises in the reconstruction of the past, very frequently the medieval past beloved of the earlier Gothic writers.

James was historiographer royal to William IV and later to Victoria, and could thus be considered to have been a historian of some note. He is also an overtly political writer, whose project throughout his works is the justification and rehabilitation of the aristocracy. Yet there is a certain unease or instability in this project: although it is true that many of the novels preach and demonstrate a chivalric ideal, and draw the obvious conclusion that such an ideal is only possible in the context of a feudal order and is also far superior to the drabness of the Victorian present day, nevertheless the chivalric hero in James is often less than successful, and some of the narrative sympathy gets extended instead – in *Corse de Leon, or, The Brigand* (1841), for instance – to more peripheral and lawless figures. Here again James shows the influence of the classic Gothic novelists and their oft-repeated figure of the *banditti*, living in splendid and sublime isolation away from the everyday demands of society.

If any fiction can be properly defined as escapist, then James's would surely fall into that category; but it is interesting how frequently in his works the qualities he finds in the feudal order seem also to entail their own opposites, so that it becomes impossible to re-energize chivalry without simultaneously representing a far darker barbarism. Even costume drama – which is what the weakest of James's works become – seems still to leave an interpretative space which gets filled in with the brutal and the demonic, despite the texts' professed ideology.

Bibliography

Ellis, S. M. 1927: *The Solitary Horseman: or, The Life and Adventures of G. P. R. James*. London: Cayne Press.

Punter, David 1996: *The Literature of Terror: A History of Gothic Fictions from 1765 to the Present Day*. Vol. 1: *The Gothic Tradition*. 2nd edn. London: Longman.

HEΠRY JAMES

(1843–1916)

While Henry James is associated primarily with the development of psychological realism, it is sometimes claimed that even his realist novels are suffused with an underlying Gothicism which is revealed primarily in psychological or metaphorical terms. His main interest for the Gothic, however, must come from what is perhaps the best known, and certainly the most analysed, of all ghost stories, the enigmatic *The Turn of the Screw* (q.v.). James, familiar with many of the debates in the contemporary spiritualist movement, also wrote several other ghost stories noted for their masterful use of irony and ambiguity. These stories, as James himself said, are characterized by the 'strange and sinister embroidered on the very type of the normal and easy'.

An early tale, 'The Romance of Certain Old Clothes' (1868), is one of his more conventional stories in terms of the Gothic, concluding with a spectacular eruption of ghostly revenge as the heroine's throat is marked by 'ten hideous wounds from two ghostly hands'. James's Gothic effects are usually far more subtle than this, however, and tend to be subordinate to the psychological drama that is his primary concern. As is often noted, the emphasis on psychology results in his frequent engagement with the idea of the double, with projections of the disturbed and divided self. Many of his stories deal with the effects of the past upon the present, the results of thwarted or repressed passions, or, a theme his supernatural fiction shares with his realist fiction, the spectral and 'unlived' life of the alienated and isolated individual. Many of these concerns come together in 'The Jolly Corner' (1908), the tale of Spencer Brydon, who leaves his comfortable life in Europe for his ancestral home in New York City in order to 'stalk a creature more subtle, yet at bay perhaps more formidable, than any beast of the forest', a creature that turns out to be the spectral self he has become.

Bibliography

Lustig, T. J. 1994: *Henry James and the Ghostly*. Cambridge: Cambridge University Press.

Savoy, Eric 1999: 'Spectres of Abjection: The Queer Subject of James's "The Jolly Corner".' In Glennis Byron and David Punter (eds), *Spectral Readings: Towards a Gothic Geography*. Houndmills: Macmillan, 161–74.

Sheldon, Pamela Jacobs 1974: 'Jamesian Gothicism: The Haunted Castle of the Mind.' *Studies in the Literary Imagination*, 7 (1), 121–34.

M. R. JAMES

(1862–1936)

M. R. James is often regarded as the master of the early twentieth-century ghost story. He had a distinguished academic career as a palaeographer and scholar of ancient manuscripts; was appointed provost of King's College, Cambridge, in 1905; and moved to the cognate position at his old school,

Eton, in 1918. His output of ghost stories was in fact quite small, consisting, apart from a handful of separately printed tales and a few that appeared for the first time in his *Collected Ghost Stories* (1931), of four volumes: *Ghost Stories of an Antiquary* (1904), *More Ghost Stories of an Antiquary* (1911), *A Thin Ghost and Others* (1919) and *A Warning to the Curious, and Other Ghost Stories* (1925).

The stories emerged in what is perhaps a unique fashion, in that most of them were initially read to small private audiences before being prepared for publication. It is probable that this method of production accounts in part for their form, for they combine a leisurely, affable, intimate habit of narration with an ending of sudden, explosive terror.

Among the best known are 'Canon Alberic's Scrap-Book' (1895), 'Lost Hearts' (1895), 'The Ash-Tree' (1904), 'Oh, Whistle, and I'll Come to You, My Lad' (1904), 'The Treasure of Abbot Thomas' (1904), 'The Tractate Middoth' (1911) and 'A Warning to the Curious' (1925). Although these stories, and the others, vary in setting and event, they all have a similar tone and, in a sense, concern an identical structure of belief, in which an initial scepticism on the part of the main character – and, it is supposed, on the part of the reader too – is swept away by inexplicable occurrences.

The ghosts, spirits and monsters (q.v.) in James are variously described, and some of them are materially more clear than others, but what is invariable about them is their malevolent violence. The human characters in the tales may occasionally behave foolishly, or even with not altogether pure intent; but rarely if ever do they do anything sufficiently dreadful to call down upon them the frightful doom that awaits. Yet having said this, it is important to reaffirm that James's tales are a very long way away from more contemporary horror stories: we may receive – and we are supposed to receive – a short, sharp shock, and some of these shocks may well reverberate in the mind for some time to come; but to dwell for too long on horrors would be entirely out of keeping with the scholarly, or gentlemanly, ambience of the tales.

Bibliography

Briggs, Julia 1977: *Night Visitors: The Rise and Fall of the English Ghost Story.* London: Faber and Faber.

Holland-Toll, Linda J. 2001: 'From Haunted Rose Gardens to Lurking Wendigos: Liminal and Wild Places in M. R. James and Algernon Blackwood.' *Studies in Weird Fiction*, 25, 2–11.

Mason, Michael A. 1982: 'On Not Letting them Lie: Moral Significance in the Ghost Stories of M. R. James.' *Studies in Short Fiction*, 19 (3), 253–60.

STEPHEN KING

(1947–)

Stephen King is probably the best known, and certainly the best selling, writer of horror fiction working today. His list of novels includes *'Salem's Lot* (1975), *The Shining* (q.v.), *Christine* (1983), *Pet Sematary* (1983), *It* (1986), *Misery* (1987), *Needful Things* (1991), *Dolores Claiborne* (1992), *Insomnia* (1994), *Bag of Bones* (1998) and *Dreamcatcher* (2001). Most of these, and others of his works including shorter novellas and short stories, have been made into films (q.v.). King has also written quite extensively about his craft, in books including *Danse Macabre* (1983) and *On Writing* (2000).

King's career had a slow start but, as the partial list above shows, he is now a prolific writer, and has not even been significantly slowed down by a recent near-fatal road accident. His novels are certainly gory, but they are also notable for being set, for the most part, in easily imaginable locations, usually in small towns in the US. Many of the books in effect use terrors and demons to test the strength of communal relations in such places: there is usually a huge amount of destruction, but also the survival of something valuable. Emblematic is *Needful Things*: here a thinly disguised devil-figure arrives in town and sets up shop, enabling the town's inhabitants to buy their hearts' desires. Predictably, this does not make them happy but simply inflames local enmities and rivalries to the point where only one product is 'needful': a gun. However, as one of the characters, who escapes the general carnage, says when asked the question, 'What really happened in this goddam town?', 'There was a sale. The biggest going-out-of-business sale you ever saw . . . but in the end some of us decided not to buy.'

The appalling violence and inexplicable supernatural disturbances in King's fiction are constantly offset by a certain indomitability on the part of a few of the human characters: indeed, the occult phenomena often seem to be only a device for depicting, time and time again, a human battle, between the forces of individualism and courage (good) and the forces of science and the military (bad). In this sense one can see King's work as an extension of a general ideological project to do with the 'American way of life'; in another, the question of why it is necessary to resort to the extremes of literary horror in order to pursue this theme remains a significantly challenging one.

Bibliography

Abbott, Joe 1995: 'Why is Stephen King so Popular? or, Meditations on the "Domestic Monsterdrama".' *Popular Culture Review*, 6 (2), 27–43.

Keesey, Douglas 2002: ' "Your Legs must be Singing Grand Opera": Masculinity, Masochism and Stephen King's *Misery*.' *American Imago: Studies in Psychoanalysis and Culture*, 59 (1), 53–71.

Nash, Jesse W. 1997: 'Postmodern Gothic: Stephen King's *Pet Sematary*.' *Journal of Popular Culture*, 30 (4), 151–60.

RUDYARD KIPLING

(1865–1936)

Kipling, often considered a spokesman for his age in giving voice to his sense of England's imperial (q.v.) destiny, was perhaps the most popular author writing in English at the end of the nineteenth and beginning of the twentieth centuries. Celebrated for such fictional works as 'The Man Who Would be King' (1888), *Kim* (1901) and the animal-fantasy stories of the *Jungle Books* (1894, 1895), Kipling was a master of the short story form and produced some of the finest supernatural stories ever written. These were published alongside the more realist tales of Anglo-Indian life in such collections as *Plain Tales From the Hills* (1888), *The Phantom Rickshaw and Other Tales* (1888) and *Life's Handicap* (1891).

Kipling's ideological position with respect to imperialism is the subject of continuing debate, and the variations in his supernatural tales could be said to show why. Such stories as 'The Strange Ride of Morrowbie Jukes' (1885), set in a nightmarish village where officially dead Indians – those who have been thought dead because of catalepsy, for example – are exiled, may be read as allegorical inversions of relationships between colonizing and colonized, master and servant. And such stories as 'Jukes', in which the supernatural is ultimately rationalized, usually end with a conservative reinstatement of conventional power relations. However, stories in which the supernatural remains unexplained tend to maintain a certain subversive force until the end. In 'The Mark of the Beast' (1890), for example, a drunken Englishman called Fleete defaces the image of the Indian Monkey god Hanuman, whose priest turns Fleete into a wolf-like creature; Fleete is saved only when the police investigator Strickland and the narrator, witnesses

135

to this horrific transformation, torture the priest to make him reverse the process. The priest's powers, however, are not explained away, and the strategies used by the colonizers result in a morally ambiguous conclusion.

In later life, Kipling generally moved away from the ghostly and macabre, although some of his most disturbing supernatural stories were nevertheless published at this time. 'The House Surgeon', from *Actions and Reactions* (1909), for example, offers an interesting turn on the concept of haunting, as a living person's morbid obsessions oppress a house and disturb and trouble its dead, while 'Swept and Garnished', collected in *A Diversity of Creatures* (1917), is a particularly grim account of guilt in which children killed in the bombing of the First World War appear in a ghostly but bloody form to a Berlin widow.

Bibliography

Crook, Nora 1989: *Kipling's Myths of Love and Death*. Houndmills: Macmillan.
Morey, Peter 2000: 'Gothic and Supernatural: Allegories at Work and Play in Kipling's Indian Fiction.' In Ruth Robbins and Julian Wolfreys (eds), *Victorian Gothic: Literary and Cultural Manifestations in the Nineteenth Century*. Houndmills: Palgrave, 201–17.

Francis Lathom

(1777–1832)

Francis Lathom is one of the more curious figures in the early history of Gothic fiction. Of uncertain origins, at a precocious age he showed signs of becoming a leading playwright, but abruptly left Norwich, where he was living and writing at the time, and settled in the Scottish highlands, where he was to remain for the rest of his life. Speculation as to the cause of this move remain unresolved, but it is possible that it was occasioned by homosexual scandal.

Presumably possessed of an independent income – perhaps because he was the illegitimate son of a prominent nobleman – he continued to write plays, and he also wrote novels. If he is remembered at all now, it is because his novel *The Midnight Bell* (1798) figures on the list of Catherine Morland's Gothic reading in Jane Austen's (q.v.) *Northanger Abbey* (1818). *The Midnight Bell* is a book which still repays reading; although on the surface it can appear a recitation of stock Gothic motifs – castles and convents, troubled and persecuted virgins, doubtful inheritances – it is none the less an odd book, and one particularly amenable to the subtleties of a 'queer reading'. Relations among and between men are presented in curious terms; and questions about inheritance, legitimacy and the family line present the reader with conundra at least as complex as anything to be found in Ann Radcliffe (q.v.).

What Lathom's life and works present to the reader and critic is, perhaps above all, a series of questions about the nature of the secret. Secrets abound in *The Midnight Bell*, as they do in most Gothic fiction; what is unusual about Lathom's writing is the multitude of ways in which these secrets seem to parallel and even at times to satirize the enforced secrecy of a life lived in the pain of denial. For Lathom, the supernatural is always – in the end – explicable; but the question that remains is about the forces of conventionality that have led these secrets to be formed in the first place, the connections between a dominant morality and the contortions of the subject as it seeks to find – and yet at the same time to avoid – expression, knowing that a fullness of such expression could lead to scandal, exposure and downfall.

Bibliography

Sadleir, Michael 1927: *The Northanger Novels: A Footnote to Jane Austen*. London: English Association Pamphlet No. 68.

Varma, Devendra P. 1968: 'Introduction.' In Francis Lathom, *The Midnight Bell*. London: Folio Society, i–xxi.

J. Sheridan Le Fanu
(1814–1873)

Journalist, editor, and writer of Irish historical fiction, Le Fanu is now best known for his ghost stories and for such sensation fictions as *Wylder's Hand* (1864), *Uncle Silas* (q.v.) and *The Rose and the Key* (1871). All these sensation novels exploit Gothic motifs and are influenced particularly by the female Gothic (q.v.) of Ann Radcliffe (q.v.), with its typical plot of the heroine's confinement and escape. Like most Victorian Gothic (q.v.), Le Fanu's novels are set in the contemporary world and exploit the Gothic for the purposes of social critique. In *The Rose and the Key*, for example, the aristocratic heroine is locked up in a lunatic asylum by her mother on the grounds that her behaviour has been unconventional. Exposing the supposedly enlightened system of moral management found in nineteenth-century asylums, where the model of the family is used to impose a moral rather than a physical straitjacket on the patient, Le Fanu indicts Victorian society generally as an insane system of repression and control.

His short stories, the best of which are collected under the title *In a Glass Darkly* (1872), are presented as extracts from the casebook of Dr Hesselius, a German physician who is a forerunner of the modern psychiatrist. Included here is 'Carmilla', usually considered to be the first lesbian vampire (q.v.) story. The other stories – which concern the haunting of male subjects and are primarily concerned with exploring the nature of the psyche – typically involve a protagonist who opens up some part of his mind in such a way that he becomes haunted by a figure that is in some sense a part of himself. The malevolent monkey that terrorizes Mr Jennings in 'Green Tea', for example, could be simply the product of his addiction to that particular substance. However, given the painfully reserved and studious nature of that clergyman, and his obsessive interest in pagan mythology, the monkey seems just as likely to be the embodiment of some aspect of his repressed self.

Bibliography

McCormack, W. J. 1980: *Sheridan Le Fanu and Victorian Ireland*. Oxford: Clarendon Press.
Milbank, Alison 1992: *Daughters of the House: Modes of the Gothic in Victorian Fiction*. Houndmills: Macmillan.

SOPHIA LEE
(1750–1824)

The daughter of two Shakespearean actors, Sophia Lee had some success as both a novelist and a dramatist; her comic drama *The Chapter of Accidents* was first produced at the Haymarket in 1780, and performed every year thereafter until the end of the century. With the proceeds, Lee and her sister Harriet opened a private school in Bath, which, some historians suggest but cannot clearly prove, Ann Radcliffe (q.v.) may well have attended. Lee's primary contribution to the Gothic is *The Recess; or, A Tale of Other Times* (1783–5). While some critics have disputed the novel's claims to belong to the genre, considering it a sentimental-domestic-historical novel with Gothic trimmings, others have argued for *The Recess* as a foundational text of Gothic fiction and as a particularly significant influence on Radcliffe.

The story concerns the lives of the fictional twin sisters Matilda and Ellinor, long-concealed children of Mary Stuart, queen of Scots, from a secret marriage to the duke of Norfolk. Hidden in the Recess, a set of sub-terranean chambers beneath the ruins of an abbey, the twins do not know the secret of their birth until they reach their late teens. The novel is in the form of a memoir written by the dying Matilda and includes Ellinor's diary; these two main narratives of unrelenting misery present a double story of female persecution. Many of Lee's character types anticipate those of Radcliffe, including the predatory male villains, suffering heroines and in-effectual heroes. So too do Lee's motifs, including the sequestered life that leaves women naïve and open to temptation and danger, the lack of a protector in a patriarchal world, and the threat of extreme passions or sen-sibilities. But for Lee's heroines, unlike Radcliffe's, there is no happy ending, no release from suffering. Furthermore, Lee exploits a far more complex narrative form than Radcliffe, and the conflicting perspectives of Matilda and Ellinor effectively suggest the distortions of subjectivity. The narrative struc-ture of *The Recess* has received particular attention with respect to the novel's positioning as female Gothic (q.v.).

Bibliography

Alliston, April (ed.) 2000: 'Introduction.' In Sophia Lee, *The Recess*. Lexington, KY: University Press of Kentucky, ix–xliv.

Issac, Megan Lynn 1996: 'Sophia Lee and the Gothic of Female Community.' *Studies in the Novel*, 28, 200–18.

Lewis, Jayne Elizabeth 1995: ' "Ev'ry Lost Relation": Historical Fictions and Sentimental Incidents in Sophia Lee's *The Recess.*' *Eighteenth-Century Fiction*, 7, 165–84.

VERNON LEE

(1856–1935)

Vernon Lee (pen name of Violet Paget) was born in France and spent most of her life in Italy. A prolific writer, she produced numerous historical studies, travelogues, pieces of literary criticism, and essays on aesthetics. She is generally credited with introducing the term 'empathy' into aesthetic studies, and this concept also plays a significant role in her supernatural fiction: her protagonists repeatedly achieve what always turns out to be an unhealthy and ultimately destructive empathy with the ghosts that haunt them. As she makes clear in the preface to her best-known collection, *Hauntings* (1890), Lee had little use for simple ghost stories about the return of the dead and considered these as misguided attempts to rationalize inexplicable phenomena. For her, a genuine haunting results from some external stimulus, such as a landscape or a work of art, acting upon a receptive imagination and prompting a series of simultaneously disturbing and desirable sensations.

Lee's stories, mostly written in a highly polished and rather florid prose style that owes something to the Decadent movement, explore psychological and usually erotically charged obsessions. She typically focuses upon a character's fascination with the past, with an imagined world which gradually takes precedent over the real present. For both character and reader, boundaries between past and present, real and imaginary, begin to dissolve. Not only does Lee write under a male pseudonym, she also typically writes from the perspective of a male narrator whose fascination with the past takes the form of an obsession with a perverse and dangerous woman. Gender boundaries are often confused, and many of the stories, most notably 'A Wicked Voice', contain androgynous spectres and homoerotic overtones.

Bibliography

Colby, Vineta 2003: *Vernon Lee: A Literary Biography*. Charlottesville: University of Virginia Press.
Robbins, Ruth 1992: 'Vernon Lee: Decadent Woman?' In John Stokes (ed.), *Fin de Siècle, Fin du Globe: Fears and Fantasies of the Late Nineteenth Century*. New York: St Martin's Press, 139–61.
Robbins, Ruth 2000: 'Apparitions Can Be Deceptive: Vernon Lee's Androgynous Spectres.' In Ruth Robbins and Julian Wolfreys (eds), *Victorian Gothic: Literary*

and *Cultural Manifestations in the Nineteenth Century*. Houndmills: Palgrave, 182–200.

M. G. LEWIS

(1775–1818)

Matthew Lewis is mainly well known today for having written *The Monk* (q.v.), one of the crucial works of the classic Gothic, which he did in a remarkably short space of time at the age of 20, while embarking on a political and diplomatic career. He belonged to a very wealthy family which had made money out of colonial estates. He eventually abandoned politics and went on to become a prominent literary figure, not just because of *The Monk*, although it was an instant scandalous success, but also because of the eighteen plays which he wrote or translated from the German, some of which were also immensely successful.

Gothic runs throughout these plays, the best known of which are *The Castle Spectre* (1798) and *Alfonso, King of Castile* (1801). Lewis was very much involved with the work of the German terror-novelists, and as well as plays also translated Heinrich Zschokke's *The Bravo of Venice* (1805). Lewis never wrote another novel himself, but his reputation continued to increase and he was much admired by such figures as Lord Byron, E. T. A. Hoffmann (q.v.) and Walter Scott (q.v.), who contributed three original ballads to Lewis's collection *Tales of Wonder* (1801). It is perhaps not easy now to see exactly why this was so: with the possible exception of *The Monk*, his work can look to the contemporary reader extremely crude, even to the point of seeming like a parody of common assumptions about Gothic characterization and machinery.

However, it needs to be said that Lewis's work has a zest, a rapidity, a power of immediate engagement which are thrown into stark relief if we compare them with the elegant *longueurs* of Ann Radcliffe (q.v.). Also, of course, Lewis's work, like that of his German masters, was transgressive; it did not shrink from descriptions of sexual activity and violence, and there is a certain freshness to it, a resistance to externally imposed rules and regulations, which is constantly mentioned in contemporary reviews and criticism. Lewis himself seems not particularly to have wanted to play up the political content of his work: none the less, there is no doubt that others saw in his fables of tyranny, incarceration and liberation a series of metaphors for more literal restrictions and imprisonments, and willingly adapted Lewis's concerns to a call for freedom which was, of course, of enormous Europe-wide concern at the time of his writing.

Bibliography

Irwin, Joseph 1976: *M. G. Lewis*. Boston: Twayne.

Lyndenberg, Robin 1979: 'Ghostly Rhetoric: Ambivalence in M. G. Lewis's *The Monk.*' *Ariel: A Review of International English Literature*, 10 (2), 65–79.

McLean, Clara D. 1999: 'Lewis's *The Monk* and the Matter of Reading.' In Linda Lang-Peralta (ed.), *Women, Revolution and the Novels of the 1790s*. East Lansing, MI: Michigan State University Press, 111–31.

David Lindsay

(1878–1945)

David Lindsay wrote six significant novels, or perhaps one should rather say fantasies, albeit of strikingly different kinds: *A Voyage to Arcturus* (1920), *The Haunted Woman* (1922), *Sphinx* (1923), *Devil's Tor* (1932), *The Violet Apple* and *The Witch*, the last of which was never finished, and the last two of which were not published until 1976. They are, it is fair to say, the products of a vivid but wildly undisciplined imagination; they might also be said to be genuinely escapist fictions in the sense that they seem to have been extrusions from a life full of disappointments of various kinds.

Only the first two seem to achieve a finished form. *A Voyage to Arcturus* is one of the most unusual fantasies in the English canon, a kind of epic in which each incident, each scenario, seems strangely disconnected from the last and which appears on the surface to bristle with allegorical reference, even though it becomes progressively difficult to see what the force of the cumulative allegory might be. Perhaps indeed it is best to think of it not as an allegory, or even perhaps as a unified work at all, but rather as a series of striking episodes, loosely linked around the development and vicissitudes of the creative mind.

Only *The Haunted Woman* can truly be seen as Gothic. It is, like *Dracula* (q.v.), an eve-of-wedding fantasy, in which the heroine Isbel Loment encounters the owner of an ancient and mysterious house. Within this house she experiences many confusions of memory, and also moments both of transcendental awareness and of sexual transport; all of this strangely coded – in a way perhaps interestingly reminiscent of Wilkie Collins's *The Woman in White* (qq.v.) – by an apparent doubt about Isbel's gendered identity. The book is at one level a meditation on the relationship between the 'human spirit' and issues of gender and sex; at another it is a remarkable incarnation of a multiply-haunted house, a version – at once supernatural and strangely down-to-earth – of the ancient castles (q.v.) of the Gothic, within which, as of old, the heroine undergoes mysterious changes of identity and intimations of powers entirely beyond her control, while at the same time, in a curious twist, also experiencing the possibility that she might in fact be able to gain her own power within the context of this very house and its mysterious owner.

Bibliography

Hume, Kathryn 1978: 'Visionary Allegory in David Lindsay's *A Voyage to Arcturus.*' *Journal of English and Germanic Philology*, 77, 72–91.

Raff, Melvin 1980: 'The Structure of *A Voyage to Arcturus.*' *Studies in Scottish Literature*, 15, 262–8.

Tigges, Wim 1995: 'The Split Personality and Other Gothic Elements in David Lindsay's *A Voyage to Arcturus.*' In Valeria Tinkler-Villani, Peter Davidson and Jane Stevenson (eds), *Exhibited by Candlelight: Sources and Developments in the Gothic Tradition*. Amsterdam: Rodopi, 243–54.

H. P. Lovecraft

(1890–1937)

Howard Phillips Lovecraft occupies an extraordinary and indeed notorious position in the history of horror fiction. He was born in Providence, Rhode Island, and this location, transmuted into a series of horrific fantasies, forms the backdrop to many of his works. These consist almost entirely of short stories, which were published in the 'pulp magazines' current during his lifetime, apart from two novellas, *The Case of Charles Dexter Ward: A Novel of Terror* (1927) and *The Lurker at the Threshold* (1945), the latter of which was finished by his disciple August Derleth (q.v.).

Lovecraft's notoriety comes from two sources. More obviously, his fiction is one that is entirely concerned with the production of horrific effects, in the service of which he invented an entire panoply of gods and demons, known as the Cthulhu Mythos. It would be difficult to mistake a Lovecraft story: his style is wordy, profuse, yet capable of delivering a short sharp shock; he has sometimes been compared to Edgar Allan Poe (q.v.), but he possesses little of Poe's gift for shocking intimacy. Instead the reader is made to feel at the mercy of vast, malign forces emanating from a universe perhaps in some ways parallel to our own, but intruding on ours only to confound all expectation and to plunge characters and readers into the pit.

Behind these effects lies a set of political attitudes which have the power to horrify all on their own: racist, misogynist, Lovecraft appears to have been conducting a one-man battle against the forces of modernization, while clearly remaining locked into an image of the past that is itself compounded of terror and destruction. The origin of his stories, critics have often said, lay in his own nightmares; certainly something of the claustrophobia and repetitiveness of nightmare is present in the best of the stories. This sense of the repetitive and the inescapable has been oddly continued in the work of Derleth and others, so that the 'Lovecraftian mode', complete with its own publishing set-up, the Arkham House Press, persists to this day, and the circles of the Cthulhu Mythos continue to spread like an unhealthy but fascinating growth on the body Gothic.

Bibliography

Burleson, Donald R. 1983: *H. P. Lovecraft: A Critical Study*. Westport, CT: Greenwood Press.

Joshi, S. T. and Clark Ashton Smith 1980: *H. P. Lovecraft: Four Decades of Criticism*. Athens, OH: Ohio University Press.

Meikle, Jeffrey 1981: ' "Other Frequencies": The Parallel Worlds of Thomas Pynchon and H. P. Lovecraft.' *Modern Fiction Studies*, 27 (2), 287–94.

GEORGE MACDONALD

(1824–1905)

Perhaps not strictly a Gothic writer in any of the more obvious senses of the term, George MacDonald was a Scottish clergyman who wrote a vast series of works in an astonishing variety of different genres. Well known in his heyday, his fame rested then largely on a series of 'realistic' novels, and also on a group of works, including *At the Back of the North Wind* (1871) and *The Princess and the Goblin* (1872), which were, or were regarded as, fairy tales for children. As time has gone on, however, two quite other works have come to seem his most important: *Phantastes*, written near the beginning of his career in 1858, and his final work, *Lilith* (1895).

Viewing those works which contain supernatural elements as a whole, it can be seen that MacDonald represented a crucial link in the evolution of the 'high imagination' of German writers such as Johann Ludwig Tieck, Novalis and E. T. A. Hoffmann (q.v.) into the twentieth-century fantasies of such writers as C. S. Lewis and J. R. R. Tolkien. MacDonald's greatest works always hover on the edge of allegory, although they often contain sudden changes of tone and development which challenge the reader's expectations. There is a constant concern with other worlds which may lie close to this one, and into which one might find oneself suddenly plunged; the question for his protagonists is then how to find a mode of action in this alternative world which will enable them to comprehend and develop through the strange experiences they encounter.

There is a long tradition in Gothic, arguably beginning with James Hogg (q.v.), which speaks to problems of the double and its foundations in religious sensibility; in MacDonald this double sometimes takes the form of the 'shadow', an alternative self by which one might be haunted, but with which it is one's duty to come to some kind of terms. This shadow may well represent the dark side of possibility; in *Phantastes* and *Lilith*, his most subtle works, it could also be said that the shadow or its avatars represent an intuition of the unconscious, of forces within the self but outside the self's control. If the conventional Gothic apparatus is missing in MacDonald, certainly the pressure of the supernatural is very much present, and the human figures in his stories often appear, in Gothic fashion, to be dwarfed by the demands placed upon them and by their intimations of a different world where human aspiration is constantly tested 'on another scene'.

Bibliography

Gunther, Adrian 1996: 'The Multiple Realms of George MacDonald's *Phantastes.*' *Studies in Scottish Literature*, 29, 174–90.

Raeper, William (ed.) 1990: *The Gold Thread: Essays on George MacDonald.* Edinburgh: Edinburgh University Press.

Robb, David 1988: 'Realism and Fantasy in the Fiction of George MacDonald.' In Douglas Gifford (ed.), *The History of Scottish Literature*. Vol. 3: *The Nineteenth Century*. Aberdeen: Aberdeen University Press, 275–90.

ARTHUR MACHEN

(1863–1947)

In his novel *The Three Imposters* (1895), Arthur Machen asks a question: 'what if the obscure and horrible race of the hills still survived, still remained haunting wild places and barren hills, and now and then repeating the evil of Gothic legend?' On the basis of this hypothesis, the notion that ancient forces of evil might still have the power to break through the texture of everyday life, Machen wrote a series of books which some critics have regarded as the most decadent in the English language.

This decadence (q.v.) takes several forms. *The Great God Pan* (1894) is a story which takes seriously the opposite of Darwinian evolution, the hypothesis that a primitive capacity for evil and horror survives in us all and can, under the right circumstances, drive us to commit the most dreadful of deeds. *The Three Impostors* is again inhabited by demons, and leaves the reader adrift in a realm where no single version of the world can be trusted, where there is no surety against slipping back into the horrors of the past. And *The Hill of Dreams* (1907), arguably Machen's masterpiece, presents us with a protagonist for whom the world is as nothing compared with the power of a single obsession, which drives him into a series of experiences of pain and sacrifice that are clearly designed to undermine any certainty in the progress and hope of the human species.

Perhaps now better known for his powerful story about the Angel of Mons, *The Bowmen* (1915), Machen's work none the less deserves to be classified with other late Victorian key works of decadent scepticism like H. G. Wells's (q.v.) *The Island of Doctor Moreau* (1896) and Oscar Wilde's (q.v.) *The Picture of Dorian Gray* (1890, rev. 1891). Machen, however, goes farther than either of these in his acceptance of a world of horror which is kept only precariously at bay by the veneer of civilized society, and in his continual suggestions of the evil to which the human may at any moment sink. Sometimes this evil is graphically depicted, sometimes it is conveyed in hints and evasions; but its power is never to be denied, and the limits of what it might be mean to be a civilized human being are constantly under siege from dark forces, arising from past, half-hidden memories that remain lodged in the individual psyche as well as being inseparable from humankind's bloody history.

Bibliography

Ferguson, Christine 2002: 'Decadence as Scientific Fulfilment.' *Publications of the Modern Language Association*, 117 (3), 465–78.

Reynolds, Aidan and Charlton, William 1963: *Arthur Machen: A Short Account of his Life and Work*. London: Richards Press.

Sweetser, Wesley D. 1964: *Arthur Machen*. New York: Twayne.

JAMES MACPHERSON

(1736–1796)

Although when we think of the Gothic today it is natural to think of the long development of Gothic themes and motifs in fiction from Ann Radcliffe and M. G. Lewis (qq.v.) on, it is also important to remember that their evolution of the Gothic had its own cultural context, in the revival of interest in particular aspects of the British past in the mid- and late eighteenth century (q.v.). One of the major manifestations of this interest focused on the series of poems published by James Macpherson in the guise of 'translations' from the ancient Gaelic poet 'Ossian'.

The controversy about the authenticity of these poems was a major literary *cause célèbre* of the age, and took increasingly subtle forms; after all, if Macpherson's poems had no real past provenance, might this not argue for the skill of the poet himself rather than for him to be convicted of fraudulence? At all events, Macpherson's poetry, wherever he gained his inspiration, was widely seen as involved in the revaluation of ancient vernacular languages, and it was this that was crucial to the larger-scale revaluation of the 'British' that was at the core of early Gothic.

If Gothic is centrally concerned, first, with voices from the past, and second, with the reinstallation of a 'native' tradition in counterpoint to the neo-classicism of the earlier eighteenth century, then Macpherson – or rather, perhaps, what we might call the 'Ossian' phenomenon – needs to take its place alongside the work of such antiquarians as Thomas Percy and Richard Hurd. It was these investigations, flawed or not, into the history of 'Britain', considered as a Celtic nation or a set of Celtic nations, that allowed for or perhaps responded to the emergence of a new cultural sensibility, which repudiated the automatic superiority of the classical and claimed to find in the history of 'Britain' a new source of passion in writing that could stand against the formality, restraint and order beloved of the neo-classicists. The Ossian poems are lengthy, wordy accounts of battles, lamentations for lost cultures and lost heroes, doomed actions fought out on the cloudy fields of a remote and uncertain past; as such, they prefigure many of the concerns of the Gothic, not least by casting into doubt the question of their own origin, thus antedating and perhaps providing a dubious progenitor for the host of 'lost manuscripts' with which early Gothic fiction is so overwhelmingly concerned.

Bibliography

Haugen, Kristine Louise 1998: 'Ossian and the Invention of Textual History.' *Journal of the History of Ideas*, 59 (2), 309–27.

Larrissy, Edward 1999: 'The Celtic Bard of Romanticism: Blindness and Second Sight.' *Romanticism*, 5 (1), 43–57.

Punter, David 1995: 'Ossian, Blake and the Questionable Source.' In Valeria Tinkler-Villani, Peter Davidson and Jane Stevenson (eds), *Exhibited by Candlelight: Sources and Developments in the Gothic Tradition*. Amsterdam: Rodopi, 25–42.

RICHARD MATHESON

(1926–)

Born in New Jersey, Matheson is a prolific writer who, in addition to producing numerous novels and stories in the genres of mystery, science fiction, fantasy, westerns and horror, has written many film (q.v.) and television scripts, including fourteen memorable episodes of *The Twilight Zone* and several of Roger Corman's Edgar Allan Poe (q.v.) films, including *House of Usher* (1960) and *The Pit and the Pendulum* (1961).

Matheson's first published story, 'Born of Man and Woman' (1950), concerns a 'freak' child that attempts to escape imprisonment by its parents, and introduces a theme that pervades Matheson's work: the isolated individual pitted against a hostile environment. Works of particular interest for the Gothic include *A Stir of Echoes* (1958), a story of paranormal experience and a paranoid fantasy about the darker side of suburban life, and *Hell House* (1971), in which a team of psychic investigators attempt to find the source of a destructive supernatural power.

Matheson is best known, however, for *I Am Legend* (1954), a chilling take on a familiar monster – the vampire (q.v.). Combing Gothic with science fiction, it is the story of Robert Neville, the last man alive in a world ravaged by a plague that has turned everyone else into vampires. The irony is that Neville, as morally suspect as the vampires, is now the alien other, the outsider who must be destroyed because he is different. Matheson suggests not only Neville's terror and his paranoia (q.v.), but also, with a spare, almost documentary style, effectively captures the monotony, the banality of Neville's life. In an interview Matheson has said that he believes the best fantasy comes from adding just a drop of the fantastic into an otherwise realistic mixture and then writing the story in as realistic a manner as possible, and this is precisely what he achieves in *I Am Legend*. While the book remains unaccountably neglected by the critics, it has certainly captured the popular imagination: it has twice been made into a film – *The Last Man on Earth* with Vincent Price in 1964 and *The Omega Man* starring Charlton Heston in 1971. It has also had a strong influence on such later horror classics as George A. Romero's *Night of the Living Dead* (1968), and, surely undeniable proof that *I Am Legend* has become part of the cultural imagination, it has even served as the basis for the lyrics of a White Zombie song and for a significant number of video games.

Bibliography

Dziemianowicz, Stefan 1994: 'Horror Begins at Home: Richard Matheson's Fear of the Familiar.' *Studies in Weird Fiction*, 14, 29–36.

Oakes, David 2000: *Science and Destabilization in the Modern American Gothic: Lovecraft, Matheson and King*. Westport, CT: Greenwood Press.

Pharr, Mary 1999: 'Vampiric Appetite in *I Am Legend*, *'Salem's Lot*, and *The Hunger*.' In Leonard G. Heldreth and Mary Pharr (eds), *The Blood is the Life: Vampires in Literature*. Bowling Green, OH: Bowling Green State University Popular Press, 93–103.

CHARLES ROBERT MATURIN

(1780–1824)

Born in Dublin and educated in the classics at Trinity College, Maturin was an ordained minister who turned to writing to supplement his income and support his growing family. His first novel was *Fatal Revenge; or, The Family of Montorio* (1807). Published under the pseudonym of Dennis Jasper

Murphy, this introduced some of the primary themes that would come to dominate his later work, including guilt, revenge and, most notably, religious persecution (q.v.) and fanaticism. In Father Schemoli, a figure combining elements of Faust and the Wandering Jew, Maturin also anticipates the type he will develop most spectacularly in his best-known work, *Melmoth the Wanderer* (q.v.), the Gothic tale of the outcast who sells his soul to the devil in return for knowledge and power.

Other works of particular significance for the Gothic include the now frequently anthologized 'Leixlip Castle' (1825), which draws upon the motif of the demon lover, and the Gothic revenge melodrama *Bertram; or, The Castle of St Aldobrand*, produced in 1816 at Drury Lane with Edmund Kean in the leading role. The play concerns a Byronic hero-villain who is dispossessed of his property and then shipwrecked; after being rescued Bertram encounters the man who was responsible for his exile and who had married the woman Bertram loved. Driven by uncontrollable passions, Bertram takes his revenge, seducing Lady Imogine, murdering Lord Aldobrand, and then killing himself, leaving Imogine to be driven mad by guilt and sorrow. The play was savagely reviewed by Samuel Taylor Coleridge, who attacked it as 'jacobinical' and objected to its apparent celebration of emotional and psychological extremes and consequent subversion of moral and social authority.

Bibliography

D'Amico, Diane 1984: 'Feeling and Conception of Character in the Novels of Charles Robert Maturin.' *Massachusetts Studies in English*, 9 (3), 42–54.

Kramer, Dale 1973: *Charles Robert Maturin*. New York: Twayne.

Nikolopoulou, Anastasia 1994: 'Medievalism and Historicity in the English Gothic Melodrama: Maturin's *Bertram; or, The Castle of St Aldobrand*.' *Poetica*, 39–40, 139–53.

HERMAN MELVILLE

(1819–1891)

In the works of the American writer Herman Melville, perhaps best known for such novels as *Typee* (1846) and *Moby-Dick* (1851), there is a persistent evocation of the Gothic tradition. The vertebrae on the skeleton of a whale in the latter are likened to the 'great knobbed blocks on a Gothic spire', while the mate or headsman is described 'like a Gothic Knight of old . . . always accompanied by his boat-steerer or harpooneer, who in certain conjunctures provides him with a fresh lance'. Ships like the *Pequod* in *Moby-Dick* or the *San Dominick* in 'Benito Cereno' (1855) are often said to become like floating equivalents of the traditional haunted castle (q.v.).

Melville's most significant links with the Gothic, however, can be seen in his central protagonists. On the one hand, there are such Promethean over-reachers as *Moby-Dick*'s Ahab, a man willing to sacrifice his crew to his obsession, to his pursuit of what he considers to be elemental evil, or Bannadonna in 'The Bell Tower' (1855), who, in a manner reminiscent of Beckford's *Vathek* (qq.v.), builds a 300-foot bell tower and, much like Mary Wollstonecraft Shelley's Victor Frankenstein (qq.v), attempts to usurp the role of God by animating a 'locomotive figure' to install in the belfry. On the other hand there are the tragic innocents, such as the eponymous heroes of *Pierre; or, the Ambiguities* (1852), a Gothic romance with incestuous and homoerotic elements, and *Billy Budd, Sailor*, published posthumously in 1924, a novella which, contemporary critics observed, seems primarily designed to demonstrate the simple impracticability of virtue. The 'welkin-eyed' Billy is doomed by the malevolent hatred of a ship's officer, John Claggart, but whether the first can be seen as a Christ-like figure of purity and the second as a simple embodiment of evil is difficult to determine, given that Billy ultimately becomes the murderer and Claggart his victim. This problematizing of the basic conflict between good and evil on moral grounds is usually considered Melville's most important contribution to the development of the Gothic tradition.

Bibliography

Fisher, Benjamin F., IV 1994: 'Gothic Possibilities in *Moby-Dick*.' In Allan Lloyd Smith and Victor Sage (eds), *Gothick: Origins and Innovations*. Amsterdam: Rodopi, 115–22.

Goldner, Ellen J. 1999: 'Other(ed) Ghosts: Gothicism and the Bonds of Reason in Melville, Chesnutt, and Morrison.' *MELUS*, 24 (1), 59–83.

Miles, Robert 1999: ' "Tranced Griefs": Melville's *Pierre* and the Origins of the Gothic.' *ELH*, 66, 157–77.

Joyce Carol Oates
(1938–)

Since the early 1960s, Oates has published over forty novels and twenty-five collections of short stories in addition to works of literary criticism, and she is celebrated as one of the leading practitioners of American Gothic today. As stated in her introduction to *American Gothic Tales* (1996), Oates considers that American Gothic's primary concern is to depict the 'assaults upon individual autonomy and identity', and this is certainly the focus of her own Gothic fiction. Whether they are set within the dangerous but seductive world of urban violence, as in *them* (1969), or in the sterile suburbs of the American dream, as in *Expensive People* (1968) and *American Appetites* (1989), Oates's stories repeatedly record the disintegration of the self in the face of the dehumanizing and alienating world of modern America. As her characters struggle for control, violence repeatedly erupts, shattering the fragile surfaces by which they desperately seek both to protect and to define themselves.

One of Oates's particular interests is the effect of family structures upon the autonomy of the individual, and this forms a significant theme in two of her most Gothic and macabre works. *Expensive People* is the extended confession of Richard Everett, a victim of the pressures of conventional suburban America and its ideals, who attempts to find some release by bringing a touch of chaos into his ordered world and becomes a matricide and sniper. *Zombie* (1995), equally disturbing in the way it brings us into distressing proximity with a psychotic mind through diary form, is modelled on accounts of Milwaukee serial killer Jeffrey Dahmer's attempts to lobotomize a victim in order to create a malleable love-slave.

Also of interest in terms of the Gothic are Oates's revisionary experiments with the works of earlier Gothic texts. In *Marriages and Infidelities* (1972), for example, she rewrites Edgar Allan Poe's (q.v.) 'The Man of the Crowd' as 'Stalking'. In *Haunted* (1994), Henry James's *The Turn of the Screw* (qq.v.) appears in a new form as 'Accursed Inhabitants of the House of Bly', focusing upon the love between Quint and Miss Jessel and their affection for the children, and offering a positive alternative family structure to set against the questionable moralities of both the governess and her employer.

Bibliography

Bender, Eileen-Teper 1987: *Joyce Carol Oates: Artist in Residence.* Bloomington: Indiana University Press.

Bloom, Harold (ed.) 1987: *Joyce Carol Oates: Modern Critical Views.* New York: Chelsea House.

Johnson, Greg 1994: *Joyce Carol Oates: A Study of the Short Fiction.* New York: Twayne.

MARGARET OLIPHANT
(1828–1897)

Oliphant, one of the most prolific women writers of the nineteenth century and Queen Victoria's favourite novelist, is primarily known for the seven-volume 'Chronicles of Carlingford', realist tales of English provincial life which included *Salem Chapel* (1863) and *The Rector and The Doctor's Family* (1863). Her importance for the Gothic comes from the supernatural tales that she called her 'stories of the seen and the unseen'. Always understated, never sensationalized, many of these stories are now considered classics of the genre; Oliphant's realist strategies, transplanted into her supernatural tales, result in the disruption of the real and the 'normal' becoming all the more disturbing and effective.

Given that Oliphant's family life was repeatedly marked by tragedy – she lost three babies, her husband died of consumption in 1859 and her 10-year-old daughter of gastric fever in 1864 – it is not so surprising that many of these stories focus on bereavement and attempts at reunion between the dead and the living. Images of gates, windows and doors pervade the stories, embodying the barriers between life and death through which contact seems tantalizingly possible but ultimately fails or remains forbidden. Despite all the efforts of both the dead and the living, the attempts to break through these barriers never result in more than what is described in 'Old Lady Mary' (1885) as 'a jar and tingle in the inanimate world'.

The impossibility of communication is particularly emphasized by the way the barriers are so frequently positioned within a linguistic space. In 'The Library Window' (1896), for example, there is a writing ghost whose manuscript is never read, while in the novella 'The Beleaguered City' (1880), the ghosts, despairing of ever communicating with the citizens of Semur, put up a large sign which is summarily dismissed; the inhabitants are eventually compelled by an unseen force to leave their homes and go outside the gates of the city while the dead return to take back their old homes as a judgement upon the living.

Oliphant frequently used her supernatural stories for the purposes of social critique. 'The Land of Darkness', part of her *Little Pilgrim* series (1882–8) about a soul's spiritual travels to heaven, hell and earth, for example, may now be too sentimental for modern tastes, but it is nevertheless notable for its effective depiction of a hell that bears a striking resemblance to industrial England.

Bibliography

Fielding, Penny 1999: 'Other Worlds: Oliphant's Spectralisation of the Modern.' *Women's Writing*, 6 (2), 201–13.

Jay, Elisabeth (ed.) 1990: *The Autobiography of Margaret Oliphant: The Complete Text*. Oxford: Oxford University Press.

Jay, Elisabeth 1995: *Mrs Oliphant: 'A Fiction to Herself'. A Literary Life*. Oxford: Clarendon Press.

Mervyn Peake

(1911–1968)

The crumbling castle, looking among the mists, exhaled the season, and every cold stone breathed it out. The tortured trees by the dark lake burned and dripped, and the leaves snatched by the wind were whirled in wild circles through the towers. The clouds mouldered as they lay coiled, or shifted themselves uneasily upon the stone skyfield, sending up wreaths that drifted through the turrets and swarmed up the hidden walls.

Thus does Mervyn Peake describe his great Gothic creation, the castle of Gormenghast, heir to the great castles (q.v.) in the line of inheritance from *Udolpho* (q.v.). Peake himself was a man as tortured as his castle, a writer and artist of the grotesque and the haunted. Gormenghast was the setting for a trilogy of novels, *Titus Groan* (1946), *Gormenghast* (1950) and *Titus Alone* (1959); most critics would agree that they are of steadily diminishing power, but none the less the castle itself, far more than the characters in it or the plot on which the trilogy is hinged, remains as a fine effigy of the twentieth-century manifestation of the Gothic.

Gormenghast follows Gothic tradition in being mapless, trackless, pathless: around every corner there are always other corners; there are no limits to its dimensions. In this sense it represents a past which is finally irrecoverable; a past which is constantly signified and resignified in a set of rituals that have lost all meaning for its present inhabitants, but by which their lives are controlled at every turn. If it might be suspected that myths of entrapment by the feudal past should have passed away over time, the (at least cult) status of Peake's fiction reminds us that the kinds of ghost he is writing about seem incapable of a final act of disappearance, that British cultural history can still be overshadowed by something which modernity has always sought to banish but which refuses to lie down. The plot is indeed vestigial; it seems more as though Peake, a haunted, obsessional writer, felt it necessary to subdue plot to the demands of a vision of stasis, of a recurring past from which escape is not possible, and in enacting this compelling scenario – a scenario that reminds us (inescapably) of Sigmund Freud's dictum that from the unconscious nothing ever goes away – he creates for the reader a world where the past continues to rule, even if significance has been drained away and reduced to a series of dead and meaningless rites.

Bibliography

Gardiner-Scott, Tanya 1989: *Mervyn Peake: The Evolution of a Dark Romantic.* New York: Peter Lang.

Redpath, Philip 1989: 'Mervyn Peake's Black House: An Allegory of Mind and Body.' *ARIEL: A Review of International English Literature,* 20 (1), 57–74.

Tolley, Michael 1999: 'Grotesque Imaginings: Peaking through Keyholes.' In Alice Mills (ed.), *Seriously Weird: Papers on the Grotesque.* New York: Peter Lang, 153–66.

Edgar Allan Poe
(1809–1849)

It would be difficult to overestimate Edgar Allan Poe's influence on the development of Gothic fiction. A writer who was continually struggling against both his own demons and the apparent recalcitrance and rejection of the outside world, constantly driven, at least in his own opinion, to produce work inferior to his own ideals, operating under continual financial, medical and addictive pressures, he nevertheless produced a series of poems and, more importantly, short stories which have ineluctably coloured the public apprehension of Gothic writing.

'The Black Cat' (1843), 'The Fall of the House of Usher' (1839), 'The Cask of Amontillado' (1846), 'Ligeia' (1838), 'The Pit and the Pendulum' (1843): these only begin the list of Poe stories that seem to have fostered a curious sense in the reader; namely, that these are stories which have, in some sense, *always* been in existence. If Gothic from its 'origins' has been concerned with, indeed obsessed by, the past, then Poe's stories seem to redouble this fixation and to attain – perhaps all too easily – the status of mental archetypes.

One reason for this is that Poe presses on a Gothic nerve: he is startlingly good – as in, for example, 'Usher' – at creating in short order a sense of an external landscape; but simultaneously the reader is led to wonder constantly whether this landscape is indeed really external or rather a projection of a particular psychological state. In Poe, things constantly return; but whether they return from an outer world or because they have never been banished from unconscious depths of the psyche remains a problem which is irresolvable, and the very brevity of the tales serves to reinforce the fundamental impossibility of answering such a question.

In Poe, then, the Gothic setting – the castle (q.v.), the monastery, even (and perhaps especially) the tomb – is taken through another turn of the screw; his stories may be redolent of, to take a major example, an uncanny fear of premature burial, but the question of whether such a fear has any relation to a world outside the psyche is left hanging. Perhaps in the end in Poe's stories there is no 'outside' at all, nothing outside and beyond the text; in this respect, then, it is perhaps unsurprising that his stories have provided rich sources for most contemporary theories of literature, from deconstruction to psychoanalysis, and have attracted extended and illuminating critiques from such theorists as Jacques Derrida and Jacques Lacan.

Bibliography

Howarth, William L. (ed.) 1971: *Twentieth-Century Interpretations of Poe's Tales: A Collection of Critical Essays.* Englewood Cliffs, NJ: Prentice-Hall.

Regan, Robert (ed.) 1967: *Poe: A Collection of Critical Essays.* Englewood Cliffs, NJ: Prentice-Hall.

Tymms, Ralph 1949: *Doubles in Literary Psychology.* Cambridge: Bowes and Bowes.

JOHn POLÍDORI
(1795–1821)

While only a minor player in the literary world, Polidori, Lord Byron's physician and friend, nevertheless had a significant impact on the Gothic through his writing of *The Vampyre* (1819). The idea of the story was borrowed from a fragment Byron wrote as a result of the ghost-story competition between Mary and Percy Shelley, Byron and Polidori, held on that famous June evening of 1816 and leading to the writing of *Frankenstein* (q.v.). Initially attributed to Byron, Polidori's novella was quickly translated into French, inspiring an anonymous sequel, *Lord Ruthwen, ou Les Vampires* (1820), and various vampire (q.v.) melodramas, including J. R. Planché's *The Vampyre, or, The Bride of the Isles: A Romantic Melodrama in Two Acts* (1820).

The publication of Polidori's *The Vampyre* could be said to mark the decisive move away from the folkloric vampire, away from the shuffling, mindless peasant of legend, and to establish the basic form of the literary vampire. Lord Ruthven, the name of the vampire, is borrowed from Lady Caroline Lamb's *Glenarvon* (1816), whose central villain, Clarence de Ruthven, is a savage portrait of her former lover, Lord Byron. Given its many connections with Byron, it is appropriate that the novella was to establish the type of the vampire as the world-weary aristocrat for whom vampirism is, on the whole, just another form of seduction. Polidori's Ruthven is above all a seducer, and the havoc he causes, interestingly anticipating Bram Stoker's *Dracula* (qq.v.) in many ways, is not completely his fault. Focusing on the overly romantic young aristocrat Aubrey, Polidori shows how Aubrey's fascination with the vampire successively leads to the deaths of his lover, his sister and finally himself; Ruthven is above all a catalyst for the repressed tendencies within those he meets, and his victims' downfall is to a great degree attributable to human weakness.

Polidori's other novel, *Ernestus Berchtold; or, The Modern Oedipus* (1819), exploits many Gothic motifs – the overreacher, incest and the supernatural – but is of much less interest. The ruthless Count Filiberto Doni goes to Asia in search of wealth and acquires it from the 'hideous form' of a spirit, who demands in return that the Count must suffer some 'domestic affliction'. Only later does the Count learn what this affliction will be: he discovers that Ernestus, who has married his daughter Louisa, is his son from a previous marriage. The novel has never received the critical attention given to *The Vampyre*, no doubt at least partly because Polidori devotes so many endless and self-indulgent pages to recounting the overwhelming despair of the distraught Ernestus.

Bibliography

MacDonald, D. L. 1991: *Poor Polidori: A Critical Biography of the Author of The Vampyre*. Toronto: University of Toronto Press.

AПП RADCLIFFE

(1764–1823)

Born in London on 9 July 1764, the year in which Horace Walpole (q.v.) published *The Castle of Otranto* (q.v.), Ann Radcliffe lived a reclusive life. Nearly all the biographical information we have about her comes from her husband William, who wrote an entry on his wife for the *Annual Bibliography and Obituary for the Year 1824* and provided the information for Thomas Noon Talford's biographical memoir, appended to the posthumously published *Gaston de Blondeville* (1826). This final work of fiction also had a framing prologue involving two contemporary travellers whose conversation reveals contrasting views on literature and the imagination. It was first published separately as an essay in aesthetic theory, 'On the Supernatural in Poetry', in the *New Monthly Magazine* for 1826, and sheds interesting light on Radcliffe's fictional techniques.

Over a period of eight years, Radcliffe wrote six major novels, including *The Romance of the Forest* (1791), which made her reputation, *The Mysteries of Udolpho* (q.v.), now her best-known work, and *The Italian* (1797). Her first novel, *The Castles of Athlin and Dunbayne* (1789), draws on the usurpation plot which looks back to Walpole's *Otranto*, and could fairly be called an apprentice work. This was followed in 1790 by *A Sicilian Romance*, where the character types and stock features of Radcliffe's Gothic begin to come together, including the persecution of the heroine by the older man, the father figure, and the search for the absent mother, suggestive of the problematic quest for identity in a world where the maternal is effaced. The central figure is now a heroine: Julia de Mazzini is imprisoned within the family castle by her father, who has arranged for her to marry a rich but distinctly unpleasant, if not outright repulsive, duke. She escapes and has various adventures, sometimes helped by Hippolitus, her rather ineffectual and bland lover, and eventually discovers her mother, who has been imprisoned in the family home by her father. Mazzini is poisoned by his new, younger wife and Julia is consequently free to marry the man she loves.

For much of the twentieth century, Radcliffe's reputation remained low, partly due to her use of the explained supernatural, which was mistakenly seen as evidence of a conservative rationalism, and partly due to the critical preference for the male Gothic, judged more transgressive and consequently more in the 'true' Gothic line of development. This position has now changed, primarily due to the pioneering work done by feminist critics in identifying an alternative tradition of female Gothic (q.v.), with its encoded expressions of female experience.

Bibliography

Miles, Robert 1995: *Ann Radcliffe: The Great Enchantress*. Manchester: Manchester University Press.

Norton, Rictor 1999: *Mistress of Udolpho: The Life of Ann Radcliffe*. London: Leicester University Press.

CLARA REEVE
(1729–1807)

The daughter of a clergyman, Reeve is best known for *The Old English Baron*, first published anonymously as *The Champion of Virtue: A Gothic Story* (1777) and offered, in a manner similar to Horace Walpole's *The Castle of Otranto* (qq.v.), in the fictional guise of a translated manuscript. When Reeve changed the title and acknowledged her authorship in the second edition of 1778, she added a new preface that included an analysis of Walpole's text and an explanation of her own quite different aims. While *Otranto*, she argued, so exceeded the limits of probability as to excite laughter, her story was to balance the fantastic with the natural world of eighteenth-century realism.

The Old English Baron is the story of a young peasant, Edmund Twyford, eventually revealed to be the heir of the estate of Lovel and restored to his true position in society. Reeve is usually credited with introducing the motif of the haunted chamber, even if, as many critics have suggested, the

159

potential for terror in the episode where Edmund holds his nightlong vigil in the forbidden apartment of Lovel Castle is somewhat spoiled by the irritatingly didactic ghost that appears to him. Characters repeatedly demonstrate their moral superiority by their self-possession in encounters with the supernatural. Sustained by virtue and prayer, Edmund and his companions remain notably untroubled by their experiences; indeed, by the third night of the vigil in the haunted chamber, 'being somewhat familiarized to it', they are able to carry on happily with their conversations and quite disregard the fearful groans that so insistently rise from beneath the floorboards.

While Walpole himself spoke disparaging of Reeve's novel as an imitation of *Otranto* reduced to reason and probability, it is clearly not quite that, and Reeve certainly made a significant contribution to the development of the Gothic novel. With her more restrained use of the supernatural and her assumption of a more overtly didactic and moral position, Reeve paved the way for the development of the female Gothic (q.v.) in the works of Charlotte Smith and Ann Radcliffe (qq.v.).

Bibliography

Berg, Temma F. 2001: 'Engendering the Gothic: Clara Reeve Redecorates The Castle of Otranto.' *Reader: Essays in Reader-Oriented Theory, Criticism, and Pedagogy*, 44, 53–78.

Clery, E. J. 2000: *Women's Gothic: From Clara Reeve to Mary Shelley.* Tavistock: Northcote House.

G. W. M. REYNOLDS

(1814–1879)

G. W. M. Reynolds was a mid-Victorian writer, newspaper proprietor and political activist. Born into a wealthy family, he spent much of his money on political causes. He was involved with the Chartists, and campaigned in his newspapers on behalf of a variety of issues, including women's rights, the rejection of anti-Semitism, the abolition of private property and the disestablishment of the state church; and against capital punishment and the powers of the peerage.

He wrote an immense amount, and was as famous and as popular in his day as Charles Dickens (q.v.). Reynolds's books included historical romances and 'social novels', but he was best known as the author of three supernatural novels, *Faust* (1845–6), *Wagner, the Wehr-wolf* (1846–7) and *The Necromancer* (1852), as well as two immensely long works, *The Mysteries of London* (1844–8) and *The Mysteries of the Courts of London* (1848–56). All of these appeared originally in serialized form, and the latter two are between them almost as long as Dickens's complete works.

Reynolds's singular achievement was to use much of the traditional Gothic apparatus – terrified heroines, threats of murder and rape, darkened and shadowy settings – and to bring them up to date, so that his terrors are situated in the present day, among the destitute and underprivileged in his own contemporary London. His Gothic works always have a political point, but this does not prevent them from being on the extreme end of literary sensationalism – on the contrary, he makes his political arguments precisely by portraying what he sees as the real horror of life in London if one is not part of the privileged elite.

Reynolds's central argument – and it is one which fits neatly with his Gothic antecedents – is that it is impossible to expect the poor to behave well if they do not have the means to live, and, perhaps more importantly, if the models they see in the upper echelons of society are depraved and tyrannical. For Reynolds, the feudal aristocracy is still alive and well in his contemporary world, and still dedicated to crushing the spirit of their social inferiors and denying them any means of escape from the claustrophobia of the mean streets.

Bibliography

Maxwell, Richard C., Jr 1977: 'G. W. M. Reynolds, Dickens and the Mysteries of London.' *Nineteenth-Century Fiction*, 32, 188–213.

Punter, David 1996: *The Literature of Terror: A History of Gothic Fictions from 1765 to the Present Day.* Vol. 1: *The Gothic Tradition.* 2nd edn. London: Longman.

Aппє Rжcє

(1941–)

Rice, christened Howard Allen O'Brien after her father, grew up in the Irish Catholic quarter of New Orleans, the place that was to provide the setting for so many of her works. An extraordinarily prolific writer, she is still best known for her first book, *Interview with the Vampire* (q.v.), the first-person narrative of Louis, a New Orleans vampire (q.v.), and his adventures in the New and Old Worlds. This initiates what would become *The Vampire Chronicles*, including such works as *The Vampire Lestat* (1985), *The Queen of the Damned* (1988), *Tale of the Body Thief* (1992), *Memnoch the Devil* (1995) and *Pandora* (1998). Other novels that have links with the Gothic in their dealing with the occult include *The Witching Hour* (1990), and other works in the continuing saga of the Mayfair Witches, which threatens to expand much as the *Vampire Chronicles* have – indeed, in recent works they have begun to merge. Rice has also written historical fictions, including *The Feast of All Saints* (1979), a chronicle of New Orleans slaves freed before the Civil War, and *Cry to Heaven* (1982), which focuses on the castrati of eighteenth-century Venice. Finally, she has written erotica under the name of Anne Rampling and a sado-masochistic trilogy playing on the fairy tale of Sleeping Beauty as A. N. Roquelaure.

Rice's prose has alternately been praised for its lush and ornate qualities and castigated as repetitive, stilted, formulaic and melodramatic. The quality of the works is undeniably variable; she has a wonderfully successful formula, but at times, she offers nothing more than precisely that formula. *Violin* (1997), for example, the story of a 50-something woman seduced by a Russian fiddle-playing ghost, written in the most pompous and contrived language imaginable, is considered numbingly unreadable even by many hard-core Rice fans.

For some critics, Rice is of particular interest for reworking Gothic conventions with a postmodern sensibility about identity. Typically focusing upon protagonists who are in some way marginalized from society, she offers subversive as well as imaginative and fantastical representations of our everyday reality. Others suggest, however, that Rice has become increasingly tentative in her critique of gender ideology and that there is, more generally, an increasingly conservative element in her work. While she began with an attempt to problematize clear-cut definitions of good and evil, more recently she has tended to reinstate these oppositions, suggesting that, as she observed in a 1992 interview, 'Evil is, after all, evil.' Her popularity, however, shows little signs of waning, perhaps indicating that the changes in her ideological positions are only a response to changes in our times.

Bibliography

Hoppenstand, Gary and Browne, Ray B. (eds) 1996: *The Gothic World of Anne Rice.* Bowling Green, OH: Bowling Green State University Popular Press.

Keller, James R. 2000: *Anne Rice and Sexual Politics: The Early Novels.* Jefferson, NC: McFarland.

Roberts, Bette B. 1994: *Anne Rice.* New York: Twayne.

WALTER SCOTT

(1771–1832)

Walter Scott is, of course, most famous for his series of historical novels – *Waverley* (1814), *Rob Roy* (1817), *The Heart of Midlothian* (1818), *Ivanhoe* (1820), *Kenilworth* (1821), *Anne of Geierstein* (1829) and many others – and for his championing of Scottish literature and Scottish culture in general. Often regarded as primarily a realist novelist, both because of his detailed depiction of life in past times and because of his concentration on equivocal protagonists, he was also, however, considerably influenced by the Gothic, and had himself a pronounced interest in the supernatural, especially in so far as it influenced legend and folk-tale.

He was a collector of folk-legends and ballads, in a direct line of descent from the eighteenth-century (q.v.) antiquarians. He contributed to M. G. Lewis's (q.v.) collection of ballads, *Tales of Wonder* (1801), and wrote two heavily Gothic plays, *House of Aspen* (1799) and *Doom of Devorgoil* (1817). He wrote three tales of terror which are still regarded as models of the genre, 'The Tale of the Mysterious Mirror' (1828), 'The Tapestried Chamber' (1828) and the disturbing 'Wandering Willie's Tale' in *Redgauntlet* (1824). He was also the author of *Letters on Demonology and Witchcraft* (1830), which addresses itself partly to the question of historical belief in ghosts; it is ostensibly a condemnation of the witch-persecutions of the seventeenth century, but along the way Scott collects together a whole series of strange accounts of supernatural events which make up most of the book's appeal.

Scott's interest in Scottish folk culture proves in the end inseparable from a concern with the supernatural. Even though in most cases this may be explained away, as in the works of Ann Radcliffe (q.v.), it none the less forms a continuing backdrop; it was crucial to Scott's sense of his own cultural mission that he investigate the belief structures of previous ages, and there can be no doubt that his portrayal of those beliefs often far exceeds their ostensible purpose. Despite his reputation as a realist novelist, Scott never-theless manages simultaneously to romanticize aspects of the past; his inter-est in feudal times, family history and heredity necessarily plunges him into the field of the Gothic, which was so vividly around him at the time that he wrote.

Bibliography

Johnson, Edgar 1970: *Sir Walter Scott: The Great Unknown*. 2 vols. New York: Macmillan.

Lockhart, John Gibson 1902: *Memoirs of the Life of Sir Walter Scott*, ed. Susan M. Francis. 5 vols. Boston: Houghton Mifflin.

Robertson, Fiona 1994: *Legitimate Histories: Scott, Gothic and the Authorities of Fiction*. Oxford: Clarendon Press.

MARY WOLLSTONECRAFT SHELLEY

(1797–1851)

Mary Shelley was the only child of two notable intellectual radicals, William Godwin (q.v.) and the pioneering feminist Mary Wollstonecraft, author of *A Vindication of the Rights of Woman* (1792), who died only eight days after her daughter's birth. Although Shelley is known primarily as the author of *Frankenstein* (q.v.), increasing critical attention is being directed to her other works. These include *Valperga; or, The Life and Adventures of Cas-truccio, Prince of Lucca* (1823), a historical romance set in fourteenth-century Italy that includes such Gothic elements as a gloomy castle (q.v.) full of secret passages, a witch, a Wandering Jew figure, and an albino dwarf; *The Last Man* (1926), an apocalyptic fantasy which follows Lionel Verney through a twenty-first-century world which has been depopulated by a plague; and the novella *Matilda*, written in 1819 but not published until 1959, which deals with father/daughter incest.

Perhaps of more importance for the Gothic, however, are Shelley's short stories, and while these stories, most of which were first published in the literary annuals of the time, were long neglected and dismissed by the critics, they too are increasingly the focus of critical attention because of their reworking of Gothic motifs and their connections with the more famous *Frankenstein*. 'The Mortal Immortal' (1833) is the story of an alchemist's apprentice that examines the meaning and consequences of immortality; 'Transformation' (1831) is a Gothic fairy tale that focuses upon a deformed, Satanic dwarf who exchanges identities with a vindictive and dissolute youth; and 'The Mourner' (1830) considers monstrosity, the double and family relationships. Two of Shelley's stories pursue the idea of the restoration of life. 'Roger Dodsworth: The Re-animated Englishman' (1826), based on a popular hoax about an alleged revival, is a rather comic tale of a man found in a glacier and reanimated; and the incomplete 'Valerius; the Reanimated Roman' considers the rebirth of a body without its soul. Many of these stories revise the motif of the double for the specific purpose of examining family relationships and re-evaluating the value and function of the domestic affections.

Bibliography

Bennett, Betty T. and Curran, Stuart (eds) 2000: *Mary Shelley in Her Times*. Baltimore, MD: Johns Hopkins University Press.

Fisch, Audrey A., Mellor, Anne and Schor, Esther (eds) 1993: *The Other Mary Shelley: Beyond Frankenstein*. Oxford: Oxford University Press.

Mellor, Anne 1988: *Mary Shelley: Her Life, Her Fiction, Her Monsters*. London: Methuen.

CHARLOTTE SMITH

(1740–1806)

Born into a prosperous family, Smith was 16 when she married Benjamin Smith, and within a few years found herself with a large family to support and an irresponsible husband in a debtor's prison. Although she had a decided preference for poetry, Smith's financial problems made it necessary to turn to the more profitable field of fiction. Her first novel, *Emmeline, the Orphan of the Castle* (1788), was received with enthusiasm, and this was followed by one novel a year for the next nine years. The degree to which these novels belong to the genre of the Gothic is sometimes debated; Diane Long Hoeveler, for example, describes *Emmeline* as 'a sentimental novel with a gothic novel buried within it struggling to emerge as a full-blown genre in its own right' (Hoeveler 1998: 38).

There is, however, no doubt that Smith exerted a significant influence on the development of the Gothic, and in particular on the works of Ann Radcliffe (q.v.) and her followers. There is, to begin with, the strategy of the explained supernatural. Smith disliked sensationalism, and the supernatural plays little role in her Gothic fiction. It is no sooner suggested than it is dismissed: such events as the appearance of a mysterious face in *The Old Manor House* (1793), for example, are quickly explained away. It would remain for Radcliffe to prolong such episodes and fully exploit their potential for creating suspense and terror. Smith had a strong interest in landscape and painting, and she was also influential in her use of sublime and picturesque settings, such as the Pyrenees in *Celestina* (1791), to intensify emotion. The pursuit and persecution of the heroine against such a backdrop, first introduced by Smith, would become a standard motif in many of the Gothic romances that followed.

Bibliography

Fry, Carrol L. 1996: *Charlotte Smith*. New York: Twayne.
Hoeveler, Diane Long 1998: *Gothic Feminism: The Professionalization of Gender from Charlotte Smith to the Brontës*. University Park: Pennsylvania State University Press.

ROBERT LOUIS STEVENSON
(1850–1894)

Scottish novelist, poet and essayist, Stevenson is best known for his children's classic, *Treasure Island* (1883), and for *The Strange Case of Dr Jekyll and Mr Hyde* (q.v.), sometimes dismissed by Stevenson himself as a 'shilling shocker' or 'Gothic gnome', but certainly the most famous and influential story of the double ever written. Much of his work, including the melodrama *Deacon Brodie, or The Double Life* (1880), written with W. E. Henley, and his finest Scottish historical novel, *The Master of Ballantrae* (1889), reveals its essentially Scottish origins in a Calvinist feeling for the immediacy of evil, and a sense of man's darker, divided self which goes back to James Hogg's *The Private Memoirs and Confessions of a Justified Sinner* (qq.v.).

Stevenson also wrote several other tales of horror and the supernatural – or 'crawlers' as he called them – in addition to *Jekyll and Hyde*, and here too the duality of human nature is a frequent concern. In 'Markheim' (1886), for example, a man who kills and begins to rob a pawnbroker is immediately haunted by a 'lump of terror' whose outlines begin to 'change and waver' while simultaneously showing 'a likeness to himself', while in 'The Tale of Tod Lapraik' (1893), an eerie figure dances on a deserted island while another figure, in the same likeness, sits at home in a trance, endlessly weaving and grinning.

Many of Stevenson's tales of terror reveal his interest in folk-lore and the superstitions and fears of the past. These tales include 'Thrawn Janet' (1881), primarily narrated in Scots dialect by an old villager and concerned with the events that led to the minister, Mr Soulis, becoming a fierce scourger of sinners in public and a 'scared' and 'uncertain' man in private. Stevenson travelled extensively, finally making his home in Samoa, and his last work, *Island Nights* (1893), is a collection of supernatural fantasies based on Samoan legends, including 'The Bottle Imp', a genie tale with a twist.

Bibliography

Bell, Ian 1995: *Dreams of Exile: Robert Louis Stevenson, a Biography*. New York: Holt.
Maixner, Paul 1981: *Robert Louis Stevenson: The Critical Heritage*. London: Routledge and Kegan Paul.

Bram Stoker
(1847–1912)

Novelist, biographer, critic, and manager of the actor Henry Irving, Stoker's reputation today rests primarily on *Dracula* (q.v.), the book that established the type of the vampire (q.v.) for future generations and produced one of the most enduring of all literary myths. In recent years Stoker's other Gothic fictions, *The Jewel of Seven Stars* (1903), *The Lady of the Shroud* (1909) and *The Lair of the White Worm* (1911), have attracted increasing critical attention. It would be fair to say, however, that none of these later works comes close to achieving the power of his most famous novel.

With *The Jewel of Seven Stars*, an orientalist Gothic tale, Stoker turns to the question of the powerful, often demonic woman – anticipated in *Dracula*'s Lucy – that would dominate his later works. The story concerns the attempt to resurrect the mummy of Tera, an Egyptian sorceress-queen, exploiting the traditional Gothic motif of the search for forbidden knowledge and reworking the double motif with the possession of the heroine, Margaret Trelawney, by the personality of her physical double, Tera. In *The Lady of the Shroud* Stoker returns to the theme of vampirism – although the female vampire is eventually revealed to be very much alive, and fully aware of the significance of, and able to exploit, the myths. *The Lair of the White Worm*, his last novel and admittedly a little incoherent in terms of plotting and characterization, is nevertheless the most compelling of these three works, and the evil Lady Arabella Marsh, the white worm of the title, is ultimately destroyed by the hero Adam Salton in a fabulously messy conclusion involving dynamite. The novel was given the tongue-in-cheek treatment it cried out for by director Ken Russell in 1988 (see 'Gothic Film'). Stoker also wrote a number of short stories of interest for the Gothic, including 'The Judge's House' (1891) and 'The Burial of the Rats' (1891), and his earlier collection of children's stories, *Under the Sunset* (1881), is full of dark and disturbing images of death, disease and monstrosity (q.v.) that interestingly anticipate many of the concerns of his later novels.

Bibliography

Belford, Barbara 1996: *Bram Stoker: A Biography of the Author of Dracula*. New York: Knopf.

Hughes, William 2000: *Beyond Dracula: Bram Stoker's Fiction and its Cultural Context*. London: Palgrave.

Hughes, William and Smith, Andrew (eds) 1998: *Bram Stoker: History, Psychoanalysis and the Gothic*. Houndmills: Macmillan.

HORACE WALPOLE

(1717–1797)

Born on 24 September 1717, Horace Walpole was the third son of the Whig politician Sir Robert Walpole, prime minister from 1721 to 1742. Best known as the author of what is usually considered the first Gothic novel, *The Castle of Otranto* (q.v.), Horace Walpole was also partly responsible for the eighteenth-century Gothic architectural (q.v.) revival. In 1749, after a summer spent visiting and studying ruins, churches and old houses, Walpole determined to reconstruct his home, Strawberry Hill, in the Gothic style. Over the following years, he doubled the size of the building, adding battlements, pinnacles, a gallery, a cloister and two towers, and filling it with art objects and rare books. It was here that he had the dream which supposedly inspired Otranto, a dream of a gigantic hand in armour resting on a banister – 'a very natural dream', Walpole wrote, 'for a head filled like mine with Gothic story'.

A rather preposterous and melodramatic story full of supernatural machinery, *Otranto* was, upon publication, interpreted by many as a burlesque – and it is admittedly easy to see why. By the 1790s, however, its significance as the originator of a new genre had become clear. As the critic Thomas Matthias complained in *The Pursuit of Literature* (1796), Walpole's 'Otranto Ghosts have . . . propagated their species with unequalled fecundity. The spawn is in every novel shop.'

Walpole was also responsible for the first Gothic drama, *The Mysterious Mother* (1768), a tragedy set in the period before the Reformation. Only fifty copies of the play were produced, on Walpole's private printing press at Strawberry Hill, and circulated amongst his friends. This limited circulation was apparently due to the possible impropriety of the subject matter. The mysterious mother of the title, the Countess of Narbonne, not only has an incestuous relationship with her unknowing son, but also deliberately plans the incest when overcome by passion caused by his close resemblance to his dead father. Her son, whom she subsequently exiles, returns and marries Adeliza, the result of the incestuous union, and the Countess, upon discovering the marriage of her children, kills herself. *The Mysterious Mother* is attracting increasing attention from the critics and can be said to show a significant advance on *Otranto*. From the rather ludicrous and laughable machinations of *Otranto*'s Manfred, Walpole moves to the tragic contemplation of

169

human desire and suffering, to a darker, more serious and more psychologically complex vision of what Edmund, in the closing speech of the drama, calls 'this theatre of monstrous guilt'.

Bibliography

Baines, Paul 1999: 'This Theatre of Monstrous Guilt: Horace Walpole and the Drama of Incest.' *Studies in Eighteenth-Century Culture*, 28, 287–309.
Clery, E. J. 2001: 'Horace Walpole's *The Mysterious Mother* and the Impossibility of Female Desire.' In Fred Botting (ed.), *The Gothic*. English Association *Essays and Studies*. Cambridge: Boydell and Brewer, 23–46.
Sabor, Peter (ed.) 1987: *Horace Walpole: The Critical Heritage*. London: Routledge.

H. G. WELLS
(1866–1946)

Herbert George Wells occupies a curious position in the history of Gothic writing. By conviction a secular humanist, and devoted to a number of radical causes, the strength of his belief in science frequently caused him to explore realms where rational explanation confronts the inexplicable, often with surprising results. Perhaps the outstanding example is *The Island of Doctor Moreau* (1896), a short novel apparently devoted to exposing the futility of trying to make animals into human beings by scientific – or quasi-scientific – means, but in fact producing some of the most enduring images of horror in the tradition.

Most of his many novels, however, have a more realist or satirical bent; it is mainly in his short stories that Wells's imagination gets the better of his rationalist convictions and the reader finds himself or herself entering strange worlds. The problems Wells confronts in these stories are the same as the ones that preoccupied him in his other works: the problems of human progress, of the justification of empire, of the nature of the bestial, of the return of the repressed. But the creatures he imagines in order to test these ideas – in, for example, 'The Empire of the Ants' (1905), 'In the Abyss' (1896), 'The Sea-Raiders' (1896) or 'The Valley of the Spiders' (1903) – are very much the material of fantasy.

Another group of stories, including 'The Crystal Egg' (1897), 'The Remarkable Case of Davidson's Eyes' (1895), 'The Flowering of the Strange

Orchid' (1894), 'The Moth' (1895) and 'Pollock and the Porroh Man' (1895), are essentially tales of hallucination (q.v.) and obsession; in 'The Moth', for example, the hallucination which afflicts and finally maddens the protagonist is directly the result of his obsession with a fellow entomologist, and what we see in this story is the way in which scientific rigour, when carried to its farthest extreme – as in *Frankenstein* (q.v.) – becomes psychologically ruinous. More directly Gothic, although at the same time providing an ironic commentary on the Gothic, is 'The Red Room' (1896); here the protagonist undertakes to spend a night in a haunted room, with frightening results, but it turns out that what he has been frightened by is not some identifiable manifestation, but rather fear itself.

Bibliography

Bergonzi, Bernard (ed.) 1976: *H. G. Wells: A Collection of Critical Essays.* Englewood Cliffs, NJ: Prentice-Hall.

Morton, Peter R. 1976: 'Biological Degeneration: A Motif in H. G. Wells and Other Late Victorian Utopianists.' *Southern Review*, 9, 93–112.

Parrinder, Patrick 1977: *H. G. Wells.* New York: Putnam.

EDITH WHARTON

(1862–1937)

Like her one-time mentor Henry James, Edith Wharton experimented with the Gothic and wrote a number of psychological ghost stories at the same time as establishing herself as a literary realist and an astute and ironic commentator on American society. Recent critics have begun to identify a Gothic strain even within such apparently realist works as *The House of Mirth* (1905) and *The Age of Innocence* (1920). The 'Gothic spirit, pushed to its logical conclusion', Wharton wrote in *A Motor-Flight Through France* (1908), aims for the 'utterance of the unutterable', and in her realist novels, Gothic becomes the vehicle through which attention is focused on the darker secrets hidden by the constraints of social structures. As she observes in her 1937 preface to *Ghosts*, what ghosts need to exist are 'not echoing passages and hidden doors behind tapestry, but only continuity and silence'. Her doomed heroine Lily Bart is not the only Wharton character to discover that the 'house of mirth' is haunted by loneliness and deception.

Wharton's short and restrained supernatural stories, like her more realist novels, frequently dramatize a particularly female perspective. In 'The Lady's Maid's Bell' (1904), Wharton's first ghost story, Alice Hartley becomes maid to the victimized Mrs Brympton; wanting but unable to help, Alice is given some direction from her dark double, the ghost of the previous maid, Emma Saxon. Although it is clearly implied that it involves sexuality, the exact nature of the secret of the house and the marriage is never revealed. Mrs Brympton suffers silently, and Emma never speaks, leaving Alice to 'carry the weight of the secret I couldn't guess'. The terrors that they experience but cannot share transforms all the women into ghosts, and here, as in so many of her other tales, Wharton appropriates the supernatural mode to show the silent terrors of marriage and the horrors that may be found within the house.

Bibliography

Carpenter, Lynette and Kolmar, Wendy K. (eds) 1991: *Haunting the House of Fiction: Feminist Perspectives on Ghost Stories by American Women*. Knoxville, TN: University of Tennessee Press.

Dyman, Jenni 1996: *Lurking Feminism: The Ghost Stories of Edith Wharton*. New York: Peter Lang.

Fedorko, Kathy A. 1995: *Gender and the Gothic in the Fiction of Edith Wharton*. Tuscaloosa: University of Alabama Press.

OSCAR WILDE
(1854–1900)

Oscar Wilde's principal claims to fame today probably rest upon, first, the extraordinary and continuing symbolic resonance of his short life and disastrous fate and, second, the continual procession of performances of his two most famous plays, *Lady Windermere's Fan* (1892) and *The Importance of Being Earnest* (1895). However, Wilde's talents were various, and despite the high comedy of his drama it is possible to trace a Gothic tendency through the darker of his stories (particularly 'Lord Arthur Savile's Crime' [1887]) and 'fairy-tales' ('The Birthday of the Infanta' [1888] and 'The Fisherman and his Soul' [1891], for example), to what many critics have regarded as a Gothic masterpiece, *The Picture of Dorian Gray* (1890, rev. 1891).

What runs through these examples is a strong sense of crime and punishment. Wilde was distantly related to Charles Robert Maturin (q.v.), from whose *Melmoth the Wanderer* (q.v.) it is sometimes said Wilde lifted the central motif of *Dorian Gray*, and through these darker works there runs something of the earlier writer's sense of the inevitability of divine judgement. In Wilde, however, these matters are complicated; he famously said that art had nothing whatever to do with morality, and thus it is not always quite clear what his characters are being punished *for*. In *Dorian Gray*, to take a major example, the eponymous hero does indeed commit appalling crimes – or at least so we are led to believe, since they are described in little detail – but whether this is the result of an innate flaw in his nature or of his exploitation by an older and more worldly character is never fully resolved.

Gothic, however, has since the beginning dealt in the corruption of the flesh and the distortion of beauty, and thus *Dorian Gray* occupies to some extent familiar terrain. What gives it its strength is the intensity of Wilde's concentration on the single – or rather, more precisely, double – image of Gray and his portrait, the one remaining apparently youthful while the other spectacularly disintegrates, until the denouement when it is demonstrated that it is impossible, however hard one tries, to escape the vengeance implicit in the idea of the *Doppelgänger*.

Bibliography

Ellmann, Richard (ed.) 1966: *Oscar Wilde: A Collection of Critical Essays. Twentieth-Century Views.* Englewood Cliffs, NJ: Prentice-Hall.

Oates, Joyce Carol 1980: '*The Picture of Dorian Gray*: Wilde's Parable of the Fall.' *Critical Inquiry*, 7, 419–28.

Poteet, Lewis 1971: '*Dorian Gray* and the Gothic Novel.' *Modern Fiction Studies*, 17, 239–48.

Key Works

HORACE WALPOLE,

THE CASTLE OF OTRANTO

(1764)

Horace Walpole is a doubly important figure in terms of the Gothic: not only did he play a significant role in the eighteenth-century Gothic revival in architecture (q.v.), he also produced what is usually considered the founding text of Gothic fiction, *The Castle of Otranto*, first published in 1764. Drawing upon the authenticating device of the discovered manuscript already common in eighteenth-century fiction, it purported to be a medieval work by one 'Onuphrio Muralto' and translated from the Italian by 'William Marshall, Gent.', who presents it in the preface as a piece of Catholic propaganda. When the book sold out in three months, Walpole, encouraged by the public's enthusiastic response, produced a second edition in April 1765, adding both a new preface admitting his authorship and the subtitle 'A Gothic Story'.

The prefaces to these two editions are considered as significant to the originating moment of Gothic fiction as the text itself. If the first preface looks back to the past through the pretence of the discovered manuscript, the second preface combines a gesture towards the past with strong claims for innovation (Clery 1995). For much of the seventeenth and early eighteenth centuries the term 'Gothic' had been used pejoratively as a synonym for the barbaric and the primitive. By the 1750s, however, there was a new interest in and re-evaluation of the idea of the Gothic. Such writers as Richard Hurd in *Letters on Chivalry and Romance* (1762) had begun to argue for a more positive reading of the Gothic age which, precisely because of its more primitive nature, had allowed for more imaginative invention than the rational and civilized present (see 'Gothic in the Eighteenth Century'). Walpole, whose interest in the Gothic had prompted him to transform his home at Strawberry Hill into a miniature Gothic castle, makes a similar point in the preface to his second edition. His aim, as outlined in a manifesto for a new kind of writing, was to combine features of the two kinds of romance, the ancient and the modern. In the former all was imagination and improbability: in the latter nature is always intended to be, and sometimes has been, copied with success. Invention has not been wanting; but the great resources of fancy have been dammed up, by a strict adherence to common life.

The 'new route he has struck out', he hopes, 'shall have paved a road for men of brighter talents'. By the 1790s his influence had indeed resulted in a flourishing school of what was then usually referred to as 'terrorist fiction' or 'modern romance'. The name eventually given to this type of fiction, however, 'the Gothic novel', far more precisely captures the conflicting impulses underlying the originating moment of the genre: to return to the past and to create something new.

Set in a southern Italian principality during the time of the Crusades, *The Castle of Otranto* tells the story of the tyrant Manfred, prince of Otranto. Fearing an enigmatic prophecy which states 'That the castle and lordship of Otranto should pass from the present family, whenever the real owner should be grown too large to inhabit it', Manfred attempts to ensure his line by marrying his only son, Conrad, to Isabella, the daughter of Frederick, marquis of Vicenza. His plans, however, are quite startlingly thwarted when, during the marriage ceremony, Conrad is crushed to death by a huge helmet that, as a young man later identified as Theodore observes, closely re-sembles that belonging to the nearby statue of Alfonso the Good in the Church of St Nicholas. Manfred, enraged by the discovery Alfonso's helmet is missing, blames Theodore for the event and imprisons him beneath the helmet. Undeterred by the death of his son, however, he resolves to ensure a new heir by divorcing his wife Hippolita and marrying the very unwilling Isabella himself.

The appearance of the disconcertingly large helmet is the first of many supernatural occurrences in the novel. A statue bleeds from the nose; a massive armour-clad foot appears in the gallery and an arm on the stairs; an ancestor in a portrait sighs, hops out of his frame, and walks away. While *Otranto* may have been an attempt to combine the fantastical elements of the old romances with the naturalistic features of the modern novel, it is the fantastical elements that predominate. Walpole's supernatural effects have, from the start, frequently been dismissed as ludicrous and self-indulgent. As Clara Reeve (q.v.) complained in the preface to her *The Old English Baron*, it might be possible to accept an enchanted sword, but not one requiring a hundred men to lift it. Admittedly, none of the many supernatural occur-rences appears particularly believable or designed to induce feelings of fear or terror. What is important for the later development of the Gothic, however, is the way the supernatural comes to represent the past, whether psychological or historical, rising up to assert its power within the present.

Equally influential were Walpole's character types – the tyrannical Manfred, a prototype for the Gothic hero-villain, his victimized wife, the bland hero and the selfless, passive heroine. However, while Walpole declares his intention of having his characters 'think, speak and act, as it might be supposed mere men and women would do in extraordinary positions', these characters have attracted as much criticism as his supernatural effects and frequently been dismissed as superficial and wooden. But while the realist novel aims to produce the effect of psychological depth, some critics argue, the Gothic emphasis on surfaces functions to suggest how subjectivity is not so much a matter of inner depths as one of public interpretation. Other critics suggest that the emotions of characters in Gothic fiction are externalized through such things as supernatural phenomena and inanimate objects: in *Otranto* it is possible to see how architecture, the labyrinthine and claustrophobic spaces of castles (q.v.), monasteries, ruins and prisons, will come to serve an important function in suggesting such emotions as fear and helplessness. When Isabella flees from Manfred though the subterranean vaults of the castle, for example, her flight introduces a motif that will repeatedly recur in subsequent Gothic fiction. The castle has even been seen as the primary protagonist of *Otranto*; all the events take place either within or near it, and its physical presence dominates the text, creating a sense of oppression that emphasizes the powerlessness of the characters to control their own lives.

Walpole's thematic concerns also had a great influence on later Gothic fiction, in particular his focus on issues of succession and inheritance. Supernatural forces emerge here primarily in order to effect the restoration of Otranto to its rightful owner, and although the plot involves numerous complications, it nevertheless moves swiftly towards this resolution. After helping Isabella escape, Theodore is recaptured and Manfred threatens his life. Manfred is stopped by Friar Jerome, and Theodore is subsequently revealed to be Jerome's son, and Jerome the count of Falconara. A troop of knights bearing the colours of Isabella's family then arrives, carrying a gigantic sword of proportions corresponding to the helmet, and, suspicious of Manfred, they join in the search for Isabella. Meanwhile Theodore has escaped with the help of Manfred's daughter Matilda. He finds Isabella in a labyrinth of caverns, and, thinking he is defending her honour, injures a knight who turns out to be her father, Frederic. They return to the castle, where Theodore and Matilda, greatly attracted to each other, are found in the chapel by Manfred. Mistaking his daughter for Isabella, he stabs and kills her, thus, with two children now dead, demonstrating how, as pointed out by the fictional translator in the first preface, 'the sins of fathers are visited on their children'. With the death of Matilda, there is a clap of thunder and the walls of the castle collapse, suggesting the final disintegration of Manfred's line. The immense form of Alfonso appears: all the supernatural pieces of armour have now come together, and this process of reconstruction replicates the restoration of the true line of inheritance. Theodore is established as the rightful heir of Otranto and Manfred revealed to have inherited the title only through the treachery of his grandfather, who poisoned Alfonso and forged a will: both he and Hippolita are despatched to neighbouring convents. A 'new' social order is consequently produced, not through revolutionary means but through the reinstatement of the rightful and uncorrupted dynastic line.

In its concern with property and ownership *Otranto* is not just looking backwards to a feudal order but also offering a complex engagement with modern aristocratic ideology. The legitimacy of the aristocracy's political and economic domination was a crucial issue in a rapidly changing society marked by the growing economic importance of the bourgeoisie. While the restitution of the rightful dynastic line seems to support the notion of power and control on the basis of genealogy, this is nevertheless compromised, as E. J. Clery notes, 'by the violent means it uses to repair the damage' and the ways in which this relentless order is shown to be at odds with the desires of the characters themselves (1995: 73–4). No one appears particularly happy in the end: even Theodore remains bereft at the loss of Matilda and finds only small consolation in marrying Isabella, a woman 'with whom he could forever indulge the melancholy that had taken possession of his soul'. The demands of self and the demands of society are, as they will be in all the Gothic fictions that follow Walpole, shown to be irrevocably at odds.

Bibliography

Clery, E. J. 1995: *The Rise of Supernatural Fiction 1762–1800.* Cambridge: Cambridge University Press.

Hogle, Jerrold E. 1994: 'The Ghost of the Counterfeit in the Genesis of the Gothic.' In Allan Lloyd Smith and Victor Sage (eds), *Gothick: Origins and Innovations,* Amsterdam: Rodopi, 23–33.

Sabor, Peter (ed.) 1987: *Horace Walpole: The Critical Heritage.* London: Routledge.

Watt, Ian 1986: 'Time and Family in the Gothic Novel: *The Castle of Otranto.*' *Eighteenth Century Life* 10 (3), 159–71.

William Beckford,

VATHEK

(1786)

The publication history of William Beckford's *Vathek* is almost as bizarre as the tale itself. Originally written in French, the work was translated into English by Samuel Henley while Beckford was still in the process of completing a series of episodes he wished to add, stories related by some of the damned in the Hall of Eblis. To Beckford's annoyance, Henley published his English translation in 1786 without Beckford's knowledge or approval, and without any mention of his name. The preface, drawing upon the fiction of the discovered manuscript, proposes that the tale is a translation of an Arabian original, 'collected in the East by a Man of letters'. Of the episodes, two were eventually completed and the fragment of a third (there is a fourth but it is doubtful that it was written by Beckford). However, they were not published in French until 1909 and in English until 1912, while a full edition incorporating the episodes did not appear until 1929. To complicate matters even further, the original version of the first episode, which concerns the love between a young man and a boy, was suppressed, and the story was rewritten around a more 'acceptable' heterosexual relationship. The full version of *Vathek with the Episodes of Vathek*, with the original version of this first episode reinstated, was not published until 2001.

Like Horace Walpole (q.v.), Beckford was interested in reviving those elements of the imaginative and marvellous that had been lost as the realist novel assumed dominance. While Walpole looked to a European medieval past for *The Castle of Otranto* (q.v.), however, Beckford looked to the Orient. An interest in the Orient was initially stimulated during the eighteenth century by the publication of the first volume of Antoine Galland's translation of *Arabian Nights Entertainment* in 1704: in complete contrast to the rational realism favoured by the eighteenth century, the *Arabian Nights* offers a world of wonders where the supernatural repeatedly invades the realm of the natural. Scholarly works on the Orient and travel accounts also began to appear, and the first English translation of the Koran was published in 1734. The Oriental tale, exotically set in the Middle or Far East, soon followed – early British examples include Samuel Johnson's *Rasselas* (1759) and Frances Sheridan's *The History of Nourjahad* (1767). Although Beckford loosely gestures towards the didactic framework typical of these previous Oriental tales, he is far more interested in the transgressive excesses he relates: in *Vathek* he produces what is usually considered the first orientalist tale of terror.

The story concerns the Caliph Vathek, who builds five magnificent palaces, each devoted to the gratification of one of the senses. His unrestrained appetites in the pursuit of pleasure are not presented in entirely disapproving terms, since they are the result of a belief that it was not 'necessary to make a hell of this world to enjoy paradise in the next'. Vathek's main fault is that he is 'of all men . . . the most curious', and desires 'to know every thing; even sciences that did not exist'. He is an overreacher; it is not his palaces of the senses that anger Mahomet, but the high tower he builds in the hope of penetrating the secrets of the heavens. Tempted by the wondrous gifts and promises of a grotesque stranger, the Giaour, Vathek soon makes a Faustian pact, abjures Mahomet, and sets off for the ruined city of Istakar, where he is told the treasures and powers of the pre-Adamite sultans await him.

Vathek's desire for knowledge, for metaphysical truths, is repeatedly equated with physical hunger and thirst. On the second of the three times he is shown ascending his tower, for example, 'instead of the visions he expected, he had acquired in these unsubstantial regions a voracious appetite'. He is, however, denied food by his mother Carathis, who, attended by her fifty one-eyed, mute black women and numerous eunuchs, is engaged in some of her characteristically unspeakable rites involving skeletons, mummies and venomous oils. Vathek consequently abandons himself 'to grief and the wind that ravaged his entrails'. Repeatedly, his attempts to reach beyond human limitations are deflated by the irruption of the physical. While *Vathek* could be basically described as a Faustian story placed within an oriental setting, it is also, more complexly, a tale of terror with a decidedly comic twist.

A particular concern of many has been the puzzling narrative voice: the tone throughout most of the text is coolly sardonic, and even the most horrific events are related with ironic reserve and understatement. When Carathis needs directions en route to Vathek, for example, she summons up ghouls and offers the dead bodies of her guides to tempt their appetites. Ghouls 'on all sides, protruded their noses to inhale the effluvia, which the carcasses of the woodmen began to emit' and finally assemble before Carathis. She receives them 'with distinguished politeness' and, Beckford adds, 'supper being ended, they talked of business'. Beckford repeatedly offsets the horror with deflating conventional expression, and the ludicrous and the horrific become disturbingly fused.

Kenneth Graham (1978) offers one possible explanation for this strange fusion when he suggests that Beckford is working primarily in the mode of the grotesque. The grotesque, in a general sense, violates the laws of nature; visually, it is a world where classifications break down, resulting in an inherent tension between the ludicrous and the fearful. The text is full of physical grotesques, most notably the Giaour, who is 'so abominably hideous that the very guards, who arrested him, were forced to shut their eyes, as they led him along', but the grotesque also repeatedly emerges within human behaviour, as in the case of Carathis and the ghouls. It suggests disorder at both the physical and moral levels of existence, and it is part of the chaos of the human condition that appears to be replicated even within Beckford's narrative style.

The tone changes quite strikingly, however, when Vathek and Nouronihar, the emir's daughter whom he has seduced and who accompanies him on his travels, finally reach the Hall of Eblis. Beckford's Eblis, chief of the fallen angels in Muslim mythology, is clearly a reworked version of Milton's Satan, and his Hall is reminiscent of Dante's Inferno. Now the sublime predominates, with its suggestions of a powerful and mysterious order and unity, and is set in opposition to the grotesque vision of chaos and disorder that defines the human world. Vathek and Nouronihar wander from 'hall to hall; and gallery to gallery; all without bounds, or limit' until finally their hearts burst into flame and they are condemned to 'an eternity of unabating anguish'.

The primary theme of *Vathek*, and indeed of the episodes, appears to be that of the alienated individual rebelling against limitations, whether these are imposed by social institutions or are the product of the human condition itself. Such individualism is ultimately punished, in the Hall of Eblis, by the damned being condemned to absolute isolation in the midst of a multitude of others. All remaining human attachments and affections are lost as they recoil from each other in horror: 'Vathek beheld in the eyes of Nouronihar nothing but rage and vengeance; nor could she discern aught in his, but aversion and despair.' The tale ends with the pronouncement of the official moral: this is the punishment for 'unrestrained passions', 'atrocious deeds', 'blind curiosity' and 'restless ambition'; 'the condition of man upon earth is to be', we are assured, 'humble and ignorant'.

After all the excesses of the text – not just in the characters' behaviour but in Beckford's writing – the moral seems notably unconvincing, and it tends to be subverted in various other ways. In the sublime Hall of Eblis it may seem quite appropriate that the condition of man is to be humble and ignorant and not strive for knowledge 'reserved for beings of a supernatural order'. However, this never appears quite so clear or straightforward in the grotesque world of the human. On the one hand, the constant deflation of Vathek's metaphysical endeavours by the irruption of the all too physical may indeed confirm the need to accept human limitation. On the other hand, however, it is precisely this constant deflation which suggests there is a need to try to transcend human limitation. Furthermore, the offering of the amoral and childishly innocent Gulchenrouz, Nouronihar's old playmate, as the ultimate example of the good in the last lines of the novel completely undercuts any remaining authority the conclusion might have. To be condemned like Gulchenrouz to 'whole ages in undisturbed tranquillity, and in the pure happiness of childhood' does not appear to be a totally desirable alternative to endless agony in the Hall of Eblis.

Bibliography

Graham, Kenneth W. 1978: 'Implications of the Grotesque: Beckford's *Vathek* and the Boundaries of Fictional Reality.' *Tennessee Studies in Literature*, 23, 61–74.

Graham, Kenneth W. (ed.) 1990: *Vathek and the Escape From Time: Bicentenary Revaluations*. New York: AMS Press.

Potkay, Adam 1993: 'Beckford's Heaven of Boys.' *Raritan*, 13, 73–86.

Roberts, Adam and Robertson, Eric 1996: 'The Giaour's Sabre: A Reading of Beckford's *Vathek.*' *Studies in Romanticism*, 35, 199–211.

Ann Radcliffe,

THE MYSTERIES OF UDOLPHO

(1794)

The Mysteries of Udolpho, while not literally the first of the major Gothic novels, is nevertheless to all intents and purposes the classic example of the genre, the *fons et origo* of much of what comes after it, and perhaps still the best-known novel from the first wave of late eighteenth-century Gothic (q.v.). It relates an essentially simple narrative, fundamentally a unitary story structured round the experience of a single character, Emily St Aubert, who lives at the beginning of the book in idyllic peace at the chateau of La Vallée in Gascony with her parents. In the year 1584 her mother dies and, after a sudden decline and a lengthy journey made for recuperative purposes, her father follows, leaving Emily in distressing financial circumstances and at the mercy of her father's unprepossessing sister, Madame Cheron. Emily has met a youth named Valancourt, with whom she has fallen in love, and while at Toulouse under Cheron's care their courtship is, for purely financial reasons, encouraged; however, Cheron herself marries a sinister Italian nobleman called Montoni, and Emily is consequently whisked away from potential happiness, first to Venice, where she is almost married against her wishes to one Count Morano, and then to Montoni's splendidly and emblematically decaying castle (q.v.) in the Apennines, Udolpho, in which she is effectually imprisoned during the central and most memorable part of the book.

It is one of the principal marks of Ann Radcliffe's skill and delicacy of treatment that the many and terrifying dangers which threaten Emily while at Udolpho are never made entirely clear. At one point, it seems to be forced marriage, at another rape, at another the theft of her remaining estates, at another supernatural terrors; but none of these actually comes to pass. Eventually, after many nights of fear and after her aunt has met a fate which the reader cannot altogether regret, Emily escapes to a further chateau, Le Blanc, which proves to have sinister connections with her own family and a cast of ghosts of its own. These, however, are duly exposed, as were the phantoms of Udolpho, and Emily rediscovers Valancourt; he conveniently repents of the moral decline which has overtaken him since their parting, and the lovers are married.

Despite the brilliant and justly praised use of suspense techniques, there are certain problems in the narrative, which were commented on at the time. The incidents at Le Blanc are rather pallid beside the richly coloured and terrifying Udolpho scenes, and it could be said that Radcliffe fails in her apparent design of using them to show how Emily has recovered from the over-credulity which has caused her so much misery earlier – the exposure of this over-credulity indeed seeming to be a large part of the moral of the tale. The removal of the almost superhuman and certainly melodramatic figure of Montoni from the action, and his subsequent death, leave a regrettable space which is never filled; and the attempt to introduce the Villefort family as a further centre of narrative interest is too cursory to succeed. But the strengths of *Udolpho* are less to do with suspense or narrative than in other areas. It is in her character psychology, her use of symbols to intensify the action, and the extraordinary use of suspicion and doubt, which constantly blur the boundaries of reality and fantasy, that Radcliffe sets the course for the future of Gothic. In terms of character, not only is Montoni an excellent, sometimes subtle, and to an extent innovatory (although he certainly looks back to precursors in Jacobean drama) version of the attractively cruel villain, but Emily herself, although she emerges as a highly conventional eighteenth-century heroine, is depicted clearly and in tremulous, moment-by-moment detail. In accordance with emergent Gothic tradition, her fearful plight is continually referred back to other stories and legends of cruelty and murder which lurk, half-told and threatening, in the background: the mysterious disappearance of the former owner of Udolpho, the murder of the marchioness de Villeroi, the fate of Madame Cheron herself, are interesting not merely in themselves but also for the terrifying parallels they offer to the various dooms which Emily barely avoids. An example of this kind of symbolic intensification occurs in a scene at Le Blanc where the servant Ludovico, locked for a night in a haunted room, reads a ghost story which eventually shades into 'reality'; the celebrated fact that Radcliffe in the end explains all her apparently supernatural machinery in no way removes the power which her ghosts have over Emily, or over the reader during the course of the book.

There is a significant point, halfway through the second book, when Emily is on the eve of being married to the undesirable Morano: alone, friendless, fearful of the malignity of Montoni, 'her mind, long harassed by distress, now yielded to imaginary terrors; she trembled to look into the obscurity of her spacious chamber, and feared she knew not what'. It is possible to read the whole of the rest of the work as the nightmare which follows that eve of terror, as the poetic and symbolic correlative of the state of Emily's over-wrought imagination, and we might say, bearing in mind the whole drift of Gothic fiction, that no amount of last-minute 'explanation' can destroy the potency of dreams. The inhabitants of Udolpho and of its ominous sur-roundings may be ghosts, bandits or devils; to Emily they are the incarna-tion of evil, and their reality can only be read through the medium offered by her dislocated mind.

In part, then, *Udolpho* is an investigation into the prominent eighteenth-century concept of sensibility. Radcliffe points out very early in the novel that Emily is possessed of 'a degree of susceptibility too exquisite to admit of lasting peace', and it is this quivering sensitivity which continually prostrates here before spectres which, the reader increasingly feels, are of her own imagining. Sensibility, Radcliffe suggests along with other early Gothic writers, is incompatible with the general fabric of social activity. A typical scene occurs when Emily, treated to a harangue by Madame Cheron, decides by means of her acute perceptions that Cheron's 'misfortunes did not admit of real consolation' and does not bother to reply. Cheron, perhaps understandably piqued by this lack of response, becomes even angrier: 'O! I suspected what all this boasted sensibility would prove to be!', she says, 'I thought it would not teach you to feel either duty, or affection, for your rela-tions, who have treated you like their own daughter!' This is, of course, a misunderstanding, but it is one which recurs again and again, for Emily's sen-sibility does in fact render her incapable of the gross and rapid responses nec-essary to active social participation, and sinks her more and more dangerously into the world of her overstimulated imagination.

The positive side of sensibility, upon which Radcliffe dwells more than does her contemporary M. G. Lewis (q.v.), is represented by its visionary quality, which is at its height in the character of Emily. Her many visions clearly show that the strength of the sensitive individual is in terms of her inner life, and that sensibility allows and encourages this to expand at the expense of communicative contact. But it is precisely because of this that Emily's perceptions of the *real* world go sadly amiss, as when, for instance, she continually imagines her fellow prisoner at Udolpho to be Valancourt. There is not the slightest reason why it should be Valancourt, except that this would fit into Emily's vision of life; and, of course, it turns out that it is indeed not Valancourt.

It is also sensibility which lays the individual open to the inroads of 'superstition', and here we come with Radcliffe to one of the crucial contradictions of Gothic writing. There is a fine irony in the text from *Julius Caesar* with which Radcliffe prefaces one of her chapters: 'I think it is the weakness of mine eyes, / That shapes this monstrous apparition. / It comes upon me!' But the implicit question raised is never answered, for although Emily is indeed prey to 'imaginary terrors' she is also assailed by real difficulties, while it is the Gothic villain Montoni who is allowed to hold the balanced and reasonable view of superstition: 'I am not superstitious', he says at one point, 'though I know how to despise the commonplace sentences, which are frequently uttered against superstition.' The reader may well spend the whole book hoping that Emily will come to a similar position, but she never really does. When Radcliffe says, quite late in the book, that Emily 'now sunk, for a moment, under the weakness of superstition', it is difficult to know what the reader is meant to think, for this is what she has already been doing for 500 pages.

In a sense, it cannot be doubted that Emily forges her own shackles: 'she looked upon Count Morano with horror', we read,

> but apart from him, a conviction, if such that may be called, which arises from no proof, and which she knew not how to account for, seized her mind – that she would never see Valancourt again. Though she knew, that neither Morano's solicitations, not Montoni's commands had lawful power to enforce her obedience, she regarded both with a superstitious dread, that they would finally prevail.

The end-point of these doubts, as many critics have said, is a kind of madness, the dislocation of the mind under pressures that cannot even be accurately categorized as internal or external. Emily blames herself 'for suffering her romantic imagination to carry her so far beyond the bounds of probability, and determined to endeavour to check its rapid flights, lest they should sometimes extend into madness', but in the end what Radcliffe demonstrates is that the entire process of sensibility, and the advocacy of it as a female 'accomplishment', is bound to end in a world of ghosts and terrors from which mere rational 'explanation' can provide no real salvation.

Bibliography

Miall, David S. 2000: 'The Preceptor as Fiend: Radcliffe's Psychology of the Gothic.' In Laura Dabundo (ed.), *Jane Austen and Mary Shelley and their Sisters.* Lanham, MD: University Presses of America, 31–43.

Miles, Robert 1995: *Ann Radcliffe: The Great Enchantress.* Manchester: Manchester University Press.

Norton, Rictor 1999: *Mistress of Udolpho: The Life of Ann Radcliffe.* London: Leicester University Press.

Townshend, Dale 2000: 'Constructions of Psychosis and Neurosis in Ann Radcliffe's *The Mysteries of Udolpho.*' *Pretexts: Literary and Cultural Studies,* 9 (2), 175–206.

William Godwin,

CALEB WILLIAMS

(1794)

William Godwin wrote six novels. *Things as They Are; or, the Adventures of Caleb Williams* is the only one still much read today, and it might initially be categorized as a work of 'political Gothic'. This is not to say that it falls within the rather different German Gothic political tradition, which hinges on dealings with the feudal past, for *Caleb Williams* is clearly set in the present; but it is deeply if somewhat ambivalently concerned with the problems of social interaction within a class-divided society, and with the injustice which that society is capable of meting out to the apparently innocent.

The plot centres on Caleb Williams, who, alone in the world, is taken on as secretary to a wealthy but reclusive squire with the pleasingly cosmopolitan name Ferdinando Falkland. Williams decides that Falkland is not all he seems and, from a motive of sheer curiosity, sets himself to discover Falkland's secret. Disastrously for Williams, he does so; an old retainer reveals that Falkland was once put on trial for the murder of an intolerably boorish neighbour named Tyrell, who had grossly insulted him, but was acquitted. By ceaseless vigilance and some remarkable strokes of luck, Williams establishes that Falkland did in fact commit the murder, but Falkland turns the tables on him by pointing out that Williams's knowledge of this secret means that he, Falkland, must keep him under his thumb for the rest of his life. Williams begins to realize the extreme peril of his situation and starts a long series of attempts, which take up the largest part of the book, to evade Falkland; but every step he takes plunges him further into the toils of misery and persecution (q.v.), Falkland's power of retaliation increasingly appearing to be infinite. Williams is propelled from humiliation to prison to temporary exile, and everywhere Falkland and his minions contrive to ruin his reputation and blast his hopes. In the end, desperate, he manages to persuade the authorities of the truth of his story, only to suffer a terrible agony of guilt at ruining Falkland, who, for all his past crimes, none the less still curiously appears to Williams as a model of nobility.

The story is extremely meticulously, even mechanically, planned; indeed, Godwin is known for, apparently, having thought of the pursuit situation first and only afterwards invented a series of events to provoke it. The last part of the book in particular moves from the effect of a received manuscript into almost direct speech in a startling fashion, making the reader feel very strongly the imminent closing in of the book's maleficent forces. It has been said that part of the concentrated power of the text stems from Godwin's intellectualism, yet this is true only in certain respects. The *plan* of the book certainly appears to work on directly Godwinian principles, according to the dictates of reason rather than of the imagination, and it has also been suggested that *Caleb Williams* is the first novel in the language without an overt love interest; but the abstractness of the text is not, in fact, that of a cold intellectual system but rather that of a world which operates according to its own immutable and barbaric – in other words, in certain respects Gothic – laws, a world in which characters find themselves for the most part far away from the reassurances of reason and instead oscillate between the most violent extremes of passion. On one occasion when Williams seems near to discovering the secret of Falkland's guilt, Falkland's behaviour is described in a way that might be considered to be at the opposite extreme from the reasonable: 'He left his employment, strode about the room in anger, his visage gradually assumed an expression as of supernatural barbarity, he quitted the apartment abruptly, and flung the door with a violence that seemed to shake the house.'

This might well remind the reader of the uncivilized manners of the average Gothic villain, and indeed the phrase 'supernatural barbarity' well summarizes the treatment that the servant Williams fears, and in part receives, at Falkland's hands. 'What was it', he expostulates at one point, 'that fate had yet in reserve for me? The insatiable vengeance of a Falkland, of a man whose hands were, to my apprehension, red with blood, and his thoughts familiar with cruelty and murder. How great were the resources of his mind, resources henceforth to be confederated for my destruction!'

But then, it is difficult to know quite how far Williams's fears are justifiable, for Godwin begins, as do many other Gothic writers, by pointing out to us that both of his principal characters are afflicted by an interest in romance, that cast of mind so fatal to Ann Radcliffe's (q.v.) heroines. Caleb, in his youth, 'panted for the unravelling of an adventure with an anxiety, perhaps almost equal to that of the man whose future happiness or misery depended on its issue'. This susceptibility makes him a somewhat unreliable witness; while in the case of Falkland, the whole of his crime is attributed to his over-serious and archaic sense of honour, which Godwin also takes care to link with a Gothic love of chivalry and romance.

There are indeed points in the book where Godwin's rationalism comes over strongly, particularly in his extended disquisition on the evils of prison, which connects directly with his publicly known political priorities. He also shows us a band of 'philosophic banditti' and enters into great detail, reminiscent of earlier eighteenth-century models, about their arguments in favour of a life of crime, and about Williams's position on this. Godwin had a strong interest in criminal psychology, and it is difficult to think of a book in which a prison escape is described in such enormous detail. But on the whole, the world of *Caleb Williams* is a curiously distorted one; although Williams himself passes through many different scenes in the course of his flight, these pass like shadows, while Falkland – who in fact is rarely physically present in the text – possesses an overwhelming material reality for Williams which he is barely able to forget for an instant.

Godwin is very skilled at building up suspense; one way in which he does it is by constantly reminding us that the book is Williams's *present account of the past*: thus, while we are watching him flee across England at some past moment we are also hearing his present voice, fraught with the burden of his wasted years: 'I have not deserved this treatment. My own conscience witnesses in behalf of that innocence, my pretensions to which are regarded in the world as incredible.' In the first part of the book, Williams often holds out promises of horrors to come, horrors which all too strongly suggest 'supernatural barbarity', as 'the death-dealing mischief advances with an accelerated motion, appearing to defy human wisdom and strength to obstruct its operation'. For Falkland, through the eyes of Williams – and that is, of course, the reader's only vantage point – appears scarcely human. That is not to say that he is melodramatically evil or Satanic, but rather that, like so many Gothic figures, he is a creature who embodies total *will*. For Falkland, there is only the smallest of gaps between decision and operation: his conviction of the necessity of hounding and silencing Williams is sufficient to enable him, apparently, to disregard all laws of probability. This leaves Williams, understandably, at a loss for words: the 'catastrophe' he is about to relate, he says at one point, 'will be found pregnant with horror, beyond what the blackest misanthropy could readily have suggested'.

What Godwin has done in *Caleb Williams* is to attempt to set up a situation from which there is no escape, in which persecution by the enemy is unavoidable. But it is, of course, very hard if not impossible to do this within a realist framework, because such an extreme situation requires the removal of any possibility of the intrusion of luck, chance, the unexpected.

Falkland's methods, then, become even more effective and terrifying than those of the political state which he in some sense represents, which in turn means that the one cannot be exactly taken as a metaphor for the other. Although the kind of power Godwin is depicting of course has a connection with political power (and is, at crucial points of the story, sustained by the authorities), it is not in itself political power. It is better described as the power of subjection, and as such it operates partly through Williams's own consciousness, through his unintentional collaboration with the forces of persecution.

It is always impossible to establish objectivity within a first-person narrative. Williams certainly is persecuted, but we find ourselves as readers looking through the cracks in his account of the persecuting universe. In the first place, it is not true that his is the position of 'conscious innocence', as he puts it; his curiosity – one might call it spying – is arguably the prime cause of Falkland's actions. Also, there are occasions when Williams entirely mistakes Falkland's intentions towards him and conjures them into an over-malevolent form. And finally, Williams's feelings are clearly bound up in a kind of rejected love; through all his vicissitudes he bears with him a still, small acceptance of Falkland's tremendous worth, which, of course, renders his feelings all the more bitter as events develop. The crucial question, however, is whether we should decide on evidence of this kind that Williams himself is an exaggerator, given to misinterpreting and over-dramatizing his situation, or whether the informing consciousness behind the whole novel is transgressing realist conventions and producing a world of deliberately heightened dimensions, and on this point, characteristically of the Gothic, the text provides the reader with no definitive resolution.

Bibliography

Bender, John 1995: 'Impersonal Violence: The Penetrating Gaze and the Field of Narration in *Caleb Williams.*' In Stephen Melville and Bill Readings (eds.), *Vision and Textuality.* Durham, NC: Duke University Press, 256–81.

Cohen, Michael 1998: 'Godwin's *Caleb Williams:* Showing the Strains in Detective Fiction.' *Eighteenth-Century Fiction,* 10 (2), 203–20.

Edwards, Gavin 2000: 'William Godwin's Foreign Language: Stories and Families in *Caleb Williams* and *Political Justice.*' *Studies in Romanticism,* 39 (4), 511–31.

Mucke, Dorothea von 1996: ' "To Love a Murderer": Fantasy, Sexuality and the Political Novel: The Case of *Caleb Williams.*' In Deirdre Lynch and William B. Warner (eds), *Cultural Institutions of the Novel.* Durham, NC: Duke University Press, 306–34.

Walsh, Cheryl 1998: 'Truth, Prejudice and the Power of Narrative in *Caleb Williams.*' *English Language Notes,* 35 (4), 22–38.

M. G. LEWIS,

THE MONK

(1796)

The Monk was written by Matthew Lewis when he was only 20, and while he was simultaneously beginning a political and diplomatic career for which he had been destined by reason of birth and wealth. It rapidly became acknowledged as the most scandalous of the early Gothic novels, on the grounds of the explicitness of its violent and especially its sexual scenes. It was strongly influenced by early German Gothic models, but although Lewis permits himself a great degree of licence in the description of violence and lust, he shows little explicit involvement with the politically radical content of the German terror-novels. *The Monk* also looks back to Shakespeare and Milton, although its use of such forebears is very much less skilful than, for example, in the case of Ann Radcliffe (q.v.).

The Monk is two stories in one and, although there sometimes seems little connection between them, their co-presence gives Lewis scope for a series of dramatic alternations which give the book a pace and energy quite foreign to the far more leisurely procedures of Radcliffe. The major story concerns the monk Ambrosio, a paragon of virtue and famous throughout Madrid for his powerful, 'sublime' sermons. His closest associate in the abbey, apparently a young and virtuous novice, reveals himself to be a woman, Matilda by name, and proceeds to seduce him, a deed which releases Ambrosio's pent-up passions and sets him on a course of violence and self-destruction. Dissatisfied with Matilda, he sets about seducing a young and naïve girl called Antonia, whereupon Matilda, to his surprise, proves capable of offering him supernatural assistance, which he accepts, albeit with initial reluctance. The scheme, however, goes wrong and Ambrosio murders the girl's mother to prevent her from publicly revealing his true character. With further demonic help from Matilda, however, Ambrosio carries Antonia off, apparently dead, to a crypt where, on her awakening, he savagely rapes her.

The second story, which is intertwined with this, is of two lovers, Raymond and Agnes. Agnes is destined from birth to enter a convent, although she increasingly dislikes the idea. By various stratagems her relatives manage to discourage her from her plans of eloping with Raymond and persuade her to take the veil. Raymond finds her in Madrid, in the convent adjoining Ambrosio's, and convinces her that he has been misrepresented; in the course of the surreptitious meetings they hold to discuss the possibility of escape, she becomes pregnant. The abbess of the convent – abetted by Ambrosio, whom she wants to impress – determines to make an example of her and subjects her to a hideous imprisonment; Raymond finds her, and she is rescued amid a bloodbath of popular anti-clerical violence during which the abbess is torn to pieces and her convent sacked. The rescuers of Agnes also find Ambrosio in the vaults with the corpse of Antonia, whom he has now murdered, and he is captured and brought before the Inquisition. Matilda, who has been captured with him, succeeds in tempting him to complete his pact with the Devil by selling his soul in exchange for freedom, whereupon Satan, with predictable jocularity, cheats him and brings him to a horrible death.

Unlike Radcliffe, Lewis makes no excuses for the supernatural, and indeed near the end of the book he even suggests that Matilda has been a demon all along, although this interpretation is not supported by much of the earlier part of the novel. Interwoven with the main stories there are elements of many other fearsome legends: the Wandering Jew, Faustus, the Water-King, the pact with the Devil. There are also lesser-known legends, like that of the Bleeding Nun, which Lewis found in German writers and wove into his fabric. But although these are materials that Radcliffe would probably have found sensationalist and implausible, they contribute in *The Monk* to a textual density which can bear comparison with that of *The Mysteries of Udolpho* (q.v.): the sufferings of Agnes and of Antonia are situated against a background of legend which both substantiates and intensifies their plight. Lewis, in fact, takes materials far more arcane and improbable than Radcliffe's and, by a terseness of style which sometimes seems almost naturalistic, contrives to make them seem oppressively convincing. We are not required precisely to come to a *belief* in the supernatural in *The Monk* – this is assumed: rather, we are required to *see* it before us, lurid and gory as a stage ghost.

Although Lewis's methods are sometimes crude, *The Monk* is a very self-consciously reflective book, much more so than Radcliffe's *Udolpho*, and delights in complications of narrative. The reader is made to move through a series of stories, and stories within stories. We are exposed, for example, to Raymond's history as told by himself to his friend Lorenzo, and within it is a further tale of banditry. Also within Raymond's narration, Agnes relates the tale of the Bleeding Nun, 'in a tone of burlesqued gravity'. But a little later, the story of the Bleeding Nun is told again, all too seriously, by the Wandering Jew, who has come to exorcise her; and furthermore the Nun herself gives a brief account of her plight (which is basically the same as in the Provençal Tale in *Udolpho*). Agnes eventually gets round to finishing her own history; and, as if Lewis were precociously determined to show us how conscious his methods are, a servant called Theodore is made to spend a couple of happy hours frightening the nuns of the convent with ridiculous tales and songs. In the first major Gothic novel, *Udolpho*, the boundaries of reality and fantasy were blurred and softened: Lewis, taking this anti-realist process a step further, begins the essentially Gothic construction of a world of mutually self-validating fictions which are texturally more 'real' than reality itself.

By contrast with the claustrophobic privacies of Radcliffe, the social world of *The Monk* is a wide and general one. Lewis places considerable emphasis on crowd scenes and on the public ramifications of private disaster and tragedy: Ambrosio's fate is not only his own but simultaneously – and here there are traces of the Gothic's political legacy – an aspect of the wider decadence and hypocrisy of a mythical Madrid. The reader is required to see himself as a spectator at a dramatic entertainment (Lewis was also a dramatist) which deliberately highlights and parades the more spectacular aspects of life. Lewis is deeply conscious of the position in which this puts the writer:

> An author, whether good or bad, or between both, is an animal whom everybody is privileged to attack, for though all are not able to write books, all conceive themselves able to judge them . . . In short, to enter the lists of literature is wilfully to expose yourself to the arrows of neglect, ridicule, envy, and disappointment. Whether you write well or ill, be assured that you will not escape from blame.

But he is, of course, not really concerned about this: the public eminence of Ambrosio and the importance of his reputation can be seen as analogies of the fate of the writer, but Lewis was clearly more interested, in his life and in his work, in the pleasure of public idolization than in its more dubious causes and effects. There are risks in sensationalism, but they are risks that he was happy to run for the sake of admiration.

And in *The Monk* the reader's admiration is frequently deflected from the characters, even the virtuous Antonia, on to Lewis's own sleight of hand. Many of the lurid qualities and sensational oppositions in the text are calculated more to show us the range of the author's dramatic abilities than to provide any profound comment on life. Satan's 'explanation' of Ambrosio's worst crimes at the end of the book has not the slightest narrative justification; it is a piece of deliberate extremism, and the same is true of Lewis's juggling with Matilda's human-ness or otherwise. The book is full of psychological contrasts which have little to do with the verisimilitude of the portrayal of particular characters, but are meant instead to enhance the general sense of precariousness that the writer wishes to encourage; he tries constantly to challenge his audience, to upset its security, to give readers a moment of doubt about whether they may not themselves be guilty of the complicated faults attributed to Ambrosio. Nothing in *The Monk* is what it seems, for any state can be revealed as the repression of its opposite. The more attractive and suitable a man or woman may seem as a potential partner, the more 'dangerous' he or she is; the sexual roles of Ambrosio and Matilda even become reversed as Matilda gains more and more control over the monk and threatens to change back into the man she had once pretended to be. The motif of this process is the double appearance of the demon; in his transformation from beauty to savagery is summarized the disturbing trickery Lewis constantly practises on his audience.

The high points of *The Monk*'s style are short, almost surreal, dramatic scenes: Lorenzo's extraordinary dream about the rape in the cathedral, Ambrosio's overheated nightmares and his vision of the naked Antonia. Lewis wants his readers to be impressionable, admiring, spectatorial, and open to sudden doubt about whether the author's paradoxes do not in fact undermine their own moral pretensions and show them unwholesome and repressed aspects of their own psyche. Above all, he wants the reader to see essentially private faults exposed mercilessly on a more or less public stage, and he wants to mock our confused reactions.

Bibliography

Blakemore, Steven 1998: 'Matthew Lewis's Black Mass: Sexual and Religious Inversion in *The Monk.*' *Studies in the Novel,* 30 (4), 521–39.

Frank, Fred (ed.) 1997: *Matthew Lewis's 'The Monk'. Romanticism on the Net* 8.

Geary, Robert F. 1992: 'M. G. Lewis and Later Gothic Fiction: The Gothic Dissipated.' In Nicholas Ruddick (ed.), *State of the Fantastic: Studies in the Theory and Practise of Fantastic Literature and Film.* Westport, CT: Greenwood Press, 75–81.

Jones, Wendy 1990: 'Stories of Desire in *The Monk.*' *ELH,* 57 (1), 129–50.

Mulman, Lisa Naomi 1998: 'Sexuality on the Surface: Catholicism and the Erotic Object in Lewis's *The Monk.*' *Bucknell Review,* 42 (1), 98–110.

MARY WOLLSTONECRAFT SHELLEY,

FRANKENSTEIN

(1818, REVISED 1831)

Frankenstein, first published in 1818, was extensively revised for the third edition of 1831 and published with an expanded introduction. While a number of recent critics and editors have preferred the 1818 edition, the 1831 edition remains the more conventional choice and will be referred to here. A useful summary and discussion of the substantive changes can be found in Marilyn Butler's appendix to her edition of the 1818 text.

The complex structure of *Frankenstein* involves a series of framed or embedded narratives. In the outermost layer, Robert Walton describes his attempt to reach the North Pole and his encounter with Victor Frankenstein, in a series of letters to Walton's sister, Margaret Saville. Within this relatively realistic layer, there is the more marvellous account of Frankenstein, who tells Walton the story of how he created and abandoned the monster, the revenge it took upon him by destroying those he loved most, and his eventual pursuit of the creature. Further narratives can be found within Victor's account, in, for example, the letters from Elizabeth, who was taken in by the Frankenstein family as a child and whom he supposedly intends to marry, and from his father. In the central layer of narrative, the creature then challenges Frankenstein's account of events as he describes his development after his flight, and his experiences of rejection. Within this story we also learn about the history of the De Lacey family and of Felix De Lacey's betrothed Safie.

In addition to all these narratives, there are numerous references to extra-textual narratives, including Samuel Taylor Coleridge's 'The Rime of the Ancient Mariner' (1798), another tale of an alienated individual and the disturbance of natural order, and the three books the creature discovers in the woods. The most important of these, Milton's *Paradise Lost* (1667), provides both an epigraph for the novel and a framework through which both the creature and Victor understand their changing situations. As many critics observe, the novel as an aggregate of narrative pieces and literary influences is closely connected to the creature, constructed from fragments of corpses. Both are hybrid forms, monstrous (q.v.) bodies, a connection made by Mary Wollstonecraft Shelley herself when she concludes her 1831 introduction by bidding her 'hideous progeny go forth and prosper'.

Frankenstein, as the subtitle to the story indicates, is a searcher after forbidden knowledge, one of those overreachers who refuse to accept limitations and are subsequently punished. But he is specifically a 'modern' Prometheus, partly because this is a notably secular world with no gods against whom to rebel, and partly because his search is conceived of in scientific terms. *Frankenstein* introduces the prototypical Gothic mad scientist and registers some anxieties about scientific progress unaccompanied by social conscience. The potential problems of Frankenstein's search for the principle of life are soon suggested: his studies alienate him from his family, and from the start lead him to charnel houses, to death and corruption. As his language implies, even Frankenstein himself feels some unease concerning his 'secret toil' in his 'workshop of filthy creation'. In creating life and imagining how a 'new species would bless me as its creator and source', he is seeking to usurp the role of God. He is also, however, seeking to usurp the role of women, and such an unnatural birth, the text suggests, can only have unnatural consequences.

At the actual moment of the creature's animation, Frankenstein is horrified. Immediately rejecting the creature as monstrous on the basis of his physical appearance, Frankenstein runs away and attempts to forget in sleep. This sleep is disturbed by a nightmare in which Elizabeth, as he tries to kiss her, transforms into the rotting corpse of his mother. Then, as he awakens, the image is replaced by that of the creature, who is seen, on the first of three such occasions, by the 'dim and yellow light of the moon' at the window.

In juxtaposing the dream with the vision of the creature, the text prophetically suggests that bringing the monster to life is equivalent to killing Elizabeth. Furthermore, as Elizabeth changes into the corpse of the mother, the dream emphasizes Frankenstein's circumvention of the normal channels of procreation: giving life to the creature has effectively eliminated the mother. The dream also implies much about the psychological state of the dreamer himself, suggesting at the very least some anxieties concerning sexuality – this is something we might remember later when, on their wedding night, Frankenstein tells his new bride 'Oh! Peace, peace, my love . . . this night, and all will be safe: but this night is dreadful, very dreadful.' As Frankenstein awakens from his dream with a start, the language used to describe his physical manifestations of fear, particularly the reference to the way his limbs 'convulsed', echoes the language used to describe the animation of the creature. This may be the first indication that the creature can be seen as Frankenstein's double, something that Victor further implies when he subsequently refers to the creature as 'my own spirit let loose from the grave ... forced to destroy all that was dear to me'. The doubling does not, however, give form only to the return of the repressed energies of an individual psyche: the monstrous other here is both psychological and social.

The creature's own narrative suggests that Frankenstein's main sin is not his act of creation but his failure to take responsibility for what he produces, and it is through the creature's account that the text most explicitly engages with the problematic question of the monstrous. Initially he appears in terms of the born innocent who will be formed by environment and circumstance. As his education proceeds and he moves from nature to culture, the creature learns about and experiences the injustices of society. He masters language, but rather than allowing him access to human society it only serves to make him aware of his unique origin and to alienate him further.

Although the creature may be physically repellent, he is initially far more natural and humane than the creator who rejects him, the villagers who stone him, and the ungrateful father who shoots him. Set oppositions between the human and the monstrous are further disturbed by demonstrations of the corruption of social institutions, including the law and the church. In the story of the De Laceys and the trial of Justine, human injustice is repeatedly emphasized. As Elizabeth declares after Justine's execution, 'men appear to me as monsters thirsting for each other's blood'. Sometimes read as a metaphor for the violent masses in times of political upheaval, the creature offers his own critique of human institutions, and initially turns away in 'disgust and loathing' from evidence of 'vice and bloodshed'. It is only when he is exposed to, and begins to suffer from, the viciousness of human society that he is gradually contaminated by a similar violence and aggression and starts to replicate the very human characteristics that initially repulse him.

The question of the monstrous is also problematized by the way in which it is repeatedly suggested to be little more than a discursive effect. Frankenstein, an unreliable narrator at best, repeatedly misreads such things as the creature's gesture towards him at the moment of animation, and the creature's words regarding his wedding night; later, he even assumes the food and clothing left for him as he pursues the creature must come from some guardian angel. They are, of course, left by the creature himself, but Frankenstein reveals a mind determined to impose coherence in accordance with his own understanding of himself as a victim and his creature as a monstrous force to be eliminated. His language, as much as any act of the creature, functions to produce monstrosity.

This is particularly notable in the scene when he destroys the female he is creating to be the mate of the creature. Contrasting markedly with his creator's evident reluctance to settle his 'union' with Elizabeth, the creature's desire for companionship is one of his most human qualities. Nevertheless, while Frankenstein is eventually persuaded by his eloquence to make the creature a companion, he repeatedly challenges this evidence of humanity with his declared revulsion for the 'filthy mass that moved and talked'. Furthermore, once Frankenstein starts his new project, he completely rewrites the creature's explanations, and convinces himself that the creation of a mate may result in 'a race of devils to be propagated upon the earth'. As the creature watches, once more from a window, and once more by the dim light of the moon, Frankenstein tears the female apart. 'I will be with thee on thy wedding night', the creature threatens, a remark that Frankenstein perhaps egoistically, perhaps purposely, perhaps inexplicably, interprets as a threat to himself. From then on, recognizing he is doomed to be excluded from the domestic world, the creature devotes himself to its annihilation.

The destruction of the female mate needs to be seen in the context of the idealizing narrative of the family revolving around Elizabeth and, in the case of Walton, Margaret Saville. The creature idealizes the domestic world, but is excluded from it. Both Frankenstein and Walton repeatedly sing the praises of the domestic world, but take great pains to escape it. Both display the egocentricity and ambition that prompt many critics to read *Frankenstein* as a critique of the underlying masculine assumptions and values of the romantic imagination. It is, nevertheless, not entirely clear that the domestic female world is presented as an ideal alternative to the individualistic male world. The responsibilities of the insular domestic sphere may place too much of a curb upon individual desires, while strictly enforced artificial role distinctions result in the creation of passive, dependent women who ultimately become monsters to be rejected. As Maggie Kilgour observes, perhaps by turning in upon itself, 'the family doesn't wall monsters out, but ends up producing its own' (1995: 202).

The creature's final revenge is the death of Elizabeth. On the wedding night, Victor leaves Elizabeth alone in the bedroom while he wanders the corridors, supposedly anticipating combat with the creature. The result is predictable: Frankenstein returns to find the body of Elizabeth 'flung by the murderer on its bridal bier'. Enacting the scene of his nightmare, he embraces her only to find that she is dead; he faints, and when he awakens, once more, by the light of the moon, the creature looks on from the window.

Frankenstein concludes his story with an account of his pursuit of the creature into the polar regions, and the narrative then returns to Walton. In the face of impending mutiny, he has reluctantly agreed to turn the ship back home. Frankenstein dies, and Walton discovers the creature, full of grief and horror, bending over the corpse. With the intention of immolating himself on a funeral pyre, the creature springs from the cabin window. Little, however, has been resolved. The boundaries between the human and the monstrous remain problematically blurred, and Shelley leaves the reader, like the creature, 'lost in darkness and distance'.

Bibliography

Baldick, Chris 1987: *In Frankenstein's Shadow: Myth, Monstrosity and Nineteenth-Century Writing*. Oxford: Oxford University Press.

Bann, Stephen 1994: *Frankenstein, Creation, and Monstrosity*. London: Reaktion.

Botting, Fred 1991: *Making Monstrous: Frankenstein, Criticism, Theory*. Manchester: Manchester University Press.

Botting, Fred (ed.) 1995: *Frankenstein. New Casebook*. Basingstoke: Macmillan.

Butler, Marilyn (ed.) 1994: *Frankenstein, or The Modern Prometheus: The 1818 Text*. Oxford: Oxford University Press.

Halberstam, Judith 1995: *Skin Shows: Gothic Horror and the Technology of Monsters*. Durham, NC: Duke University Press.

Kilgour, Maggie 1995: *The Rise of the Gothic Novel*. London: Routledge.

Knoepflmacher, U. C. and Levine, George (eds) 1979: *The Endurance of Frankenstein: Essays on Mary Shelley's Novel*. Berkeley, CA: University of California Press.

Charles Robert Maturin,

MELMOTH THE WANDERER

(1820)

Charles Robert Maturin's *Melmoth the Wanderer* was a vastly influential book, both in its own time and later: Honoré de Balzac, Charles Baudelaire, Edgar Allan Poe (q.v.) and Robert Louis Stevenson (q.v.) were among the many writers who have spoken of its enduring power. Despite its enormous size and extremely complex and difficult narrative structure, it is in fact a highly organized work, and to understand it requires the uncovering of that heavily encrusted principle of organization which sustains its rococo decoration.

To recount the 'story', however, is not easy. The character known as young Melmoth, attending at the decease of an aged relative in Ireland, inherits a manuscript. With the lack of wisdom and forethought conventional in the Gothic genre, he reads it and finds that it relates the story of one Stanton and his encounters with a mysterious figure who, first, promises Stanton that he will encounter much misfortune, culminating in a spell in a madhouse, and then, when this prophecy is fulfiled, appears to him in the depth of his adversity offering to give him his freedom in exchange for his soul. The figure who thus tempts him is identified as a relative of young Melmoth's, also called Melmoth, who ought by rights to have been dead long before. While young Melmoth is wondering at this manuscript, a shipwreck brings to his door a Spaniard called Monçada, who tells him his own story, which is even more horrific than Stanton's but which involves the Wanderer in a similar capacity, in other words, as a figure who appears at the point of death to offer his final bargain.

At this point, the book has barely started; the stories come thick and fast, most of them now related by Monçada to young Melmoth. They are set across 150 years, and range through Europe to the Indian Ocean. Most of them are – as indeed they have to be in order to expose their protagonists to the kinds of fate that prompt the elder Melmoth's interest and appearance – highly coloured and grim with death and horror, although it has to be said that one or two minor tales are tedious in the extreme. It is all grist to Maturin's mill; almost at the end of the book, Monçada shows signs of starting all over again, with a second series of stories, as it were. In all the tales the Wanderer features; in all of them he is a figure of superhuman powers who appears at moments of the most profound despair, making his devilish offer. Maturin remains gentlemanly to the end in not fully revealing the Wanderer's terms, although it is perfectly clear from the first encounter that he is a seeker of souls, and it is reasonably assumed that the reader will be familiar with the story of the Wandering Jew that lies behind the construction of the figure of Melmoth.

In the end the Wanderer himself appears to his young relative, announcing that his quest has failed and that he has come home to await the end; the end consisting in his being dragged away by demons, initially into the sea but, we presume, thence to the flames which he has failed to avoid; the only way, of course, in which he could have escaped his fate would have been by persuading somebody else to take his place.

Above all other themes, and perhaps more so than many other Gothic novels despite their frequent conventionalized setting in abbey, monastery and convent, *Melmoth* is a book about religion. To Melmoth, all religions are equally delusory in their promises of beneficence and salvation; the only reality behind religion is divine vengeance. Maturin's own position as a writer – he was a Protestant clergyman – is clearly against Catholicism in particular and all its works, but one of the most interesting features of the book is the way in which time and time again particular characters go beyond what is necessary to defend this specific position. At one point a dying and very evil monk offers a neat summary of his views on the falsity of religious belief: 'All saints, from Mahomet down to Francis Zavier, were only a compound of insanity, pride, and self-imposition; – the latter would have been of less consequence, but that men always revenge their impositions on themselves, by imposing to the utmost on others.'

This speech is partly undercut by Maturin's implications about the unpleasant nature of the speaker, but the response from Monçada, who is by no means an evil character, is to comment that 'there is no more horrible state of mind than that in which we are forced by conviction to listen on, wishing every word to be false, and knowing every word to be true'; in context the reader can see that this adds conviction to the dying monk's words, and again the problem within Catholicism overspills its apparent boundaries. Certainly the overall impression derived from the book is that Maturin vastly exceeds his brief against the Catholic Church, and brings most of the edifice of religion, or perhaps indeed of belief itself in a more general sense, down on his head.

Like William Godwin's *Things as They Are; or, The Adventures of Caleb Williams* (qq.v.), *Melmoth* is a book in which sheer intensity and savagery of feeling – feeling which is essentially anti-tyrannical in both the theological and political spheres – overwhelm any attempt at fine doctrinal discrimination. There is indeed a power of discrimination in *Melmoth*, but it lies elsewhere: what is most startling in it is the depiction of the complexity, and often the paradoxical nature, of extreme emotional states – generally, of course, states of extreme terror and despair. There are many examples that could be cited. Monçada is tortured at one point by monks who, in order to break his resistance to taking the vows, enter into a communal pretence that he is mad and affect to be frightened of him. For Monçada, this hideously compounds his own terror:

> The terror that I inspired I at last began to feel. I began to believe myself – I know not what, whatever they thought me. This is a dreadful state of mind, but one impossible to avoid. In some circumstances, where the whole world is against us, we begin to take its part against ourselves, to avoid the withering sensation of being alone on our own side.

He attempts to escape with a companion, and is thwarted at the last moment when their light expires: 'we lay', he says,

> not daring to speak to each other, for who could speak but of despair, and which of us dared to aggravate the despair of the other. This kind of fear which we know already felt by others, and which we dread to aggravate by uttering, *even to those who know it*, is perhaps the most horrible sensation ever experienced. The very thirst of my body seemed to vanish in this fiery thirst of the soul for communication, where all communication was unutterable, impossible, hopeless.

In each of these cases – and they are both, perhaps, cases where one can detect the way in which Maturin influenced – the writer takes a psychological commonplace – the terror of being regarded as mad, the longing for communication in moments of stress – and turns the screw one notch further, a technique he displays to greatest advantage where he is talking about insanity and the fear of insanity.

We may refer to *Melmoth*, again like *Caleb Williams*, as a paranoiac (q.v.) text, in which persecution is everywhere and vastly exceeds any pretext for it. What is critical is that the world is not purged by the eventual death of Melmoth – as it is, for example, by the death of Ambrosio in M. G. Lewis's *The Monk* (qq.v.) or of Schedoni in Ann Radcliffe's (q.v.) *The Italian* – because Melmoth is not a *principal* of evil in himself but rather an agent and indeed a product of the perennial evil of others; were it not for this greater evil he would have no hoped-for victims to whom to offer his bargain. His absence will thus in no way affect the existence of the 'enormous engine' of persecution which Monçada at one point describes, and which beats at its strongest in those secret places of the soul, those 'monasteries' characterized by the midnight search and the carefully placed interrogation lamp.

Melmoth is thus largely an instrument of the evil of others, but he does have his own moments of sadism. About to consummate his demon-marriage to the innocent Immalee, he exults in the evil which will result:

> Perish to all the world, perhaps beyond the period of its existence, but live to me in darkness and in corruption! Preserve all the exquisite modulation of your forms! all the indescribable brilliancy of your colouring! – but preserve it for me alone! – me, the single, pulseless, brooder over the dark and unproductive nests of eternal sterility, – the mountain whose lava of internal fire has stilled, and indurated, and enclosed for ever, all that was the joy of earth, the felicity of life, and the hope of futurity!

But these are mere words; Melmoth is actually powerless to harm Immalee unless she acquiesces. Meanwhile, the real horror of the world goes on regardless: the consigning of the innocent to the madhouse, the hideous lynching of the parricide, the behaviour of the 'amateur in suffering', the gentleman who makes a point of being present at every execution to savour the screams of the dying – these practises and incidents owe nothing to Melmoth's agency; he merely exults in them, and indeed offers a way of escape, even though the reader knows that it would involve consignment to worse torture hereafter.

As the book goes on, the reader finds experiences of increasingly dream-like states. There is, for example, a crucial comment made by Immalee (her name now changed to Isidora) on her death-bed. She claims to have been visited by Melmoth on the previous night, and her confessor suggests that this must have been a dream. 'My father, I have had many dreams', answers Isidora, 'many – many wanderings, but this was no dream.' At this moment, 'dream' and 'wandering' become the same word, and the being of the Wanderer fades into the chimerical world of the unconscious, whence perhaps he came. We might be reminded of some phrases in Herbert Marcuse's *Eros and Civilisation* where, summarizing Sigmund Freud's theory of the return of the repressed, Marcuse says that 'the memory of pre-historic impulses and deeds continues to haunt civilisation: the repressed material returns, and the individual is still punished for impulses long since mastered and deeds long since undone' (1969: 52). This, surely, is the microcosmic form of the world displayed in *Melmoth* in macrocosm: a world in which suffering is in no way proportionate to guilt, in which no amount of civilized behaviour can prevent the breaking out of those forces which still haunt the mind of the individual and the mind of the culture.

Bibliography

Fowler, Kathleen 1986: 'Hieroglyphics in Fire: *Melmoth the Wanderer.' Studies in Romanticism*, 25 (4), 521–39.

Hennelly, Mark M. 1981: '*Melmoth the Wanderer* and Gothic Existentialism.' *Studies in English Literature*, 21 (4), 665–79.

Lew, Joseph W. 1994: '"Unprepared for Sudden Transformations": Identity and Politics in *Melmoth the Wanderer.' Studies in the Novel*, 26 (2), 173–95.

Marcuse, Herbert 1969: *Eros and Civilisation: A Philosophical Inquiry into Freud.* New edn. London: Sphere Books.

Miles, Robert 2002: 'Europhobia: The Catholic Other in Horace Walpole and Charles Maturin.' In Avril Horner (ed.), *European Gothic: A Spirited Exchange, 1760–1960*. Manchester: Manchester University Press, 84–103.

Scott, Shirley Clay 1980: *Myths and Consciousness in the Novels of Charles Robert Maturin.* New York: Arno.

James Hogg,

THE PRIVATE MEMOIRS AND CONFESSIONS OF
A JUSTIFIED SINNER
(1824)

James Hogg's *The Private Memoirs and Confessions of a Justified Sinner* is a novel centrally con-cerned with the evil the author sees as produced by anti-nomianism, the extreme Calvinist doctrine that those who are Elect, 'saved by God', will remain so regardless of their works on earth. But this is only the starting-point of the *Confessions*, for on this basis Hogg also produces what has often been since taken to be a detailed and terrifying account of schizo-phrenia, tracing it through its stages of development with remarkably prescient psychological skill.

The book falls into two principal parts: the so-called 'Editor's Narrative' and the 'Confessions' proper. The editor's narrative tells the story of the Colwan family. This is headed by an old laird who marries, late in life, a younger woman who is a strict Calvinist, much under the influence of a 'fire and brim-stone' preacher named Wringhim. The couple are rapidly estranged, but she bears the laird two sons. The elder, George, is acknowledged as his father's son and brought up as heir to the estates. The younger, however, the laird does not acknowledge: his wife brings him up with the assistance of Wringhim, who bestows on him his own name. The younger Wringhim, as he will now be known, begins to 'haunt' his brother, claiming to regard him as one of the 'Reprobate' – those not elected to be saved – and using every means to taunt and provoke him. For a long time George refuses to retaliate; when he finally does so, albeit mildly, he is found dead under mysterious circumstances. Wringhim, who is by now associating with a mysterious friend called Gil-Martin, who appears to have shape-changing powers, succeeds to his father's estates, whereupon his conduct becomes even more extreme and rep-rehensible. The authorities are persuaded of the possibility that he murdered his brother. A search for Wringhim is ordered, but fails; he has disappeared.

Thus runs the 'editor's' narrative; then follow the 'confessions' proper, which are the account of the same, and other, events apparently written by

208

Wringhim himself. He tells how he was brought up by the elder Wringhim, the preacher, to regard himself as one of the Elect, and how he meets his mysterious friend Gil-Martin. By dint of various sophistries, Gil-Martin persuades Wringhim that his work on earth is to purge it of the Reprobate, and provokes him into murdering a recalcitrant preacher. Gil-Martin then aids and abets Wringhim in his harassment of his brother, and eventually in his murder. All the time, Wringhim persuades himself that Gil-Martin is a benefactor who is helping him to perform the work of God in purging the world of the Reprobate. When Wringhim has succeeded to the lairdship, however, things start to go oddly wrong. He begins to suffer from memory lapses and other curious symptoms, and his life becomes progressively nightmarish. He also begins to be beset by demons; Gil-Martin claims that it is only by accepting his protection that they can be held at bay. Wringhim is forced to flee the estate, Dalcastle, on being accused of murder, rape and other crimes, and roams the country in the utmost misery, pursued by demons and, since his presence anywhere leads to supernatural disturbance, unable ever to stay in one place. He eventually succumbs to the temptation of suicide, which Gil-Martin claims, again, will be forgiven him because he is of the Elect.

The relationship between the two accounts is not simple and has excited a great amount of critical controversy. Clearly Wringhim's story is unreliable; principally what remains in doubt is the extent to which Gil-Martin really 'appears' (if such a thing can be said to happen in a novel) or is a figment of his imagination. The editor's account appears the more objective of the two, but it has been argued that even this is not a voice that we can indubitably ascribe to Hogg. It has been suggested that Hogg is trying to draw a line between an acceptable and an unacceptable form of Calvinism; but over against Wringhim's antinomianism he places an 'editor' who is very little impressed by religion at all. Early in the editor's narrative, the old laird rebukes Wringhim senior in robust terms – 'in short, Sir, you are a mildew, – a canker-worm in the bosom of the reformed Church, generating a disease of which she will never be purged, but by the shedding of blood' – but the laird himself seems to regard religion as merely a matter of form. It may be, however, that Hogg's own opinion emerges more clearly when the narrator remarks that the tenets of the young Lady Dalcastle 'were not the tenets of the great reformers, but theirs mightily overstrained and deformed'; and this emphasis on the eventual tendencies of Calvinist doctrines, when taken to extremes, runs right through the book. When Wringhim first meets Gil-Martin (if he does), they conduct theological discussions: 'in every thing that I suggested', says Wringhim, 'he acquiesced, and, as I thought that day, often carried them to extremes, so that I had a secret dread he was advancing blasphemies'. But he fails to act upon this doubt; and since he remains convinced of the angelic purposes of Gil-Martin, his perception of the world is correspondingly distorted.

Hogg's witty portrayal of the younger Wringhim's self-righteousness comes out emblematically in the latter's account of an incident when he is harassing George by getting in his way during a tennis match. The 'editor' has already told the story in a way that suggests that Wringhim was acting out of pure malice, but Wringhim claims that he was 'fired with indignation' at seeing his brother engaging in 'ungodly' sports – fired to the point of blows:

> Yes, I went boldly up and struck him with my foot, and meant to have given him a more severe blow than it was my fortune to inflict. It had, however, the effect of rousing up his corrupt nature to quarrelling and strife, instead of taking the chastisement of the Lord in humility and meekness, He ran furiously against me in the choler that is always inspired by the wicked one; but I overthrew him, by reason of impeding the natural and rapid progress of his unholy feet, running to destruction.

Needless to say, this is distinctly different from the previous account, according to which George, trying to reach a ball, fell over Wringhim, Wringhim aimed a vicious kick at him, and George hit him lightly with his racket.

In effect, the book is the story of a dual persecution; in the first narrative the persecution of George by Wringhim, in the second Wringhim's persecution by Gil-Martin. George is bewildered by Wringhim's ability – which it turns out that he owes, of course, to Gil-Martin – to pursue him with supernatural accuracy; he becomes 'utterly confounded; not only at the import of this persecution, but how in the world it came to pass that this unaccountable being knew all his motions, and every intention of his heart, as it were intuitively'. Indeed, 'the attendance of that brother was now become like the attendance of a demon on some devoted being that had sold himself to destruction', and Wringhim comes to seem a demon to George in much the same way as Wringhim himself becomes demon-haunted.

Wringhim's fate, however, could be said to prove much the worse. George is 'merely' murdered, but Wringhim suffers the graphically described tortures of the damned on earth. From being a friend, Gil-Martin becomes an inescapable and implacable pursuer, and this, of course, again raises the central ambivalence of the *Confessions*, as to the objective existence of Gil-Martin. This is a question which the text does not answer. It is true that other people seem to see Gil-Martin, in various guises, as a physical being; but equally, Wringhim is clearly progressively subject to what would usually be termed a religious mania. From the outset of his narrative, he demonstrates megalomaniac tendencies in his account of his own past – 'I was born an outcast in the world, in which I was destined to act so conspicuous a part' – and throughout his narrative he sees his life as a testimony to the glory of God. Any potential resolution of the various interpretations that might be placed on the book is left in the hands of the 'editor', but his is clearly not meant to be the last word. Instead, he expresses a careless scepticism which is clearly ironic:

> in this day, and with the present generation, it will not go down, that a man should be daily tempted by the devil, in the semblance of a fellow-creature; and at length lured to self-destruction, in the hopes that this same fiend and tormentor was to suffer and fall along with him. . . . In short, we must either conceive him not only the greatest fool, but the greatest wretch, on whom was ever stamped the form of humanity; or, that he was a religious maniac, who wrote and wrote about a deluded creature, till he arrived at that height of madness, that he believed himself the very object whom he had been all along describing. And in order to escape from an ideal tormentor, committed that act for which, according to the tenets he embraced, there was no remission, and which consigned his memory and his name to everlasting detestation.

On this note, the reader is left with what might be termed an 'undecidable' account, a story – or perhaps a set of stories – from which no final interpretation may be derived.

Bibliography

Duncan, Ian 1997: 'Scott, Hogg, Orality, and the Limits of Culture.' *Studies in Hogg and his World*, 8, 56–74.

Fox, Warren 2001: 'Violence and the Victimisation of Women: Engendering Sympathy for Hogg's Justified Sinner.' *Studies in Scottish Literature*, 32, 164–79.

Garside, Peter 2001: 'Hogg's Confessions and Scotland.' *Studies in Hogg and his World*, 12, 118–38.

Groves, David 1988. *James Hogg: The Growth of a Writer.* Edinburgh: Scottish Academic Press.

Kearns, Michael S. 1978: 'Intuition and Narration in James Hogg's *Confessions.*' *Studies in Scottish Literature*, 13, 81–91.

Mackenzie, Scott 2002: 'Confessions of a Gentrified Sinner: Secrets in Scott and Hogg.' *Studies in Romanticism*, 41(1), 3–32.

Emily Brontë,

WUTHERING HEIGHTS

(1847)

Wuthering Heights is often considered a hybrid form: the novel appears formally split down the middle, with the first-generation plot frequently considered the Gothic story and that of the second generation a rewriting of this story as domestic realism. For many, this is a rewriting that involves a decided loss of narrative power. Rosemary Jackson, for example, argues that *Wuthering Heights* ultimately harnesses Gothic 'to serve and not subvert a domestic ideology' and that it silences the fantastic elements 'in the name of establishing a normative bourgeois realism' (1981: 124).

For other critics, the split into first- and second-generation narratives is part of Emily Brontë's reworking of female Gothic (q.v.). Brontë is seen to appropriate the Gothic in order to represent and investigate women's fears about a restrictive and sometimes threatening domestic space. For the female characters, most particularly the first Catherine, being a woman involves only a choice of different kinds of imprisonment. After a childhood of relative freedom roaming the moors with Heathcliff, Catherine Earnshaw's meeting with the Lintons and the attempt to transform her from a rebellious 'wild, hatless little savage' into a proper young lady initiate a process of confinement that will end only with death. She marries Edgar Linton and returns to the Grange, but her transformation is far from complete and she remains torn between Heathcliff and Linton. As Lyn Pykett observes, 'the denouement of her particular Gothic plot involves her imprisonment in increasingly confined spaces: the house, her room, and finally "this shattered prison", her body, from which she longs to escape as she does from womanhood itself' (1989: 77).

Significantly, it is complications resulting from childbirth, another kind of 'confinement', that finally lead to her death. With her daughter, also named Catherine, and Hareton Earnshaw, her brother's son, the second-generation narrative begins. The first story is rewritten to show the civilizing process now working and Hareton and the second Catherine functioning effectively within the domestic world. For some critics, this rewriting of the story as domestic realism simply involves a restoration of patriarchy. For others, more affirmatively, it involves a redefined space that is 'more feminine and more egalitarian' and in which 'women are no longer the victims of patriarchal authority' (Senf 1985: 209).

There are some problems with seeing a clear-cut division between the Gothic and domestic realism in *Wuthering Heights*, since the Gothic is actually appropriated throughout as a means of constructing psychological depth and intensity. Uncanny (q.v.) repetitions of names and the reproduction of physical characteristics produce a doubling that repeatedly works against any sense of narrative division. Furthermore, the character of Heathcliff spans both narratives and becomes increasingly otherworldly, lost in a land of ghosts, as the second, supposedly 'realist' narrative progresses. To insist on a clear division between the Gothic and the realist plots is to introduce precisely the kind of boundary line that *Wuthering Heights* repeatedly pushes against.

And it is in its concern with boundaries that *Wuthering Heights* most clearly reveals its status as a Gothic text. In John Matthews's words, the novel 'haunts the sites of division' (1993: 54). It continually questions, transgresses or attempts to dissolve boundaries, boundaries between self and other, nature and society, barbaric and civilized, natural and supernatural. The concern with boundaries is even given formal expression through the use of a frame narrative to enclose the central story of the Earnshaws and Lintons, but here too boundaries are repeatedly crossed. Lockwood, who listens to the story of Nelly Dean, previously housekeeper for the Earnshaw family, intrudes upon the world of the Heights as soon as he arrives. Uninvited and unwelcome, he pushes past a locked gate and proceeds over the 'threshold' into the 'penetralium' of Wuthering Heights. Past these boundaries, the codes and conventions of Lockwood's world prove inadequate for interpretation: cats turn out to be dead rabbits while the supposed 'beneficient fairy' responds to him with mute hostility. Lockwood, who understands neither himself nor others, is immediately set up as an unreliable narrator. The second narrator, Nelly, may initially seem more reliable; she is not just telling the story, she is a character within it. However, her common-sense perspective frequently undercuts her authority, and in a world full of dreams and ghosts, her insistence that 'We're dismal enough without conjuring up ghosts and vision to perplex us' proves her to be an equally limited guide to events. At the same time as Lockwood and Nelly strive to frame or contain events within the central story and render them comprehensible, they repeatedly raise the ghosts of something that remains unaccountable within their normalizing perspectives.

The very title of the novel directs attention to landscape and weather, and the wild, desolate and stormy moors suggest the irruption of passions and natural energies that cannot be contained by social structures or interpreted through conventional perspectives. Nevertheless, Brontë actually makes far more use of the house, with the divisions and boundaries of its rooms and enclosures, than of the wide open spaces of the surrounding landscape. When Lockwood, undeterred by his first reception, makes a second visit to the Heights, he finds even further barriers to access. Unable to remove the chain, he must jump over the gate to reach the door, where he knocks for admittance until his 'knuckles tingled and the dogs howled', and shakes the latch in frenzy.

The dangers of crossing boundaries for someone like Lockwood soon become clear within the panelled bed into which he retreats for the night. First, he is disoriented by the names he finds scratched on the window ledge and is assailed by an uncanny 'glare of white letters' that 'started from the dark, as vivid as spectres' as the 'air swarmed with Catherines'. His subsequent dreams reveal a world of shifting boundaries. The tapping of the preacher on the pulpit in his first dream merges into the tapping of a branch against the window. This in turn becomes the knocking of the ghostly Catherine at the pane as, replicating Lockwood's own previous demands, she cries to be let in. Distinctions between dream and reality dissolve. Dorothy Van Ghent, in a seminal essay on boundaries in *Wuthering Heights*, argues that doors, windows and gates are vulnerable points in the barriers between the civilized and social spaces of houses and the wild, savage landscape outside. The window pane in particular she sees as a treacherously transparent site of separation between the inside and the outside, the human and the alien other (1953: 168). But these boundaries are repeatedly dissolving, and the differences between human and other constantly problematized. When the terrified Lockwood rubs the ghostly child's arm against the broken pane until it bleeds, his civilized veneer breaks down to reveal a savagery at least equal to that he finds at the Heights.

While the shifting boundaries of reality and dream problematize the status of the ghost for the reader, Heathcliff has no doubts about the truth of Lockwood's experience. Wrenching open the lattice, he bursts 'into an uncontrollable passion of tears. "Come in! come in!" he sobbed. "Cathy, do come. Oh, do – *once* more. Oh! My heart's darling, hear me *this* time – Catherine, at last!' If Lockwood desperately tries to lock out the ghost, but fails, Heathcliff has no more success in persuading the ghost to come in. What Lockwood fears is precisely what Heathcliff desires. Lockwood is terrified by evidence of the shifting and unreliable boundaries between self and other and natural and supernatural, and determines to leave a safe distance between himself and the Heights in the future; Heathcliff, however, wants nothing more than the dissolution of those boundaries Lockwood so anxiously seeks to reinstate.

The relationship of Catherine and Heathcliff reveals a strong desire for the dissolution of the boundaries of the self. 'Nelly, I am Heathcliff', the young Catherine declares, while Heathcliff asserts that she is his soul, his life. In Lacanian terms, Catherine's and Heathcliff's relationship looks back to the mirror stage when the self is defined not through language but through the reflecting gaze of an other, who is, in Catherine's words, 'more myself than I am'. Exiled from this world of imaginary unity, they struggle repeatedly to recover it. When Catherine is forced to choose between Heathcliff and Linton, she loses the other self that gives her the sense of wholeness. Her only hope lies in death and a spiritual reunion: 'they may bury me twelve feet deep, and throw the church down over me, but I won't rest till you are with me', she tells him. Heathcliff, who much prefers possession to separation, insists 'haunt me then! . . . Be with me always.' The haunting, however, only serves to reaffirm those boundaries between them that constitute desire. Catherine is everywhere for Heathcliff. He is 'surrounded by her image' and the world 'a dreadful collection of memoranda that she did exist'. However, although he repeatedly speaks of 'absorbing' her and 'dissolving' with her, Catherine simultaneously remains totally inaccessible. Like her, Heathcliff soon looks only to a reunion in death. Loosening one side of her coffin and bribing the sexton to ensure their remains can intermingle when he is laid next to her, he tells Nelly that 'by the time Linton gets to us he'll not know which is which!' His self-willed death replicates that of Catherine: refusing to eat, he withdraws to the panelled bed they once shared, anticipating a final end to separation.

On one level, the imminent marriage of Catherine and Hareton and their removal to the Linton family home, Thrushcross Grange, ultimately seems to banish the Gothic ghosts and dispel all uncanny presences. But the novel actually ends on a far less conclusive note, using the frame narrative to revive the spectral even as it lays it to rest. The country folk believe there has been no quiet resolution, and that Heathcliff and Catherine still walk the moors. Nelly and Lockwood sensibly agree to dismiss such 'idle tales' as 'nonsense', and in the final lines Lockwood lingers around the graves 'watching the moths fluttering among the heath, and harebells' and wondering 'how anyone could ever imagine unquiet slumbers for the sleepers in that quiet earth'. Given the reader's knowledge of the limitations of both frame narrators, however, their comforting reassurances fail to dispel the disturbing sense that, in the world of *Wuthering Heights,* something unresolved and unaccounted for remains.

Bibliography

Jackson, Rosemary 1981: *Fantasy: The Literature of Subversion.* London: Methuen.

Matthews, John 1993: 'Framing in *Wuthering Heights.*' In Patsy Stoneman (ed.), *Wuthering Heights: New Casebook.* Basingstoke: Macmillan, 54–73.

Napier, Elizabeth R. 1984: 'The Problem of Boundaries in *Wuthering Heights.*' *Philological Quarterly,* 63 (1), 95–107.

Pykett, Lyn 1989: *Emily Brontë.* Basingstoke: Macmillan.

Senf, Carol 1985: 'Emily Brontë's Version of Feminist History: *Wuthering Heights.*' *Essays in Literature,* 12, 204–14.

Van Ghent, Dorothy 1953: *The English Novel, Form and Function.* New York: Holt, Rinehart and Winston.

WILKIE COLLINS,

THE WOMAN IN WHITE

(1860)

The close connection between Gothic fiction and the Victorian sensation novel is best illustrated in the work of Wilkie Collins, regarded in his time as 'Mrs Radcliffe brought down to date'. We can see Collins at his best as a writer in a novel popular in its day and right down to the present time, *The Woman in White*. The most obvious strength of the book is its intricate story, which it would be impossible to recount in any detail here, but equally impressive is Collins's creation of a genuinely Victorian successor to the by then traditional, if not somewhat outdated, Gothic villain. Count Fosco is, like many another Gothic villain, a foreign nobleman with mysterious origins and equally mysterious sources of power. He turns out to be partly motivated by political intrigue and the need to escape the consequences of having betrayed a pseudo-Rosicrucian 'Brotherhood', again a lingering Gothic theme, but Collins invests this fat, foppish, grandiose and eloquent figure with a startling amount of life. He is (like, of course, Victor Frankenstein [q.v.]) a chemical experimenter, well versed in 'medical and magnetic science' and callous of other lives when carrying out his secret purposes; but what gives a unique level to his personality is his thoroughgoing enjoyment of his own melodramatic potential, which Collins brings to the fore in sections of the book where Fosco himself takes over the narrative.

He is enabled to come out with statements like, 'I accomplish my destiny with a calmness which is terrible to myself', without any of the hesitation and agonizing which used, in the tradition, to accompany the machinations of a Montoni or an Ambrosio. He is also granted by Collins entire confidence in his own powers of persuasion: 'women can resist a man's love, a man's face, a man's personal appearance, and a man's money', Fosco points out (although he manages to make full use of even these supposedly inferior assets), 'but they cannot resist a man's tongue, when he knows how to talk to them'. Fosco is above all a talker, a persuader. He is also conscious of, and reflective about, the inherently melodramatic power of the actions which he undertakes. At one point he recounts his abduction of one of the novel's heroines, Marian Halcombe, with a panache derived from total self-admiration: the scene, he says, of her removal 'was picturesque, mysterious, dramatic, in the highest degree'; and, a little later, of another part of his deeply laid plan: 'What a situation! I suggest it to the rising romance writers of England. I offer it, as totally new, to the worn-out dramatists of France.'

Fosco is, in fact, himself a 'writer of romance', in the sense that he organizes the raw material of his own and other people's lives into theatrical, even melodramatic, actions. He takes over the narrative on two occasions, and they are both connected with this facility. The first one is when he discovers a diary in which Marian has been recording her own opinions of the mystery, and himself writes on its final page a commendation of her intellectual powers and of her skill in unfolding mystery. The second is when the hero (albeit one who is decidedly pallid compared with Fosco), Walter Hartright, exposes Fosco's schemes and forces him to write a confession, which, as it turns out, he thoroughly enjoys: 'habits of literary composition', he says, 'are perfectly familiar to me. One of the rarest of all the intellectual accomplishments that a man can possess is the grand faculty of arranging his ideas. Immense privilege! I possess it. Do you?'

This becoming modesty might suggest the extent to which Fosco is a 'projection' of Collins himself; although if this is so there are other aspects of Fosco's personality which, in a thorough psychological analysis, might well give pause for thought. One of the outstanding features of *The Woman in White* is its very curious sexual emphases. Almost all the characters are in one way or another deviant within their own gender, even if only in appearance. When Walter is first introduced to Marian, he sees her from the back and admires the femininity of her figure, only to be sharply disappointed when she turns round, revealing a face that is dark, even 'swarthy', and 'masculine'. Her stepfather, on the other hand, is part of the line which runs from Roderick Usher to decadent transvestitism, a person of acute and feminine sensibilities, and of a degree of fractiousness and petty irritability which, in the range of Victorian stereotypes, is normally associated only with women. On another occasion Marian sees Fosco himself indulging in one of his odder habits, wandering through the woods singing Figaro's song from *The Barber of Seville* and dressed for relaxation so curiously that she compares him to 'a fat St Cecilia masquerading in male attire'.

The political significance of Fosco is perfectly clear: he is in the long line of aristocratic hero/villains portrayed by Ann Radcliffe (q.v.), Lord Byron,

Edward George Bulwer-Lytton (q.v.) and so many others, but Collins is even more explicit about Fosco's role as a successor to the long-departed order of feudal privilege than his predecessors had been. When Fosco dies, his adoring wife writes an expurgated biography of him which concludes with the resounding judgement: 'His life was one long assertion of the rights of the aristocracy, and the sacred principles of Order – and he died a Martyr to his cause.' Collins even ironically underlines the 'tragedy' of the displaced aristocrat by having him die in a peasant's costume which he was using as a disguise. In gender terms, it is almost unsurprising in terms of the coordinates that Collins sets up that Fosco, who combines in himself the dandy and the man of traditional privilege, should find himself attracted to Marian, the masculine 'New Woman', but also a woman resigned to spinsterhood and for this reason – so we are told – capable of real converse with males. It is also for the same reasons unsurprising that Marian feels nothing for Fosco but revulsion, for in many ways she really *is* a new woman, whatever that may mean, of a kind quite foreign to previous sensation fiction. The reader's sense of this derives partly from the skill with which Collins impersonates her at those points when the narrative is told through her diary, partly from the fact that she has a role, as discoverer and rationalist, that had rarely been attached to women in more traditional literary genres. The other 'heroine' of the book, Marian's half-sister Laura, reminds us far more of the traditional Gothic persecuted (q.v.) and timid figure: she is 'sensibility' to her fingertips, and it is again a mark of Collins's indebtedness to the Gothic tradition that the figure of Fosco's English wife, the cowed but mutedly ferocious Madame Fosco, seems almost uncannily similar to Radcliffe's Madame Cheron. Marian, however, is quite different. When the righteous but insipid Walter feels the onset of paranoid uncertainties familiar to earlier Gothic heroes – 'I began to doubt', he says in connection with the mysterious appearances of Anne Catherick, the woman in white of the title, 'whether my own faculties were not in danger of losing their balance. It seemed almost like a monomania to be tracing back everything strange that happened, everything unexpected that was said, to the same hidden source and the same sinister influence' – Marian is far more clear-minded. When she speaks of the wicked Sir Percival's 'active persecution' of herself and Laura, his wife, she is quite sure – and thus makes the reader quite sure – that real persecution is what is taking place, a certainty underlined by having her narrative contribution precisely in the form of a day-to-day diary rather than of the remembered accounts which make up most of the rest of the book.

But, as with earlier Gothic fiction, the presence of rational characters and their accounts, and the absence of events that turn out to be actually supernatural, is not allowed to cheat the reader of supernatural thrills, even if these are later explained. Most of these thrills centre on the early appearances of the woman in white, the wraithlike and disturbed Anne, and Collins's tone can be judged from Walter's reflections on her death:

> Through what mortal crime and horror, through what darkest windings of the way down to Death, the lost creature had wandered in God's leading to the last home that, living, she never hoped to reach! . . . *That* rest shall be sacred – that companionship always undisturbed! . . . So the ghostly figure which has haunted these pages as it haunted my life, goes down into the impenetrable Gloom. Like a Shadow she first came to me, in the loneliness of the night. Like a Shadow she passes away, in the loneliness of the dead.

It is significant that it is only really in connection with Anne that Collins adopts this stance of high reflection, which has reminded some critics of Charles Dickens and Nathaniel Hawthorne (qq.v.). In general Collins is by no means an intrusive narrator, as indeed is evident from the surprisingly modern skill with which he allows the narrative to impersonate different characters' voices.

In terms of location, Collins takes the Gothic ideal of isolation and gloom and brings it to England in the lowering shape of Blackwater Park, with its disused wings and dark lake, the house to which Sir Percival brings his less than willing bride, and also in the setting of the earlier part of the book, Limmeridge House. Limmeridge is situated in pure Brontë (q.v.) country, which seems to have had an effect on Marian's freedom from social constraint: 'in our wild moorland country', she says, 'and in this great lonely house, we may well claim to be beyond the reach of the trivial conventionalities which hamper people in other places'. But these locations are invested with a distinctive quality: they are drawn in with a firm hand, and the mysterious management of large households which appeared to provoke so many difficulties in the eighteenth century is depicted in naturalistic and convincing detail, a partial domestication of the Gothic which remains one of the most enduring aspects of Collins's legacy.

Bibliography

Gindele, Karen C. 2000: 'Wonders Taken for Signs: Marian and Fosco in *The Woman in White.*' *Literature and Psychology*, 46 (3), 65–76.

Hughes, Winifred 1980: *The Maniac in the Cellar: Sensation Novels of the 1860s.* Princeton, NJ: Princeton University Press.

Lim, Soonhee 2002: 'Wilkie Collins's *The Woman in White* and the Politics of the Borderline: The Process of Deterritorialisation in the Sensation Novel.' *British and American Fiction to 1900*, 9 (1), 217–37.

O'Neill, Philip 1988: *Wilkie Collins: Women, Property and Propriety.* Basingstoke: Macmillan.

Pedlar, Valerie 2001: 'Drawing a Blank: The Construction of Identity in *The Woman in White.*' In Dennis Walder (ed.), *The Nineteenth-Century Novel: Identities.* London: Open University Press and Routledge, 69–94.

Taylor, Jenny Bourne 1988: *In the Secret Theatre of Home: Wilkie Collins, Sensation Narrative and Nineteenth-Century Psychology.* London: Routledge.

J. Sheridan Le Fanu,

UNCLE SILAS

(1864)

Uncle Silas: A Tale of Bartram-Haugh is now perhaps the best known of
J. Sheridan Le Fanu's Gothic sensation novels. It is the story of Maud
Ruthyn, who, upon the death of her father, is sent to live with her Uncle
Silas. With an eye on Maud's fortune, Silas first plots to marry her to his
brutal oaf of a son, Dudley, and then, when it emerges Dudley is already
married, he and Silas conspire to murder Maud with the help of her former
governess, Madame de la Rougierre. The plot fails. Dudley mistakes the governess in a drunken stupor for Maud in a drug-induced sleep, and murders
Madame de la Rougierre with a spiked hammer.

As this brief summary suggests, Le Fanu is working in the mode of the
female Gothic (q.v.) and offers many of the same motifs and themes as Ann
Radcliffe's *The Mysteries of Udolpho* (qq.v.), but in a revitalized form. Le
Fanu, unlike Radcliffe, has his female protagonist relate the events herself in
retrospect, and, partly through this emphasis upon Maud's mind and the
accompanying revelation of the dangerous limits of her vision, he pushes the
Gothic towards a more conscious engagement with psychology. An uncanny
(q.v.) sense of doubling pervades the text, suggested even through the pre-
sentation of two Mauds, the one who experiences events and the older and
wiser one who recollects and guides the narrative, commenting upon the
mistakes and fears of her younger self. Like *Udolpho*, *Uncle Silas* sets up two
secluded houses associated with two patriarchal representatives. One is the
pastoral world of Knowl, where Maud initially lives with her father, Austin.
The other is the decaying Gothic mansion of Bartram-Haugh, full of secret
chambers and hidden passages, where she lives after Austin's death under
the guardianship of the sinister Silas. But while the novel would seem to fall
into two separate parts, defined by Maud's stay in the two houses, these parts
are in fact closely related.

A complex patterning characterizes the way in which Le Fanu sets up one against the other. Both Knowl and Bartram-Haugh are remote country houses; the characters that appear in the first half of the novel reappear in the second; most importantly, there is a curious doubling of Austin and Silas. At Knowl, Silas is literally absent and yet still present, in the portrait that fascinates Maud and initially inspires her with thoughts of redeeming his ruined reputation and the family name. Similarly, at Bartram-Haugh, the dead Austin is strangely present. The night before Maud leaves Knowl, she dreams of her father, whose face is inexplicably threatening, alternately white, sharp, transparent, 'hanging in cadaverous folds', but always marked by 'the same unnatural expression of diabolical fury'. Falling asleep again, she hears her father's voice say sharply, 'Maud, we shall be late at Bartram-Haugh.' Later, when she swoons upon first becoming aware of her uncle's schemes, she comes to consciousness confused: 'I did not in the least know where I was. I thought my father was ill, and spoke to him, Uncle Silas was standing near the window, looking unspeakably grim.'

With Silas, Le Fanu offers a masterful reworking of the Gothic villain. A religious fanatic, ageing, dissolute and addicted to laudanum, Silas has been shunned by society ever since a notorious gambler was found dead on his estate; although it was declared a suicide, it turns out, as popularly suspected, to have been murder. What is particularly interesting about Silas is that, as W. J. McCormack (1980) observes, he appears to be called into being by Austin's death. Appropriately, then, Silas is described primarily in terms associated with death and the spirit world; he appears above all to be a living corpse. On first meeting Silas, for example, Maud describes him as having a 'face like marble, with a fearful monumental look', like an 'apparition, drawn as it seemed in black and white'. The connections between Silas and Austin and the spectrality of the former, McCormack suggests, may be explained in terms of the Swedenborgian doctrine that suffuses the text. According to the Swedish theologian and visionary Emanuel Swedenborg (1688–1772), the events of a man's life are repeated in his consciousness after death to reveal his true spiritual condition. The doubling of Austin and Silas may consequently imply that Austin is the earthly existence of a soul whose real nature is exposed in the figure of Silas.

However, the text's relationship with Swedenborgianism is ambiguous; it is, after all, strongly implicated in Le Fanu's attack on religious fanaticism. Furthermore, this explanation does not take into account the fact that it is through Maud's perspective that we are offered a spectral Silas. The connection that she makes between her uncle and father suggests a possible underlying awareness of something her conscious mind cannot admit, something that contradicts all her taught systems of belief. Both brothers actually represent a danger to Maud. Silas is tempted by her inheritance and willing to kill her, but it is Austin who is willing to expose her to risks in the first place for the sake of the family name. Maud is determined to believe in Silas, in order to fulfil the trust placed in her by her father, and her inability to recognize or admit that he constitutes a threat to her nearly leads to her death. She can see Austin no more clearly than she can Silas. She may repeatedly insist that she experiences a close and loving relationship with her father, but Austin, constantly described in terms of rigidity and shadows, shows little emotional warmth towards her. As the portraits that line the walls of the Ruthyn parlour suggest, family tradition and responsibility define and circumscribe Austin's social world. Ultimately, he is much like Silas and sees his daughter as little more than a pawn to manipulate in his quest to redeem the family name.

Austin's apparent inability to see anything wrong with the woman whom he retains as his daughter's governess is one of many indications of his failure as a father. Despite Maud's fears, he dismisses Madame de la Rougierre only when she is discovered rifling through his desk. To both Maud and the reader, there is something disturbing about this female grotesque from the start, even when the horror is placed in uneasy juxtaposition with farce. There is little psychological subtlety in Le Fanu's portrayal of the governess: large, bald and bony, she is an unsettling parody of the feminine, a 'great raw-boned hannimal' resembling, as Alison Milbank suggests, more a pantomime dame than an actual woman (1992: 180). She is nevertheless a horrific figure, never more so than when she sings the ballad about the lady with a pig's head and then takes Maud into the graveyard, where she capers around amongst the stones: 'I am Madame la Morgue – Mrs. Deadhouse! I will present you my friends, Monsieur Cadavre and Monsieur Squelette. Come, come leetle mortal, let us play.'

Although *Uncle Silas* is a long book, surprisingly little actually happens: the emphasis is less on action than on the creation of a brooding and threatening atmosphere. Descriptions become heavily symbolic, particularly the references to pictures that recur throughout the text. Both Austin and Silas are described as resembling figures painted in the style of Rembrandt or Wouvermans, setting up a series of reflections and shadows that not only emphasize the sense of insistent doubling but also draw attention to questions of representation. There seems to be no possibility of objective vision for Maud; her understanding of people and events is always to some degree mediated through the perceptions of others or her properly socialized beliefs. Like the picture, the other primary motif, the window, is used to suggest these limitations. Windows in *Uncle Silas,* rather than offering clear visions, become barriers to perception, offering a 'framed' view of the world, and emphasizing the way in which each character's vision is in some way limited or directed by a constraining set of attitudes and beliefs.

Only at the very close of the novel does Maud's vision appear to clear. After she escapes with the help of the peasant girl Meg to the house of her cousin Monica Knollys, the main narrative concludes with Maud falling unconscious; she loses all memory of what follows. The story resumes, years after the events, in the conclusion: 'I have penned it. I sit for a moment breathless.' Maud looks out now 'on the sweet green landscape and pastoral hills', on 'images of liberty and safety', and 'the tremendous nightmare of my youth melts into air'. It is, for the first time in the narrative, a summer scene, and the paradisiacal landscape previously described by the Swedenborgian Dr Bryerly as existing after death is now seen here. Only with the conclusion, Alison Milbank suggests, is a sense of 'ubiquitous spectrality finally lifted from the narrative' (1992: 160). It is also precisely at the moment when Maud seems to see the world around her clearly, however, that she reveals her own acceptance of Swedenborg, in particular the idea that the earthly points to a more 'real' supernatural. 'This world is a parable – the habitation of symbols', Maud concludes, 'the phantoms of spiritual things immortal shown in mortal shape.' Given the previous treatment of Swedenborg within the text, the conclusion seems strangely unsatisfactory. Maud appears to have exchanged faith in one father for faith in another, and whether she now indeed sees clearly or has simply adopted an equally suspect frame of vision is ultimately left unclear.

Bibliography

McCormack, W. J. 1980: *Sheridan Le Fanu and Victorian Ireland.* Oxford: Clarendon Press.

Milbank, Alison 1992: *Daughters of the House: Modes of the Gothic in Victorian Fiction.* Basingstoke: Macmillan.

Robert Louis Stevenson,

DR JEKYLL AND MR HYDE

(1886)

The best-known of all *Doppelgänger* stories, Robert Louis Stevenson's *The Strange Case of Dr Jekyll and Mr Hyde* emerges from a Gothic tradition which includes such works as James Hogg's *Confessions of a Justified Sinner* (qq.v.) and Edgar Allan Poe's (q.v.) 'William Wilson' (1839). It is also, however, firmly located in a particular historical moment, and shares many features with other Gothic works of its time. The story is told through multiple narratives that combine to create a mystery to be solved. Gothic, as both the full title and many of the chapter headings suggest, here merges with detective fiction. Events are related primarily from the perspectives of John Utterson, Jekyll's lawyer, and Dr Lanyon, his friend and colleague, and the story concludes with 'Henry Jekyll's Statement of the Case'.

Like much Victorian Gothic (q.v.), *Dr Jekyll and Mr Hyde* locates its Gothic horror in a contemporary metropolitan setting. The city, resounding with a 'low growl', is both primitive and threatening. Hyde lives in the 'dismal quarter of Soho', described 'like a district of some city in a nightmare', and Jekyll's windowless laboratory is a 'sinister block of building' that shows signs of prolonged and sordid neglect. The story begins when Utterson is taking his weekly walk with Richard Enfield, a 'well-known man about town', and the two men walk by this building. Enfield points out the door and begins to describe an incident he witnessed in which a man trampled over a child's body 'like some damned Juggernaut' and left her screaming on the ground. After Enfield threatened scandal and insisted on financial compensation to the child's family, the man went in this particular door and came out with a cheque bearing the signature of another man, one 'in the very pink of the proprieties'. While Enfield recognizes Henry Jekyll's name on the cheque, he does not know, as Utterson does, that this door, most appropriately in terms of this story of psychic splitting, leads into the old dissecting room of Jekyll's laboratory. What neither man can comprehend, and what is set up as the central mystery of the story, is the nature of the relationship between Jekyll and Hyde.

It is a question of particular interest to Utterson, since Jekyll has made a will leaving everything to Edward Hyde. Utterson determines to seek Hyde out, and when he meets him, the dreadful nature of the creature is confirmed. From the start, Hyde is presented as something barely human; he gives a 'strong feeling of deformity' and produces revulsion in all who meet him. Elaine Showalter suggests that from one perspective he can be seen as the embodiment of late Victorian anxieties about the homosexual. In 'the most famous code word of Victorian sexuality', she observes, the other male characters 'find something *unspeakable* about Hyde' (1990: 112). There is also, more obviously, something rather atavistic about him. Repeatedly he is described in terms of the bestial and the primitive. Darwinian elements abound and Hyde's animal nature is suggested not only through his name but through a striking series of images: he is described as 'troglodytic' and 'apelike', as 'hissing' like a snake, and 'snarling' into a 'savage laugh'. Evolution becomes a central issue here, or, more correctly, the possibility of devolution. When Jekyll later describes taking the drug that effects the split for the first time, he notes 'the most racking pangs succeeded: a grinding in the bones, deadly nausea, and a horror of the spirit'. The repeated associations of Hyde with the primitive and bestial suggest that what happens here is some kind of reversion of the species. At this point in the story, however, Utterson is unaware how closely Jekyll and Hyde are connected. He assumes that for Jekyll to be associating with such a creature, he must be haunted by another kind of past, suffering for 'the ghost of some old sin, the cancer of some concealed disgrace'.

Following Hyde's murder of Sir Danvers Carew, and prompted by his suspicion that Jekyll is helping a murderer, Utterson consults their mutual friend Dr Lanyon, who mysteriously declares he has had a shock from which he will never recover and refuses to speak of Jekyll. On Lanyon's death, he leaves Utterson an envelope containing yet another sealed envelope, with the direction that it is not to be opened until the death or disappearance of Jekyll. Eventually, Jekyll's manservant, hearing only a strange voice behind the laboratory door, tells Utterson he fears that his master has been murdered; Utterson recognizes the voice of Hyde, the door is broken down, and they find Hyde dead inside. The story ends with the two accounts that explain the mystery: Dr Lanyon's narrative, in which he tells of witnessing Hyde transform into Jekyll, and Jekyll's own statement of the case.

To some extent, *Dr Jekyll and Mr Hyde*, like many Gothic texts of the Decadence (q.v.), engages with and aggravates cultural anxieties about the dangers associated with scientific progress, particularly if such progress is not directed by clear moral guidelines. Jekyll realizes that the drug succeeds not because of his advanced knowledge and expertise, but because of an impurity in a particular batch of chemicals: it is simply a disastrous mistake. However, we learn little about the scientific side of his experiments, and Jekyll shows little interest in describing them; he, like the text as a whole, is far more interested in analysing the nature of the relationship between himself and Hyde.

While dabbling in science is implicated in Jekyll's disastrous splitting, Jekyll himself suggests it is the repressive forces of social convention that are primarily responsible. Initially, he writes, 'the worst of my fault was a certain impatient gaiety of disposition' that was difficult to reconcile with 'my imperious desire to carry my head high, and wear a more than commonly grave countenance before the public'. Since Jekyll desires to be seen as entirely respectable, he must, as the name of his alter ego suggests, 'hide' his private self, and this he does by splitting it off from his public self. Jekyll's problems echo those of numerous earlier Gothic protagonists, like Victor Frankenstein (q.v.), whose aspirations render them particularly susceptible to fragmentation. They are also, however, more specifically the product of a particular historical moment, when the strict policing of morality needed to uphold the sense of Victorian middle-class superiority inevitably resulted in the intensification of various psychic pressures.

Jekyll suggests the potential exists for even more fragmentation: 'I hazard the guess that man will be ultimately known for a mere polity of multifarious, incongruous, and independent denizens.' Although the story mainly encourages us to think in terms of duality and duplicity, a far less disturbing concept than multiplicity, the nature of the split is nevertheless complex, and problematizes the whole issue of identity. While Hyde is Jekyll's double, he is not his opposite; even the fact that Hyde is smaller and younger suggests he is only a part while Jekyll is a more complex whole. When the 'very fortress of identity' is shattered, the result is not a simple opposition between good and evil. Even Jekyll observes that while one character may be 'wholly evil', the other is 'the same old Henry Jekyll, that incongruous compound of whose reformation and improvement I had already learned to despair'. What Hyde embodies remains a part of Jekyll, a point most clearly made when Jekyll recalls sitting in the sun on a bench, 'the animal within me licking the chops of memory'. Writing complicates the division even further: Hyde retains the same hand as Jekyll, and so a new signature must be created for him, but when Hyde writes the letter to Lanyon it is not only in the hand of Jekyll, it is also entirely in Jekyll's voice.

The idea of a clear split, however, is increasingly emphasized by Jekyll himself as his statement progresses. Initially, he is not repulsed by Hyde, and even celebrates their connection; when he looks upon 'that ugly idol in the glass' he feels a 'leap of welcome. This, too, was myself. It seemed natural and human.' Hyde is first viewed primarily as a disguise; Jekyll speaks of him as a body he wears, and talks of sharing in his pleasures and adventures. The change in his attitude comes when he begins to lose control over Hyde's emergence, and fears he is losing hold of his original self and 'becoming slowly incorporated with my second and worse'.

At this point he determines to avoid the drug and, for two months, leads a life 'of such severity as I had never before attained to'. The results are predictable: 'My devil had been long caged, he came out roaring.' While the murder of Carew makes Jekyll even more resolved to live a 'beneficent and innocent life', Hyde begins to emerge without the drugs, and the transformation becomes increasingly difficult to control. Jekyll's statement now demonstrates his complete rejection of any connection with his other, and his desperate attempt to reassert some separate identity of his own. Describing Hyde's activities, it is 'he' of whom Jekyll speaks: 'He, I say – I cannot say, I. That child of Hell had nothing human; nothing lived in him but fear and hatred.' As he runs out of the powder that gives him some vestige of control, and comes to the end of his statement, Jekyll writes that 'this is my true hour of death'. By conflating himself with his narrative, and identifying himself as its true subject, Jekyll makes one last attempt to distinguish himself as a separate and distinct 'I'. The end of the narrative is the end of Jekyll, he says, and what remains 'concerns another than myself'. This final separation, however, seems quite as superficial as those he has suggested before, 'far more', as Jerrold Hogle suggests, 'a hope than a fact' (in Veeder and Hirsch 1988: 189).

Bibliography

Geduld, Harry M. (ed.) 1983: *The Definitive Dr Jekyll and Mr Hyde Companion.* New York: Garland.

Showalter, Elaine 1990: *Sexual Anarchy: Gender and Culture at the Fin de Siècle.* Harmondsworth: Penguin.

Veeder, William and Hirsch, Gordon (eds) 1988: *Dr Jekyll and Mr Hyde After One Hundred Years.* Chicago: University of Chicago Press.

Bram Stoker,

DRACULA

(1897)

In *Dracula*, Bram Stoker established the prototype of our modern vampire (q.v.) and created one of the most potent of all literary myths. Few Gothic figures have been so repeatedly revived and reworked as Stoker's vampire, and after more than one hundred years interest still shows no signs of abating. Even in a formal sense, *Dracula* is an extraordinary narrative. The novel begins with Jonathan Harker's diary, in which he keeps a shorthand account of his journey to Transylvania, his meeting with Count Dracula, who is purchasing the ancient estate of Carfax, and his experiences in the Count's castle. From chapter 5 onwards the novel becomes a compilation of a wide range of genres, including letters, journals and newspaper clippings. Dracula disembarks at Whitby, and proceeds to attack Lucy, the friend of Jonathan's fiancée Mina. In spite of all the efforts of Professor Van Helsing, and multiple blood transfusions, Lucy eventually dies, or, rather, becomes one of the undead. She is 'saved' only by being staked through the heart by her fiancé, Arthur, under Van Helsing's direction and with the support of her other admirers, the American Quincey Morris and John Seward, the superintendent of the lunatic asylum at Purfleet. The remainder of the narrative is concerned with Dracula's advances on Mina and the attempt of the vampire hunters to save her, to find and neutralize the boxes of earth which give the Count sanctuary, and to destroy him. The chase eventually leads them to Transylvania, where the vampire is finally despatched.

Like most Victorian Gothic (q.v.), Stoker's *Dracula* insists on the modernity of its setting. The opening section, as Jonathan details his trip through Transylvania, may return to a feudal world populated by fearful and superstitious peasants, but the text soon leaves this alien land and locates itself firmly in back in England. There is a particular emphasis on London, the urban nucleus of the modern world, a world that would have been eminently familiar to the contemporary reader. Repeatedly, the modernity of the text is emphasized by references to recent technological advances: telegraphs, typewriters, telephones, phonographs and Kodak cameras are all drawn upon in the struggle against the vampire. Like the shorthand diary that Jonathan keeps, the text is 'nineteenth century up-to-date with a vengeance'.

Set against the orderly and civilized modern world is the atavistic vampire himself. Like all vampires, Dracula is associated with the disruption and transgression of accepted limits and boundaries. As shapeshifter he resists any stable, fixed identity; as 'undead' he straddles that seemingly ultimate boundary between life and death. He is usually absent and yet strangely present. Although central to the opening section set in Transylvania, he practically disappears after arriving in London. His presence is felt thereafter primarily as a troubling presence in the mind, first of Lucy and then of Mina. When Arthur observes of Lucy that 'There is something preying on my dear girl's mind', he unknowingly points out the primary problem with Dracula: it is not just bodies that he penetrates and disturbs. His significance ultimately lies not so much in the way he embodies transgression as in the way he functions as the catalyst for transgression in others: he prompts the release of energies and desires normally repressed in the interest of both social and psychic stability.

Such transgression is a source of both pleasure and fear. When Jonathan begins to succumb to the female vampires, for example, he feels 'a wicked, burning desire that they would kiss me with those red lips'. The experience is nevertheless as repulsive as it is thrilling and both the encounter and his own reaction cause him to question his sanity, as he turns to his diary to record his experience in the seeming fixity offered by the text. Even Mina, that 'good, good woman', demonstrates ambivalence: while she recalls the moment when Dracula forces her to feed from a wound in his breast with horror, she has to admit that 'strangely enough, I did not want to hinder him'.

If *Dracula* is above all concerned with the breaking of taboos, it nevertheless needs to be read as an expression of specifically late Victorian concerns. It is, for example, persistently anxious about the breakdown of gender roles. Victorian middle-class gender ideology tended to police the boundaries of male and female quite rigorously, aiming to control by defining and delimiting the nature and roles of the sexes in a manner that particularly constrained women. Throughout the century women had nevertheless reacted against these restrictions, and the challenge to gender ideology led to the emergence of the New Woman, referred to upon several occasions in *Dracula*, who was characterized by her demands for both social and sexual autonomy. The anxiety caused by the breakdown of traditional roles pervades the text. Female vampires feeding on children, for example, a rather obvious rejection of maternity, provokes some of the vehement expressions of horror, while Lucy's flirtatiousness makes her suspect from the start, and Dracula's visits only serve to release a barely repressed sensuality as she turns into a voluptuous wanton 'nightmare of Lucy'.

This was not only the age of the New Woman, however, it was also the time when the homosexual was first constructed as a category. What was then termed 'sexual inversion' began to enter into discourse in such texts as John Addington Symonds's *A Problem in Greek Ethics* (1883) and Havelock Ellis's *Sexual Inversion*, published and then suppressed in 1897. The confusion of gender categories, many critics have noted, is most clearly demonstrated by Jonathan's feminine passivity in the scene where he is seduced by the three female vampires; here the conventions of sexual difference are inverted as the fluttering Jonathan awaits the moment of penetration. For Christopher Craft, what is always threatened in the text is that Dracula will seduce and penetrate another male. This desire, however, is never directly enacted and instead finds its fulfilment in a series of heterosexual displacements (in Byron 1999: 110).

This breaking down of traditional gender roles was just one factor in what was seen as a more widespread degeneration of society, of growing cultural and social decay and corruption (see 'Gothic and Decadence'). The discourse of degeneration pervades *Dracula*, with Stoker even making reference to two key figures in the debate: the criminologist Cesare Lombroso, who argued that habitual criminals were throwbacks to the primitive, and Max Nordau, whose *Degeneration* (1895) extended Lombroso's arguments and further saw evidence of degeneration through excessive emotionality in many of the writers of the time.

While many of the threats to society in *Dracula* are seen to come from within, the text also enacts late Victorian society's most important and persistent narrative of decline: the narrative of reverse colonization, the fear of a racial degeneration which would corrupt and destabilize identity. Dracula clearly has plans for colonization: 'Your girls that you all love are mine already', he tells the vampire hunters, 'and through them you and others shall yet be mine – my creatures, to do my bidding and to be my jackals when I want to feed.' Dracula's 'foreignness' is made quite clear, and descriptions link him to the 'monstrous Jew' constructed by nineteenth-century anti-Semitic discourse. And this 'foreigner' blends just a little too easily into the modern Victorian world, strolling down Piccadilly in full daylight and watching the pretty girls pass by.

Dracula's modernity lies both in its emphasis on a contemporary setting and in its concern with technology and data accumulation: the acquisition of power is closely associated with the collection of data. The vampire hunters defeat the Count partly because they learn enough about him to predict his movements and responses. All the information comes together in the typescript Mina produces, and even Dracula, as he demonstrates with his attempts to destroy their hoard of information, is aware of the power such information confers. As well as drawing upon these recent technological advances, however, Stoker also engages with many of the most recent theories and developments in the mental sciences.

Published one year after the term 'psychoanalysis' was introduced, *Dracula* participates in many of the debates in the field then known as 'mental physiology', the study of the workings of the mind. Seward studies madness and is interested in the unconscious; dreams, hypnotism and telepathy all play a significant role in the text. The study of such issues was a growing part of a movement away from a more materialist science. Many scientists were reluctant to shift completely from a materialist explanation of behaviour, however, and *Dracula* also articulates such reluctance, appearing to swing between the two sides of the debate. While Dracula's ultimate defeat is partly due to Van Helsing placing Mina in the hypnotic trance that allows them to track the vampire's movements, it is also partly due to the more materialist science of physiognomy. Mina, with her knowledge of the theories of Nordau and Lombroso, is able to identify Dracula as a criminal type and consequently to make certain assumptions about his responses and behaviour. Nevertheless, the text also repeatedly questions the validity of this science. The sleeping Lucy, her face full of sweetness and purity, awakens to snarl and seduce; lines of difference, such moments suggest, are not so easily stabilized. Furthermore, as Van Helsing notes when Seward insists there must be a rational explanation for Lucy's condition, it is the vampire hunters' very reliance on the rational sciences that makes them vulnerable to Dracula: 'in this enlightened age, when men believe not even what they see, the doubting of wise men would be his greatest strength'.

Boundaries must ultimately be reconfirmed, social and psychic order restored. The staking of Lucy provides the most brutal enactment of the restoration of gendered boundaries. As Arthur, supported by his friends, pounds in the 'mercy-bearing stake', Lucy's writhing body is released from the grip of desire and restored to 'holy calm'. Mina, suitably punished for her momentary lapse when feeding at Dracula's breast by being branded with the sacred wafer, is ultimately restored to her proper role as nurturing mother. The female vampires in Dracula's castle are, like Lucy, despatched with the appropriate penetrating stake. Dracula himself, however, is destroyed not with a stake, which would suggest further transgression, but with the weapons of empire (see 'Imperial Gothic'), with Jonathan's kukri knife and Quincey's bowie knife; he dies like a man. And as the primary alien threat is neutralized in this final struggle, it is notable that Quincey, representative of the rising imperial power of America, is the one vampire hunter who does not survive. The novel ends with a 'Note' from Harker which appears to place us back in the secure Victorian bourgeois world, but the restoration of order is nevertheless problematized. As Van Helsing is well aware, the oppositional terms of good and evil depend upon each other: 'it is not the least of its terrors', he observes, 'that this evil thing is rooted deep in all good'. The threatening other, which ultimately resides within the characters themselves, is not destroyed in *Dracula*: it is simply repressed once more.

Bibliography

Byron, Glennis (ed.) 1999: *Dracula: New Casebook.* Basingstoke: Macmillan.

Glover, David 1996: *Vampires, Mummies, and Liberals: Bram Stoker and the Politics of Popular Fiction.* Durham, NC: Duke University Press.

Hughes, William and Smith, Andrew (eds) 1998: *Bram Stoker: History, Psychoanalysis and the Gothic.* Houndmills: Macmillan.

Senf, Carol 1998: *Dracula: Between Tradition and Modernism.* New York: Twayne.

HENRY JAMES,

THE TURN OF THE SCREW

(1898)

The Turn of the Screw is one of the most extensively discussed works in modern litreature. One of the questions about it is how one might consider its relation to the tradition of the Gothic. The essence of the story concerns a governess – the narrator of almost all of the story – who is appointed by a mysterious gentleman to look after two children, Miles and Flora. She is granted a completely free hand, provided she under no circumstances troubles her employer. She finds a housekeeper on the premises, Mrs Grose, and encounters the children; her attempts, however, to settle into her position are hindered by a series of curious events and half-events – in the sense that they are only partly seen, or partly validated, as will of course always be the case with a first-person narration – which make her fear the children. In particular, they have been exposed in the past to the influences of the previous governess, a Miss Jessel, and a fellow servant named Quint, both of whom have disappeared, or died, under mysterious circumstances, and who, perhaps, had an affair of which the children could not have remained ignorant (this, though, might only be in the mind of the governess, a projection of her own compoundly lonely position). The governess comes to feel that this couple, even perhaps after their deaths, are continuing their influence over the children, and her apparent concern for them gradually turns into a bitter struggle for control, which culminates in the removal of Flora and the death of Miles.

This, though, is by no means to give a flavour of the story, which is full of strange glimpses and conflicting interpretations. Such supernatural apparitions and portents as there are, of course, are recounted solely by the governess, and even she is often doubtful of their reality; the whole story moves in a miasma of uncertainty, and most of the critical debate has effectively centred on the main question: to what extent is the governess a reliable interpreter of the signs she claims to observe? That the matter should remain unresolved is, of course, a central part of Henry James's purpose; his habitual subtleties of style interlock with this motif in such a way as to manipulate the reader into a situation of chronic doubt which is in no way resolved by the end of the tale. This, however, does not prevent the reader from trying to see the governess more clearly, and the character-structure that might be seen to emerge is one which is not unfamiliar from previous Gothic works – Emily in Ann Radcliffe's *Mysteries of Udolpho* (qq.v.), Charlotte Brontë's (q.v.) Jane Eyre, and Maud Ruthyn in J. Sheridan LeFanu's *Uncle Silas* (qq.v.) are all similarly characters placed in situations for which they are unfitted by reason of birth, expectation and/or training. James's governess, whatever else she may do, clearly approaches her task with a set of preconceptions that make her handling of the delicacies of the situation with the children highly questionable.

Like earlier Gothic heroines, she prides herself on her 'sensitivity', yet in her actual dealings with the children and with Mrs Grose this sensitivity is sometimes hardly apparent, despite – or sometimes because of – her own versions of events. She claims to find Mrs Grose totally transparent, and considers herself justified in overriding the housekeeper's more experienced view of the situation at all points, even suspecting her of collusion with the children, although the reader may frequently question her judgement on these points. The consequence of this – which flows, at least in part, from her assumption of Mrs Grose's social inferiority – is that she (the governess) becomes, or perhaps one should say remains, an isolated figure, relying solely on her own perceptions and confident of her skill in unravelling the 'mystery' – which in turn, of course, assumes that there is a mystery to unravel. Yet the skilful detective work which the reader might feel this situation to require is not helped by her habit of jumping to extreme conclusions; phrases like 'the strangest thing in the world' abound, suggesting very strongly her determination to place herself at the 'heart' of a highly charged emotional situation, whether such a situation already exists or not. Whatever this situation may be, the force of her narrative is to place herself at the centre of it, although we are given repeated suggestions that her importance to the children, in their eyes, is at best peripheral. It is precisely their self-sufficiency to which she continually objects: although the only mode of existence that Quint and Miss Jessel may have is as part of the children's private mythology (possibly, or possibly not, shared by Mrs Grose), the governess determines to read in the relationships between the four a perversion of 'natural' order, and sees her role as keeping apart worlds which 'ought not' to meet according to her own standards of late Victorian propriety.

In this respect, her role as governess is clearly symbolic. It is at least possible that she is, and perhaps increasingly becomes, less than sane, but this is connected with an obsessive rationality which, despite her own 'sensitivity', she is determined to instill into the children. The misty figures of Quint and Miss Jessel appear to symbolize several things to her: the tendency of the children, or perhaps of any or all children, to develop a private world of their own; their growing awareness – only hinted at – of sexual and emotional life; the perpetual threat to her of their own independence and adulthood. She is in many respects a typified Victorian figure, totally self-righteous in her insistence on the necessary repression of children and in her confidence in her own approach to education. For her Miss Jessel is a 'horror of horrors', despite the fact that she knows next to nothing about Miss Jessel and despite the even more damning fact that the little she does know derives from Mrs Grose, whose word the governess normally – that is, when it does not coincide with her own opinions – professes to doubt and even despise.

The governess's final, lethal fury with the children is, seen from one perspective, the frustrated rage of one who has failed to convince others of the validity of her own mode of perception. Whether Miles or Flora 'see ghosts' may be a moot point, but it is clear that they do not see the world as the governess does, and that she fails in her struggle to make them do so. And as with so many Gothic texts, the roots of this frustration are convoluted: to say that she is herself deranged would be to discount the elements of derangement which exist in the situation around her, a situation in which she is expected to act as professional inductor into a world to which she is herself denied the key. There are suggestions in the text that she may be infatuated with her employer, and this may be the case; at any rate, the possibility that she might be serves symbolically to strengthen the dislocation in her relationships with the children, and thus to underline the synthetic and displaced elements in her emotional position.

To ask the crucial question of whether the ghosts in *Turn of the Screw* are 'real' is merely to run into paradox and to miss the principal points of the text. That text is given as the governess's account, and what it chiefly displays is a set of psychological problems in her position within the microcosmic society of the book. Within that society, she is required to fulfil all the duties of social reinforcement. She it is who is entrusted with the guardianship of the 'line', that is, with the production of 'suitable' successors for her employer, although she herself near the beginning of the book seems doubtful of her fitness for such a role. It is she who is responsible for educating the children into a sense of their 'station' in life, although she has little idea of what that station is, and even less of her own. She discharges these duties by conventional means, through the instilling of fear of 'tabooed' objects and relationships; this also implies, however, the implicit and probably deeply unconscious attempt to redirect the children's affections onto herself. These tasks prove, as the reader may early suspect, incompatible: as she deploys all her strength to dissolve the children's world, she naturally renders their love impossible, and then in turn condemns them for the lack of that quality of feeling which she feels herself to possess in superabundance. And as she classifies their other relationships, real or imagined, as impure, she sets herself an ideal of purity which is disabling and cold to the point of cruelty.

There are indications in the text that she thinks that Quint and Miss Jessel had offered the children a different kind of 'education', less pure, perhaps, but also more 'real'. The reader is thus presented with a fable of isolation and its paranoiac (q.v.) content; what is particularly distinctive in *Turn of the Screw* is its minuteness of attention, its insistence on the apparent viability and coherence of different views of the same events. What takes place, perhaps, is a mutual struggle for exploitative power: moment by moment the governess and the children perceive, sometimes dimly, each other's weaknesses and move in on them when they are only half-formed. Within a single sketchy conversation the balance of power swings giddily as the rival participants gradually accept that the stake is getting higher and higher, and even that strength may lie eventually in their own ability to impose their individual fictions as the truth. Interpretation of events becomes pragmatic, particularly in the case of the governess, who comes to wield her perceptions like weapons, weapons which attain in the end the power of life and death.

What *The Turn of the Screw* suggests in remarkable detail is that there is no transcendent truth *behind* interpretation; the psychology of the story appears to claim that the 'real' is composed of the interrelations between event and account, and it is these interrelations that the text insistently probes. And if this is the structure of reality, then the 'ghosts' are neither more nor less real than anything else in the book; they are among the forms in which consciousness apprehends, and are thus elements in a process of psychological selection, a Gothic world in which nothing is certain and every emotion or behaviour may be victim to a process of apparently surreal exaggeration.

Bibliography

Brooke-Rose, Christine 1976–7: 'The Squirm of the True.' *PTL: A Journal for Descriptive Poetics and Theory,* 1, 265–94, 513–46; 2, 517–62.
Curtsinger, E. C. 1980: '*The Turn of the Screw* as Writer's Parable.' *Studies in the Novel,* 12 (4), 344–58.

Haralson, Eric 2000: ' "His Little Heart, Dispossessed": Ritual Sexorcism in *The Turn of the Screw.*' In Peggy McCormack (ed.), *Questioning the Master: Gender and Sexuality in Henry James's Writing.* Newark, DE: University of Delaware Press, 133–48.

Williams, Jeff 1998: 'Narrative Games: The Frame of *The Turn of the Screw.*' *Journal of Narrative Technique*, 28 (1), 43–55.

Robert Bloch,

PSYCHO

(1959)

Robert Bloch's *Psycho* is the story which formed the basis for Alfred Hitchcock's rather better-known film of that name. In it, a woman called Mary Crane, engaged to marry her boyfriend Sam Loomis but compelled to wait to marry him because of Sam's financial problems, steals $40,000 and drives off to join him. On the way she stops at a lonely motel, run by a man called Norman Bates and, apparently, his sick mother. Bates rents her a room which is connected by a peep-hole to his own office. Observing her undress and go into the shower, he starts to drink while meditating on the dirtiness of women, and appears briefly to pass out; perhaps, though, he passes into a hypnotic, somnambulistic state in which he could be said to be no longer aware of his actions.

When he wakes up, he sees that Mary Crane has been brutally murdered, and concludes, it would appear, that only his mother could have done it. To protect her, he disposes of the body. Meanwhile, Sam is disturbed at his hardware store by the arrival of Lila, Mary's younger sister, who is searching for Mary; and they are simultaneously visited by Arbogast, a private detective hunting for the stolen money, who has tracked Mary this far but has not found her.

Arbogast discovers the motel, the last on his list of places where she may have stayed, and suspects Bates. While Arbogast goes up to the house behind the motel where Bates and his mother live, a worried Bates again starts to drink and, as before, passes out. When he too heads for the house, he finds Arbogast also killed, and goes through the same procedure as before to protect his mother from the consequences of her apparently deranged crimes.

When Arbogast does not return to town, Lila persuades Sam to come to the motel with her, where they book into the room Mary had occupied and discover enough to make them too suspect Bates of murder. They plan for

Sam to keep Bates in conversation while Lila goes off to phone for help. Bates is again drinking, and as he does so he tells Sam something of the truth. However, before Sam can act, Bates knocks him out; before doing so he has warned Sam that, in fact, Lila has not gone for the sheriff but has instead decided to explore the house on her own in a search for further clues.

We next switch to Lila, who explores the house; we have, of course, been present at this scene of the 'exploration of the house' before in many previous literary and filmic (q.v.) manifestations of the Gothic. She discovers Bates's bedroom, which is oddly untouched although the bed itself bears traces of recent occupancy. She eventually goes down to the cellar and, while searching this most remote yet most intimate fastness of what we might think of as the body of the dream-house, she discovers instruments of the taxidermist's craft (we have already been told that this is a hobby of Bates's). She then, however, hears footsteps overhead and, in her panic, accidentally finds herself in a room still further inside the cellar.

Within it, she finds to her horror the decomposed corpse of Bates's mother, and screams 'Mrs Bates' – surely by any account a rather odd thing to scream under the circumstances, but an answer comes; not from the corpse but from Bates himself, who is descending the cellar steps, wearing his mother's clothes and wielding a knife. Before he can get to Lila, however, he is overpowered by Sam, who has conveniently 'come round' in the nick of time.

The book has several epilogues which are, however, perhaps better described as aftermaths. In the first one, we are told that 'in fact' Bates's mother has died some twenty years before, along with a man who was her lover. It was supposed at the time that they had made a suicide pact; Bates, her son, had then been committed to hospital because of his supposed grief, loss and mourning – which had, however, been transformed, Hamlet-like, into madness. However, it now emerges that Bates had forged the all-important suicide note and had himself killed the couple, and had subsequently, in a fit of remorse, exhumed his mother's body; it is this body he has been living with ever since, and thus it is he himself, as we have now been told, who has killed Mary and the detective; or at least this is what one is led to believe, although the Norman Bates who stands thus convicted may, it would seem, have been pretty much unaware of the events in which he has played such a bloody part.

A psychiatrist's explanation follows, as a second aftermath, and takes fairly conventional lines, dwelling on Bates's early domination by his mother, who had conceived a morbid hatred of men when Bates's father had walked out on her shortly after her son's birth. Bates, we are told at this point, had developed a triply fragmented personality after murdering his mother: the

241

conventional adult who ran the motel, the child who could not escape from under his mother's jurisdiction, and the mother herself.

In a chilling final footnote which constitutes the third aftermath, we encounter Bates in his psychiatric hospital (which itself has certain crucial resemblances to a motel). The previous gaps in his fragmented personality are now closing over as adult and son vanish into the psyche of the mother; a mother who, having, as 'she' says, been silent for these twenty years, must now remain silent for the rest of her life, and so motionless that everybody will realize that she, rather like Renfield in *Dracula* (q.v.), 'wouldn't even harm a fly'.

Overall, this narrative of psychic splitting is told tersely and even conventionally: the characters of the Crane sisters and Sam Loomis step straight from the pages of pulp fiction, while Arbogast with his cigarettes and trilby is another avatar of Humphrey Bogart. The power lies in Bloch's ability to manipulate our uncertainties; although quite early on we learn that Bates's version of his mother's life and death does not square with other known facts, the reasons for this discrepancy remain in doubt until the denouement.

There are also a number of significant blurrings of boundaries. At the beginning Bates is in conversation with his mother, and one could say that this hardly squares with 'external' reality as it is apparently revealed later in the text. But Bloch could have a ready answer for this: the personality with which he is dealing is so far disintegrated that rival accounts proliferate, and the conversation between Bates and his mother may be seen as a spur to his actions as much as anything which happens in an outer world that can be validated.

Psychoanalytically, though, *Psycho* could be seen – and in this respect it would not be unique in the Gothic – as the story not mainly of the disintegration of a personality, but rather of a massive attempt by the psyche to *reseal* itself, to find some way of disguising and recovering from the gaping wounds in its construction; and, of course, it could be said that in this it depicts a successful strategy of the unconscious, albeit a strategy which reminds us of a master/slave dialectic in which the ego, unknowingly and uncomplainingly, walks direct into the trap (death) which it has all along existed to avoid. Faced by the strain of maintaining a multiplicity of personalities, Bates has to perform actions that will make this situation unsustainable and will make possible its replacement by a forcible reunification on one side or the other of the border of psychosis. We might think here of the extraordinary strains of story-telling evidenced in the text of, for example, Henry James's *The Turn of the Screw* (qq.v.).

Again, it is no accident that this resealing takes place in a mental hospital, precisely the place where the original splitting occurred as a paradoxical effect of Bates's attempt to heal the gaps in his *outer* world through the original double murder – a double murder itself replicated in the text by the slaying of Mary and the detective. Further than these uncanny doublings, one might say, Bates cannot go, because to encounter triplicity, the one step beyond these locked pairings, would be to encounter a replication of the pattern on which his own inner life has stabilized and become modelled, a pattern in which all three corners of the Oedipal triangle have to be held together, because to let any of them go would be to permit once again the possibility of 'loose ends', ends (of the narrative) which can never be picked up and which therefore leave all the personality's hopes of order shattered.

It is at this point that one might think more deeply about what is told in this 'tale of the unexpected', this Gothic exploration of the uncanny (q.v.), and this would involve looking not only at the 'story' itself, but also at the triple structure – account, diagnosis and aftermath/'footnote' – into which the text itself, in some ways like Bates's psyche, falls. We would need to see *Psycho* as a drama of the vicissitudes of the psyche entrapped in a wish to be loved; and more particularly, of a male psyche caught between images of the woman-as-mother and the woman-as-lover. Under the circumstances described, what is experienced is a mismatch between the inner and the outer, between the presumed full splendour of the 'adult' inner self, as a (Gothicized) adolescent may often experience it, and the accidentally acne-pitted outer countenance which will render this splendid inner person invisible. In Bates's case, the split is floridly displayed in transvestitism, a transvestitism which not only hides the shamed male contour from the outside world but also hides Bates's own actions from himself – in, perhaps, a guise of 'female' passivity which again reminds us of the ambiguities of Gothic's treatment of its vulnerable heroines.

Bibliography

Bloch, Robert 1998: 'On Horror Writers.' In Clive Bloom (ed.), *Gothic Horror: A Reader's Guide from Poe to King and Beyond.* New York: St Martin's Press, 77.

Joshi, S. T. 1995: 'A Literary Tutelage: Robert Bloch and H. P. Lovecraft.' *Weird Fiction,* 16, 13–25.

Punter, David 1990: 'Robert Bloch's *Psycho*: Some Pathological Contexts.' In Brian Docherty (ed.), *American Horror Fiction: From Brockden Brown to Stephen King.* New York: St Martin's Press, 92–106.

ANNE RICE,

INTERVIEW WITH THE VAMPIRE

(1976)

Interview with the Vampire, the first in Anne Rice's series of *The Vampire Chronicles*, offers one of the most significant rewritings of the traditional myth since it was established by Bram Stoker in *Dracula* (qq.v.). Shifting the narrative perspective to the vampire himself, a move anticipated by Fred Saberhagen in his 1975 *The Dracula Tape* when he retells Stoker's story from the perspective of his vampire, the text begins to dissolve the conventional boundaries between the vampire and the human. *Interview* is the story of Louis de Pointe du Lac as told to a young reporter, later identified in *The Queen of the Damned* (1988) as Daniel. Part one begins in 1791 and is set in New Orleans, the city that plays a central role in much of Rice's work. Presented as a cosmopolitan part of the new world but simultaneously somehow ancient, imbued with history and decadent, New Orleans becomes the ideal Gothic space for a new vampire fiction. Louis, in despair over the death of his brother, a religious fanatic whose visions he had disparagingly dismissed, accepts the 'dark gift' of the vampire Lestat and is made into a vampire.

The relationship between the two men, as critics have frequently noted, has clear homoerotic overtones. But whether Rice in fact challenges or reproduces the boundaries of either sexuality or gender in this novel is something that has been much debated. For some critics, the characters only parodically re-enact gender conventions. Louis is feminized, presented as passive, delicate and sensitive, and speaks about his feelings at some length. Lestat's masculinity is strongly emphasized; the consummate hunter, he is aggressive, arrogant and unfeeling. (This perspective on Lestat is adjusted, however, when he tells his own story in *The Vampire Lestat* [1985] and advises us, with respect to Louis's narrative, to read between the lines.)

Other critics have seen Rice's vampires more in terms of androgyny and sexual ambiguity. Sandra Tomc, however, suggests this is achieved only

244

through the exclusion of adult female sexuality. Each time an adult female appears in the text, the androgynous ideal is threatened: the usually feminized Louis begins to respond in terms of more conventional heterosexual behaviour, and the adult female is summarily rejected and ejected. Rice, Tomc argues, 'apparently *can't* introduce women characters as significant players in the drama without her own representation of androgyny showing signs of dismantling itself' (1997: 99).

The avoidance of adult female sexuality is first signalled through Claudia, the child vampire that Louis and Lestat create. The three function for a while as a strange family with Louis and Lestat as both her 'fathers' and her 'lovers'. Claudia is condemned to live forever as a powerless victim, 'enslaved', as she says, by her fathers; her growing rage at being a woman with adult desires trapped in a child's body leads to her revolt against Lestat. Her decision to destroy him has been read as both a protest against the kind of femininity offered to women in a patriarchal culture, and a desire to assume the father's authority for herself. 'Such blood, such power', she says to Louis. 'Do you think I'll possess his power and my own power when I take him?'

Part two focuses on the travels of Louis and Claudia through Europe as they try to find others like themselves and some clues to the meaning of their existence. All they find in eastern Europe, however, are 'mindless, animated' corpses who prey on the peasants in the surrounding countryside. 'I had met the European vampire', Louis says as he describes killing the last one: 'He was dead.' Disillusioned, they travel to Paris, the 'mother of New Orleans', and find others of their kind at the Théâtre des Vampires, where real vampires act out vampire behaviour in front of unknowing, mesmerized human audiences. In a sense, vampirism throughout the novel is presented as primarily a spectacle. While Louis yearns for some sense of identity, a clear demarcation of vampire from human is only effected through a series of conventions and performances. Separation is enforced precisely in order to produce the illusion of a distinct identity. The female Parisian vampires tell Claudia that her pastels are tasteless, for example, and as Louis notes, all the Parisian vampires have died their hair black, giving an impression of identity and conformity. Spectacle becomes all. 'To be a vampire is,' Ken Gelder suggests, nothing more than to *act* like a vampire' (1994: 112).

Claudia, disenchanted with Paris and fearing the loss of Louis, insists upon him creating a surrogate mother for her, and the doll-maker Madeleine, who has lost her own child, is made into a vampire. In the meantime, Louis grows increasingly closer to Armand, the oldest of all living vampires, and Lestat has made his way over to Paris. When it is discovered that Louis and Claudia tried to destroy Lestat, the Parisian vampires expose Claudia and Madeleine to the sunlight. After torching the theatre in revenge, Louis leaves, with Armand, and eventually returns to New Orleans.

Armand needs Louis, he tells him, in order to make contact with the nineteenth century: 'You are its spirit, you are the heart.' When Louis objects that far from being the spirit of any age he is 'at odds with everything and always [has] been', Armand points out that it is precisely this that makes him representative: 'Everyone feels as you feel. Your fall from grace and faith has been the fall of a century.' As Louis becomes representative of the nineteenth century for Armand, so the vampires generally become representative of Rice's contemporary world. And as the text initiates a search for both origins and meaning, the vampire is reworked to become a vehicle for philosophical speculation about the origins, the point and the condition of human existence. Louis's quest replicates the human quest for truth, for community, and for moral codes and values by which to live. Connections between the vampire and the human worlds are frequently and explicitly signalled. Louis finds vampire life little different from human life: 'a narrow materialistic and selfish existence'; indeed, he suggests, 'the gods of most men' are just like those of vampires: 'Food, drink, and security in conformity.'

Undercutting the boundaries between vampire and human simultaneously involves a problematizing of questions of good and evil. The traditional vampire and Christian iconography that underwrites any clear distinctions between these oppositions is removed. Bats and wolves are conspicuous only by their absence; unlike Stoker's vampires, these vampires can see themselves in the mirror; garlic and crucifixes have no effects upon them; indeed, as Louis notes, he can look on anything he likes, and 'I rather like looking on crucifixes in particular.' The apparent absence of both God and the Devil, however, is a source of torment to Louis; once the notion of the vampire as damned is removed, there is no explanation for either the origin or the meaning of the vampire's existence. Rice consequently suggests nostalgia for lost certainties at the same time as, at this stage at least, refusing to reinstate these certainties. Later in Rice's *Chronicles,* however, at least by the time of *The Queen of the Damned,* the old oppositions of good and evil have been reinstated, even if in a displaced form.

Finding no answers to his questions, Louis remains in a state of despair. Part four serves as an epilogue to his story as he relates a reunion with Lestat, arranged by Armand, attempting to restore Louis's capacity for feeling. The interview then concludes, with the young reporter asking to be turned into a vampire. Louis, who attacks him and leaves, is horrified at the boy's inability to understand the despair of the vampire life, but the boy's desire to be transformed is something for which we have been prepared throughout. The reader is placed on much the same level as the 'titillated crowd' watching the young woman stripped and vampirized on the stage of the Théâtre des Vampires: Louis, as he watches, can actually 'taste' her. As Rice here collapses the boundaries between performers and audience, so with her lush descriptions she invites the reader to experience with the vampire and share in the sensual pleasures that are opened up to the vampire's expanded senses. In transforming the monster (q.v.) into a site of identification, Rice participates in one of the most significant transformations in the Gothic fiction of today.

Bibliography

Doane, Janice and Hodges, Devon 1990: 'Undoing Feminism: From the Preoedipal to Postfeminism in Anne Rice's Vampire Chronicles.' *American Literary History,* 2 (3), 422–42.

Gelder, Ken 1994: *Reading the Vampire.* London: Routledge.

Haggerty, George E. 1998: 'Anne Rice and the Queering of Culture.' *Novel,* 32 (1), 5–18.

Hoppenstand, Gary, and Browne, Ray B. (eds):1996: *The Gothic World of Anne Rice.* Bowling Green, OH: Bowling Green State University Popular Press.

King, Maureen 1993: 'Contemporary Women Writers and the "New Evil": The Vampires of Anne Rice and Suzy McKee Charnas.' *Journal of the Fantastic in the Arts,* 5 (3), 75–84.

Roberts, Bette B. 1994: *Anne Rice.* New York: Twayne.

Tomc, Sandra 1997: 'Dieting and Damnation: Anne Rice's *Interview with the Vampire.*' In Joan Gordon and Veronica Hollinger (eds), *Blood Read: The Vampire as Metaphor in Contemporary Culture.* Philadelphia: University of Pennsylvania Press, 95–113.

Waxman, Barbara Frey 1992: 'Postexistentialism in the Neo-Gothic Mode: Anne Rice's *Interview with the Vampire.*' *Mosaic,* 25 (3), 79–97.

Stephen King,

THE SHINING

(1977)

In *The Shining*, Stephen King brings together one of the key characters in his fiction, the writer, with one of his most recurrent concerns, child abuse, complicated here by the addition of substance and wife abuse (q.v.). The story begins with Jack Torrance applying for and obtaining a position as winter caretaker at the Overlook Hotel in the Colorado Mountains. Jack, a recovering alcoholic, has a violent temper which is not completely under control; in the past he has broken his son's arm for spilling beer on his papers, and more recently he has been dismissed from a school for a savage attack on one of his students.

The Overlook Hotel, however, has an even shadier history. An 'inhuman place [that] makes human monsters', it provides a reworking of the traditional Gothic castle (q.v.). Full of sinister passages, forbidden rooms, and a basement with a pointedly symbolic old boiler that, if steam is not let off regularly, will explode, the hotel seems to have absorbed and become a repository of the malevolence of its perverse and frequently criminal guests. The previous caretaker succumbed to its influence and murdered his family with an axe – Jack's problems soon make him equally susceptible.

Jack's 5-year-old son, Danny, possesses psychic abilities, the 'shine' of the title, which allow him to read the minds of others. And he has an invisible friend, Tony, who would appear to be some kind of double for Daniel *Anthony* Torrance. More specifically Tony, who initially appears deep down in the bathroom mirror, seems to represent, as Steven Bruhm points out, 'the discourse of the Other, the barely intelligible voice that proceeds from the space opened up in the mirror stage' (1998: 80). Danny cannot remember precisely what Tony shows him, but he knows it has something to do with 'that indecipherable word he had seen in his spirit's mirror': 'Redrum' (murder). Danny's mind is open to visions of both past and future horrors in the hotel. He has, for example, dreams of a terrifying figure chasing him with a rocque mallet, a figure that will turn out to be his father. And when Danny gives in to his obsessive curiosity about the forbidden room 217, a moment full of echoes of 'Bluebeard', he sees and is attacked by the rotting corpse of an old suicide.

The Shining frequently signals that the horrors of the Overlook are the product of psychological disturbance. Whether it is Danny's psychic abilities, or Jack's barely repressed frustration and rage, or both that wind up the 'clockwork mechanism' of the hotel and become the 'charge' which powers the hotel's 'battery' is not completely clear. However, the ghosts tend to emerge primarily when Jack's repressed feelings are released. Danny's encounter in room 217, for example, takes place when Jack is having a nightmare about breaking his son's arm and being urged on by the voice of his dead father to further violence. Numerous literary references further imply that in some way the horror lies within. There are many echoes of Edgar Allan Poe's (q.v.) 'Masque of the Red Death', where the nobles who attempt to shut out the plague that is devastating their country find they have locked it in with them, and here the cry to 'unmask, unmask' becomes particularly suggestive. Similarly, Lewis Carroll's Wonderland is rewritten to become a 'land full of sick wonders' that is reached through mirrors, or through 'a round black hole' that leads 'deep down in yourself in a place where nothing comes through'.

But for all the emphasis on the psyche, there is nevertheless something quite tangible about the effects produced by the ghosts of the Overlook; Danny's neck is bruised when the woman in room 217 attempts to strangle him, and his clothes are quite definitely left damp. To strip the text of its supernatural elements and rationalize all the events simply as projections of the disturbed psyche would be difficult. Rather, King seems to be working within the terms of Todorov's fantastic in that both characters and reader hesitate between a supernatural and a psychological solution. When Jack in turn goes to room 217, he refuses to believe the doorknob of the locked room is turning, since that would confirm the presence of the supernatural. Nevertheless,

> below the tumble of his chaotic thoughts, below the trip-hammer beat of his heart, he could hear the soft and futile sound of the doorknob being turned to and fro as something locked in tried helplessly to get out, something that wanted to meet him, something that would like to be introduced to his family.

The language here seems to suggest that whatever is locked in yet striving to get out is simultaneously within Jack and within the room.

The text complicates simple conclusions of any kind about the source of the horror. When Jack falls increasingly under the influence of the hotel, gradually turning into a maniacal 'thing' stalking the hotel corridors seeking to 'correct' his son, Wendy attempts to reassure Danny that what threatens them is 'not your daddy talking, remember; it's the hotel'. Danny in turn, waiting for Jack to come and kill him, defines the evil force 'hiding behind Daddy's face' as 'not his daddy'. Overall, however, this is something that the text does not entirely support.

Just as the text undercuts any clear distinctions between psychological and supernatural explanations, so it questions any clear distinctions between the supposedly civilized social world and the primitive forces of the psyche. Working on the hotel roof, Jack is stung when he uncovers a wasp's nest, and uses the experience as a way of rationalizing and excusing his behaviour. 'When you stuck your hand into the wasp's nest', he muses,

> you hadn't made a covenant with the devil to give up your civilized self with its trappings of love and respect and honor. It just happened to you. Passively, with no say, you ceased to be a creature of the mind and became a creature of the nerve endings; from college educated man to wailing ape in five seconds.

But the civilized world here is shown to be just as dangerous as the primitive. Jack is the product of a patriarchal world that defines men precisely in terms of the control, power and aggression that produce his violent behaviour.

Most readings of *The Shining* to date have been psychoanalytical. Clare Hanson, for example, provides a Lacanian reading of King's concern with 'the construction of the subject in the unconscious and conscious mind' and the way in which Danny's entry into the symbolic is problematized because of the disruption caused by his father (1990: 145). More recently, Steven Bruhm has suggested that one of the features which marks contemporary Gothic is that the Freudian machinery has become much more than a critical tool for analysing Gothic narratives. It is, rather, frequently the subject matter of the narrative itself; *The Shining*, he points out, is 'consciously Freudian', offering a 'textbook case of the oedipal conflict' (2002: 262–3).

If Danny is locked in the Oedipal moment, so are his parents. Wendy has failed to move beyond her attachment to her father, and Jack's present problems are certainly closely connected to unresolved past problems with his own father. He too is a victim of an alcoholic and abusive parent who still has power over him, and, having learned his lessons well, he recreates the same scenario with his own son. Jack's own grasp on the symbolic is shaky, something emphasized by the way in which he, a writer, begins to lose his grip on language while Danny desperately tries to learn to read in order to decipher the messages of his visions. As Jack's insecurities increase, so does his identification with his father's power and rage, and the blame is placed upon the submissive wife/mother who is seen as too easily falling into the role of victim. For Jack, assuming control increasingly means asserting authority, and in this he is encouraged by various voices: by Delbert Grady, the previous caretaker who murdered his family with an axe, and by his own father, who instructs him through the radio. The chaos that ensues at the Overlook Hotel is as much the product of the 'civilized' patriarchal world as it is the product of irrational forces within Jack or supernatural forces within the hotel.

In his critical work *Danse Macabre,* Stephen King suggests that horror functions to reaffirm our sense of community and to restore order and harmony. It is, he asserts, as 'conservative as a Republican in a three piece suit', with a 'moral code so strong it would make a Puritan smile' (1982: 368). Ultimately, however, it is difficult either to see *The Shining* as an affirmative text or to identify what conservative values are being promoted. The resolution is brought about as Danny remembers what his father has forgotten, or 'overlooked': the boiler. The hotel, along with Jack Torrance, blows up. Clare Hanson concludes that Danny is finally securely placed within the symbolic order, allowing for the establishment of a 'stable and unified self' (1990: 148). If so, this is a far from affirmative ending. In *The Shining* the law of the father is associated primarily with the axes and mallets used to deliver corrective 'medicine'.

The family is by no means recuperated as a potential source of redemption and harmony. On the contrary, like much contemporary Gothic, the text signals the impossibility of family harmony, and nothing is offered to replace this loss. *The Shining* may well be one of King's darkest stories: it is about disintegration and fragmentation, not reconstruction or redemption. It reveals such institutions as the family to be only constructs built in an attempt to impose some kind of order upon the dark and threatening forces associated with Jack's 'wailing ape'. Even more disturbingly, however, given the nature of the authoritative discourses that underwrite these 'civilized' institutions, it also suggests they are, in the end, at least as dangerous as those primitive forces they seek to control.

Bibliography

Bruhm, Steven 1998: 'On Stephen King's Phallus, or The Postmodern Gothic.' In Robert K. Martin and Eric Savoy (eds), *American Gothic: New Interventions in a National Narrative.* Iowa City: University of Iowa Press.

Bruhm, Steven 2002: 'The Contemporary Gothic: Why We Need It.' In Jerrold E. Hogle (ed.), *The Cambridge Companion to Gothic Fiction*. Cambridge: Cambridge University Press, 259–76.

Grixti, Joseph 1989: *Terrors of Uncertainty: The Cultural Contexts of Horror Fiction*. London: Routledge.

Hanson, Clare 1990: 'Stephen King: Powers of Horror.' In Brian Docherty (ed.), *American Horror Fiction: From Brockden Brown to Stephen King*. New York: St Martin's Press, 135–54.

Holland-Toll, Linda J. 1999: 'Bakhtin's Carnival Reversed: King's *The Shining* as Dark Carnival.' *Journal of Popular Culture*, 33 (2), 131–46.

King, Stephen 1982: *Danse Macabre*. New York: Signet.

Bret Easton Ellis,

AMERICAN PSYCHO

(1991)

One of the epigraphs which Bret Easton Ellis provides for *American Psycho*, a book which caused a considerable stir when it was first published in 1991, provides an extraordinarily exact gloss on the novel's terrain. It is from Dostoevsky's *Notes from Underground*:

> Both the author of these *Notes* and the *Notes* themselves are, of course, fictional. Nevertheless, such persons as the composer of these *Notes* not only exist in our society, but indeed must exist, considering the circumstances under which our society has generally been formed. I have wished to bring before the public, somewhat more distinctly than usual, one of the characters of our recent past. He represents a generation that is still living out its days among us. In the fragment entitled 'Underground' this personage describes himself and his views and attempts, as it were, to clarify the reasons why he appeared and was bound to appear in our midst. The subsequent fragment will consist of the actual 'notes', concerning certain events in his life.

Patrick Bateman, Ellis's protagonist, is a wealthy and successful Wall Street investment banker; he is also a psychopath who rapes, mutilates and kills, leaving a trail of atrocity behind him. What is even more telling, however, is the note of *necessity* to which Dostoevsky alludes and which conditions Bateman's story from the start. It is as though, in a world where every material goal has been achieved and every need is capable of being satisfied virtually instantaneously, it is necessary that these achievements and satisfactions turn directly into their opposite, that the desire that should apparently have been slaked mutates into ever more bizarre forms.

American Psycho is therefore, despite the bloodthirsty Gothic descriptions for which it is most famous, above all a work of social critique, a devastating indictment of a society that allows characters like Bateman's to develop, indeed requires their development. For what is chilling in the novel is not, in the end, its violence, even when this extends to torture and cannibalism. It depends rather both on the way in which Bateman describes his crimes, and on the way in which they are received in what passes in the novel for a public context. To take the second point first: although he becomes ever more reckless in his self-advertisement – wearing a placard saying 'Mass Murderer' to a party, for example – nobody in the novel ever admits to believing that he is actually guilty of anything. This is partly because he is protected by his own social status: it would, the text seems to say, be impossible for somebody of his background and position to be a murderer. It is also, though, because there is a sense in the novel that, if Bateman were to be exposed, then it would be tantamount to an exposure of a whole caste of the super-rich: although the point is left tellingly undeveloped, it would nevertheless then be possible for the 'public' to speculate as to how many other psychopaths might lurk in the 'underground' of success.

But it is perhaps Bateman's own self-descriptions that constitute the most extraordinary feature of the text, and here the situation differs a little from Dostoevsky's, for it is not obvious that Bateman does clarify – or indeed really wishes to clarify – the 'reasons why he appeared'; in this respect his coldness, his dissociation from himself, take him one step beyond his literary forebear. Here too the reader senses that the problem may not be an individual one at all, but again a social condition, for one of the main features of Bateman's psyche and discourse is that he is constantly *distracted*: he is, as he puts it himself at a key moment of the text in a deeply ambiguous phrase, 'beside himself'; not only deranged, but also watching his own behaviour without understanding it, constantly at the mercy of the flow of media images and brand names that seem to be the only things truly to engage his attention.

This is how *American Psycho* begins:

> Abandon hope all ye who enter here is scrawled in blood red lettering on the side of the Chemical Bank near the corner of Eleventh and First and is in print large enough to be seen from the backseat of the cab as it lurches forward in the traffic leaving Wall Street and just as Timothy Price notices the words a bus pulls up, the advertisement for *Les Misérables* on its side blocking his view, but Price who is with Pierce & Pierce and twenty-six doesn't seem to care because he tells the driver he will give him five dollars to turn up the radio, 'Be My Baby' on WYNN, and the driver, black, not American, does so.

These endlessly accretive sentences are typical of the text: in them the place-names and similar details of description constantly take precedence over and threaten to occlude any possible attribution of personality. In the case of the character named Timothy Price, the crucial fact is that he is 'with Pierce & Pierce'; his professional status, especially in the context of his age – or rather, youth – is the only truly defining feature for anybody in a cast where all the participants are essentially the same, where individual difference has been varnished away in the name of wealth and success. Advertisements for *Les Misérables* recur constantly in the text, reminders of a world of poverty and degradation (but transmuted into 'art') that – except when it is victimized by Bateman's acts of apparently meaningless violence – serves as a mere backdrop to the rarefied heights of Wall Street.

In *American Psycho,* the city of New York is in a state of constant gridlock; just so, Bateman and his colleagues are gridlocked, stuck in a world where there is nowhere to go, no further heights to be conquered, nothing more to worry or care about except whether one is wearing the right expensive suit, being seen at the right parties, having sex with the most appropriate (and appropriately named) people. In a sense, the entire novel feels like a single sentence, without an origin and without a potential ending – the last phrase reads 'THIS IS NOT AN EXIT' – in which even the most violent of actions fails to puncture the cocooned life of money-making, champagne, designer mineral water and cocaine.

American Psycho takes place in a vacant, hollowed, corporate space, a place of total privilege where one is responsible to no one for one's actions, where nobody would dare – or bother – to question the integrity of the contemporary 'masters of the universe', successors to the endless power of the earlier aristocracies of Gothic fiction. This, one might then fairly say, is one contemporary equivalent of the Gothic castle (q.v.), where a total, brutal power holds sway: in one sense, Bateman merely enacts the uncaringness about individual life and the human body which is at the root of the extreme version of international capitalism of which he is an operative. What is frightening is that there is nothing but surface to Bateman: when he thinks, when he fantasizes, it is only to trivialize and fall into unending repetition, to refuse – if only implicitly – any discrimination between the important and the unimportant:

> In this office right now I am thinking about how long it would take a corpse to disintegrate right in this office. In this office these are the things I fantasise about while dreaming: Eating ribs at Red, Hot and Blue in Washington, D.C. If I should switch shampoos. What really is the best dry beer? Is Bill Robinson an overrated designer? What's wrong with IBM? Ultimate luxury. Is the term 'playing hardball' an adverb? The fragile peace of Assisi. Electric light. The epitome of luxury. Of ultimate luxury. The bastard's wearing the same damn Armani linen suit I've got on. How easy it would be to scare the wits

out of this fucking guy. Kimball is utterly unaware of how truly vacant I am. There is no awareness of animate life in this office, yet still he takes notes. By the time you finish reading this sentence, a Boeing jetliner will take off or land somewhere in the world. I would like a Pilsner Urquell.

There are questions here that might be best expressed in terms of the origin and the replica. How is it possible for anything, including one's self, to be 'original', or is one condemned to being merely a replicated version of the other? In his Wall Street terms, Bateman is uncannily posing precisely the questions we might find at the forefront of poststructuralist criticism. Bateman has no memory, no recollection, at all. Sucked into the corporation, he does not know how he came to be here, in *this* office, wearing *this* suit – if indeed it *is* his suit and not one of a collection of somebody else's clothes hanging in the corporate wardrobe.

What we are aware of here is that there is an impossibility of desire, a vacancy, a gap to be filled only by addictions of various kinds – addictions to the name, to the brand, to the hierarchy as much as to methamphetamines and mood-swingers. The world of *American Psycho* can be accurately compared to a Gothic labyrinth, a maze within which it is no longer possible to ask the vital questions. A more 'romantic', or even existentialist, view might suggest that Bateman's multiple acts of slaughter are in some way liberating; but here all possibility of liberation has been foreclosed, there is no escape from the castle and no possibility of a recognition of one's own monstrosity (q.v.), either by oneself or by the other.

Bibliography

Brusseau, James 2000: 'Violence and Baudrillardian Repetition in Bret Easton Ellis's *American Psycho.*' In Michael T. Carroll and Eddie Tafoya (eds), *Phenomenological Approaches to Popular Culture.* Bowling Green, OH: Bowling Green State University Popular Press, 35–47.

Leypoldt, Gunter 2001: *Casual Silences: The Poetics of Minimal Realism from Raymond Carver and the New York School to Bret Easton Ellis.* Trier: Wissenschaftlicher.

Price, David W. 1998: 'Bakhtinian Prosaics, Grotesque Realism, and the Question of the Carnivalesque in Bret Easton Ellis's *American Psycho.*' *Southern Humanities Review,* 32 (4), 321–46.

Warner, Michelle 1996: 'The Development of the Psycho-Social Cannibal in the Fiction of Bret Easton Ellis.' *Journal of Evolutionary Psychology,* 17 (1–2), 140–6.

THEMES AND TOPICS

The Haunted Castle

If there is such a thing as a general topography of the Gothic, then its central motif is the castle. The genre has often been said to 'originate', for example, with Horace Walpole's *The Castle of Otranto* (qq.v.), a site of spectres and miracles, whose 'lower part . . . was hollowed into several intricate cloisters', and thus contains a 'long labyrinth of darkness', and whose upper part provides a scene, if often a tormented one, of feudal magnificence. Ann Radcliffe's Udolpho's (qq.v.) 'massy and gloomy walls' give Emily 'terrible ideas of imprisonment and suffering'; its 'broken walls, and shattered battlements . . . mingled with the loose earth, and pieces of rock', in a scene in which the sublime of nature seems to generate the castle as a necessary accompaniment to terror, that terror to which Emily is a constant prey as she tries to find her way through the maze of secrets that constitutes the castle's ill-lit interior. Warwick Castle, in Radcliffe's *Gaston de Blondeville* (1826), presents in its disarray a more picturesque aspect:

> On the left, the shattered walls of that lofty pile, built by Leicester and still called by his name, advance proudly to the edge of the eminence that overlooked the lower court, hung with the richest drapery of ivy; on the right, stands the strong square tower, called Caesar's, which, though the most ancient part of the castle, appears fresher and less injured by time, than parts that were raised some ages later. This was the keep, or citadel, of the castle; and the prodigious thickness of the walls appears through the three arches in front, proportioned and shaped like some which may yet be seen in aqueducts near Rome.

In this castle, then, as in many others, centuries of history are compressed into a single image, albeit one that never quite comes together. A common feature of many Gothic castles is that they seem to distort perception, to

259

cause some slippage between what is natural and what is human-made; they act as unreliable lenses through which to view history and from the other side of which may emerge terrors only previously apprehended in dream. When the Countess of Leicester arrives at Kenilworth in Walter Scott's (q.v.) 1821 novel of that name, she finds 'the tower, beneath which its ample portal arch opened, guarded in a singular manner'; on the battlements are 'gigantic warders, with clubs, battle-axes, and other implements of ancient warfare, designed to represent the soldiers of King Arthur', but some of these warders are 'real men, dressed up with vizards and buskins' while others are 'mere pageants composed of pasteboard and buckram'. In the context of the castle, nothing is what it seems; even commonly accepted definitions of the human and the non-human, the natural and the supernatural, drop away like the rotting fortifications themselves.

In William Harrison Ainsworth's (q.v.) *The Tower of London: An Historical Romance* (1840), the reader is treated to an entire chapter of descriptive detail about the Tower, which almost threatens to overwhelm any possible narrative that could go on within its walls. We are to learn of 'its antiquity and foundation; its magnitude and extent; its keep, palace, gardens, fortifications, dungeons, and chapels; its walls, bulwarks, and moat; its royal inmates; its constables, jailers, wardens, and other officers; its prisoners, executions, and secret murders', information that clearly fascinated Ainsworth and his readers even if today it seems to belong more to the world of heritage and guidebooks than to the realm of historical reality. The action, such as it is, of Edgar Allan Poe's (q.v.) 'The Masque of the Red Death' (1842) takes place admittedly in an abbey, belonging to Prince Prospero, but it is a 'castellated abbey', an 'extensive and magnificent structure, the creation of the prince's own eccentric yet august taste'. It is, of course, designed to repel all potential entrants, especially the plague itself, although this proves a predictably futile hope. Again, the action of Robert Louis Stevenson's (q.v.) 'Olalla' (1885) takes place in a building known only as a 'residencia', an 'antique and dilapidated mansion', but its literary provenance is not in doubt: the lower storey, for example, is 'naked of windows, so that the building, if garrisoned, could not be carried without artillery', and the entire building reeks of the decay of a previous historical order:

> It was a rich house, on which Time had breathed his tarnish and dust had scattered disillusion. The spider swung there; the bloated tarantula scampers on the cornices; ants had their crowded highways on the floor of halls of audience; the big and foul fly, that lives on carrion and is often the messenger of death, had set up his nest in the rotten woodwork, and buzzed heavily about the rooms.

The confusion of tenses here is symptomatic: does the Gothic castle belong to the present or to the past, and with what suppressed denizens of our own pasts does it menace us as we try to 'read' its ambiguous signs? The impression made upon Jonathan Harker by that other major Gothic symbol, Castle Dracula (q.v.), is well known; it is after a period of what appears to be sleep or unconsciousness that he becomes 'conscious of the fact that the driver was in the act of pulling up the horses in the courtyard of a vast ruined castle, from whose tall black windows came no ray of light, and whose broken battlements showed a jagged line against the moonlit sky', and the Count himself issues Harker with a quintessentially paradoxical instruction that echoes down the whole long line of Gothic castellans: 'You may', he says, 'go anywhere you wish in the castle, except where the doors are locked, where of course you will not wish to go.'

Following the line into the twentieth century we encounter perhaps the largest, wildest and least well-defined of all Gothic edifices, Mervyn Peake's (q.v.) Gormenghast, a castle for which no plan exists, or perhaps ever has existed:

> Stone after grey stone climbed. Windows yawned: shields, scrolls, and legendary mottoes, melancholy in their ruin, protruded in worn relief over arches or doorways; along the sills of casements, in the walls of towers or carved in buttresses. Storm-nibbled heads, their shallow faces striated with bad green and draped with creepers, stared blindly through the four quarters, from between broken eyelids.

And carrying on closer to the present day, Iain Banks's (q.v.) *A Song of Stone* (1997) features a castle as its main protagonist, a castle which admittedly is finally destroyed but which while it stands, even sullied by barbarian invaders, provides some model of solidity, survival, at least for its troubled and linguistically ornate inhabitant:

> Dark in dark the castle stands, held in suspension in the air's warped symmetry, of some solution no guarantee, but letting me, soiled but unearthed, enter it by its unlocked door. In the lower hall, lit by a last few fitful stumps of candles, something like a massacre is tableau'd. Bodies, littered, lie; wine pools, dark as blood. Only a snort and something muttered deep in sleep witnesses that the scene is one of torpor rather than murder.

Here there is room to list only a few of the castle's symbolic referents. The castle is a labyrinth, a maze, a site of secrets. It is also, paradoxically, a site of domesticity, where ordinary life carries on even while accompanied by the most extraordinary and inexplicable of events. It can be a place of womb-like security, a refuge from the complex exigencies of the outer world; it can also – at the same time, and according to a difference of perception – be a place of incarceration, a place where heroines and others can be locked away from the fickle memory of 'ordinary life'. The castle has to do with the map, and with the failure of the map; it figures loss of direction, the impossibility of imposing one's own sense of place on an alien world.

The castle represents desubjectification: within its walls one may be 'subjected' to a force that is utterly resistant to the individual's attempt to impose his or her own order. It frequently is, or contains, a hall of mirrors: as one sees the ghost fleeing down its darkened corridors, it may all too often be a vision of oneself that one sees, a previous self perhaps, a childhood self, victim of anxieties that should long since have disappeared or been overcome. It is a sign of antiquity, of a life that has preceded our own but appears never to have gone away, and as such it refers as much to a condition of the unconscious as to a historical moment of feudalism. In its figuring forth of our own vulnerable childhood, it afflicts us with problems of size and scale; it threatens us with measureless boundaries, and yet at the same time, with the most tomb-like claustrophobia, it enacts the hovering possibility of premature burial. It challenges all notions of rescue and salvation; it exposes us before an excess of patriarchal power, while at the same time it conveys to us that even the utmost monuments of human grandeur become, or perhaps always have been, ruins.

Bibliography

Ellis, Kate Ferguson 1989: *The Contested Castle: Gothic Novels and the Subversion of Domestic Ideology.* Urbana: University of Illinois Press.

Mehrotra, Kewal Krishna 1934: *Horace Walpole and the English Novel: A Study of the Influence of 'The Castle of Otranto', 1764–1820.* Oxford: Oxford University Press.

Oakes, David A. 1999: 'Ghosts in the Machines: The Haunted Castle in the Works of Stephen King and Clive Barker.' *Studies in Weird Fiction*, 24, 25–33.

Railo, Eino 1927: *The Haunted Castle: A Study of the Elements of English Romanticism.* London: Routledge.

Shelden, Pamela J. 1974: 'Jamesian Gothicism: The Haunted Castle of the Mind.' *Studies in the Literary Imagination*, 7 (1), 121–34.

The Monster

While the term 'monster' is often used to describe anything horrifyingly unnatural or excessively large, it initially had far more precise connotations, and these are of some significance for the ways in which the monstrous comes to function within the Gothic. Etymologically speaking, the monster is something to be shown, something that serves to demonstrate (Latin, *monstrare*: to demonstrate) and to warn (Latin, *monere*: to warn). From classical times through to the Renaissance, monsters were interpreted either as signs of divine anger or as portents of impending disasters. These early monsters are frequently constructed out of ill-assorted parts, like the griffin, with the head and wings of an eagle combined with the body and paws of a lion. Alternatively, they are incomplete, lacking essential parts, or, like the mythological hydra with its many heads, grotesquely excessive. By the eighteenth century the horrific appearance of the monster had begun to serve an increasingly moral function. As Alexander Pope writes in his *Essay on Man* (1733–4), 'Vice is a monster of so frightful mien / As, to be hated, needs but to be seen' (217–18). By providing a visible warning of the results of vice and folly, monsters promote virtuous behaviour.

What is primarily important for the Gothic is the cultural work done by monsters. Through difference, whether in appearance or behaviour, monsters function to define and construct the politics of the 'normal'. Located at the margins of culture, they police the boundaries of the human, pointing to those lines that must not be crossed. In most Gothic fiction of the eighteenth and nineteenth centuries (see 'Gothic in the Eighteenth Century' and 'Victorian Gothic'), there is a relatively predictable if variable narrative strategy that has, Christopher Craft observes, a tripartite structure. The text 'first invites or admits a monster, then entertains and is entertained by monstrosity for some extended duration, until in its closing pages it expels

263

or repudiates the monster and all the disruptions that he/she/it brings' (in Byron 1999: 94). Limits and boundaries can therefore be reinstated as the monster is despatched, good is distinguished from evil and self from other. However, the very dependence of the one term upon the other introduces an ambivalence that becomes increasingly notable in Gothic of the twentieth century.

Monsters, as the displaced embodiment of tendencies that are repressed or, in Julia Kristeva's sense of the term, 'abjected' within a specific culture not only establish the boundaries of the human, but may also challenge them. Hybrid forms that exceed and disrupt those systems of classification through which cultures organize experience, monsters problematize binary thinking and demand a rethinking of the boundaries and concepts of normality. Gothic texts repeatedly draw attention to the monster's constructed nature, to the mechanisms of monster production, and reveal precisely how the other is constructed and positioned as both alien and inferior. In turn, this denaturalizes the human, showing the supposedly superior human to be, like the monster's otherness, simply the product of an ongoing struggle in the discursive construction and reconstruction of power.

Representations and interpretations of monstrosity repeatedly change over time. The literally monstrous body, for example, begins to take on a particularly significant role in Gothic fiction of the Victorian Decadence (q.v.), a move that seems tied in with the discoveries of the evolutionary sciences, and accompanying anxieties about the autonomy and stability of the human subject. During the 1950s, a sense of Cold War paranoia is articulated through numerous alien invasion narratives, most notably perhaps, Don Siegel's 1956 film *Invasion of the Body Snatchers*. Like the most effective horror films, Siegel's *Invasion* works on more than one interpretative level: the image of terror here, a soulless and unindividuated vegetable life form, not only suggests Cold War paranoia but also offers a chilling commentary on social conformity.

Conformity is central to one of the earliest of Gothic monsters established in the twentieth century: the zombie. Emerging out of the myths of the walking dead associated with the voodoo religion of Haiti, the zombie is initially most obviously identified with slavery, allowing for a critique of colonialism, and is frequently used this way in postcolonial Gothic (q.v.) texts. In its first Gothic appearance, Victor Halperin's 1932 film *White Zombie*, this connection is clarified by Bela Lugosi's portrayal of a Haitian sorcerer who uses zombies to work his sugar fields. He also, however, gains possession of a young white woman – Madeline, the white zombie of the title – and here the implications of the monstrous figure begin to shift. Since the film makes it difficult to detect much difference between Madeline pre-

and post-zombification, the zombie begins to suggest anxieties about dein-dividuation. This is also central to George Romero's cult classic *Night of the Living Dead* (1968) and the subsequent *Dawn of the Dead* (1978), which takes place in a shopping mall overrun by zombies and begins to move towards an engagement with anxieties concerning a culture defined by consumption. On the whole, zombies proliferate more in film (q.v.) than in printed fiction, a point that, given the image of a cinema full of viewers gazing at the screen, could be said to have its own underlying irony.

One of the most notable changes in more recent representations of Gothic monstrosity involves a shift in sympathies and perspectives. While Mary Wollstonecraft Shelley's *Frankenstein* (qq.v.) was probably the first to invite sympathy for the monster, to allow him to speak and explain the origins of his monstrous behaviour, there is usually little attempt to do this in most eighteenth- and nineteenth-century Gothic. Modern criticism may rewrite such figures as the vampire (q.v.) as heroic rebels against conformity and repressive moral systems, but Stoker's *Dracula* (qq.v.) actually offers little encouragement for readers to align themselves with this monstrous force. In recent Gothic, Fred Botting observes, however, monstrous figures are now much 'less often terrifying objects of animosity expelled in the return to social and symbolic equilibrium'. Instead, they are 'sites of identification, sympathy, and self-recognition. Excluded figures once represented as malevolent, disturbed, or deviant monsters are rendered more humane while the systems that exclude them assume terrifying, persecutory, and inhuman shapes' (Botting 2002: 286). While Botting demonstrates the shift through a discussion of the gradual movement towards a 'posthumane' identification with the other in the *Alien* series of films, it is equally evident in recent Gothic works as varied as the stories of Angela Carter (q.v.), Anne Rice's (q.v.) *Vampire Chronicles*, Francis Ford Coppola's 1992 reworking of Stoker's *Dracula* and Toni Morrison's *Beloved* (1987).

Where this move towards establishing the monstrous other as a site of identification becomes particularly disturbing is with the serial killer, the monster that dominates the last part of the twentieth century. While 'sympathy' is not precisely the word to describe the response encouraged by serial killer narratives, there is often nevertheless a certain ambivalence in the representations of these modern monsters. Often seen as symptomatic of an increasingly violent and alienated society, the serial killer might seem to call for the most emphatic reassertion of social norms and the strongest reaffirmation of conservative values within the text. This is, however, rarely the case.

In the most chilling manifestations of the serial killer narrative, such as Bret Easton Ellis's *American Psycho* (qq.v.), Joyce Carol Oates's (q.v.) *Zombie*

(1995), and John McNaughton's 1986 film *Henry: Portrait of a Serial Killer*, there is no move to contain or expel the monster. Rather than being established as the demonic other to mainstream society, the monster is explicitly identified as that society's logical and inevitable product: society, rather than the individual, becomes a primary site of horror. These killers are rarely made accountable, and attention is directed as much to the institutions that create such monsters as to the killers themselves. To emphasize connection rather than distance further, the reader or viewer, instead of being positioned on the side of the normal and the human with the monstrous other located as the external threat, is forced into an uncomfortable intimacy with the monster's perspective. There is rarely any assurance that the threat can be contained; in McNaughton's *Henry*, for example there is not even a sign that the police are aware of what Henry is doing. Henry shows not a flicker of remorse, and the film itself offers no judgement and no closure, simply ending bleakly with the murder of his girlfriend and the disposal of her body. Rather than being ejected from society, the serial killer, its representative, is simply left to carry on.

Even in the more reassuring serial killer narratives, often those in which a criminal profiler is offered as encouraging evidence that the monstrous can be identified and contained, the majority of texts remain at the very least ambivalent about the repudiation of the monstrous. The stability of self and other, good and evil, is frequently undercut through a particularly emphatic use of the traditional Gothic double. The killer may ultimately be caught and punished, but this is often brought about by the profiler's overidentification with the killer. Emphasis is placed less on scientific deduction than on irrational intuition, an almost psychic connection that dangerously destabilizes boundaries. As FBI trainee Clarice Starling is repeatedly reminded in Thomas Harris's *The Silence of the Lambs* (1988), the last thing you want is serial killer Hannibal Lecter inside your mind. And yet that is precisely where the killer usually ends up. Moral boundaries become particularly unstable in Harris's *Red Dragon* (1981) as a result of FBI agent Will Graham's even closer empathic connection with serial killer Francis Dolarhyde, and Graham is intensely aware of his own murderous impulses, recognizing that 'in the bone arena of his skull there were no forts for what he loved'. These narratives insist that the potential for corruption and violence lies within all, and the horror comes above all from an appalling sense of recognition: with our contemporary monsters, self and other frequently become completely untenable categories.

Bibliography

Botting, Fred 2002: 'Aftergothic: Consumption, Machines, and Black Holes.' In Jerrold E. Hogle (ed.), *The Cambridge Companion to Gothic Fiction*. Cambridge: Cambridge University Press, 277–300.

Byron, Glennis (ed.) 1999: *Dracula: New Casebook*. Basingstoke: Macmillan.

Cohen, Jeffrey Jerome (ed.) 1996: *Monster Theory: Reading Culture*. Minneapolis: University of Minnesota Press.

Huet, Marie-Hélene 1993: *Monstrous Imagination*. Cambridge, MA: Harvard University Press.

Ingebretsen, Edward 1998: 'Monster-Making: A Politics of Persuasion.' *Journal of American Culture*, 21 (2), 25–34.

Simpson, Philip L. 2000: *Psycho Paths: Tracking the Serial Killer Through Contemporary American Film and Fiction*. Carbondale, IL: Southern Illinois University Press.

The Vampire

Vampire legends appear nearly everywhere, including India, China and Tibet, but the vampire of today has its roots specifically in the folk-lore of Eastern Europe. Usually little more than a shambling and mindless creature, the revenant, nosferatu or vrykolakas, as it is variously called, was of peasant stock, preyed on his or her immediate family or neighbours, and functioned primarily to explain the spread of disease and sudden deaths in the community. Reports of such real vampires led in the eighteenth century to an investigation by various doctors and scholars, most notably perhaps the Benedictine Augustin Calmet, who produced a treatise on vampires in 1746, translated into English as *The Phantom World*. Calmet, like most investigators, concluded that the most likely explanation for vampiric behaviour was premature burial.

During the romantic period, this creature of folk-lore combined with the tradition of the demon lover, and began to edge closer to a figure recognizable as our modern vampire. Vampires moved out of anthropology and into poetry, appearing in such works as Goethe's 'The Bride of Corinth' (1797), Southey's 'Thalaba the Destroyer' (1801) and Byron's *The Giaour* (1813). John Polidori's (q.v.) *The Vampyre* (1819), however, saw the first appearance of the vampire in English fiction. The success of Polidori's tale was soon consolidated by numerous stage versions that introduced vampires to an even wider, non-literate audience and gave them a popularity that has continued up to the present day. No other monster has endured, and proliferated, in quite the same way – or been made to bear such a weight of metaphor. Confounding all categories, the vampire is the ultimate embodiment of transgression, but while most critics agree in reading the vampire as a transgressive force, the psychological or social significance they attach to this figure varies considerably.

One of the most significant shifts in the movement from folk-lore to literature is the vampire's transformation from peasant to aristocrat. Polidori's Lord Ruthven was most notably followed first by James Malcolm Rymer's Sir Frances Varney in his 109-part serial published during the 1840s, *Varney the Vampire, or The Feast of Blood*, and then by Sheridan Le Fanu's (q.v.) Countess in 'Carmilla' (1871), and by Stoker's Count in *Dracula* (q.v.). Such a shift immediately opens up the possibilities for political readings. *Dracula*, for example, has been read as the tyrannical aristocrat seeking to preserve the survival of his house and threatening the security of the bourgeois family represented by the vampire hunters. However, as Marx first suggests with his repeated use of vampire imagery in *Das Capital* (1867), the vampire also perfectly embodies the way in which human life nourishes the machine of capitalist production. Connections between the vampire and capitalism continue today as production has given way to consumption. Not only has the vampire itself become a highly marketable commodity, but, as Rob Lathan puts it, 'Marx's gluttonous capitalist rat has been transformed into an army of consuming mall-rats' (in Gordon and Hollinger 1997: 131). In Tony Scott's glossy and upmarket 1983 film of Whitley Strieber's *The Hunger* (1981), the vampire as consumer is chillingly exemplified in the characters played by David Bowie and Catherine Deneuve and their world of glamour, elegance and privilege. The excesses of lifestyle here are matched only by excesses of blood as they feed on their victims in an orgy of slaughter.

Early vampires are not only aristocrats, but also seducers, and from the start the vampire has been associated with sexuality. Lord Ruthven ruins reputations as well as drinking blood, while Varney has a particular interest in attractive young women, and Carmilla seduces Laura in such highly erotic terms that at one point Laura even wonders if she is a young man in disguise. Early criticism also noted the connections between the vampire and sexuality, Ernest Jones opening the Freudian floodgates in *On the Nightmare* with his reminder that 'one of the most important of Freud's discoveries was that morbid dread always signifies repressed sexual wishes' (1929: 106). In the unconscious mind, he adds, 'blood is commonly an equivalent for semen' and the vampire superstition 'yields plain indications of most kinds of sexual perversions' (1929: 98, 119). Christopher Bentley's early Freudian reading of *Dracula* – notorious for being far more titillating than the book itself – elaborates on this to include, among other violated taboos, necrophilia, incest, oral and genital rape, sadism and masochism.

Throughout the nineteenth century, the vampire functions to police the boundaries between 'normal' and 'deviant' sexuality, with the narrative voice firmly positioned on the side of the 'normal'. In particular, as Sue-Ellen Case argues, the 'apparatus of representation' belongs to the unqueer (1990: 9). Le Fanu's 'Carmilla' is narrated by the victim, Laura, and while she is both repulsed and thrilled by the vampire's advances, Carmilla must ultimately be expelled. Same-sex desire between men can be encoded only through women, as Aubrey and Lord Ruthven's relationship must be negotiated through Aubrey's sister in Polidori's *The Vampyre*. While the homosexual has continued to be figured as what threatens the 'norm' in some twentieth- and twenty-first-century fiction, the vampire has nevertheless become a significant site of resistance for queer and lesbian theory, and traditional texts have been seen to offer opportunities for queer critical rewritings. As often observed, the vampire is particularly well adapted to signify 'deviant' sexuality. With the penetrating teeth set in the softness of the mouth, the vampire mouth problematizes any easy distinctions between the masculine and the feminine. In addition, a number of queer and lesbian writers, including Jeffrey McMahan, Gary Bowen, Jody Scott and Pat Califia, have offered their own oppositional vampire texts, while Jewelle Gomez's black working-class lesbian in *The Gilda Stories* (1991) has functioned more generally as a metaphor for marginality.

In nineteenth-century vampire fiction, the representation of the vampire as monstrous, evil and other serves to guarantee the existence of good, reinforcing the formally dichotomized structures of belief which, although beginning to crumble under the impact of an increasingly secular and scientific world, still constituted the dominant world view. Vampire fiction of the later twentieth century becomes increasingly sceptical about such categories. The old-type vampire as the embodiment of both evil and otherness certainly still appears – John Skipp and Craig Spector's *The Light at the End* (1986) is an example that immediately springs to mind – but more usually the oppositions between good and evil are increasingly problematized. The Christian ideology that underlies these distinctions begins to disappear and vampires move further away from their folk-lore connections with such things as garlic and crucifixes. Rather than being the devil's work, vampirism is explained in new ways: it might be some kind of viral infection, for example, as in Barbara Hambly's *Those Who Hunt the Night* (1988), or the product of evolutionary processes, as in Suzy McGee Charnas's *The Vampire Tapestry* (1980). What these new vampires do is an expression of their own condition, not of any metaphysical conflict between good and evil, and there can consequently be vampires that edge alarmingly close to the good – Chelsea Quinn Yarbro's Saint Germain does not kill when he feeds, for example, and, in exchange for the blood he takes, offers his victim some rather good sex.

Perhaps the most significant transformation of the vampire in such works as Fred Saberhagen's *The Dracula Tape* (1975), Anne Rice's *Interview with the Vampire* (qq.v.) and Jody Scott's *I, Vampire* (1984) results from a shift in narrative perspective. Vampires start to tell their own stories and consequently become more sympathetic, closer to the human and much less radically the 'other'. They are more likely to offer a site of identification than a metaphor for what must be abjected, and with the movement from the metaphorical to the metonymical, the vampire increasingly serves to facilitate social commentary on the human world.

As well as becoming the subject rather than the object of the narrative, the modern vampire, rather than being solitary like Stoker's Count, desires companionship. In part, this can be seen as a return to the origins of vampire fiction. As Auerbach (1995) argues, early vampires cultivate an insidious intimacy with humans, and it is only Stoker's Dracula who breaks with this tradition, remaining aloof, alien, cold and impersonal. If it is a return, however, it is a return with a difference, since while contemporary vampires again desire intimacy, it is primarily with others like themselves. In Strieber's *The Hunger*, for example, Miriam, last of her kind, attempts to overcome her loneliness by taking one human companion after another, trying, and always ultimately failing, to transform them into creatures like herself. The solitary vampire often gives way to a community, and this process of socialization humanizes vampires further as they become motivated not only by hunger or the desire for power, but also by such feelings as jealousy or fear.

Frequently, as in Poppy Z. Brite's *Lost Souls* (1992) or Jewelle Gomez's *The Gilda Stories*, the establishment of a vampire community serves to register a disaffection with, and a search for an alternative to, the modern family and its values. At other times, the vampire is appropriated in the service of a more conservative moral agenda that aims to reinforce threatened values in much the same way as Stoker's *Dracula*. Such popular vampire films as *The Lost Boys* (1987) and *Near Dark* (1987), for example, in spite of offering the attractions of a more anarchic world, are ultimately completely complicit with the Reaganite values of the era in which they were produced. Demonic vampire communities function as a metaphor for the contemporary dysfunctional family and are set against, and vanquished by, 'good' human families. The father in *Near Dark* reverses the threat to his vampirized son with a transfusion of his own wholesome blood, while Grandpa saves the day in *The Lost Boys* when he kills the head vampire.

On the whole, however, the demonization of the vampire gives way to the modern humanization of the vampire, something that, Angela Carter's (q.v.) 'The Lady of the House of Love' (1979) suggests, is in a sense the death of the vampire. Her reluctant Nosferatu, 'Queen of the Vampires', is 'both death and the maiden', both the monster and its victim. Helplessly she re-enacts the life of her ancestors: she is 'a cave full of echoes, she is a system of repetitions, she is a closed circuit'. All she longs for is to evade her nature as the other and become human. Made all too human by her love for a touring English cyclist, however, she dies rather than destroy him, ironically leaving him instead to 'a special, exemplary fate in the trenches of Europe'. Metaphysical notions of evil may be ejected, the story suggests, but human evil always lies waiting to slide into the space it vacates.

Bibliography

Auerbach, Nina 1995: *Our Vampires, Ourselves*. Chicago: University of Chicago Press.

Case, Sue-Ellen 1990: 'Tracking the Vampire.' *Differences*, 3 (2), 1–20.

Day, William Patrick 2002: *Vampire Legends in Contemporary American Culture*. Lexington, KY: University Press of Kentucky.

Frayling, Christopher 1991: *Vampyres: Lord Byron to Count Dracula*. London: Faber and Faber.

Gelder, Ken 1994: *Reading the Vampire*. London: Routledge.

Gordon, Joan and Hollinger, Veronica (eds) 1997: *Blood Read: The Vampire as Metaphor in Contemporary Culture*. Philadelphia: University of Pennsylvania Press.

Heldreth, Leonard G. and Pharr, Mary 1999: *The Blood is the Life: Vampires in Literature*. Bowling Green, OH: Bowling Green State University Popular Press.

Persecution and Paranoia

From its beginnings, the literary Gothic has been concerned with uncertainties of character positioning and instabilities of knowledge. Far from knowing everything, like an omniscient narrator, characters – and even narrators – frequently know little or nothing about the world through which they move or about the structures of power which envelop them. We can point, for example, to three classic works, William Godwin's *Things as They Are; or, The Adventures of Caleb Williams*, Charles Robert Maturin's *Melmoth the Wanderer* and James Hogg's *The Private Memoirs and Confessions of a Justified Sinner* (qq.v.) as representations of persecuted victims, subject to violence and pursuit for incomprehensible reasons. These types of fiction can be referred to as paranoid in that they enact a classic psychology of paranoia whereby the self is threatened and pursued by its own unaccommodated residues. We can further extend the usefulness of this description if we think of some more recent fictions, for example those of Thomas Pynchon, as again representing the individual as helpless in the grip of powerful forces – in this case military and international; in the case of other fictions like, for example, those of William Gibson or Will Self, technological and cybernetic – which represent the self as dissolved in a web of uncomprehended power structures. Gothic could be seen as having proved fertile in adapting its descriptions as the historical representations of power have themselves altered and developed, and as the discourses through which power is transmitted have shifted terrain according to a logic of scientific and economic development, within which the self experiences itself as at the mercy of forces beyond its control.

As one example of these more recent modes, we might look at the Gothic traces in Joseph Heller's terrifying representation of corporate dehumanization in *Something Happened* (1974). Corporate life, according

273

to Heller's protagonist Bob Slocum, is a matter of relative but quantifiable fear:

> In the office in which I work there are five people of whom I am afraid. Each of these five people is afraid of at least four people (excluding overlaps), for a total of twenty, and each of these twenty people is afraid of six people, making a total of one hundred and twenty people who are feared by at least one person. Each of these one hundred and twenty people is afraid of the other hundred and nineteen, and all of these one hundred and forty-five people are afraid of the twelve men at the top who helped found and build the company and now own and direct it . . . Nobody is sure who really runs the company (not even the people who are credited with running it), but the company does run.

The arithmetic may appear ridiculous, but the fact remains that Slocum is so hollowed out by the corporate that he kills his own son by smothering him in order to protect him from the persecutory 'real world' of competition, death and pain. The main source of fear, as we might possibly expect, is called the 'Corporate-Operations Department'; but the problem for Slocum is that there no longer appears to be any alternative in his life to what are known as 'corporate operations', in the sense that all possible authenticity has become subsumed within the many masks of the replica:

> I always dress well [he says]. But no matter what I put on, I always have the disquieting sensation that I am copying somebody; I can always remind myself of somebody else I know who dresses much the same way. I often feel, there-fore, that my clothes are not my own. (There are times, in fact, when I open one of my closet doors and am struck with astonishment by the clothes I find hanging inside).

The great skill of Heller's book is that while in a sense subscribing to a generally developing argument about the neo-Gothic inclusiveness of the 'corporation', the text both finds a language, a discourse of flattening, of draining, in which to represent the fate of the subject at the mercy of the process of corporate hollowing, and also deconstructs the subject's mono-logue through the very evasions and uncertainties that striate Slocum's ago-nizing attempts to locate the 'something' that, he suspects, 'happened' in the past – whereas we know as readers that it is something that is still hap-pening, that will continue to happen, that is doomed to repetition, to secrecy and disavowal.

It is also Heller who produces one of the most extraordinarily Gothic images of what happens when corporate man is hollowed out, and more particularly of the ghosts and phantoms that inevitably come to populate the vacated space:

> I have a universe in my head. Families huddle there in secret, sheltered places. Civilisations reside. The laws of physics hold it together. The laws of chemistry keep it going. I have nothing to do with it. No one governs it. Foxy emissaries glide from alleys to archways on immoral, mysterious missions. No one's in charge. I am infiltrated and besieged, the unprotected target of sneaky attacks from within. Things stir, roll over slowly in my mind like black eels, and drop from consciousness into inky depths. Everything is smaller. It's neither warm nor cold. There is moisture. Smirking faces go about their nasty deeds and pleasures surreptitiously without confiding in me. It gives me a pain. Victims weep. No one dies. There is noiseless wailing. I take aspirins and tranquillisers. I am infested with ghostlike figurines (now you see them, now you don't), with imps and little demons. They scratch and stick me. I'd like to be able to flush the whole lot of them out of my mind into the open once and for all and try to identify them, line them up against a wall in the milky glare of a blinding flashlight.

And so it continues, a mixed rhetoric of the valley of death and the concentration camp, quiet, almost unheard murmurings, sharp stabs of pain. The body, as so often in Gothic, has been somewhere taken over and 'virally' infected; the self has been emptied out and replaced by a 'replicated' multitude.

Aspects of this scenario might remind us of a very different novel, Paul Auster's *City of Glass* (1985). Here, a man named Quinn follows a man named Stillman. At first, rather in the manner of Edgar Allan Poe's (q.v.) 'man of the crowd', Stillman's movements appear random, nonsensical, but eventually it appears that his tracks through the city spell out a series of giant letters, which Quinn eventually manages to piece together to find a meaning which is simultaneously the destruction of all meaning, the paranoid's plunge into despair at the task of making sense of the world and his or her consequent construction of an alternative set of realities: 'Tower of Babel'.

This double-take on meaning would seem to be the key to the paranoid problems and complexities of *City of Glass*, and it is intricately connected with problems of subjectivity. One morning, near the beginning of the book, Quinn, having received a baffling and indeed frightening phone call the night before summoning him to a 10 o'clock appointment,

> found himself doing a good imitation of a man preparing to go out. He cleared the table of the breakfast dishes, tossed the newspaper on the couch, went into the bathroom, showered, shaved, went on to the bedroom wrapped in two towels, opened the closet, and picked out his clothes for the day . . . It was not

until he had his hand on the doorknob that he began to suspect what he was doing: 'I seem to be going out', he said to himself.

In passages such as this, the subject is revealed as merely the persecuted effect of its own locations, its own trajectories. There is nothing intrinsic to Quinn (he has been called to the appointment under a different name: Auster, the name of the author, of his own creator) that can be separated from the places in which he appears, and these are frequently incomprehensible to him. As the text goes on, one might say that Quinn begins to disintegrate; but this is never put to us in terms of anything we might recognize as character, but rather in terms of a pressure of persecution from outside and paranoid fantasy from within.

Towards the end of the story Quinn, having become interested (despite himself, as it were) in the mysteries, pursuits and flights happening around him, is abruptly told that they are no longer any concern of his. Shocked by this and unable to think about it, he decides that 'for now, the only thing that seemed to matter was going home. He would return to his apartment, take off his clothes, and sit in a hot bath.' Then, perhaps, 'he would begin to think about it'. But Quinn's transition between different worlds, his persecution at the hands of, *inter alia*, his own author, has fatally dislocated him in space as well as in time, and he steps into his apartment to find that

> everything had changed. It seemed like another place altogether, and Quinn thought he must have entered the wrong apartment by mistake. He backed into the hall and checked the number on the door. No, he had not been wrong. It was his apartment; it was his key that had opened the door. He went back inside and took stock of the situation. The furniture had been rearranged. Where there had once been a table there was now a chair.

Very much in the manner of the early Gothic of the explained supernatural, it turns out that there is indeed an explanation for this; but this does not prevent Quinn from experiencing this moment as a paranoid culmination, a removal of all his sure and secure bearings in the world, and as precipitating him into a final and catastrophic decline as his subjectivity disintegrates under the pressure of paranoid fantasies, just as the persecuted hero, or more usually heroine, of early Gothic fiction, is continually faced with the prospect of the dissolution of all expectation and hope.

Bibliography

Flieger, Jerry Aline 1997: 'Postmodern Perspective: The Paranoid Eye.' *New Literary History*, 28 (1), 87–109.

Nadel, Alan 2002: 'Paranoia, Terrorism, and the Fictional Condition of Knowledge.' *Contemporary Literature*, 43 (2), 406–21.

Nicol, Bran 1999: 'Reading Paranoia: Paranoia, Epistemophilia and the Postmodern Crisis of Interpretation.' *Literature and Psychology*, 45 (1–2), 44–62.

O'Donnell, Patrick 2000: *Latent Destinies: Cultural Paranoia and the Contemporary US Narrative*. Durham, NC: Duke University Press.

Simons, Jon 2000: 'Postmodern Paranoia? Pynchon and Jameson.' *Paragraph: A Journal of Modern Critical Theory*, 23 (2), 207–21.

Female Gothic

When Ellen Moers first used the term 'female Gothic' in *Literary Women* (1976), she defined it simply as the work that women writers had done in the Gothic mode since the eighteenth century (q.v.). Since then, there has been a continuing and vigorous debate about whether female Gothic can be considered as a separate genre and, if so, what the characteristics of that genre might be.

Underlying many critical attempts to theorize a female Gothic is the idea that male and female Gothic differ primarily in the ways they represent the relationship of the protagonist to the dominant Gothic spaces depicted. Male Gothic tends to represent the male protagonist's attempt to penetrate some encompassing interior; female Gothic more typically represents a female protagonist's attempts to escape from a confining interior. Elaborating upon this basic distinction, however, critics have posited various more detailed differences in terms of both plot patterns and narrative conventions.

The plot of the male Gothic, typified by such novels as M. G. Lewis's *The Monk* (qq.v.), primarily focuses on questions of identity, and on the male protagonist's transgression of social taboos. It involves the confrontation of some isolated overreacher with various social institutions, including the law, the church and the family. In such texts women characters tend to be objectified victims, their bodies, like the Gothic structures, representations of the barriers between inside and outside that are to be broached by the transgressive male. Like the protagonist himself, the male Gothic text, both in its subject matter and in its narrative conventions, is usually considered to be particularly transgressive: violence, especially sexual violence, is dealt with openly and often in lingering and lascivious detail. The reader is frequently denied any fixed or stable position from which to interpret the text by the use of multiple points of view. And while male Gothic generally has a tragic

278

plot, with the protagonist punished for his breaking of the taboos, the text in many ways nevertheless resists narrative closure – the supernatural, for example, tends to be left unexplained.

In the female Gothic plot, the transgressive male becomes the primary threat to the female protagonist. Initially, she is usually depicted enjoying an idyllic and secluded life; this is followed by a period of imprisonment when she is confined to a great house or castle (q.v.) under the authority of a powerful male figure or his female surrogate. Within this labyrinthine space she is trapped and pursued, and the threat may variously be to her virtue or to her life. This basic scenario is, of course, present in the Gothic from the very start. In Horace Walpole's *The Castle of Otranto* (qq.v.), Isabella is placed in precisely this situation when, after the death of her intended husband Conrad, she flees from the attentions of his father, the tyrant Manfred, prince of Otranto, through a dark labyrinth of passages under the castle. In the female Gothic, however, as established by Ann Radcliffe (q.v.) in such novels as *A Sicilian Romance* (1789) and *The Mysteries of Udolpho* (q.v.), and as developed by her numerous imitators in the late eighteenth century, this scene of a woman trapped and pursued is not just adopted but transformed. The emphasis changes from general identity politics to a more specific concern with gender politics: it is the heroine's experiences which become the focus of attention, and her experiences are represented as a journey leading towards the assumption of some kind of agency and power in the patriarchal world, or alternatively as a search for an absent mother. Female Gothic tends to emphasize suspense rather than outright horror, and this is often generated by limiting the reader's understanding of events to the protagonist's point of view. It is her fears and anxieties upon which the text focuses rather than on violent encounters or rotting corpses. The presence of the supernatural is often suggested, but all mysterious events tend ultimately to be rationalized and explained. A resistance to ambiguous closure is also found in the preference for the happy ending; usually, the protagonist is reintegrated into a community and acquires a new identity and a new life through marriage.

The summary of female Gothic plot patterns and conventions outlined above cannot be taken as absolutes, and may well be applicable primarily to the work of Radcliffe and her followers and, more recently, to the popular Gothic romances of such writers as Victoria Holt. Even in the case of these writers, some qualifications are often required. Women writers frequently exploit motifs and conventions from both male and female Gothic. They may well even produce male, rather than female Gothic. Charlotte Dacre's (q.v.) *Zofloya, or The Moor* (1806) and Mary Wollstonecraft Shelley's *Frankenstein* (qq.v.) for example, would both appear to have more links to the former than the latter, even if *Frankenstein* was the text upon which Moers focused in her seminal discussion of female Gothic. Furthermore, female Gothic is no longer considered to be restricted to female writers. J. Sheridan Le Fanu's *Uncle Silas* (qq.v.) and Wilkie Collins's *The Woman in White* (qq.v.) are just two examples of male-authored books which fit quite neatly into the category of female Gothic: the confinement of Maud at Bartram-Haugh in the former, and of Laura at Blackwater Park in the latter, could both be said to play variations on Emily's experiences at Radcliffe's Udolpho.

While it is generally accepted that the primary defining trait of female Gothic is the consistent focus on the heroine and the house, there has, nevertheless, been much critical debate over the way this focus should be interpreted and the functions it serves. Whether female Gothic should be seen as radical or conservative has been an issue of particular concern. Since the initial attempt to theorize a female Gothic was linked to the change in consciousness resulting from the women's liberation movement of the late 1960s, early critics tended to focus upon female Gothic as a subversive genre which expressed women's fears and fantasies, their protests against the conditions of patriarchy.

The subversive element of the texts was particularly emphasized when critics in the late 1970s and 1980s began to theorize female Gothic through psychoanalytical readings of the female protagonist. These critics read the typical plot of confinement and escape as representing the daughter's struggle towards psychic individuation. Norman Holland and Leona Sherman's influential article on 'Gothic Possibilities', for example, sees the female Gothic as a rewriting of the male Oedipal struggle – the female protagonist's problematic attempt to separate from the mother. Claire Kahane (1985) in 'The Gothic Mirror' similarly reads female Gothic in terms of the mother–daughter relationship, with the spectral presence of the mother representing the problems of femininity that the protagonist must confront. For Kahane, all the female characters in such texts as *The Mysteries of Udolpho* can be read as doubles for the heroine: the madness and crimes of the Lady Laurentini, the rightful owner of Udolpho, consequently become suggestive of Emily's own potentially transgressive nature. A similar proposition was put forward by Gilbert and Gubar in *The Madwoman in the Attic* when they influentially argued for Bertha, the madwoman of Charlotte Brontë's (q.v.) *Jane Eyre*, as Jane's double, acting out both the rage and the desire that Jane herself must repress.

Critics who focus more on the socio-cultural contexts of female Gothic include Kate Ellis (1989), who reads the Gothic castle (q.v.) as the site for the contestation of the discourses of gender, a place where the ideological conflicts of the domestic sphere are enacted in a displaced form. Many critics, including Ellis, are ambivalent over the degree to which such ideology is ultimately subverted. As Eugenia DeLamotte argues in *Perils of the Night* (1990), that almost compulsory happy ending, the protagonist's marriage and reintegration into society, appears to reinforce precisely the domestic ideology which, throughout the narrative, is suggested to be the cause of all her problems and suffering.

Both psychological readings and socio-cultural readings that focus on domestic ideology have tended to enforce an identification of the female Gothic with the private, and in many ways this has worked to emphasize the conservative rather than the subversive element of the genre. Even more disturbingly, as E. J. Clery rightly points out, the tendency to read the works of female Gothic writers as 'parables of patriarchy involving the heroine's danger from wicked father figures, and her search for the absent mother' take us rather tediously back to family relations. 'In this way, "Female Gothic" can be absorbed into the notion of a distinctive women's tradition' (Clery 2000: 2). Part of this problem is resolved by the recognition that both male and female writers can produce male and female Gothic, but this nevertheless does not ultimately avoid the easy association of the female with the private world of the family.

Some recent critics have consequently suggested the need to relocate the genre in relation to the more public world. Teresa Goddu (1997), for example, argues that female Gothic has as much to do with economic concerns as with gender and family issues, and she has used the Gothic tales of Nathaniel Hawthorne (q.v.) and Louisa May Alcott to demonstrate how the anxieties of a new commodity culture were mediated through the female body. Alison Milbank's *Daughter of the House* (1992) analyses the appropriation of female Gothic by such authors as Charles Dickens and J. Sheridan Le Fanu (qq.v.), and demonstrates how the genre functions to critique not only gender ideology but also capitalism.

Ultimately, however, the use of the term 'female Gothic' remains contentious, and as Robert Miles suggests in his introduction to a special issue of *Women's Writing*, it should be taken neither as a 'commonsense category' nor as a 'self-evident literary classification' (1994: 1). At the very least, any discussion of female Gothic needs to take into account the fact that, as with any genre, once a certain set of conventions has been established, subsequent writers tend to experiment with and react against, rather than simply replicate, what they inherit.

Bibliography

Clery, E. J. 2000: *Women's Gothic: From Clara Reeve to Mary Shelley*. Tavistock: Northcote House.

DeLamotte, Eugenia 1990: *Perils of the Night: A Feminist Study of Nineteenth-Century Gothic*. Oxford: Oxford University Press.

Ellis, Kate 1989: *The Contested Castle: Gothic Novels and the Subversion of Domestic Ideology*. Urbana: University of Illinois Press.

Fleenor, Julian (ed.) 1983: *The Female Gothic*. Montreal: Eden Press.

Gilbert, Sandra and Gubar, Susan 1979: *The Madwoman in the Attic*. New Haven, CT: Yale University Press.

Goddu, Teresa 1997: *Gothic America: Narrative, History, and the Nation*. New York: Columbia University Press.

Hoeveler, Diane Long 1988: *Gothic Feminism: The Professionalisation of Gender from Charlotte Smith to the Brontës*. University Park: Pennsylvania State University Press.

Holland, Norman and Sherman, Leona 1977: 'Gothic Possibilities.' *New Literary History*, 8, 279–94.

Kahane, Claire 1985: 'The Gothic Mirror.' In Shirley Nelson Garner, Claire Kahane and Madeleine Sprengnether (eds), *The (M)Other Tongue: Essays in Feminist Psychoanalytic Interpretation*. Ithaca, NY: Cornell University Press, 334–51.

Miles, Robert (ed.) 1994. *Female Gothic Writing*. Special Issue of *Women's Writing*. 1 (2).

Milbank, Alison 1992: *Daughters of the House: Modes of the Gothic in Victorian Fiction*. London: Macmillan.

Moers, Ellen 1976: *Literary Women*. New York: Doubleday.

Williams, Anne 1995: *Art of Darkness: A Poetics of Genre*. Chicago: University of Chicago Press.

†he Uncanny

The history of the uncanny as an instrument of literary criticism was essentially fixed by Freud's great essay, 'The Uncanny' (1919), with its development of the theme of the *heimlich* and the *unheimlich*, its descriptions of the ways in which feeling or 'sentiment' may turn readily into its opposite, its detailed exploration of uncanny themes in E. T. A. Hoffmann's (q.v.) story 'The Sandman' (1816), and its suggestive distinction between the experience of the uncanny and its representation.

The Freudian *topos* forms the basis for a useful later elaboration of the uncanny in the work of Andrew Bennett and Nicholas Royle. Following the assertion that 'literature is uncanny', they describe the uncanny in terms of 'making things *uncertain*: it has to do with the sense that things are not as they have come to appear through habit and familiarity, that they may challenge all rationality and logic' (1999: 37). While such a view may create problems for any systematization of the uncanny, none the less Bennett and Royle do produce a list of 'a few forms that the uncanny takes', which can be broadly reproduced as follows:

> repetition (including the doublings of déjà vu and the *Doppelgänger*);
> coincidence and fate;
> animism;
> anthropomorphism;
> automatism;
> uncertainty about sexual identity;
> fear of being buried alive;
> silence;
> telepathy;
> death. (1999: 37–40)

It may be argued that there is an idiosyncratic quality to this list, or at least an imbalance between the scope and scale of some of the items. One might ask whether déjà vu is not in fact a more central category, certainly as far as the popular imagination is concerned; one might also ask whether the fear of being buried alive is not a specific instance of a more generalized claustrophobia, with its own complex aetiologies. None the less the list is indeed suggestive, and we can make ready application of it as the source of many 'Gothic effects'.

When beginning by thinking of repetition, however, one immediately runs up against a difficulty. For repetition is indeed a feature of many Gothic works: one might think of the repetitive structure of Charles Robert Maturin's *Melmoth the Wanderer* (qq.v.), or of the formal repetitions that arise when looking at M. R. James's (q.v.) ghost stories, which, excellent though they are, nevertheless work according to a repetitive logic that runs right through them. But on the other hand, it could be – and has been – claimed that repetition is at the heart of all writing, whether we are thinking in terms of the relation between representation and its absent original – itself a repetition of a sort – or of the more obvious ways in which most, if not all, poetic devices rely on variants of repetition for their effect. One might then go further and suggest that the culturally haunting quality of a poem like Samuel Taylor Coleridge's 'The Rime of the Ancient Mariner' (1798) arises from its conjunction of these two levels of repetition, the Gothic repetitiveness of the Mariner's wanderings and his story-telling and the formal repetitiveness of the ballad verse.

With coincidence and fate, again, one might say that this haunts most literature; the example of Thomas Hardy's novels might be the most obvious one to spring to mind. But here again one could perceive a specifically Gothic inflection, in, for example, the sense of imminent doom that haunts so many characters in, say, the novels of Ann Radcliffe (q.v.). There is indeed an added sense of fate – or perhaps in this context one might better refer to it as 'doom' – in the way in which many of these characters, especially those in the tradition of the Wandering Jew, appear to have foreknowledge of their own future.

By 'animism' is meant the way in which apparently inanimate objects come to seem to have a life of their own. Here an example that might come to mind would be the book and film of Stephen King's *The Shining* (qq.v.), based throughout on a version of animism whereby the Overlook Hotel itself seems to have its own memories, its own modes of action – indeed its own qualities and possibilities of repetition – and even, apparently, such subservient entities as the garden topiary can attain to an animate stature in the overheated imagination of the mad and violent Jack Torrance.

Anthropomorphism, one could say, is simply a subspecies of animism, whereby the inanimate is not merely invested with animate qualities but specifically 'impersonates' the human. In Gothic terms, what we would have here is the figure of the dead coming back to life; one of the most vivid images would be in George Romero's cult film, *Night of the Living Dead* (1968), but the wider tradition drawn on is that of the zombie, of the body without mind or soul that nevertheless impersonates the human. Clearly here we are dealing with the later outcroppings of age-old fears, primitive terrors that we can imagine as continuing to exist in the depths of the unconscious even when they have apparently been banished from the civilized world; or, in parallel, as continuing to haunt the child portion of the adult brain, especially under conditions of terror and darkness.

The classic example of automatism comes from Hoffmann's 'The Sandman' itself. In this story the hero apparently falls in love with a girl whom he believes to be human but who in fact turns out to be an extremely sophisticated doll. Although to attempt any interpretation of the complexities of the story would be beyond the space here available, none the less one might say that it is this mistake that eventually causes the hero's doom to fall upon him. Whether, or in what sense, he ever consciously *realizes* his error remains a moot point; perhaps it is so important for him to remain in his land of fantasy that even death is preferable to the violent reawakening, the relocation of his desires and aspirations, that would be necessary if he were to renounce his belief, however fantastical it might appear in the context of the world around him.

Again, with the question of uncertainty about sexual identity, one can find this theme running through the literary: an outstanding example would be Virginia Woolf's *Orlando* (1928), with its narrative told from the viewpoint of a person who is alternately – and without any satisfactory explanation – female and male. A Gothic version of this might be found in Wilkie Collins's *The Woman in White* (qq.v.), where many of the characters seem to have attributes more usually and stereotypically assigned to the opposite gender. It would be on these grounds that one might suggest that the Gothic plays a specific part in the challenging of conventional gender boundaries, and although it is always dangerous to have recourse to the 'writer's life', none the less it is striking how many masterpieces of Gothic have been written by authors – from Francis Lathom and M. G. Lewis to Bram Stoker and Oscar Wilde (qq.v.) – whose sexual identity offers to transgress the boundaries of the 'normal'.

When thinking of the fear of being buried alive, the figure who comes most immediately to mind is of course Edgar Allan Poe (q.v.), many of whose short stories revolve around this *topos*. Indeed Poe, we might say, takes us through a further uncanny 'turn of the screw' in that many of his revenants – in 'Ligeia' (1838), for example, or in 'The Fall of the House of Usher' (1839) – may not, for all we as readers know, be exactly the same people as those who died and were buried. Then again, perhaps this is an essential condition of the genre, emblematised by Stephen King in *Pet Sematary* (1983), where the form of the small boy who returns from the grave has gone through a horrifying transmutation as well as remaining, in some haunting sense, the same being as he was before.

Perhaps silence is too general a category to form a subset of the uncanny at all without further elaboration; but on the other hand it is clear that many ghost stories – perhaps the whole tradition of ghost stories – revolve around moments of silence, which somehow allow a sense of the 'other' to intrude. Emblematic here would be the stories of Walter de la Mare (q.v.); the silence which inhabits the great cathedral in his 'All Hallows' (1926), for example, seems to be the very medium within which the devilish work of distorted rebuilding can proceed.

Telepathy, Royle claims elsewhere (1991), is an essential condition of all narrative fiction: in other words, the sense the text engenders, and in which we as readers have no choice but to share, that characters understand each other's minds and feelings in ways that constantly challenge probability. But again, telepathy lies at the very heart of the Gothic, in the sense of barely understood intimations, the sense of one's mind being possessed by another, the schizophrenic phenomenon of 'thought broadcasting'. For an example, one might look to Charles Brockden Brown's (q.v.) *Wieland: or, The Transformation* (1798), where the entire plot hinges on telepathy and its avatars in the forms of hypnosis and mesmerism.

And so, finally – of course! – to death. But perhaps the obsession of Gothic with death needs no elaboration. What is in general certain is that these phenomena of the uncanny form the background and indeed the *modus operandi* of much Gothic fiction. Whether one could go so far as to claim on these grounds that Gothic is itself the emblematic form of fiction might be too controversial; but certainly the representation of the uncanny is at the core of Gothic, since it, like the uncanny, deals in the constant troubling of the quotidian, daylight certainties within the context of which one might prefer to lead one's life.

Bibliography

Bennett, Andrew, and Royle, Nicholas 1999: *Introduction to Literature, Criticism and Theory*. 2nd edn. London: Prentice-Hall.

Freud, Sigmund 1919: 'The Uncanny.' In James Strachey et al. (eds), *The Standard Edition of the Complete Psychological Works of Sigmund Freud*. Vol. XVII. London: Hogarth Press, 219–52.

Punter, David 2000: 'Shape and Shadow: On Poetry and the Uncanny.' In Punter (ed.), *A Companion to the Gothic*. Oxford: Blackwell, 193–205.

Royle, Nicholas 1991: *Telepathy and Literature: Essays on the Reading Mind*. Oxford: Blackwell.

Royle, Nicholas 2003: *The Uncanny*. Manchester: Manchester University Press.

The History of Abuse

Gothic, from its inception, has provided a range of images of social violence. The Gothic castle (q.v.) can be seen as a location where such violence can flourish, in one sense – at least in its earlier manifestations – safely contained by its distancing in time and place, yet at the same time inextricably entwined with more contemporary histories. The monastery or convent, an equally frequent Gothic location, similarly provides a scenario within which all manner of deprivation and violence can proceed, safely quarantined by supposed geographical and historical distance, and also by its relocation under the sign of a different religion, usually a parody of Catholicism that exists partly to provide an overt demonstration that such social ills and psychological perversions could not possibly flourish within the boundaries of Protestant England.

One contemporary way, however, in which one might seek to reconfigure these motifs would be by looking at them as the outcroppings of a consciousness that is not entirely immune to the frightening prospect that such abuses – of individuals, of social groups, of the relatively powerless – might in fact not be so remote from the contemporary or the local. Most obviously, of course, the tales that Gothic recounts have all too frequently to do with the violent abuse of women. One could take the 'originating' text here to be M. G. Lewis's *The Monk* (qq.v.), with its revoltingly detailed depictions of the monk Ambrosio's treatment of his female victims:

> With every moment the friar's passion became more ardent, and Antonia's terror more intense. She struggled to disengage herself from his arms: her exertions were unsuccessful; and finding that Ambrosio's conduct became still freer, she shrieked for assistance with all her strength. The aspect of the vault, the pale glimmering of the lamp, the surrounding obscurity, the sight of the

tomb, and the objects of mortality which met her eyes on either side, were ill-calculated to inspire her with those emotions, by which the friar was agitated. Even his caresses terrified her from their fury, and created no other sentiment than fear.

It is perhaps difficult to tell in *The Monk* where the worst abuse lies: in the fictional rape of Antonia by Ambrosio, or in the fascinated, gloating tone Lewis uses to portray such events and to complicate their relations with desire. The point, however, is brought out more clearly by Ann Radcliffe (q.v.), when Vivaldi in *The Italian* (1797) is driven to meditate on how and whether such acts can truly be regarded as the prerogative of a class or type of person entirely foreign to 'civilized' norms, or whether the implications go much further:

> Can this be in human nature! – Can such horrible perversion of right be permitted! Can man, who calls himself endowed with reason, and immeasurably superior to every other created being, argue himself into the commission of such horrible folly, such inveterate cruelty, as exceeds all the acts of the most irrational and ferocious brute.

Put in its most general form, this is perhaps one of the key questions posed by Gothic fiction: namely, to what extent are we – as citizens of a 'civilized' nation, and also as writers and readers of scenes of depravity and cruelty – implicated in the perpetuation of these violences? In one sense, indeed, Gothic distances, relocates, reterritorializes these scenes; in another, of course, it ceaselessly incarnates precisely the material which it claims to be banishing, and in doing so provides us with a kind of secret history of what goes on beneath the veneer of culture.

If women are abused in the Gothic, then it is perhaps unsurprising to find that the fate of children, their powerlessness in the face of persecution, is another recurring Gothic theme. One might think, for example, of one of the most Gothic-influenced of Charles Dickens's (q.v.) novels, *The Old Curiosity Shop* (1840), and the appalling tribulations of Little Nell, tribulations eventually ended only, to the wild dismay of Dickens's contemporary readers, by her death. That Dickens had in mind not only the miseries so many children faced in Victorian Britain but also his lifelong memories of some of his own childhood experiences needs no documentation: from the very beginning *The Old Curiosity Shop* is grounded in a hideous, haunting image. 'It would be a curious speculation', the narrator tells us, 'to imagine [Nell] in her future life, holding her solitary way among a crowd of wild grotesque companions . . .'; he checks himself,

> But all that night, waking or in my sleep, the same thoughts recurred, and the same images retained possession of my brain. I had, ever before me, the old dark murky rooms – the gaunt suits of mail with their ghostly silent air – the faces all awry, grinning from wood and stone – the dust, and rust, and worm that lives in wood – and alone in the midst of all this lumber and decay and ugly age, the beautiful child in her gentle slumber, smiling through her light and sunny dreams.

But smile though Nell might, the text cannot banish but can only intensify this image of the lost, persecuted child, adrift on a sea of menace, imaged here precisely in the Gothic paraphernalia of the 'curiosity shop' itself, including the remains of an undead past which will in the end provide her with no place of safety, but consign her to a fate that lethally underlines the evasions characteristic of much of the earlier Gothic, with its miraculous escapes and comedically reconciliatory endings.

In Stephen King's *The Shining* (qq.v.) both forms of abuse come together in the hands of Jack Torrance, whose pathological condition finds its first emblem in his violence towards his son Danny, and works its way through his treatment of both Danny and his wife. In a sense the problem Torrance confronts, yet simultaneously evades, throughout is to do with his self-recognition as an abusive parent and husband. Remembering – yet also not 'truly' remembering – the moment when he broke Danny's arm, he muses:

> He had denied doing it. He had been horrified at the bruises, at Danny's soft and implacable disconnection. If he had done it, a separate section of himself had been responsible. The fact that he had done it while he was asleep was – in a terrible, twisted way – encouraging.

There is here a multiple play on the notion of 'disconnection'. There is Danny's arm; there is Danny's retreat before the horrific images with which he is plagued by the hotel; and then there is Jack's own 'disconnection', his tortured refusal of agency, of responsibility. The self that acts in a Gothic fashion, the self that brings onto the stage of the real the most violent of fantasies, must be *another* self; it must be a self that, after the fashion of Dr Jekyll and Mr Hyde (q.v.), is somehow disconnected, dislocated from us: these actions are, after all, ones that we only perform in our sleep, they have no place in the waking world.

Torrance, we might reasonably say, is in a state of denial; he is also in a state of addiction, and the history of abuse tells us that these two things go hand in hand. The question of agency in *The Shining* is a complicated one: in one sense it is true that the hotel itself is a malevolent entity, drawing and funnelling power from past events within its walls. But in another sense it is Torrance himself, the 'torrent' that bursts forth when the hotel's boiler finally explodes (because it has not been properly cared for), who is the originating force behind events, although the rule of addiction dictates that it is not, as he sees it, really his *self* that is responsible, but some other, some foreign body within him that cannot be kept fully under control.

We might finally think of Henry James's *The Turn of the Screw* (qq.v.), for here the notion of abuse itself takes a further turn, or twist. For the governess who tells the story of her experiences is, we might suppose, herself ripe for abuse: 'the youngest of several daughters of a poor country parson' who 'inevitably' regards her employer as 'gallant and splendid', for all his refusal of all contact with her and his apparent abandonment of his own children. Quite where this cycle of abuse ends in *Turn of the Screw* is, of course, notoriously obscure: what is clear, however, is that the governess's powerlessness revisits itself upon the children, with fatal consequences. The complexity of her perceptions, the apparent delicacy of her emotional responses, her peculiar version of 'care' for her charges: all of these are presumably effects of her own position, but they are redoubled by the suggestions of a different kind of abuse, the abuse of abandonment and loneliness which – perhaps as always with James – have produced in the child Miles precisely the symptoms of precocious sexual maturity (even if only in the governess's imagination) which are the documented effects of abuse.

Gothic, then, contains and partially enacts all manner of 'secret stories'; the fact that these stories are difficult to tell – or even to remember – against a 'realist' background has been seen by some critics as rendering them all the more powerful when they emerge within the more dreamlike parametres of Gothic. There denial is both expressed and secluded, the secret is laid bare, albeit within a system of signs that allows the reader to collude in evasions that the form itself permits, even encourages, while leaving a haunting doubt as to whether the distantiation of these events is produced precisely by the self-protections of the abusive, the addicted, the pathological.

Bibliography

Kincaid, James 1998: 'Producing Erotic Children.' In Henry Jenkins (ed.), *The Children's Culture Reader*. New York: New York University Press, 241–53.

Kuribayashi, Tomoko and Tharp, Julie (eds) 1997: *Creating Safe Space: Violence and Women's Writing*. Albany, NY: State University of New York Press.

Ronell, Avital 1992: *Crack Wars: Literature, Addiction, Mania*. Lincoln, NE: University of Nebraska Press.

Scheper-Hughes, Nancy and Stein, Howard F. 1998: 'Child Abuse and the Unconscious in American Popular Culture.' In Henry Jenkins (ed.), *The Children's Culture Reader*. New York: New York University Press, 178–95.

Sturken, Marita 1999: 'Narratives of Recovery: Repressed Memory as Cultural Memory.' In Mieke Bal, Jonathan Crewe and Leo Spitzer (eds), *Acts of Memory: Cultural Recall in the Present*. Hanover, NH: University Press of New England, 231–48.

Hallucination
and the Narcotic

In many ways, we might say that the Gothic is grounded on the terrain of hallucination: this would be another way of saying that it is a mode within which we are frequently unsure of the reliability of the narrator's perceptions, and thus of the extent to which we as readers are enjoined to participate in them or to retain a critical distance. This uncertainty, this swaying of the curtain, is perhaps at its most extreme in the stories of Edgar Allan Poe (q.v.), where it is constantly and indissolubly linked to a sense of the narcotic, of impending sleep, to a world where all sense of differentiation and vivid colour is in continual danger of slipping away, beyond our grasp. There is, for example, the territorial description Poe offers us in 'Silence: A Fable' (1837):

> The waters of the river have a saffron and sickly hue; and they flow not onward to the sea, but palpitate for ever and for ever beneath the red eye of the sun with a tumultuous and convulsive motion. For many miles on either side of the river's oozy bed is a pale desert of gigantic water lilies. They sigh unto the other in that solitude, and stretch towards the heaven their long and ghastly necks, and nod to and fro their everlasting heads. And there is an indistinct murmur which cometh out from among them like the rushing of subterrene water.

We might aptly contrast this with the subterranean waters of Samuel Taylor Coleridge's 'Kubla Khan' (1798), which at least have the possibility of bursting forth in some form of eruption from the compressed unconscious; or we might compare it with the scenarios of Algernon Blackwood's (q.v.) stories, where the indistinctness of worlds of water and island produces a unique landscape in which the premonition of terror is indistinguishable from terror itself. At all events, what we appear to have in this becalmed scene is an intimation of a world wherein sleeping and waking are not separate; here there is, as Poe says, silence, or at least a sound which bears no differentiation, which is therefore in itself the opposite of language. Here there is also, as in so many of Poe's best-known tales, no possibility of escape, because the narcotic motion of the waters leaves them stuck for ever in position, no matter how they might heave and boil with frustration.

It would also be at this peculiar, narcotized still point, wherein all differentiated human feeling has been drowned, that the denouement of Poe's 'Berenice' (1835) (like, indeed, the beginning of Charles Dickens's (q.v.) *The Mystery of Edwin Drood* [1870]) takes place: it is 'an afternoon in the winter of the year, – one of those unseasonably warm, calm, and misty days which are the nurse of the beautiful Halcyon'. There is something about these surroundings of motionless warmth, the arrested river, which endlessly replays the warmth that preceded exile, and thus points the way to an identification between these narcotized states in which all willpower disappears and some infantile, imaginary state which preceded the frettings of the birth of the symbolic order. There is something about the quality of the air in these conditions which renders the memory peculiarly susceptible to an indelible engraving, like the repetitions of the narcotic, which is desperately unwanted but which cannot be avoided. A similar thing happens in Poe's 'The Assignation' (1834), when the hero gets his first glimpse of the Marchese Aphrodite:

> a snowy-white and gauze-like drapery seemed to be nearly the sole covering to her delicate form; but the mid-summer and midnight air was hot, sullen, and still, and no motion in the statue-like form itself, stirred even the folds of that raiment of very vapour which hung around it as the heavy marble hangs around the Niobe.

The plot of 'The Assignation' consists of the hero stumbling into knowledge of a relationship between the Marchese and another young man, a relationship which is about to issue in a death-pact of which the narrator is called upon to be an unwilling witness. But perhaps the very word 'witness' is specifically inadequate when trying to see with clarity the uncertain worlds that Poe and other Gothic writers bring to our attention, for it is made 'clear' to us – if such a thing is possible – that the narrator's senses have been confused by a specific hallucinatory environment, of a kind which we could also find in 'Ligeia' and others of Poe's stories:

> Rich draperies in every part of the room trembled to the vibration of low, melancholy music, whose origin was not to be discovered. The senses were

oppressed by mingled and conflicting perfumes, reeking up from strange convoluted censers, together with multitudinous flaring and flickering tongues of
emerald and violet fire. The rays of the newly risen sun poured in upon the
whole, through windows formed each of a single pane of crimson-tinted glass.

In such a world, it is impossible for narrators – or indeed other characters –
to become or remain certain of what they are seeing, or sensing, or feeling.
All senses are more or less numbed, and it is under these conditions that hallucinations flourish – the hallucination, for example, which might or might
not be the figure of Ligeia in 'Ligeia', or the ghostly forms that walk through
an uncertain light in 'The Fall of the House of Usher' (1839).

What can also happen in much Gothic fiction is that a condition of hallucination or trance – whether overtly caused by drugs or represented as the
spontaneous emergence of a 'different' state of mind – can confuse the perception not only of others or of the world around, but also of ourselves as
readers. This seems to be what happens, for example, at a crucial moment
in David Lindsay's (q.v.) *The Haunted Woman* (1922), when the heroine
Isbel Loment looks at herself in a mirror:

> Abstractedly she walked over to the mirror to adjust her hat . . . Either the glass
> was flattering her, or something had happened to her to make her look dif-
> ferent; she was quite startled by her image. It was not so much that she
> appeared more beautiful as that her face had acquired another character. Its
> expression was deep, stern, lowering, yet everything was softened and made
> alluring by the pervading presence of sexual sweetness. The face struck a note
> of deep, underlying passion, but a passion which was still asleep . . . It thrilled
> and excited her. It was even a little awful to think that this was herself, and
> still she knew that it was *true*.

One question here would be about what it might mean for a person in this
'altered' state to know something to be 'true'. What, one might wonder,
might truth actually mean when the senses have been changed, and when,
indeed, the sense of passion, although apparently all-powerful, is none the
less still 'asleep' (as, perhaps, are most of the characters in *The Haunted
Woman*, who may from time to time be figures in the dreams of one
another)?

One thing we might say about such Gothic moments – and we might
pause to wonder whether numbers of texts that we would hesitate to call
'Gothic' in themselves might nevertheless have 'Gothic moments' – is that
they serve to reveal something about the possibilities and depths of human
misrecognition, something about the degree to which life is pursued 'in the
light of' a certain degree of untruth, of misunderstanding, whether of

295

ourselves or of others, or of the perceptions that govern our relations with others.

Sometimes, of course, these 'different' recognitions are taken to be not so much missings, evasions, but rather the signs of a different access to a greater or clearer truth; this would be emblematically the case in Arthur Conan Doyle's (q.v.) Sherlock Holmes stories, where the great detective's senses are improved to a fine pitch by the ingestion of drugs. Actual drugs, then, from laudanum through opium to cocaine, can bear a double sign in the world of Gothic hallucinations; they may narcotize, reduce one to sleep, but at the same time they can clear the brain of the irrelevant and allow for a fine focus. The process of narcosis and the development of intellectual clarity thus enter into a curious symbiosis: the dulling of the senses is inseparable from what some writers would refer to as the opening of the inner eye, an outward blinding inseparable from the freeing of a 'different' way of seeing things, a seeing of 'different' things. Whether those 'different' things are in fact hallucinations would, of course, be a question without a simple answer: if, like the many half-seen monsters of Gothic, they appear all too vividly before the eye of the reader, then perhaps this is reality enough.

We might in conclusion turn briefly to Coleridge's poem 'Christabel' (1798), a poem in which, for most of the time, most of the protagonists are asleep, under the influence of some unspecified general narcotic. At the crucial moment towards the end of the poem at which light seems about to break on Christabel, and thus on the reader, as to the true nature of the intruding phantom Geraldine, the result is a revelation which is simultaneously no revelation at all, because it cannot be recounted in words but instead is sucked back into the unaccountable substance of the dream:

> Her silken robe, and inner vest,
> Dropt to her feet, and full in view,
> Behold! Her bosom and half her side –
> A sight to dream of, not to tell!
> O shield her! Shield sweet Christabel! (244–8)

Yet this is, of course, a situation of deep textual ambiguity: in the absence of a clear account, the imagination is left to dream, to hallucinate what the 'forbidden sight' might be.

Bibliography

Hayter, Alethea 1968: *Opium and the Romantic Imagination*. London: Faber and Faber.

Hill, John S. 1963: 'The Dual Hallucination in 'The Fall of the House of Usher'.' *South-West Review*, 48, 396–402.

Johae, Antony 1990: 'Hallucination in *Oliver Twist* and *Crime and Punishment*.' *New Comparison*, 9, 128–38.

Potter, Russell 1994: 'The Hallucination of Textuality.' *Nomad: An Interdisciplinary Journal of the Humanities, Arts and Sciences*, 6, 23–8.

Thomson, A. W. 1965: '*The Turn of the Screw:* Some Points on the Hallucination Theory.' *Review of English Literature*, 6 (4), 26–36.

Gᴜɪᴅᴇ ᴛᴏ Fᴜʀᴛʜᴇʀ Rᴇᴀᴅɪɴɢ

Works that focus on specific authors or texts may be found in individual bibliographies in sections on 'Writers of the Gothic' and 'Key Texts'.

Collections of Gothic writing

Baldick, Chris (ed.) 1992: *The Oxford Book of Gothic Tales*. Oxford: Oxford University Press.

Clery, E. J. and Miles, Robert (eds) 2000: *Gothic Documents: A Sourcebook, 1700–1820*. Manchester: Manchester University Press.

Cox, Jeffrey N. (ed.) 1992: *Seven Gothic Dramas, 1789–1825*. Columbus: Ohio State University Press.

Crow, Charles (ed.) 1999: *American Gothic: An Anthology, 1787–1916*. Oxford: Blackwell.

Morrow, Bradford and McGrath, Patrick (eds) 1991: *The New Gothic: A Collection of Contemporary Gothic Fiction*. New York: Random House.

Ryan, Alan (ed.) 1991: *The Penguin Book of Vampire Stories*. London: Bloomsbury.

Thompson, G. Richard (ed.) 1979: *Romantic Gothic Tales 1790–1840*. New York: Harper and Row.

Collections of Gothic criticism

Bloom, Clive (ed.) 1998: *Gothic Horror: A Reader's Guide from Poe to King and Beyond*. Houndmills: Macmillan.

Botting, Fred (ed.) 2001: *The Gothic*. English Association *Essays and Studies*. Cambridge: Boydell and Brewer.

Byron, Glennis and Punter, David (eds) 1999: *Spectral Readings: Towards a Gothic Geography*. Houndmills: Macmillan.

Docherty, Brian (ed.) 1990: *American Horror Fiction: From Brockden Brown to Stephen King*. New York: St Martin's Press.

Fleenor, Julian (ed.) 1983: *The Female Gothic*. Montreal: Eden Press.

Gelder, Ken (ed.) 2000: *The Horror Reader*. London: Routledge.

Gordon, Jan and Hollinger, Veronica (eds) 1997: *Blood Read: The Vampire as Metaphor in Contemporary Culture*. Philadelphia: University of Pennsylvania Press.

Graham, Kenneth W. (ed.) 1989: *Gothic Fictions: Prohibition/Transgression*. New York: AMS Press.

Grant, Barry Keith (ed.) 1996: *The Dread of Difference: Gender and the Horror Film*. Austin: University of Texas Press.

Grunenberg, Christoph (ed.) 1997: *Gothic: Transmutations of Horror in Late Twentieth Century Art*. Cambridge, MA: MIT Press.

Hogle, Jerrold E. (ed.) 2002: *The Cambridge Companion to Gothic Fiction*. Cambridge: Cambridge University Press.

Horner, Avril (ed.) 2002: *European Gothic: A Spirited Exchange, 1760–1960*. Manchester: Manchester University Press.

Kerr, Howard, Crowley, John W. and Crow, Charles L. (eds) 1983: *The Haunted Dusk: American Supernatural Fiction, 1820–1920*. Athens, GA: University of Georgia Press.

Magistrale, Tony and Morrison, Michael (eds) 1996: *A Dark Night's Dreaming: Contemporary American Horror Fiction*. Columbia, SC: University of South Carolina Press.

Martin, Robert K. and Savoy, Eric (eds) 1998: *American Gothic: New Interventions in a National Narrative*. Iowa City: University of Iowa Press.

Punter, David (ed.) 2000: *A Companion to the Gothic*. Oxford: Blackwell.

Riquelme, John Paul (ed.) 2000: *Gothic and Modernism*. Special Issue of *Modern Fiction Studies* 46, 585–799.

Robbins, Ruth and Wolfreys, Julian (eds) 2000: *Victorian Gothic: Literary and Cultural Manifestations in the Nineteenth Century*. Houndmills: Palgrave.

Sage, Victor (ed.) 1990: *The Gothick Novel: A Casebook*. Houndmills: Macmillan.

Sage, Victor and Smith, Allan Lloyd (eds) 1996: *Modern Gothic: A Reader*. Manchester: Manchester University Press.

Smith, Allan Lloyd and Sage, Victor (eds) 1994: *Gothick: Origins and Innovations*. Amsterdam: Rodopi.

Smith, Andrew and Hughes, William (eds) 2003: *Empire and the Gothic: The Politics of a Genre*. London: Palgrave.

Smith, Andrew and Wallace, Jeff (eds) 2001: *Gothic Modernisms*. London: Palgrave.

Thompson, G. R. (ed.) 1974: *The Gothic Imagination: Essays in Dark Romanticism*. Olympia: Washington State University Press.

Tinkler-Villani, Valeria, Davidson, Peter and Stevenson, Jane (eds) 1995: *Exhibited By Candlelight: Sources and Developments in the Gothic Tradition*. Amsterdam: Rodopi.

Waller, Gregory A. (ed.) 1987: *American Horrors: Essays on the Modern American Horror Film*. Urbana: University of Illinois Press.

General studies of the Gothic

Aguirre, Manuel 1990: *The Closed Space: Horror Literature and Western Symbolism*. Manchester: Manchester University Press.

Auerbach, Nina 1995: *Our Vampires, Ourselves*. Chicago: University of Chicago Press.

Badley, Linda 1996: *Writing Horror and the Body: The Fiction of Stephen King, Clive Barker, and Anne Rice*. Westport, CT: Greenwood Press.

Baldick, Chris 1987: *In Frankenstein's Shadow: Myth, Monstrosity and Nineteenth-Century Writing*. Oxford: Clarendon Press.

Bayer-Berenbaum, Linda 1982: *The Gothic Imagination: Expansion in Gothic Literature and Art*. London: Associated University Presses.

Becker, Susanne 1999: *Gothic Forms of Feminine Fictions*. Manchester: Manchester University Press.

Birkhead, Edith 1921: *The Tale of Terror: A Study of the Gothic Romance*. London: Constable.

Botting, Fred 1996: *Gothic*. London: Routledge.

Botting, Fred 1999: *Sex, Machines and Navels: Fiction, Fantasy and History in the Future Present*. Manchester: Manchester University Press.

Brennan, Matthew C. 1997: *The Gothic Psyche: Disintegration and Growth in Nineteenth-Century English Literature*. Columbia, SC: Camden House.

Briggs, Julia 1977: *Night Visitors: The Rise and Fall of the English Ghost Story*. London: Faber and Faber.

Bronfen, Elisabeth 1992: *Over Her Dead Body: Death, Femininity and the Aesthetic*. Manchester: Manchester University Press.

Bruhm, Steven 1994: *Gothic Bodies: The Politics of Pain in Romantic Fiction*. Philadelphia: University of Pennsylvania Press.

Büssing, Sabine 1987: *Aliens in the Home: The Child in Horror Fiction*. New York: Greenwood Press.

Carroll, Noël 1990: *The Philosophy of Horror, or Paradoxes of the Heart*. London: Routledge.

Castle, Terry 1995: *The Female Thermometer: Eighteenth-Century Culture and the Invention of the Uncanny*. Oxford: Oxford University Press.

Cavaliero, Glen 1995: *The Supernatural and English Fiction*. Oxford: Oxford University Press.

Clemens, Valdine 1999: *The Return of the Repressed: Gothic Horror from The Castle of Otranto to Alien*. Albany, NY: State University of New York Press.

Clery, E. J. 1995: *The Rise of Supernatural Fiction, 1762–1800*. Cambridge: Cambridge University Press.

Clery, E. J. 2000: *Women's Gothic: From Clara Reeve to Mary Shelley*. Tavistock: Northcote House.

Clover, Carol J. 1992: *Men, Women and Chainsaws: Gender in the Modern Horror Film*. London: BFI.

Cohen, Jeffrey Jerome 1996: *Monster Theory: Reading Culture*. Minneapolis: University of Minnesota Press.

Cornwell, Neil 1990: *The Literary Fantastic: From Gothic to Postmodernism*. London: Harvester Wheatsheaf.

Creed, Barbara 1993: *The Monstrous-Feminine: Film, Feminism and Psychoanalysis*. London: Routledge.

Day, William Patrick 1985: *In the Circles of Fear and Desire: A Study of Gothic Fantasy*. Chicago: University of Chicago Press.

DeLamotte, Eugenia C. 1990: *Perils of the Night: A Feminist Study of Nineteenth-Century Gothic*. Oxford: Oxford University Press.

Edmundson, Mark 1997: *Nightmare on Main Street: Angels, Sadomasochism, and the Culture of Gothic*. Cambridge, MA: Harvard University Press.

Edwards, Justin D. 2003: *Gothic Passages: Racial Ambiguity and the American Gothic*. Iowa City: University of Iowa Press.

Ellis, Kate Ferguson 1989: *The Contested Castle: Gothic Novels and the Subversion of Domestic Ideology*. Urbana, IL: University of Illinois Press.

Ellis, Markham 2000: *The History of Gothic Fiction*. Edinburgh: Edinburgh University Press.

Fiedler, Leslie A. 1960: *Love and Death in the American Novel*. New York: Criterion.

Gamer, Michael 2000: *Romanticism and the Gothic: Genre, Reception, and Canon Formation*. Cambridge: Cambridge University Press.

Geary, Robert 1992: *The Supernatural in Gothic Fiction: Horror, Belief, and Literary Change*. Lewiston: Edwin Mellon.

Gelder, Ken 1994: *Reading the Vampire*. London: Routledge.

Goddu, Teresa A. 1997: *Gothic America: Narrative, History, and the Nation*. New York: Columbia University Press.

Grixti, Joseph 1989: *Terrors of Uncertainty: The Cultural Contexts of Horror Fiction*. London: Routledge.

Haggerty, George E. 1989: *Gothic Fiction/Gothic Form*. University Park: Pennsylvania State University Press.

Halberstam, Judith 1995: *Skin Shows: Gothic Horror and the Technology of Monsters*. Durham, NC: Duke University Press.

Halttunen, Karen 1998: *Murder Most Foul: The Killer and the American Gothic Imagination*. Cambridge, MA: Harvard University Press.

Heiland, Donna 2000: *Gothic Novels: A Feminist Introduction*. Oxford: Blackwell.

Heller, Terry 1987: *The Delights of Terror: An Aesthetics of the Tale of Terror*. Urbana, IL: University of Illinois Press.

Hendershot, Cyndy 1998: *The Animal Within: Masculinity and the Gothic*. Ann Arbor: University of Michigan Press.

Hoeveler, Diane Long 1988: *Gothic Feminism: The Professionalization of Gender from Charlotte Smith to the Brontës*. University Park: Pennsylvania State University Press.

Howard, Jacqueline 1994: *Reading Gothic Fiction: A Bakhtinian Approach*. Oxford: Clarendon Press.

Howells, Coral Ann. 1978: *Love, Mystery, and Misery: Feeling in Gothic Fiction*. University of London: Athlone Press.

Hurley, Kelley 1996: *The Gothic Body: Sexuality, Materialism and Degeneration at the Fin de Siècle*. Cambridge: Cambridge University Press.

Ingebretsen, Edward J. 1996: *Maps of Heaven, Maps of Hell: Religious Terror as Memory from the Puritans to Stephen King*. Armonk, NY: M. E. Sharpe.

Jackson, Rosemary 1981: *Fantasy: The Literature of Subversion*. London: Methuen.

Kilgour, Maggie 1995: *The Rise of the Gothic Novel*. London: Routledge.

King, Stephen 1982: *Danse Macabre: The Anatomy of Horror*. London: Futura.

Kristeva, Julia. 1982: *Powers of Horror: An Essay on Abjection* (1980), trans. Leon S. Roudiez. New York: Columbia University Press.

MacAndrew, Elizabeth 1979: *The Gothic Tradition in Fiction*. New York: Columbia University Press.

Malchow, H. L. 1996: *Gothic Images of Race in Nineteenth-Century Britain*. Stanford, CA: Stanford University Press.

Massé, Michelle A. 1992: *In the Name of Love: Women, Masochism and the Gothic*. Ithaca, NY: Cornell University Press.

Mighall, Robert 1999: *A Geography of Victorian Gothic Fiction: Mapping History's Nightmare*. Oxford: Oxford University Press.

Milbank, Alison 1992: *Daughters of the House: Modes of the Gothic in Victorian Fiction*. Houndmills: Macmillan.

Miles, Robert 2000: *Gothic Writing, 1750–1820: A Genealogy*. Manchester: Manchester University Press. Morgan, Jack 2002: *The Biology of Horror: Gothic Literature and Film*. Carbondale, IL: Southern Illinois University Press.

Napier, Elizabeth 1987: *The Failure of Gothic: Problems of Disjunction in an Eighteenth-Century Literary Form*. Oxford: Clarendon Press.

Navarette, Susan J. 1998: *The Shape of Fear: Horror and the Fin de Siècle Culture of Decadence*. Lexington, KY: University Press of Kentucky.

Palmer, Pauline 1999: *Lesbian Gothic: Transgressive Fictions*. London: Cassell.

Pirie, David 1973: *A Heritage of Horror: The English Gothic Cinema, 1946–1972*. London: Gordon Frasier.

Prawer, S. S. 1980: *Caligari's Children: The Film as Tale of Terror*. Oxford: Oxford University Press.

Praz, Mario 1970: *The Romantic Agony* (1933), trans. Angus Davidson. Oxford: Oxford University Press.

Punter, David 1996: *The Literature of Terror: A History of Gothic Fictions from 1765 to the Present Day*. 2nd edn. 2 vols. London: Longman.

Punter, David 1998: *Gothic Pathologies: The Text, the Body and the Law*. London: Macmillan.

Railo, Eino 1927: *The Haunted Castle: A Study of the Elements of English Romanticism*. London: Routledge.

Ringe, Donald A. 1982: *American Gothic: Imagination and Reason in Nineteenth-Century Fiction*. Lexington, KY: University Press of Kentucky.

Roberts, Marie 1990: *Gothic Immortals: The Fiction of the Brotherhood of the Rosy Cross*. London: Routledge.

Sage, Victor 1988: *Horror Fiction in the Protestant Tradition*. Houndmills: Macmillan.

Schmitt, Cannon 1997: *Alien Nation: Nineteenth-Century Gothic Fictions and English Nationality*. Philadelphia: University of Pennsylvania Press.

Sedgewick, Eve Kosofsky 1986: *The Coherence of Gothic Conventions*. London: Methuen.

Skal, David J. 1993: *The Monster Show: A Cultural History of Horror*. New York: Norton.

Smith, Andrew 2000: *Gothic Radicalism: Literature, Philosophy, and Psychoanalysis in the Nineteenth Century*. Houndmills: Macmillan.

Sullivan, Jack 1978: *Elegant Nightmares: The English Ghost Story from Le Fanu to Blackwood*. Athens, OH: Ohio University Press.

Summer, Montague 1938: *The Gothic Quest: A History of the Gothic Novel*. London: Fortune Press.

Todorov, Tzvetan 1973: *The Fantastic: A Structural Approach to a Literary Genre*, trans. Richard Howard. Ithaca, NY: Cornell University Press.

Tudor, Andrew 1989: *Monsters and Mad Scientists: A Cultural History of the Horror Movie*. Oxford: Blackwell.

Varma, Devendra P. 1957: *The Gothic Flame: Being a History of the Gothic Novel in England*. London: Barker.

Varnado, S. L. 1987: *Haunted Presence: The Numinous in Gothic Fiction*. Tuscaloosa: University of Alabama Press.

Voller, Jack G. 1994: *The Supernatural Sublime: The Metaphysics of Terror in Anglo-American Romanticism*. De Kalb: Northern Illinois University Press.

Watt, James 1999: *Contesting the Gothic: Fiction, Genre and Cultural Conflict, 1764–1832*. Cambridge: Cambridge University Press.

Wein, Toni 2002: *British Identities, Heroic Nationalisms and the Gothic Novel, 1764–1824*. London: Palgrave.

Wiesenfarth, Joseph 1988: *Gothic Manners and the Classic English Novel*. Madison: University of Wisconsin Press.

Williams, Anne 1995: *Art of Darkness: A Poetics of Gothic*. Chicago: University of Chicago Press.

Winter, Kari J. 1992: *Subjects of Slavery, Agents of Change: Women and Power in Gothic Novels and Slave Narratives 1790–1865*. Athens, GA: University of Georgia Press.

Wolstenhome, Susan 1993: *Gothic (Re)visions: Writing Women as Readers*. Albany, NY: State University of New York Press.

Gothic bibliographies

Barron, Neil (ed.) 1990: *Horror Literature: A Reader's Guide*. New York: Garland.

Fisher, Benjamin F. 1987: *The Gothic's Gothic: Study Aids to the Tale of Terror*. New York: Garland.

Frank, Frederick S. 1984: *Guide to the Gothic: An Annotated Bibliography of Criticism*. Metuchen, NJ: Scarecrow Press.

Frank, Frederick S. 1987a: *The First Gothics: A Critical Guide to the English Gothic Novel*. New York: Garland.

Frank, Frederick S. 1987b: *Gothic Fiction: A Master List of Twentieth-Century Criticism and Research*. Westport, CT: Meckler.

Frank, Frederick S. 1990: *Through the Pale Door: A Guide to and through the American Gothic*. Westport, CT: Greenwood Press.

Frank, Frederick S. 1995: *Guide to the Gothic II: An Annotated Bibliography of Criticism, 1983–1993*. Lanham, MD: Scarecrow Press.

McNutt, D. J. 1975: *The Eighteenth-Century Gothic Novel: An Annotated Bibliography of Criticism and Selected Texts*. New York: Garland.

Spector, Robert D. 1984: *The English Gothic: A Bibliographic Guide to Writers from Horace Walpole to Mary Shelley*. Westport, CT: Greenwood Press.

Thomson, Douglass H., Voller, Jack G. and Frank, Frederick S. (eds) 2002: *Gothic Writers: A Critical and Bibliographical Guide*. Westport, CT: Greenwood Press.

Tracy, Ann B. 1981: *The Gothic Novel, 1790–1830: Plot Summaries and Index to Motifs*. Lexington, KY: University Press of Kentucky.

Index

Abernethy, John, 21
'abhuman', the, 23, 24, 41
abjection, 5, 24, 264, 271
abuse, 248, 250, 288–91
addiction, 138, 156, 256, 290, 291
Afghanistan, 71
Aids, 63
Ainsworth, William Harrison, 28, 79,
    110, 260
Alaric, 3
alchemy, 165
alcoholism, 248, 250
Alcott, Louisa May, 281
American Civil War, the, 116, 162
American Gothic, 54, 68, 123, 127,
    152
androgyny, 244
Angel of Mons, the, 146
animism, 283, 284–5
anthropomorphism, 283, 285
antinomianism, 208, 209
anti-Semitism, 232
apparitions, 235
architecture, 4, 8, 9, 32–8, 55, 169,
    177, 179
Ariosto, Ludovico, 8
aristocracy, 17, 18, 26, 28, 66, 98,
    114, 117, 131, 138, 157, 161, 180,
    218, 255, 269

Arkham House, 109, 144
art, 36–8
artificial intelligence, 119
Atwood, Margaret, 55
Aubrey, John, 72
Auerbach, Nina, 271
Augustanism, 10
Austen, Jane, 80–1, 136
Auster, Paul, 51, 53, 275–6
automata, 20
automatism, 283, 285

Baddeley, Gavin, 61
ballads, 9, 13, 14, 107, 141, 163, 224,
    284
Ballard, J. G., 82
Balzac, Honoré de, 203
Banks, Iain, 51–3, 83–4, 261
Banville, John, 84–5
barbarism, 4–5, 7–8, 10, 39, 52, 54,
    73–4, 83, 131, 177, 191, 213, 261
Barker, Clive, 85–6
Bastille, the, 14
Batcave, The, 59
Bath, 87, 138
Baudelaire, Charles, 203
Bauhaus, 59
Beckford, William, 10, 87, 151, 181–3
Bennett, Andrew, 283

Benson, E. F., 88–9
Bentley, Christopher, 269
bereavement, 153
Berlin, 136
Bierce, Ambrose, 89–90, 103
black magic, 91
Blackwood, Algernon, 90–1, 293
Blair, Robert, 10, 13
Blake, William, 9, 13–14, 15, 71, 72
Blatty, W. P., 69
Blixen, Karen, *see* 'Dinesen, Isak'
Bloch, Robert, 91–2, 240, 242
Bogart, Humphrey, 242
Booth, William, 22, 40
Botting, Fred, 24–5, 265
bourgeoisie, 26, 180, 234, 269
Bowen, Elizabeth, 92–3
Bowen, Gary, 270
Bowie, David, 59, 269
Braddon, Mary Elizabeth, 26, 27, 29,
    94–5
Brantlinger, Patrick, 39
Brathwaite, Edward Kamau, 58
Briggs, Julia, 27
Brite, Poppy Z., 62, 271
Brontë, Anne, 95
Brontë, Branwell, 95
Brontë, Charlotte, 30, 44, 95, 236,
    280
Brontë, Emily, 30, 95–6, 212–16
Brontë, Patrick, 95
Brontë, sisters, the, 30, 95, 220
Brown, Charles Brockden, 54, 97,
    286
Browning, Tod, 65
Bruhm, Steven, 248, 250
Buddhism, 90
Bulwer-Lytton, Edward George, 28,
    86, 98–9, 110, 219
Bürger, Gottfried August, 107
Burke, Edmund, 5, 11–12
Burton, Richard, 74
Butler, Marilyn, 21, 198
Byrne, Nicholas, 106

Byron, George Gordon, Lord, 17–18,
    95, 141, 150, 157, 218, 268
Byzantine, the, 36

Cabell, James Branch, 99–100
Calcutta, 48, 57
Califia, Pat, 270
Calmet, Augustin, 268
Calvinism, 166, 208, 209
Campbell, Ramsey, 100–1
Canada, 91
cannibalism, 115, 254
Canterbury, 35
capitalism, 20, 22, 63, 255, 269,
    281
Caribbean, the, 44
Carroll, Lewis, 249
Carter, Angela, 101–2, 265, 271
Case, Sue-Ellen, 270
Castle, Terry, 30
castles, 47, 49, 51, 111, 123, 151, 154,
    156, 158, 164, 177, 179–80, 248,
    255–6, 259–62, 279, 280, 288
catalepsy, 135
cathedrals, 34, 47, 197, 286
Catholicism, 35, 98, 111, 162, 177,
    204, 288
Chambers, Robert W., 103
Chandler, Raymond, 119
chapbooks, 111
Charnas, Suzy McGee, 270
Chartism, 160
Chaucer, Geoffrey, 9, 17
childbirth, 212
China, 268
chivalry, 18–19, 131, 192
Christianity, 270
circus, 102
city, the, 21, 26, 28, 40, 226
classicism, 4, 7, 10, 32, 34, 36, 147
claustrophobia, 55, 88, 91, 144, 161,
    196, 262, 284
Clery, E. J., 180, 281
Cold War, the, 66, 264

Coleridge, Samuel Taylor, 9, 14–16, 37, 72, 150, 198, 284, 293, 296
Collins, Wilkie, 26, 27, 29, 104–5, 113, 143, 217–20, 280
colonialism, 264
colonization, 232
Columbine High School, 60
comics, 71, 73, 86
communism, 66
Conrad, Joseph, 44
convents, 180, 195–6, 204, 288
Coppola, Francis Ford, 265
Corelli, Marie, 105–6
Corman, Roger, 66–8, 148
counterfeit, 34, 62
Craft, Christopher, 232, 263
crime, criminality, 22–3, 26–7, 29, 39–40, 42, 84, 89, 111, 115, 118, 123, 127, 173, 191–2, 197, 232–3, 240, 248, 266, 280
Crowe, Catherine, 28
Crusades, the, 178
crypts, 79, 194
Cthulhu mythos, 109, 144
Cure, The, 59
Curtis, Ian, 63
cyber-fiction, 119
cybernetic, the, 273
cyborg, the, 24

Dacre, Charlotte, 16, 27, 105, 106–7, 279
Dadd, Richard, 37
Dahmer, Jeffrey, 152
Damned, The, 59
dandy, the, 219
Dante Alighieri, 37, 183
Dark Ages, the, 3, 7
Darwin, Charles, 42, 146, 227
'Darwinian Gothic', 42, 46, *see also* evolution
de la Mare, Walter, 24, 108, 203
decadence, 23, 26, 39, 41, 42–3, 103, 140, 146, 196, 218, 227, 244, 264

deconstruction, 156
degeneration, 39, 42, 232
déjà vu, 283–4
DeLamotte, Eugenia, 198
Delibes, C. P., 127
demon lovers, 107, 150, 268
demons, the demonic, 88, 91, 97, 107, 123, 134, 144, 146, 194, 197, 204, 209, 244, 266, 271
Deneuve, Catherine, 68, 269
Depression, the, 116
Derleth, August, 109–10, 144
Derrida, Jacques, 53, 156
detective fiction, 226
deviance, 22–3
Devil, the, 69, 99, 114, 127, 134, 150, 195, 246, 270
devils, 187
Dickens, Charles, 22, 27–8, 79, 98, 110–11, 160, 220, 281, 289, 294
'Dinesen, Isak', 111–12
disease, 38–9
Doppelgänger, 41, 173, 226, 283, *see also* double, the
Doré, Gustave, 37
Dostoevsky, Fyodor, 253–4
double, the, 24, 41, 51, 63, 104, 118, 127, 132, 145, 165, 166, 168, 172–3, 197, 200, 213, 222–3, 224, 228, 243, 248, 266, 280, 283, *see also Doppelgänger*
Doyle, Arthur Conan, 48, 113, 296
dreams, 37, 50, 83, 84–5, 88, 90, 99, 104–5, 107, 127, 169, 187, 199, 206, 214, 233, 241, 260, 291, 296
drugs, 296
Drury Lane theatre, 150
Dublin, 149
Dunsany, Lord, 114–15
Dylan, Bob, 71

East End Horrors, 40
Eastlake, Charles, 35
Ellis, Bret Easton, 115–16, 253, 265

Ellis, Havelock, 232
Ellis, Kate, 280
empire, 170, *see also* 'imperial fiction';
  'imperial Gothic'; imperialism
Engels, Friedrich, 22
enlightenment, 7, 12, 36, 53, 97
Eton, 114, 133
evolution, 22, 28, 42, 46, 146, 227,
  264, 270
exorcism, 69
expressionism, 55, 65, 73

fairy tales, 145, 162
family secrets, 29
fantastic, the, 28, 249
fantasy, 50, 56, 80, 89, 93, 99, 106,
  114, 121, 123, 125, 127, 135, 142,
  143, 145, 148–9, 159, 162, 164,
  167, 170, 178, 186, 196, 212, 276,
  280, 285, 290
Faulkner, William, 116–17
Faust, 150, 182, 195
Faust, Christa, 62
female Gothic, 26, 60, 137, 139, 159,
  160, 212, 222, 278–82
feudalism, 17, 36, 52, 54, 112, 131,
  155, 161, 164, 180, 190, 219, 230,
  259
film, 61, 65–70, 86, 106, 121, 125,
  134, 148, 240–1, 264–6, 269, 284,
  285
film noir, 119
First World War, the, 93, 125, 136
Fisher, Terence, 67
Flammenberg, Laurence, 81
folk-lore, folk-tales, 128, 157, 163–4,
  167, 268–9, 270
folk tradition, 8–9
Fonthill Abbey, 9, 87
forgery, 152
France, 140
fraudulence, 147
French Revolution, the, 129

Freud, Sigmund, 127, 155, 206, 250,
  269, 283
Freund, Karl, 65
Fuseli, John Henry, 36–7

Gaiman, Neil, 72–3
Galas, Diamanda, 63
Galland, Antoine, 181
galvanism, 21
Gaskell, Elizabeth, 27–9, 118
Gein, Ed, 92
Gelder, Ken, 245
genetic engineering, 24
Genghis Khan, 50
German Gothic, 194
Germany, 39
Getes, the, 3
Ghosh, Amitav, 56–7
ghost story, the, 27–8, 30, 50, 94–5,
  106, 110, 113, 118, 125, 131,
  132–3, 137, 140, 157, 172, 186,
  286, *see also* ghosts; ghouls;
  haunting; phantoms; wraiths
ghosts, 15–16, 27, 30, 34, 52, 55–8,
  79, 89, 92, 94, 95–6, 108, 125,
  128, 132, 133, 136, 140, 153, 155,
  160, 162, 163, 171–2, 186–8,
  195, 213–15, 237, 238, 249, 262,
  275, 295, *see also* ghost story, the;
  ghouls; haunting; phantoms;
  wraiths
ghouls, 30, 182–3, *see also* ghosts;
  ghost story, the; haunting; phantoms;
  wraiths
Gibbons, Dave, 71
Gibson, William, 119–20, 273
Gilbert, Sandra, 280
Gilman, Charlotte Perkins, 24
Giotto di Bondone, 36
Gladstone, William, 106
Gluck, C. W., 127
Gober, Robert, 38
Goddu, Teresa, 281

Godwin, William, 16, 97, 120–1, 164, 190–3, 205, 273
Goethe, J. W. von, 94, 268
Gomez, Jewelle, 270, 271
Gothic Revival, the, 34–6, 62, 177
Goths, the, 3–5, 7, 32, 59
Goya y Lucientes, Francisco José de, 37, 85
Graham, Kenneth, 183
Graham of Claverhouse, John, 128
graphic novels, 62, 71–5, 86
graveyard poetry, 10–11, 13, 17
Gray, Thomas, 9, 10, 14
Greece, 4
Grosse, Karl, 81
grotesquerie, the grotesque, 110, 116, 154, 182–4, 224, 263
Grunenberg, Christoph, 37–8
Gubar, Susan, 280
Gunn, Joshua, 60

Haggard, H. Rider, 44–6, 121–2
Haiti, 264
Halberstam, Judith, 63
hallucination, 93, 122, 171, 293–6
Halperin, Victor, 65, 264
Hambly, Barbara, 270
Hammer Studios, 67–8
Hannaham, James, 59, 61, 63
Hanson, Clare, 250–1
Hanuman, 135
Hardy, Thomas, 36, 284
Harris, Thomas, 266
haunting, 52–3, 54–5, 57, 92, 94, 117, 118, 123, 125, 136, 138, 140, 143, 145, 151, 154–5, 159–60, 171, 186, 208, 210, 215, 227, 284, 285, 291, *see also* ghosts; ghost story, the; ghouls; phantoms; wraiths
Hausenstein, Wilhelm, 33
Haworth, 95
Hawthorne, Nathaniel, 123–4, 127, 220, 281

Haymarket theatre, 138
Hebdige, Dick, 62
Heilman, Robert, 30
Heller, Joseph, 273–4
Henley, Samuel, 181
Henley, W. E., 166
Herbert, James, 124–5
Hervey, James, 10
Heston, Charlton, 149
historical novels, 28, 79, 103, 109, 128, 130, 137, 139, 160–1, 162, 163, 164, 166
Hitchcock, Alfred, 68, 92, 238
Hoban, Russell, 50–1, 53
Hodgson, William Hope, 125–6
Hodkinson, Paul, 62
Hoeveler, Diane Long, 166
Hoffmann, E. T. A., 127, 141, 145, 283, 285
Hogg, James, 97, 104, 128–9, 145, 167, 208–11, 226, 273
Hogle, Jerrold E., 29, 34, 62
Holland, Norman, 280
Holt, Victoria, 279
homoeroticism, 244
homosexuality, 39, 227, 232, 270
Hurd, Richard, 8–9, 18, 147, 177
Hurley, Kelly, 23, 41
hypnotism, 233, 240, 286
hysteria, 37

'imperial fiction', 44, *see also* empire
'imperial Gothic', 39, 44, 48, 121; *see also* empire
imperialism, 30, 44–9, 57–8, 113, 135, *see also* empire
incest, 157, 164, 169, 269
India, 106, 268
industrial Gothic, 60, 63
Industrial Revolution, the, 39
industrialization, 20–1, 36, 118, 154
Inquisition, the, 121, 195

insanity, 23, 27, 29, 37, 103, 107, 127, 138, 205
Institute of Contemporary Art, the, 37
International Gothic Association, the, 62
Irving, Henry, 167
Irving, Washington, 127, 129–30
Italy, 140, 164

Jack the Ripper, 40, 42
Jackson, Rosemary, 212
Jacobean drama, 186
Jacobinism, 150
James, G. P. R., 130–1
James, Henry, 24, 27–8, 130, 131–2, 152, 171, 235–8, 242, 291
James, M. R., 132–3, 284
Johnson, Samuel, 4, 182
Jones, Ernest, 269
Jordanes, 3
Joy Division, 63
Jung, Carl, 127

Kahane, Claire, 280
Karloff, Boris, 65
Kean, Edmund, 150
Keats, John, 9, 18–19
Kennedy, John F., 82
Kenton, Erle C., 65
Kernan, Caitlin, 62
Kilgour, Maggie, 201
killers, serial, 265–6
King, Jonathan, 106
King, Stephen, 52, 124, 134, 248–51, 284, 286, 290
King's College, Cambridge, 35, 132
Kipling, Rudyard, 44, 135–6
Kliger, Samuel, 3
Koran, the, 180
Kristeva, Julia, 264

labyrinths, 28, 55, 82, 256, 261, 279
Lacan, Jacques, 53, 156, 215, 250
Lamb, Lady Caroline, 157

Lancashire, 79
Langley, Batty, 34
Lathan, Rob, 269
Lathom, Francis, 81, 136–7, 285
Lavoisier, Antoine, 20
Lawrence, William, 21
Le Fanu, J. Sheridan, 27, 30, 113, 137–8, 222–5, 236, 269–70, 280, 281
Lee, Harriet, 138
Lee, Sophia, 138–9
Lee, Vernon, 24, 140
Lewis, C. S., 145
Lewis, M. G., 15, 17, 45, 60, 68, 79–80, 98, 105, 107, 111, 127, 141–2, 147, 163, 187, 194–7, 205, 278, 285, 288–9
Lindsay, David, 142–3, 295
Liverpool, 100
Lombroso, Cesare, 22–3, 232–3
London, 28, 36, 40, 56, 61, 98, 106, 114, 124–5, 158, 161, 230–1
Lovecraft, H. P., 67, 91–2, 100, 109–10, 126, 143–4
Lugosi, Bela, 63, 65, 264

MacDonald, George, 144–5
Machen, Arthur, 40, 146
Macpherson, James, 9, 147–8, *see also* 'Ossian'
Madoff, Mark, 5
'magic realism', 102
Magna Carta, 4
Mahomet, 182
male Gothic, 60, 159, 278–9
Mallet, P. H., 9
Mamoulian, Reuben, 65–6
manuscripts, 51, 71, 80, 127, 132, 148, 153, 159, 177, 181, 191, 203
March, Fredric, 66
Marcuse, Herbert, 206
Martin, Sara, 61, 62
Marx, Karl, 269
masochism, 269

materialism, 20–1, 24, 27, 29, 42, 58, 233
Matheson, Richard, 24, 148–9
Matthews, John, 213
Matthias, Thomas, 169
Maturin, Charles Robert, 26, 149–50, 203–7, 273, 284
Maxwell, John, 94
McConnell, Frank, 73
McCormack, W. J., 223
McMahan, Jeffrey, 270
McNaughton, John, 266
méconnaissance, 53
megalomania, 103, 211
melancholy, 14–15, 97
melodrama, 16, 28, 45, 55, 65, 110–11, 116, 150, 157, 162, 166, 186, 192, 217–18
Melville, Herman, 124, 150–1
memorials, 56
memory, 256, 294
'mental physiology', 23
mesmerism, 123, 245, 286
Mighall, Robert, 29
Milbank, Alison, 224–5, 281
Miles, Robert, 40, 281
Milton, John, 9, 183, 194, 198
Milwaukee, 152
misogyny, 89
misrecognition, 295
Mississippi, 116
Modernism, 36, 37, 43, 53, 103
modernity, 8, 16, 36, 50, 53, 155, 230–1, 232
Moers, Ellen, 278, 280
monasteries, 111, 179, 204, 206, 288
monasticism, 17, 35
Monroe, Marilyn, 82
monsters, the monstrous, 23–4, 27, 40–1, 45, 63, 65, 66, 116, 119, 133, 165, 168, 198–201, 202, 256, 263–6, 268, 270, 272, 296
Montesquieu, Charles-Louis de Secondat, 4

monuments, 56
Moorcock, Michael, 75
Moore, Alan, 71
Morrison, Grant, 74
Morrison, Toni, 55, 265
mourning, 112, 123, 241
Mozart, Wolfgang Amadeus, 127
'Murphy, Dennis Jasper', 149–50
music, 59–61, 63
mysticism, 90, 99

narcotic, the, 293–6
nationalism, 4, 10, 35, 54–5
Nazism, 59
necrophilia, 269
New Jersey, 148
New Orleans, 162, 244
'New Woman', the, 39–40, 219, 231–2
New York, 115–16, 129, 132, 255
Newgate novels, 28, 110
Newstead Abbey, 18
Nietzsche, Friedrich, 71
nightmares, 15, 19, 28, 37, 82, 88, 104, 135, 144, 187, 197, 199, 201, 209, 249
Nine Inch Nails, 63
Nordau, Max, 42–3, 232–3
Norton, André, 92
Norwich, 136
'Novalis', 145

Oates, Joyce Carol, 152, 265
O'Brien, Howard Allen, 162
obsession, 171, 237
occult, the, 27, 59, 105, 134, 162
Oedipal, the, 243, 250, 280
Offenbach, Jacques, 127
Oliphant, Margaret, 28, 153–4
Order of the Golden Dawn, the, 90
orientalism, 48, 87, 168, 181, 182
'Ossian', 9, 13, 14, 17, 147–8

Paget, Violet, 140
pain, 46, 74, 86, 146, 274–5

painting, 36, 166
paranoia, 66, 68, 119, 148–9, 205, 219, 235, 264, 272, 275–6
paranormal, the, 148
Parlour Library, 130
Parnell, Thomas, 11, 14
parody, 61, 81, 141
Parsons, Eliza, 81
pathology, 83, 126, 290, 291
patriarchy, 81, 118, 122, 139, 213, 222, 245, 250–1, 262, 280
Peake, Mervyn, 154–5, 261
'penny-dreadfuls', 94
Percy, Thomas, 9, 128, 147
periodicals, 27
persecution, 82, 97, 110, 120, 139, 150, 158, 166, 190, 192–3, 205–6, 210, 219, 272, 273–4, 276, 290
Perth, 105
perversion, 288
phantomatic, the, 93
phantoms, 17, 29, 55, 58, 186, 275, 296, *see also* ghosts; ghost story, the; ghouls; haunting; wraiths
phobias, 37
physiognomy, 233
Piccadilly, 232
Pichel, Irving, 65
picturesque, the, 166
Planché, J. R., 157
Poe, Edgar Allan, 63, 65, 67–8, 103, 104, 113, 123, 127, 130, 144, 148, 152, 155–6, 203, 226, 249, 260, 275, 285, 293–4
Polanski, Roman, 68
Polidori, John, 157–8, 268–70
'political Gothic', 190
Pope, Alexander, 10–11, 263
Porter, Alicia, 61
possession, 68
postcolonial, the, 45, 54–8, 264
postmodernism, 50–3, 63, 74, 82, 84, 162
poststructuralism, 256

Powell, Michael, 68
premature burial, 156, 262, 268
Price, Vincent, 149
Priestley, Joseph, 20
prisons, 29, 179, 190, 192, 195, 226
Prometheus, 199
Protestantism, 35, 204, 288
Providence, Rhode Island, 143
psychiatry, 23, 69, 138, 241–2
Psychic TV, 63
psychoanalysis, 156, 233, 242, 250, 280
psychology, 24, 36–7, 54, 69, 88, 91, 94, 96, 107, 121, 123, 128, 130, 131–2, 140, 150, 156, 170, 179, 186, 192, 197, 199–200, 205, 208, 213, 218, 222, 224, 237, 238, 249–50, 268, 273, 281, 288
psychopathology, 67, 91, 116, 125, 253
psychosis, 53, 91, 124, 152, 242
Pugin, Augustus, 33, 35
pulp magazines, pulp fiction, 82, 91, 143, 242
Punter, David, 65
Pykett, Lyn, 212
Pynchon, Thomas, 273
Pyrenees, the, 166

queer reading, 270

Radcliffe, Ann, 14, 17, 34, 60, 79, 80–1, 98, 110–11, 123, 137, 138–9, 141, 147, 158–9, 164, 166, 185–8, 191, 194–6, 205, 218–19, 222, 236, 259, 279, 284, 289
Railway Library, 130
'Rampling, Anne', 162
rationalism, 170, 177, 181, 188, 191, 219, 233, 237
Reagan, Ronald, 271
realism, 28, 30, 96, 99–100, 104, 110, 118, 123, 131, 132, 135, 144, 149,

153, 159, 163–4, 170, 171–2, 179, 181, 192–3, 212–13, 291
Reeve, Clara, 159–60, 178
Reformation, the, 169
religious mania, 211
Rembrandt van Rijn, 224
Renaissance, the, 263
repetition, 55, 74, 117, 144, 162, 213, 274, 283–4, 294
replica, the, 256, 274, 275
revenant, the, 268, 286
Reynolds, G. W. M., 22, 28, 160–1
Rice, Anne, 162–3, 244–7, 265, 271
Rickman, Thomas, 35
Riley, Joan, 58
Robinson, James, 73
Roche, Regina Maria, 81
Roman Empire, the, 3, 7, 10
romance, 123
romanticism, 13, 16, 37, 71, 89, 99, 127, 201
Rome, 3, 4, 5
Romero, George, 149, 265, 285
'Roquelaure, A. N.', 162
Rosicrucianism, 99, 217
Royal Academy, the, 36–7
Royle, Nicholas, 283, 286
Rucker, Rudy, 24
ruins, 9, 14, 56–7, 89, 139, 169, 179, 262
Rushdie, Salman, 55
Ruskin, John, 33, 36
Russell, Ken, 168
Rymer, James Malcolm, 269

Saberhagen, Fred, 244, 271
Sade, marquis de, 72
sadism, 86, 89, 206, 269
sado-masochism, 162
Sadleir, Michael, 81
St Denis, monastery of, 32
Salem, 123
Samoa, 167
Sandhurst, 114

Satan, 98, 192, 195, 196
satanism, 68
Sauk City, 109
Schiller, Friedrich, 15–16
schizophrenia, 208, 286
Schoedsack, Ernest, 65
science, scientists, 20–5, 26, 27, 29, 41–2, 119, 125, 134, 170–1, 199, 225, 233, 266, 270, 273
science fiction, 66, 82, 83, 91, 105, 148
Scotland, 105
Scott, Jody, 270
Scott, Tony, 269
Scott, Walter, 79, 130, 141, 163–4, 260
Second World War, the, 57, 93
secrets, 14, 51, 68, 70, 86, 94, 137, 172, 182, 190, 206, 222, 259, 261, 289, 291
Self, Will, 273
sensation novels, 26–7, 28–9, 94, 104, 110, 137, 217, 219, 222
sensationalism, 196
sensibility, 187–99, 219
shadow, 145, 224, *see also* double, the; *Doppelgänger*
Shakespeare, William, 9, 194
Shanghai, 82
Shelley, Mary Wollstonecraft, 16, 20–1, 24, 26, 65, 120–1, 151, 157, 164–5, 198–202, 265, 279
Shelley, Percy Bysshe, 9, 16–17, 18, 120, 157
Shelleys, the, 97
Sheridan, Frances, 182
Sherman, Cindy, 38
Sherman, Leona, 280
Showalter, Elaine, 227
Siegel, Don, 264
'silver-fork' fiction, 98
Siouxsie and the Banshees, 59
Sisters of Mercy, The, 60
Skipp, John, 270

Slave Labour, 62
slavery, 56, 264
Sleath, Eleanor, 81
Smiles, Samuel, 22
Smith, Charlotte, 160, 165–6
social problem novels, 118
Soho, 94
somnambulism, 240
Southern Gothic, 100, 116
Southey, Robert, 268
Soviet Union, the, 71
Specimen, 59–60
Spector, Craig, 270
'spectral technology', 30
spectres, the spectral, 15, 56, 58, 79,
    104, 140, 215, 223, 259, 280
Spenser, Edmund, 9, 13, 18
spirits, 90, 128, 133, 137, 223
spiritualism, 27, 113, 131
stained glass, 33–4, 36
Stanley, Henry, 40
Stevenson, Robert Louis, 22, 24,
    39–40, 65, 80, 92, 166–7, 203, 226,
    260
Stoker, Bram, 23, 39, 44, 65, 157,
    167–8, 230, 232, 244, 246, 265,
    269, 271, 285
Strawberry Hill, 10, 34, 169, 179
Strieber, Whitley, 269, 271
sublime, the, 11, 47, 55, 87, 131, 166,
    183–4, 259
Suger, Abbot, 32
suicide, 88, 97, 209, 223, 241, 249
supernatural, the, 28, 29, 30, 41–2, 47,
    55, 68, 79, 86, 88, 89, 90, 91,
    95–6, 101, 104, 106, 107, 109–10,
    118, 120, 121, 122, 126, 128,
    129–30, 132, 134, 135–6, 137, 140,
    143, 145, 148, 153–4, 157, 159,
    160, 163–4, 166, 167, 169, 172,
    178–80, 181, 185, 186, 194–5, 209,
    210, 213, 215, 220, 225, 249–50,
    260, 276, 279
superstition, 167, 188, 230, 269

surrealism, 37, 197
Swedenborg, Emanuel, 223, 225
Symonds, John Addington, 232

taboo, 213, 238, 278–9
Tacitus, 4
Talford, Thomas Noon, 158
Tasso, Torquato, 8
taxidermy, 241
Tchaikovsky, Peter Ilich, 127
'techno-Gothic', 82
technology, 24, 30, 63, 66, 71, 82,
    116, 119–20, 231–3, 273
telepathy, 113, 283, 286
terror, 9–12, 34, 37–8, 55, 68, 72, 86,
    87, 97, 100, 103, 104, 110, 111,
    113, 120, 126, 133, 134, 144, 149,
    160, 161, 163, 166, 167, 172, 178,
    182, 185, 187, 188, 205, 234,
    259–60, 264, 285, 293
Test Department, 63
Thompson, G. R., 34
Thomson, James, 5
'thought broadcasting', 286
Tibet, 268
Tieck, Johann Ludwig, 125
Todorov, Tzvetan, 249
Tolkien, J. R. R., 114, 145
Tomc, Sandra, 244–5
Toth, Csaba, 63
Tower of London, the, 260
transvestitism, 218, 243
Transylvania, 230
trauma, 56, 58, 126
Trinity College, Dublin, 149
Tutuola, Amos, 58
Tyrwhitt, Thomas, 9

uncanny, the, 37–8, 41, 156, 213–15,
    219, 222, 243, 283–6
unconscious, the, 37, 42, 145, 155,
    156, 206, 233, 238, 242, 262, 269,
    285, 293
'undead', the, 230–1

United States, the, 39, 65, 66, 99, 134
Universal Studios, 65

vampires, 23–4, 30, 88, 94, 96, 102,
    109, 138, 148–9, 157, 162, 167–8,
    230–4, 244–7, 265, 268–72
Van Ghent, Dorothy, 214
Vasari, Giorgio, 33
Vasquez, Jhonen, 63
Venice, 162
ventriloquism, 97
Victoria, Queen, 58, 106, 130, 153
Victoria Memorial (Calcutta), 57
video games, 149
virtuality, 115–16
virus, 24, 270, 275
vivisection, 42, 45
voodoo, 91, 264

Walcott, Derek, 58
Wall Street, 115, 255–6
Walpole, Horace, 10, 29, 34, 118, 123,
    158, 159–60, 169–70, 177–80, 181,
    259, 279
Walpole, Sir Robert, 169
Wandering Jew, the, 150, 164, 195–6,
    204, 284
Wandrei, Dennis, 109
Warton, Thomas, 10
Wells, 35

Wells, H. G., 41, 44, 146, 170–1
werewolves, 23
Westminster, 35
Whale, James, 65
Wharton, Edith, 171–2
White Zombie, 149
Whitechapel, 40
Wilde, Oscar, 24, 39–40, 88, 103, 146,
    172–3, 285
William IV, King, 130
Windsor, 35
Wisconsin, 92, 109
witches, witchcraft, 73–4, 79, 88, 118,
    123, 163, 164
Wollstonecraft, Mary, 120, 164
women's liberation movement, the, 280
Wood, Ellen, 26
Woolf, Virginia, 285
Wordsworth, William, 108
wraiths, 93, *see also* ghosts; ghost story,
    the; ghouls; haunting; phantoms

Yarbro, Chelsea Quinn, 270
York, 35
Yorkshire, 95
Young, Edward, 10–11, 13, 15
Ypres, 125

zombies, 66, 264–5, 285
Zschokke, Heinrich, 141